ADVERTISING

Advertising, once seen as 'the official art of capitalist society', is an increasingly commonplace component of a characteristically promotional culture. Iain MacRury's *Advertising* offers the means to explore and evaluate this transition with an introduction to advertising for the contemporary reader.

*Advertising* provides a clear and easy guide to a changing cultural and commercial genre. It explores how advertising can be studied as a cultural industry, and as a sign system, and how adverts and the reception of adverts can be considered, drawing on approaches from literary criticism, structuralism, post-structuralism, psychoanalysis and ethnography.

Written in an accessible and interesting style, *Advertising* is the ideal introductory book for students of media, communication and journalism.

**Iain MacRury** is Principal Lecturer in Cultural Studies and Creative Industries in the School of Social Sciences, Media and Cultural Studies at the University of East London. He has co-authored *The Dynamics of Advertising* (2000) and co-edited *Buy This Book: Studies in Advertising and Consumption* (1996).

# ROUTLEDGE INTRODUCTIONS TO MEDIA AND COMMUNICATIONS

Edited by Paul Cobley
*London Metropolitan University*

This new series provides concise introductions to key areas in contemporary communications. Each book in the series addresses a genre or a form of communication, analysing the nature of the genre or the form as well as reviewing its production and consumption, outlining the main theories and approaches that have been used to study it, and discussing contemporary textual examples of the form. The series offers both an outline of how each genre or form has developed historically, and how it is changing and adapting to the contemporary media landscape, exploring issues such as convergence and globalisation.

*Videogames*
James Newman

*Youth Media*
Bill Osgerby

*News*
Jackie Harrison

*Internet*
Lorenzo Cantoni and Stefano Tardini

*Brands*
Marcel Danesi

*Cyberspace*
Mike Ledgerwood

# ADVERTISING

*Iain MacRury*

Routledge
Taylor & Francis Group

LONDON AND NEW YORK

First published 2009
by Routledge
2 Park Square, Milton Park, Abingdon, Oxon OX14 4RN

Simultaneously published in the USA and Canada
by Routledge
270 Madison Ave, New York, NY 10016

*Routledge is an imprint of the Taylor & Francis Group,
an informa business*

© 2009 Iain MacRury

Typeset in Perpetua and Univers by
Florence Production Ltd, Stoodleigh, Devon

Printed and bound in Great Britain by
TJ International Ltd, Padstow, Cornwall

*British Library Cataloguing in Publication Data*
A catalogue record for this book is available from the British Library

*Library of Congress Cataloging in Publication Data*
MacRury, Iain.
   Advertising/Iain MacRury.
      p. cm. – (Routledge introductions to media and communications)
   Includes bibliographical references and index.
   Advertising.  I. Title.
   HF5823.M132 2009
   659.1 – dc22                                    2008031536

ISBN10: 0–415–25125–7 (hbk)
ISBN10: 0–415–25126–5 (pbk)
ISBN10: 0–203–49319–2 (ebk)

ISBN13: 978–0–415–25125–9 (hbk)
ISBN13: 978–0–415–25126–6 (pbk)
ISBN13: 978–0–203–49319–9 (ebk)

# CONTENTS

# ILLUSTRATIONS

## FIGURES

## TABLES

## BOXES

# SERIES EDITOR'S PREFACE

There can be no doubt that communications pervade contemporary social life. The audio-visual media, print and other communication technologies play major parts in modern human existence, mediating diverse interactions between people. Moreover, they are numerous, heterogeneous, and multi-faceted.

Equally, there can be no doubt that communications are dynamic and ever-changing, constantly reacting to economic and popular forces. Communicative genres and modes that we take for granted because they are seemingly omnipresent—news, advertising, film, radio, television, fashion, the book—have undergone alarming sea changes in recent years. They have also been supplemented and reinvigorated by new media, new textualities, new relations of production and new audiences.

The *study* of communications, then, cannot afford to stand still. Although communications study as a discipline is relatively recent in its origin, it has continued to develop in recognisable ways, embracing new perspectives, transforming old ones, and responding to – and sometimes influencing – changes in the media landscape.

This series of books is designed to present developments in contemporary media. It focuses on the analysis of textualities, offering an up-to-date assessment of current communications practice. The emphasis of the books is on the *kind* of communications which constitute the modern media and the theoretical tools which are needed to understand them. Such tools may include semiotics (including social semiotics and semiology), discourse theory, post-structuralism, post-colonialism, queer theory, gender analysis, political economy, liberal pluralism, positivism (including quantitative approaches), qualitative methodologies (including the 'new ethnography'), reception theory and ideological analysis. The breadth of current communications media, then, is reflected in the array of methodological resources needed to investigate them.

Yet the task of analysis is not carried out as a hermetic experiment. Each volume in the series places its topic within a contextual matrix of production and consumption. Each allows readers to garner an understanding of what that communication is like without tempting them to forget who produced it, for what purpose, and with what result. The books seek to present research on the mechanisms of textuality but also attempt to reveal the precise situation in which such mechanisms exist. Readers coming to these books will therefore gain a valuable insight into the present standing of specific communications media. Just as importantly, though, they will become acquainted with analytic methods which address, explore, and interrogate the very bases of that standing.

# ACKNOWLEDGEMENTS

I would like to thank present and former colleagues who worked with me on both undergraduate and postgraduate Media and Advertising degree courses at the University of East London. Writing this book would have been impossible without them, and without the practical and collegial support upon which academic writing depends. I am indebted to Helen Powell, above all, and to Julia Dane, Catherine Yoon and Marta Rabikowska, for their support and encouragement over recent years and for laughter and inspiration as we have worked day by day to deliver to our students. I would also like to thank Barry Richards, Jackie Botterill, Helen Powell, Candy Yates, Jonathan Hardy, Andrew Blake and Mica Nava who made foundational contributions to create a sound teaching and research base for consumption and advertising studies at UEL. I would also like to thank Lena Kasapi, Mirsini Trigoni and Joy Roles. Their recent doctoral work has been a source of many enjoyable conversations about different aspects of advertising and culture. I would like to thank Colin Campbell and the staff team at York University's Sociology Department who, some years ago now, helped me begin to understand the value of academic engagements with consumption and contemporary culture.

Thanks also to other friends and colleagues including David Butler, Christine Clegg, Paul Gormley, Andrew Blake, Gavin Poynter, Karina Berzins, Mike Rustin, Emma Roberts, Barbara Harrison, Penny Bernstock, Cathy Blackford, Alan White, Marianne Wells, Graham Barnfield, Helena Blakemore, Lowri Gregg, Colin Lever, Helen Gregory, Andrew Calcutt, Emma Burchfield, David Dorrington, Stacey Pogoda, Gill Addison, Sylvie Prassad, Heather Price, Jo Brown, Jo Sherman, Angela Lambert, Pat

Clare, Linda Talbot and Fiona McAnally. All, in their different and valuable ways, have given me friendship, care and support while I have been writing this book, including during a period of illness. Thanks also for tolerance on occasions when writing has distracted me from work, rest and play.

I would like to thank the many students who have asked and answered questions about advertising in lectures and seminars at UEL, and who, in so doing, have taught me a good deal of what I understand to be important about advertising studies. In many ways this book is a record of these classroom conversations. I hope that some of this spirit – of inquiry and critical discussion – is preserved in Advertising, and in a form that will be helpful to future students.

I would like to thank Ellen Gartrell, formally of John W. Hartman Center for Sales, Advertising & Marketing History at Duke University, for expert assistance and advice on historical advertisements and for friendship and hospitality during my visits to North Carolina. This resource, along with the History of Advertising Trust Archive in Beccles, Suffolk, United Kingdom provides an important resources for advertising students and researchers and is much appreciated.

Thanks also to Fiona Isaac and the editorial production team at Florence Production for excellent and professional work in producing the book. Particular thanks go to Aileen Storry at Routledge for her patient encouragement and supportive help as the final draft was assembled, and in particular for help and advice on image permissions. All of her and her colleagues' thoughtful support in getting this title to print is much appreci- ated. I would also like to thank Susannah Wight for valuable assistance on the manuscript.

Finally I'd like to record my gratitude to Paul Cobley for giving me the opportunity to write this book and for the work he has done developing the Media and Communications series. I hope this title will be a worthy contribution alongside the other titles. I would like to thank Paul for his patient and careful editing, and for his, thoughtful input as both a scholar and a friend as I worked to finish the book.

It is certainly the case that the strengths of this book, such as they are, are to be credited to those who have supported and helped. Any un-clarity or inaccuracy is the responsibility of its author. I would like to thank my parents for their supportive care over the years. Finally, I would like to dedicate this book, with love and gratitude, to Laura Anne Bunt.

Every effort has been made to trace and contact copyright holders. The publishers would be pleased to hear from any copyright holders not acknowledged here so that this acknowledgements page may be amended at the earliest opportunity.

Nina Simone lyrics reproduced by kind permission:
Ain't Got No – I Got Life
Words by Gerome Ragni and James Rado;
Music by Galt MacDermot
© 1968 United Artists Music Co. Inc.
Alfred Publishing Co (Print) and EMI United Partnership Ltd (Publishing)
Administered in Europe by Faber Music Ltd.
All Rights Reserved.

Figure 0.1 with thanks to Michelin.
Figures 2.2, 4.3, 4.4 and 4.5 Courtesy of the J. Walter Thompson archive at the Hartman Center, Duke University.
Figure 4.1 © The Andy Warhol Foundation for the Visual Arts, Inc./ DACS, London, 2008. Trademarks Licensed by Campbell Soup Company. All Rights Reserved.
Figure 7.3 © 1992 Benetton Group S.p.A. Photo: Lucinda Devlin. Concept: Oliviero Toscani.
Figure 8.5 © Divine Chocolate Ltd/St Lukes.

# INTRODUCTION

This book introduces some of the many ways that have developed to help people think about 'advertising'. An aspect of *Advertising* common to many media-based books, though unusual in most other disciplines, is the inevitable and extensive experience, even before starting, that readers will have had with the main topic. In a media intensive society advertisements are rarely entirely out of sight or mind, and the industry, its personnel and practices frequently feature as objects of casual reflection (direct or indirect) within other media products. The advertising industry and its outputs have provided foci for many kinds of widely consumed analysis. Social satirists, comedians (from Tony Hancock to Bill Hicks and Eddie Izzard), journalists and filmmakers, as well as academic theorists, have often considered the subject. Advertising is culturally emblematic in a way that enables it to become an engaging carrier of various more or less contemporary myths: the greedy shallowness of life; the non-productive emptiness of many kinds of contemporary work; or, in more optimistic views, the excitement and energy of contemporary societies.

Advertising provides an iconography of the present; it offers reflective composite objects to pepper narratives of modernisation, westernisation, urbanisation and the trans-global extensions of consumerist society. It can play many roles – good, bad and glamorous – and has frequently emerged in filmmakers' attempts to display and explore the contemporary world, refracting audiences' examinations of social change, consumerism and the moral life and reflecting contemporary preoccupations with 'creative' lifestyles. Popular cinema has produced some brief semi-serious and evaluative glimpses of 'advertising' and associated lives and cultures;

visions of the highly pressurised experience of modern life, for instance in *How to Get Ahead in Advertising* (1989); a treatise on advertising banality in *Keep the Aspidistra Flying* (1997)[1] and a quick satirical jab at the futility of the profession in *The Idiots* (1998). In a more sustained examination, the gently bland comedy of *Crazy People* (1990) rehearsed myths of commerce and creativity and reprised debates about audiences' boredom with advertising clichés. *Quiz Show* (1994) looks back to the 1950s to examine the interference of advertisers in TV programme content. With the future in mind advertising is used to lend cultural ambience in science fiction films; new advanced marketing technologies and the (further) expansion into popular culture of ads are common indices of future dystopia, as seen for example in *Minority Report* (2002), *Robocop* (1998) or *Demolition Man* (1993). A recent US TV drama *Mad Men* (2007) opens up the moral and personal dramas of the advertising business, with a retrospective exploration of the 'golden age' of advertising in the Madison Avenue of the 1960s – an era captured at the time in two highly popular non-fiction books *Madison Avenue* (Mayer 1958) and The *Hidden Persuaders* (Packard 1957). Such examinations of advertising contribute to and help consolidate its status as one of the rare instances of a kind of 'mass expertise' – expertise at once studied and accidental.

Advertising is one of the most obvious examples of humans' deliberate efforts at representation and communication; as such it has become an occasion to try to test and develop general theories of how things mean, what impacts and effects communications might have. Advertisements provide an endless source for the elaboration of practical and hypothetical theories of communication – inside and outside the academy. Neither wondering about advertising, nor laughing at it will stop. Its triviality will continue to abut a sense of its importance; the myth of 'hidden persuaders' remains on the agenda (Packard 1957; Robinson 1998; Davenport and Beck 2001: 93–111) even in an era when advertising, as genre and as industry, has become as confessional and publicly self-reflective as any modern day celebrity. Advertising has sold its story many times, and it will do so again (e.g. Hopkins 1966; Gundlach 1931; Mayer 1958; Wight 1972; Ogilvy 1964; Arlen 1980; Mayle 1990; Hamilton 1994; Rothenberg 1994; Zyman 2002; Roberts 2004; Saatchi 2006; Delaney 2007).

Advertisements, even as they provoke so much discussion and reflection, are, primarily, nothing more than one media-based means deployed towards a limited number of commercial ends: raising and maintaining consumer awareness, distributing information and, usually, putting the case for a particular product, service or brand. The (typical) aim: increasing consumption of an advertised product. Advertisements appear in many various forms and across all media (new and traditional). They are, basically, short messages inserted into the flow of a broadcast programme, or in a magazine or newspaper. These messages invite the audience to consider the advertising proposition (for 30 seconds during the 'break', or as their eyes drift over a story feature towards a half-page photograph) – a commercial 'interlude' to the main media communication – and against the flow of other advertising communications.

A good deal of advertising and promotional material appears across non-media spaces – sometimes described as 'ambient' advertising – a term to capture the fact that we find logos and other promotional 'gestures' – in a growing variety of places and spaces: shopping trolleys, petrol pumps, toilet walls and so on. All advertising is placed, more or less strategically, by an industry committed to increasing the scope and effectiveness of advertising communications, to improve the success of their clients, however this is defined for the campaign, and to enhance personal and advertising agency reputations.

One of the aims of the book is to convey, at a basic level, some idea of the practices and some of the terms of reference typically employed in the 'advertising' industry today. It is a cliché that 'advertising' is in a state of constant flux, one repeated just more often than another which says 'advertising' *never* changes (Himpe 2006); nevertheless emphasis is given to considering some of the issues the advertising industry and its critics face in a changing world – where new media and global branding strategies are changing some key points of orientation.

The book includes a number of examples; ads that help exemplify issues under discussion. While it is a mistake to imagine that an account of advertising can simply be read off from such selected examples, looking at ads closely can be helpful, even when this is clearly not a way of looking or reading that maps easily onto most ordinary experiences of ads. Typically, people neglect and ignore more ads than they scrutinise and digest; most are glimpsed, half-registered and bypassed in busy lives, absorbed among other communications (Fowles 1996) – this despite the compelling image of the 'couch potato' which pervades much thinking about advertising audiences.

Many ads can repay a closer look. The claim that advertising provides a form of 'entertainment' (Enright 1988) has been questioned many times (for example by McGuigan 1992; Lodziak 2002). Certainly, and side-stepping this debate for the moment, ads *do* demand attention and represent a constitutive part of popular commercial culture (Fowles 1996; O'Donohoe 1997; Richards *et al.* 2000; Alperstein 2003). In an academic context, at least, when inevitably advertising comes under a different mode of attention than is usual, different that is from when it emerges in its 'natural habitats' – outdoors, or on TV, radio, and in cinema, press and most recently online – there can be some value in looking at ads in a different way and at a different pace. This may provide a kind of 'entertainment' and such reflection can also be an aid to the kinds of critical thinking that in daily life (as critics fear) can elude us as 'everyday' members of advertising audiences.

The word 'advertising' in this book is placed in quotation marks. This is not an attempt at some kind of ironic cleverness: there *is* such a thing as advertising. It is merely to highlight the multiple uses that the word 'advertising' has, and the need for caution about defining 'advertising' as a singular field or general object of study.

One ambiguity in 'advertising' has been summed up by pointing to two of its main meanings. One sees 'advertising' as an *instrument*, an economic tool, used in marketing. The other sees 'advertising' as a socio-cultural *institution*, one that in a market-based society takes on the tasks of 'persuading' but also of 'educating' and socialising consumers (Sandage 1961: 146) circulating the values and uses, the meanings and attractions, of goods and services produced and made available for sale – in order to bind these to our ways of living. This institution is also an *industry* – a cultural industry. An instance of commerce and a subset of marketing, advertising takes its place among those fields of work that have come to be known as 'the creative industries' (Davis and Scase 2000; Beck 2003; Hesmondalgh 2002). In the UK advertising is largely London-based. It employs over 10,000 men and women (Davis and Scase 2000: 45) in a variety of roles: from account administration to creative direction, to media sales, research and strategic planning. The core of industry practitioners is part of an even larger concern than is indicated by the figure 10,000. Davis and Scase provide a further estimate, quoting a survey suggesting 'that all companies whose business depends on advertising employ a total of 4.5 million people' (Davis and Scase 2000: 45). This is a consequence of the increasing significance and centrality of branding and other marketing tasks in commercial management processes. Madison Avenue, the New York-based hub of the US advertising industry, is a centre of comparable magnitude. Both London and Madison Avenue act globally, as the structure and focus of the advertising industry increasingly requires, just as large airports serve as 'centres' of traffic. The networks of international agencies, responsible for the organisation and circulation of the greater part of the brand communications we see, hear and read, belong to global corporations, which have international centres, but no national centre, and which increasingly tie in with more local and regional advertising offices, forming a complex and dispersed nexus in which the global attempts to meet the local, and local engages the global (Frith and Mueller 2003; Malefyt and Moeran 2003; Kemper 2003; Mazzerella 2003b; Seabrook 2004; O'Barr 1994).

There is a further major use of 'advertising': images, copy and slogans; the expressive and persuasive 'art' of commercial culture; *advertisements*. 'Advertising', defined now as the output, the product of the industry of the same name, is a multi-sensory and multi-media genre for communication which must, at least in part, be understood in aesthetic terms – with reference to conceptions from criticism in the arts. Advertising is especially and most often considered a part of the *visual* culture of our times (Rose 2001; Messaris 1997; Nava 1997; Frosch 2003). A hallmark of modern metropolitan life and a backdrop to suburban TV culture, advertising characterises the 'look' of contemporary consumer society, just as older ads capture (in fragmentary ways) some (nostalgic) elements of earlier phases of social and personal history. Advertising's 'sonic' life is less often explored – but is a contribution of equal measure to the mediascape (Van Leeuwen 1999).

Although people rarely stop to articulate it, it is inevitable that we engage with advertising. To do so is basic to participation in 'consumer society'. Even studied disengagement *from* consumer cultures has become a defining stance *within* contemporary experience (Lewis and Bridger 2001), one reflected by advertising practice and thinking (Goldman 1992; Klein 2000; Langer 2003). Guy Cook has helpfully described the properties of advertisements as a 'discourse type', arguing convincingly that any member of a consumer society requires tacit knowledge of the nature of advertising texts (Cook 1992: 221–2). So we *expect* that ads will usually occur in an accompanying media communication, like a magazine or a TV programme, and we are vaguely aware that someone has paid for the space or airtime (and, therefore, for any attention given to the message). Ads are expected to be brief and bounded in time (for instance, a 30-second TV ad) or on a designated page space, which frames the ad, dividing it off from the main communication.

Advertising is usefully considered as a 'genre', as one form of cultural and social communication. Myers (within his helpful treatment on the linguistics of advertising) suggests, like Cook (1992), that advertising is a specific and 'stereotypical act of communication – a genre' (Myers 1994: 6) by which he means, not that advertising uses stereotypes (which it undoubtedly does), but that within the variety and diversity of advertisements, there remains a formal stereotypical sameness, including but not restricted to:

- repeated typical purposes (to sell, to inform, to gain attention);
- repeated typical communications situations (between producers and consumers);
- and repeated typical communications intent (to represent products in terms of and by association with distinct cultural meanings).

Myers (1994), Cook (1992) and others (Bruthiaux 1996; Leech 1966) who have identified typical and generic features of advertising are right: ads are often quite 'samey', the typical products of a 'cultural industry' and the social (and sometimes global) relations of modern, media-intensive, market-based society. However, and in a way that does not disturb the identification of advertising as a 'genre', it is useful to consider (and this is timely, as from a text-focused point of view, advertising has undoubtedly developed in some interesting ways in the past decades) that within this generic stability some very significant formal variability is (on occasion) evident: variablities of purpose; of communications situation; and of communicative intent – not to mention cultural 'style'. Advertising is a genre; but one constituted in its many (and changing) sub-genres. Subsequent chapters will look at the various uses and forms (including evolving forms) of advertising communications and will consider the different ways advertising appears in different media, when it is required to perform different tasks, for different product sectors. The book will also look at changing advertising formats and consider the extensions and (partial) transmutations that confront the genre in the face of new media, new audiences and new cultural and consumer relations – in particular arising from Internet connectivity.

Depending on the medium, advertisements can combine a variety of modes, including images, music and the printed word. Contemporary ads (of some types), although this is neither a new nor universal development, often tend towards the elliptical, artful and indirect in their communicative style (more regularly than for example TV documentaries, or newspapers' editorial features). Such approaches characteristically allow advertisements to link up ideas and images which ordinarily are not associated with one another, for instance cars and the opera, or rare animals and a soft drink. Such incongruities appear condensed together in advertisements without comment or surprise – indeed this quasi-surrealist tendency (Williamson 1986: 67–74) is a key and common feature of advertising as a genre – one made routine today by the availability of digital technologies and editing packages.

The more or less unshakeable capacity of today's audiences to recognise ads' generic signatures has meant that adverts are routinely and often able to talk about themselves reflexively. Clever ads disarm us by announcing 'Hey look I'm an advert!', or by using parodic mimicry of outdated or over the top styles. Ad-makers try to make an advertising virtue out of the necessary irritation built up in audiences after a lifetime of exposure to formulaic advertising. Any such humorous self-parody exemplifies a now routine strategy long deployed by advertising creatives in an attempt to engage audience attention, and to solicit some sense of a 'special' relationship – part of either a pseudo-sophisticated cultural complicity flattering to deceive, or as an honest attempt to humanise and energise market relations – ads working to enlarge conceptions of consumers' imaginative relationship to things, and in some sense to affirm consumers' engaged role in the marketing (and meaning-making) process (see Chapter 6 below) – this to the advantage of product, brand and consumer.

Ads can take on the mannerisms of other kinds of communication. They can look like news programmes, feature films or children's cartoons – normally without being mistaken for anything but an advertisement, but necessarily declaring some cultural affinity with the modes they clone. Again this typically passes without comment. Audiences have learnt to accept and even find mild enjoyment in such playful feigning, noting key prompts such as logos to distinguish the ads from the media that surrounds them.

Ads are a 'natural' part of the media landscape, but this is not to say they are not troublesome. There is an important and influential discourse around regulating advertisements (Cronin 2004a; White 2000). Advertising for specific 'dangerous' products (cigarettes, alcohol and lately some foods and financial services) is threatened with ever-tighter restriction, and even banning. Likewise, particular audiences, especially children, are to be protected from over exposure to advertising persuasion (Cronin 2004; Ofcom 2004), as materially affluent societies try to work out ways of managing problems of over consumption.

Such lobbying and attendant threats to ban this or that advertising strategy, or to prevent certain products from being advertised, are a daily problem for the industry, but they powerfully legitimate the belief that advertising works especially effectively on some people, to sell them things against their better judgement and against their best interests. While advertising (and its texts) provide the major sites for such controversies, the industry can be fairly secure that its claimed position as the institution best placed to manage and manipulate consumer demand is broadly unchallenged.

Governmental and lobbyists' complaints about the powerful influence of advertising (in specific instances) can serve in a more general sense to consolidate the view that individuals in general (Klein 2000) and certain 'target' groups in particular are routinely susceptible to advertising influence – e.g. children (Schor 2004) and teenagers (Quart 2003). In this regard advertising, as a widely distributed communicative genre, has often been singled out for special scrutiny, with other more embedded forms of marketing, promotional and retail techniques (which arguably inform consumption in at least equal measure) appearing less often as objects of public debate or government intervention. Thus advertisements receive more detailed (official) scrutiny than the patter of a telesales caller would, or a sales pitch from a car dealer or garage mechanic, or even than the sponsorship of a sporting event.[2]

To a great extent, and in the face of ongoing pressure for more government intervention, the advertising industry regulates itself, via bodies such as the Advertising Association, to protect the public from instances of misleading or 'indecent' advertising[3] and to build trust in 'good' advertising (by an actual as well as ritual of censorship of the 'bad'). Advertising professionals no doubt also bring their own (informal and experienced-based) judgements to bear as they work towards the production of ad campaigns – balancing knowledge of cultural sensibilities, and of explicit regulations, against creative, commercial and aesthetic decisions. In different countries different governments take a more or less direct role in regulating advertising – not always trusting the industry to be sufficiently rigorous in policing itself.

Threats of increased regulatory scrutiny made to the advertising industry are not entirely undeserved. The history of advertising is peppered with incidences of advertising operating to circulate misrepresentation of fact, and also, in its pursuit of sensation and attention, misrepresentation of women, of children, of speed, sex and danger. When it goes unchecked, advertising shows a tendency to attempt to challenge the bounds of communally agreed decency, not in the name of cultural liberation, but for marketing purposes (Lears 1994). In the UK however the industry continues to be permitted (broadly) to regulate itself – the provisional and contingent nature of any kind of statement of communal agreement chief amongst the arguments against more rigid frameworks for advertising governance.

Advertising is often considered, whether as an institution or as a body of promotional communications 'items', to constitute a singular field of practice, providing various industries with a particular and specific type of communications service. Reflections on the sheer volume of this 'advertising' abound. The impression sometimes given is that this volume is (in the end) 'all the same', the infliction on society of a quantity of communication, a quantity that exhausts, or saturates, our attention and which thereby reduces our (proper) apprehension, imagination and experience of the world's objects and potentials.

From an industry point of view, to study advertising is partly to try to dissect and disaggregate this 'quantity'. This can reveal that advertising, as it is used at certain times, for example when launching a new product or in maintaining an established brand and in certain sectors, requires, case by case, a different 'art'. Likewise advertisers must contrast financial services, charity and perfume ads; to work in these product sectors is, to an extent, to engage in *different* activities, performing a variety of communicative tasks relying on a variety of sector specific techniques and know how. There are formal similarities (it's all advertising after all), but the context and purpose of any individual ad in the processes of production and consumption in each case is likely to be different. Thus it is important to be sensitive to the variability of advertising forms and functions – to consider the differing ways advertising is used and understood by marketers, advertising professionals and their audiences. An ad for perfume after all has a very different communicative function from an ad for a complex insurance product. It *delivers* something qualitatively different.

'Advertising' also describes a body of institutional *knowledge*. It is the primary professional discipline, alongside marketing and public relations, of those explicitly engaged in the widespread activity of *promotion* (Wernick 1991; Nixon 1997, 2003). Advertising expertise ranges across business and academic disciplines: psychology, research methodologies, the dynamics of individual product sectors (from dog food to funeral parlours), the practical economics of the media market and the aesthetics of contemporary design. This expertise is usually not the property of a single individual. Instead such a package of expertise is lodged in teams and agencies (and in their 'branded' reputations), and traded, to those needing such services, by advertising agency directors in a competitive marketplace.

This characterisation may appear to elevate the advertising industry – and its agencies – in some way as, say, an intellectual and artistic 'hothouse'. Certainly, at times, advertising pretends to, and in many ways *does*, inhabit a privileged and powerful position from which to 'know' and even shape society. Such a characterisation is used both by critics of advertising, who want to emphasise the industry's power and guile, and by the industry itself, which craves respect for its professional activities and credibility for its promised capacity to manage the consumer mind – its special 'knowledge' (and the capacity to turn the theory into practice) is an important element of what the advertising industry brings to market (Lury and Warde 1997; Cronin 2004a). Every profession lays just claim to a special understanding of people (think of the differing conceptions and insights available to medics, tax inspectors, teachers and the legal profession). It is primarily as *consumers* that advertising claims to know us – our various struggles with our sense of ourselves as consumers, and with our sense of society and culture as primarily and increasingly arenas for commercial consumption. Perhaps it is this limiting definition of people as 'the consumer' that determines some elements of our suspicion of advertising.

What distinguishes advertising from the other component industries of consumer society (such as market research, customer relationship management and the various techniques of retail) is that its stock in trade – brand imagery and communications, by virtue of visibility and insistence – is more routinely evident in our everyday experience than those elements of market society embedded in commercial and political bureaucracy, architecture, planning policies and the transformations of social space, or stores of information and consumer research. In our everyday imagination *advertising* comes to stand for a far broader set of processes than, strictly, it merits. As an industry, it is taking both more credit and more blame than, in isolation, its activities could actually warrant.

In its typical imageries, in its speech and in its gestures, advertising is a highly familiar phenomenon. But it is also an irredeemably strange part of the cultural landscape. Advertising is an expected part of everyday life, but it is also alien to it: the ever-expected but uninvited guest; on magazine pages, during TV programmes, and round each city corner. As an instance of the 'strange familiar', i.e. as something we see every day but which nevertheless can feel unexpected or out of place, advertising inhabits a peculiar place in experience. A genre which must at once blend in *and* stand out, advertising provokes a good deal interpretation and explanation – some of this attention is as intended by advertisers, some is informed by critical concerns about wider consequences of this kind of communication – suspicion that advertising might affect us (or others) more deeply than ordinarily could be expected. Individuals devise explanations and analyses and these circulate as part of the popular philosophies of advertising – in published books and papers, in conversation and, recently, in web-based discussions. This book examines some portion of the large volume of explanation and analysis advertising has provoked. To illustrate the range of opinion and some of the considerations informing debates about advertising, consider the following three images (see Figures 0.1, 0.2 and 0.3).

There are few better known signs that the first of these: the Michelin Man (see Figure 0.1). What could be more familiar? Speaking anecdotally, this seems to be a widely significant character. At a recent lecture in China I presented this figure and suddenly, smiles.

**Figure 0.1** 'The Michelin Man' with thanks to Michelin.

**Figure 0.2** Salvador Dali's *Esclave de Michelin*.

**Figure 0.3** Pirelli 'Original equipment on the world's finest'.

Sounds of recognition filled the room – the opportunity to share a globally recognised sign gratefully taken up, amongst, no doubt, a good deal of cross-cultural miscommunication. There can be little doubt that brand images such as this one, often affectionately known across the world, provide common reference points – even when other aspects of culture, politics and social life (e.g. language, religion and consumer habits), not to mention differing economic conditions, highlight the complexity and the division underpinning some of those processes described under the heading 'globalisation'.

This logo in particular helps to articulate something interesting about advertising taken in general. The familiar Michelin logo is a celebrated instance of the art of 'advertising personification'.[4] A person or cartoon character becomes the embodiment of a product or brand – here Michelin, manufacturers of rubber products and, notably, tyres. The figure is familiar in itself and audiences routinely read this logo – depicting a cartoon 'man' made of tyres – as a friendly character; he personifies the product range (in particular Michelin tyres) and animates both product and brand, representing a culturally recognised, practical and commercial presence – reliably *there*, friendly and trusted. This movement of personification is close to the heart of what all good advertising tends to try to achieve.

The Michelin logo is a classic instance which illustrates more generally a conjunction that advertising routinely performs (as a genre) – one which we routinely accept and understand. Advertising imagery binds persons to products – in the case of Michelin man, so intimately that the thing and the person are one and the same. Sometimes advertising does this less directly – but a defining feature of the genre is that it works to bring the world of people and the world of things together, using imagery, words and sounds to signify connections – between 'you' and 'the product' – held (if just for a moment) by the image and for the duration of the attention provoked by, or leant to an advertisement.

That advertising might provoke and even secure such elisions has concerned some commentators, whose critical analyses have insisted that there is something problematic in a genre apparently able, if only in mind and feeling, to bring the world of people and the world of things together – intimately (but also) repetitively and on a mass scale. A theme in this book (to which we will return) examines advertising as a means designed to connect people to things – to link us, by information, imagery, imagination and by desire, to the objects of the marketplace. Something of this critical anxiety is captured in Figure 0.2.

In 1966 the famous surrealist painter Salvador Dali attempted to articulate a sense of the absurdity of people's 'enslavement' (as he saw it) to the objects and ends of consumerism. Dali did this in the form of a small bronze sculpture (Figure 0.2) titled *Esclave de Michelin*, i.e. 'slave of Michelin'. The iconic status of the Michelin company in 1960s France no doubt partly inspired this satirical piece of art.

The Pirelli ad (Figure 0.3) shows a more recent play on the theme of personification, highlighting a specific branded take on the person-tyre conjunction (one perhaps consistent with Pirelli's association with sexual imagery established through its famous calendars).

These images, in different ways, show people linked to objects – as it happens here, to tyres. Half human, half material, Dali's figure shows someone 'enslaved' by Michelin tyres, bound to and by them. In a slightly different way, the Michelin logo shows an image that merges a person with tyres, a 'Michelin man'. Unlike Dali's slave, the Michelin man, of course, appears cheerful. The Pirelli ad likewise is an image in which man and tyre are merged – symbolically at least – a hybrid tyre–person – in this latter case emphasising the power afforded to man (or woman) in his (or her) conjunction with machines.

What critics of advertising and its cultural impact have argued is that advertising images such as these euphemise and provoke a process, whose reality is most closely captured by Dali's figure – a reality of captivation by, and subservience to, consumer objects – a reality of living humanity compromised. This reality is not apparent to us directly, because (critics argue) we are routinely inducted within the total processes of promotional communication, and best attuned to its attendant habits of thought. We can only barely apprehend the extent and nature of our contorted relation to consumer objects, and the 'goods' they have come to represent to us.

Critics propose that advertising processes bind us to products by provoking identifications with the values and imageries invested in and symbolically carried by advertised goods. We pursue the cultural qualities embodied in goods – for instance health, security and happiness – understanding the consumption of market-produced objects as the only reliable and culturally acceptable means towards the realisation of personal and social ends. Like the tyres round Dali's figure (Figure 0.2), consumer society encircles and distorts proper human movements – of body and mind. The recent Pirelli advertisement (Figure 0.3) demonstrates the persistence of such a strategy; in truth it is the fundamental role of advertising to try to provide links between the world of human values and the world of market-produced goods – advertising performs some of the everyday cultural work of animating the objects of the market (Cronin 2004a; Williams 1980) – and connecting them to us. While in everyday cultural practice we make these connections, in principled reflection we are perhaps wary that the objects of consumption might overtake us (or others). Academic critics have defensively underplayed the counter-argument: that the market extends and liberates human potential, so that outside the marketing industry advertising is rarely celebrated as a cultural spur, focusing aspiration and prompting positive elaboration of desire – the 'extensions of man'[5] (McLuhan 1964) through a (potentially healthy) engagement with culturally enervated and enervating products. It is this latter sense of the relations between people and things that, no doubt, is in the minds of advertisers as they strive (via ads) to weave their products into living cultures with (sometimes) aesthetically ambitious textualities and gestures.

Debates about advertising can move quite rapidly from a discussion of the everyday and into some rather grand themes about contemporary experiences (as we have seen). It is worthwhile remaining conscious of the way 'advertising', as a topic, can provoke over-dramatic generalisation, and it is helpful to return to the everyday, and to particulars as a helpful context for more general analysis. One useful particular context to ground ideas about advertising is to be found in the industry – and especially in the detail of practices which constitute this broad area of work; another is in the everyday conjectures and experiences circulating in daily life. From the perspectives afforded by either of these contexts broad generalisations about enslavement and domination are at a distance.

The first sections of the book are about the different ways advertising is understood and evaluated – introducing some 'practical theories' circulating and constituting 'advertising'; in media output, amongst consumers and in the industry. Chapter 1 explores some accounts of the ways people have tried to understand advertising as a part of everyday life, looking at some of the 'common sense' discourses and presumptions which typically circulate around 'advertising'. Chapter 2 looks at creative and commercial processes in the advertising industry and outlines some of the typical preoccupations and tensions surrounding the conception and execution of an advertising campaign – outlining a brief picture of the advertising process.[6] Some profession-based understandings of advertising are explored in relation to advertising agency processes and structure(s).

Advertising should be understood as a part of broader processes of cultural promotion. Chapter 3 identifies advertising as a specialist part of marketing and examines the place of advertising alongside its partner promotional modes, from retail, to public relations, to sponsorship. The transformative role of the Internet (and more recent forms of digital mediation) complements but also potentially destabilises the role of media-based advertising. This, alongside marketers' increased focus on *branding* (and integrative marketing), has had consequences for thinking about how advertising operates – with ever more ingenious 'media' spaces emerging and with subtle new advertising strategies ever more common (Langer 2003). Nevertheless advertising remains basic to the main media and vice versa. Historically and functionally advertising does not exist without media; this chapter outlines the different advertising media and briefly examines how they support advertising, and the impacts advertising has on its 'hosts'. Chapter 4 examines some lines academic criticism has pursued in relation to advertising. Criticism of advertising has emerged (in various forms) since advertising practices became identified as common-place elements in everyday life. This chapter also briefly outlines some of the processes and conditions informing the emergence of advertising, in particular providing more detail of the institutional structures that have developed in the 150-year history of modern advertising. While the advertising industry, in its practices and in its rhetoric, is largely oriented towards the 'now' and to the future, a historical narrative provides a useful way of grasping some of the main features of the genre.

Chapter 5 examines the prominence of advertising in culture and society. This prominence is such that it has been dubbed, sardonically, 'the official art of capitalist society' (Williams 1980), a label aimed at capturing its inflated roles and apparent ever-presence. Academics, arguing from a variety of political positions, have been united, broadly, in seeing advertising as damaging. Advertising is typically understood as being a part of 'culture', in that it is a constitutive element identifiable within life – a 'signifying practice' and an everyday fact of experience. Contradictorily advertising is identifiable (in some quarters) as the antithesis of culture. Some of these arguments about advertising, as 'culture' and as signification are given shape and focus in academic writing which attempts to address the impacts the genre at times unleashes – this chapter explores some of these ideas.

There are some key arguments which have gained prominence at different times, but all continue to inform debate. Academic critique has long urged vigilance in the face of the immense *power* of advertising: Denys Thompson warned in 1932 that advertisers are 'the Lords of creation' (Thompson 1932: 241); seventy years on Ziauddin Sardar identified advertising as 'the new lord of the manor' (Sardar 2002: 7). Advertising is often seen as inhabiting a position formally held by prior authorities, especially religion (Thompson 1932; Williamson 1978; Twitchell 1999) and also magic (Williams 1962; Alperstein 2003). This chapter identifies some of the reasons why advertising has been held up for scrutiny; these are outlined here in summary:

- sustaining economic systems where over-pricing and standardisation or non-differentiation of mass-produced goods operates against consumers' best interests;
- advertisers' production of meaningless symbolic differences between products as a more profitable alternative to providing *materially* excellent goods that people *really* need;
- consumers' (over)investment in such (apparently) valueless symbolic-ally enriched advertised products – at the expense of other cultural 'goods';

- the maintenance of a culture where individual spending is privileged readily and at the expense of more substantial social and collaborative 'projects' and objectives;
- anxiety about consumer-driven commercial colonisation of real and virtual spaces, cities, towns and, ultimately, eroding inhabitants' sense of place;
- concerns about the erosion, displacement and disappearance of global cultural diversity, i.e. the role of advertising in the production (by signs and logos) of 'non-places' (Auge 1995) – supporting the McDonaldisation effect which allows us to feel, in London, Seattle, Beijing and Kuala Lumpur, that we could be anywhere (and therefore nowhere) (Ritzer 2000);
- advertising is held as a contributor to the decay of the public capacity for sound political judgement (Mayhew 1997) revealed partly in the 'tabloid' quality of much commercially driven journalism and other public broadcasting (Leavis and Thompson 1964; Williams 1969; Curran 1981, 2002; Curran and Gurevitch 2005; Bogart 2000).

Chapter 5 looks in particular at the questions of how and in what ways advertising impacts on culture, and its tendency to appropriate or mask the signs and cultural forms on which people have depended to secure meanings and value. Advertising's capacity to transform important cultural symbols into exchangeable commodities raises some wider issues about the genre's unintended cultural consequences. This chapter also looks at one very frequently considered topic – representations of people in advertising – and extends one strand of cultural analysis to examine the impact of the idea that advertising has had a role to play in the 'construction' and endorsement of social identities – especially around gender and ethnicity – in line with the traditional preoccupations of much critique. The advertising industry has operated, since the early twentieth century, with some working assumptions about targeting, representation and product imagery. Since the 1960s critical analysis has been alert to some of the potential problems attached to these modes and habits of representation. It is a routine objection for instance to find advertising complicit in the affirmation and production of stereotypical images of people and limited views of 'the good life'. The chapter examines questions of representation and considers some advertising analyses concerned with representation of distinct groups, for instance, women, ethnic minorities and the family.

While 'culture' and representation of people remain central to thinking about advertising it is its character as assertively a signifying activity – as a genre shaping and organising *signs* – that has preoccupied a number of critics in most recent decades. Towards the end of the 1960s work on advertising drew on the insights of 'structuralism'. A 'semiotics of advertising' grew out of this moment, thus enabling an interrogation of the way in which the relationships between signs in individual advertisements and in advertising in general were constructed. Advertising language tells us about products in a way that, says Barthes, 'transforms simple use into an experience of the mind' (Barthes 1988: 178). One copywriter describes his work as changing a shoe from 'a mere lump of leather' into 'a footwear statement' (Cadley 1992: 149). Such transformational processes can be termed 'semiotic' – which refers to the movement of signs and ideas, as we engage with them and are engaged by them – in objects, texts and their contexts. Advertising – like other cultural signification – operates in and upon a (notional) semiotic and cultural 'space' that can be conceived as existing 'between' objects, texts and our experience of them. It is through signs that, as it were, we 'open up' and 'navigate' this 'space' in a sign-based process which affords a pivotal component in all our engagement with the world; with culture, experience, objects and meaning. The centrality of this semiotic 'space' in people's relations to things has ensured that it is also a primary preoccupation of those seeking to market goods – with advertising a genre assertively committed to dissemination of advertising signs via the various media and aiming (in innumerable ways) to manage and inflect the meaning of goods as consumers navigate innumerable 'marketplaces' real and imaginary – in moments of decision, anticipation, reflection and contemplation. Chapter 6 looks at ways of understanding such processes in more detail and in particular at the ways in which analysis of advertising signs has begun to grow out of its original 'structuralist' limitations, and into a broader account of processes of 'semiosis' and interpretation.

The sociocultural developments labelled 'post-modern' and located historically in the latter decades of the twentieth century have wrought havoc with many of the functional and analytical categories deployed in the production, consumption and critical analysis of advertising. Chapter 7 attempts to grasp some of the complexity of so-called 'post-modernism'. From the academic point of view the most important changes in advertisements have been to do with the adoption of ways of communicating borrowed from, and compatible with, 'post-modern' culture. Among the responses to the post-modern was the addition of a new emphasis within advertising studies; this involved thinking about audiences, not in the abstract, but as 'live', 'active' spectators. So academics began (more concertedly from the 1980s onwards) to talk to (and not just about) those whose role in life was to 'receive', 'decode', 'be positioned by' and variously take in advertising 'texts'. The interest in audiences was one part of a broader turn in academic work about media, culture and identity. Chapter 8 looks at some aspects of this set of approaches. The renewed interest is in subjectivity and 'the subject', that is, in the notional and embodied 'place' from which we think, experience, speak and see the world; this was in part a political strategy (within academia): reclaiming the specificities of everyday living from the generalities routinely asserted by abstract academic critiques and other cultural and political 'authorities'. Aside from talking to audiences about their experiences, this return to the subject invited the application of various kinds of psychology to thinking about relationships with advertising. One branch of psychology, psychoanalysis, has been used with some success to help elaborate various accounts of advertising as a media and cultural genre.

Academic criticism of advertising enters debate in two areas in particular: socio-political theory and cultural aesthetics. Critics consider the (economic and political) impact advertising has on processes guaranteeing individual freedom; the seductive textures of advertising have been theorised as provoking widespread diminution of individual autonomy. In a world in which advertising is one of the major modes of public speech, what impact might this have on the possibilities for citizenship? Can consumers (the implicit subject addressed by advertising) be good citizens? It should be recalled that 'citizen' is defined in relation to its earliest uses, as the word describing free, politically entitled men (and eventually women) living in and linked by the (open, public and democratic) communications processes of civil society. The negative opposite of 'citizen' is 'slave' – 'man' (and especially women and children) as property, without rights, voice or humanity – there to serve others' ends and not their own. Institutionally advertising connects people to public and social life, but in the world for which advertising speaks, people (it is argued) are not equal as a matter of inalienable human right; instead full inclusion and participation in *consumer* society is largely a matter of wealth. People *buy* this mode of 'citizenship' – and are graded by the market both in terms of an entitlement to participate (to buy things) and in terms of their value as potential consumers – the extent to which we are worth talking to by advertisers. Increasingly it is in hybrid mode, as 'consumer-citizens' that individuals participate to express 'freedom', 'choice' and 'identity', including the registration of 'political' and moral distinctions – for instance via 'green' or 'fair trade' options. Advertising takes on a crucial function in mediating such participation/ non-participation – and as such merits some analysis.

The anxiety pervading critical discourse is that advertising diminishes and distorts individuals' capacities for full civil citizenship (en masse). We are variously socialised to become *consumers* and not citizens, and 'consumer' describes our predominant states and modes of subjectivity and relationship (Williams 1980: 170–95), perhaps enjoyable, energised and offering choice, but which are not free, in the formal sense of political agency – the autonomous subject as citizen. Crucially also the misuse of resources to satisfy illusory desires leads to a global problem – as low waged labourers work to service the need for abundant cheap goods for sale in the richest economies – at the expense of more locally focused (sustainable) productivity. Advertising, as a key tactic serving the strategic management of demand (and so also the supply) for goods in the (global) marketplace, is frequently identified as close to the heart of some serious global political-economic problems.

Thinking about advertising, in the industry, in popular discourses and in academic writing, offers insight into the ways in which contemporary society manages and imagines the relations between 'people' and 'things' (Cronin 2004a) – what is made and not made, where investments go and how resources flow – locally and globally. These are not just questions for global economists or for distant boardrooms – they are everyday questions. Advertising has become one important locus for our engagement with such questions – and understanding it in detail matters for that reason. 'People' and 'things' denotes a simple terminology which belies the existence of an important debate underlying the academic study of advertising. To connect analysis with this debate it has sometimes been necessary to adopt less usual terminologies. So for 'people' and 'things', 'consumers' and 'products', 'audiences' and 'advertisements' (which are by no means interchangeable pairings), the analysis in this book intermittently refers to 'subjects' and 'objects'. This terminology may require brief explanation. Raymond Williams gives a detailed account of 'subject' considered as a political term (see Williams 1976: 308–12) describing (as an ideal) an active individual connected intimately to social life through a living culture and productive work.

A further helpful definition of the 'subject and object' pairing (originating in discussion of art) can be found in the work of psychoanalyst Marion Milner who distinguishes a relation between 'incorporated environment' and 'external environment' (Milner 1957: 129). Thoughts and feelings within the body, the self, constitute *subjects*, the source of and vehicle for subjectivities. 'Outside' is the external environment; where 'the things we come across, the things "out there"', *objects* existing independently of our presence and perception, but which we engage with in different ways subjectively, exist. Objects move us, and we work (in turn), usually interpretively and in relations to signs and signification processes, to make the world of objects intelligible and sensible. The definition of 'objects' can be extended to include:

> Anything that can be sensed reacted to or thought about, whether directly or indirectly . . . objects may be of an intellectual (mental) nature . . . Also a goal or purpose.
>
> (Cobley 2001: 230)

As Milner argues, typically, there is a continuing interchange between subjective and objective worlds, involving subjects' engagements and shaping experience. The array of 'products' on the market, and the images and ideas represented in advertising are objects in this sense – but market exchange is perhaps not a sufficient measure of the interchange Milner describes. These terms (subject and object) are perhaps alien to most discussion about advertising, which has existed primarily in the discourses of commerce and economics (which operate with quite complex but certain understandings of the relations between people, advertising and products).

Yet, the conceptual frames of economics and marketing-based under-standing (however sophisticated and detailed) do not fully permit the closer engagement with those aspects of advertising and consumer experience that can be apprehended within broadly 'cultural' analysis. Do not advertisements exist, in the end, to mediate between consumers' subjective experiences and products – providing (fleetingly) in texts and images, *cultural* and experiential spaces where desire, interpretation and representations play out? There is more to such transactions than simply market-based choice – even while marketplace decision-making is at the heart of the process. 'Subject' and 'object' are useful and conventional shorthand terms in the academic discussion of both 'political' and 'aesthetic' activities. And while advertising is often understood as being exactly *neither* of these kinds of activity (i.e. neither art nor politics), much academic criticism of advertising has typically required that this 'genre' be re-considered as *both*. So this book is finally about beginning to work to try and help to locate and reflect on 'advertising' in its many comple-mentary contexts: in everyday life and talk, in ad agency practices and working tensions; in academic critique; and as a significant genre shaping, informing and reflecting the most ordinary aesthetic, cultural, commercial and social experiences.

# 1

# ADVERTISING AND COMMON SENSE

## DILEMMAS

What do you already know about advertising? Probably quite a lot; there are a number of sources of information and analysis in circulation, including our everyday knowledge and experience of advertisements. In addition you might have come across professional and technical information, as well as advertising discussions in current affairs coverage and, possibly, academic analysis of advertising. In tone as much as in substance there are some considerable differences between the accounts provided by such sources. Thus the analysis of advertising that circulates in academic writing can differ widely in approach and language when compared with professional industry commentary or newspaper reports. Similarly more popular reflections on advertising, for instance in comedic satire, provide information and analysis in a variety of ways, which we readily consume, and which thus feed our thinking. However none of these modes necessarily deliver coherent or uncomplicated accounts or representations of the advertising genre.

As suggested above, advertising is a genre, an everyday feature and format across contemporary media, alongside other genres and sub-genres, such as news, sitcoms, fashion features, celebrity interviews and including films, games and – as yet more difficult to classify – various other Internet communications-based formats. Advertising's function, as we know, is to promote and often to sell a product, a service or perhaps an idea. We understand ads to be a crucial element in contemporary processes towards the dissemination of information, and we are well aware that ads are paid-for communications intended to win our attention and consent to marketing or other propositions. As private messages appearing in 'public' places and framed by more or less creditable host media and in sanctioned spaces – such as on billboards, commercial TV and radio broadcasts or in the press – we perhaps tacitly ascribe legitimacy, and so also a certain authority, to the advertising genre. Such authority is underscored by the typically high production values on show in commercial advertising relative to many other kinds of informal (and unfunded) communications genres we might come across. Further credibility is gained when the people featured in advertising embody, through celebrity, status, look and voice, subtly selected cultural characteristics and styles, signs to authenticate and legitimate the advertising appeal.

However, advertising is also a genre whose legitimacy and authority is always also in doubt. The pervasive presence of ads undermines authority and legitimacy, inviting charges of media clutter, of insistent hectoring and tacky commercialism. If 'less is more' in some communications contexts, then, and as a whole, advertising has not taken this maxim seriously – an industry strategy provoking indifference, condemnation and indiscrimination across audiences. In these conditions of ad overkill distinctions between individual advertisements and 'advertising in general' can collapse (each one becoming a sign of the other within viewers' responses and irritability) contributing to intermittent experiences of advertising as a discredited communications genre. Similarly 'glamorous' celebrities' marketing 'Midas Touch' can, over time, be seen to erode the very public image and trust upon which this or that personality's credibility rests. Advertising is part of marketing discourse – of the array of communications and actions designed to manage relations between producers and consumers. As such it has a role to play in providing us with information about and a feeling for goods and ideas in circulation. However the legitimacy of advertising propositions must always be understood to be compromised by audiences' capacities to assess the advertising promise up against information, ideas and ideals developed and affirmed in our engagements with other discourses; science, politics, family and social custom, religion and so on. Advertising attempts to operate in dialogue with such competing discourses, and mimics and appropriates some of their surface elements, or challenges and undermines their basic assumptions. The point is that advertising communications occur in contexts where our beliefs about advertising's credibility typically temper the legitimacy that we might confer upon its claims and the seriousness with which we might respond to its initial impacts.

The nature of advertising as a genre then depends to a degree on a tense and dynamic process, one in which individuals and audiences, as well as legislators confer limited or no legitimacy and consent to the genre and its propositions. This tension is evident in the frequent comments made by individual viewers who 'like' this or that advertisement, but who also 'despise' advertising 'in general'. Nor is such contradiction restricted to audiences. Advertising industry professionals' reflections on 'run of the mill' or 'pretentious' advertising – especially if made by competitor agencies – often echo the scornful indifference that the genre provokes in other audiences.

Academic and journalistic debates on advertising typically feed the maelstrom of opinion about 'advertising' ensuring that everyday reception of advertisements is shadowed by a penumbra of debate and dissent – however tacit.

So it is useful to consider for a moment the extent to which the opinions and ideas about advertising, which we might have taken on from any or all these sources, are likely to lead us to draw a variety of sometimes contradictory conclusions about what advertising is and how it functions in society as well as in commercial life. How is advertising represented and thought about in popular TV programmes, for instance in documentaries, comedy and current affairs? In this chapter we will consider some different and contradictory accounts of advertising as they circulate in everyday media genres, and outside the academic critiques which make up the major part of this book.

Advertising is a regular focus for comedy. A four-part sitcom *If You See God Tell Him*, broadcast by the BBC in 1993, was not a success, in terms of either audiences or critical opinion. It has rarely been repeated. It depicted the misfortune of the main character, Godfrey Spry, a typical suburban sitcom male, played by Richard Briers, who received a bump on the head, lost his memory and could then retain an attention span of just 30 seconds. This resulted in a further (comedic) mental disorder: Spry began to exhibit a peculiar relationship to advertisements; he developed a bizarre literal-minded belief in the promises of all 30-second TV commercials, with various amusing consequences.

What does this comic proposition, the figure of a man whose attention span is cut to the typical duration of an advert, and who thus takes ads' promises literally, tell us about how we commonly think and feel about advertising? The aim of *If You See God Tell Him* was to make us laugh. Like many comedies this series portrays an *exception* that proves the rule. The rule here is that ordinarily, people expect and are expected to retain a 'natural' capacity to process and recognise adverts with judgement and to respond appropriately – 'normal' people do not take adverts as gospel. Anyone not exercising alert discrimination in the marketplace deviates from this norm. Such attribution of deviance, and its comedy value, depends on the fact that a good part of the common sense about our relationships with advertising assumes a healthy mistrust and a casual indifference. To the audience of *If You See God Tell Him* Godfrey Spry was laughable because he deviated (quite widely) from this shared, common-sense understanding. He is puppet-like and advertising pulls his strings. Audiences' laughter – at his vulnerability, loss of autonomy and naïve trust – stands as a sign of, and marks off, a normative sense of our confident scepticism in the face of ads. *If You See God Tell Him* would make no comic sense unless this capacity to recognise advertisements, and to grasp and manage their generic purposes, formed an important part of our common sense.

But common sense is not simple. The complication? There is *another* common sense about our relationship to advertising. What is *also* believed about advertising, at times, contradicts the optimistic 'water off a duck's back' view implicit in our laughter at Godfrey Spry. This can be illustrated by looking again at *If You See God Tell Him*. According to this other 'common' sense, Godfrey Spry's 'disorder' highlights the widely held view that people (including at times ourselves) become, in some sense, 'gullible' when faced with advertising. In this alternative reading the comedy is to do with self-recognition. Spry becomes the object of a satire, a caricature reflecting, and reflecting *on,* individual and social weaknesses. We see *society's* faults exposed and personified in Spry. At a personal level, the comedy allows us to reflect on an exaggerated depiction of our own vulnerability to the advertising promise. In this vision advertising is (comically) revealed as 'a threat to autonomy': our own and that of others. Undefended against the persuasive powers of advertisements, the comedy warns us, we are *all* Godfrey Spry. Viewed as satire, *If You See God Tell Him* is a gentle nudge, a readjustment in the 'community', aimed at an apathetic society becoming ever more complacent about the influence of advertising.

When assessing advertising, and its social impact, arguments move back and forth between the first optimistic view and this second more pessimistic one. Regarding this common variability, as much a function of mood, or social habit, as of any definitive evidence, one thing is clear: in establishing what 'advertising' is, and our relationship to it, in dissecting its 'character', its 'effects' and its 'functions', common sense cannot provide definitive answers.

While in most cases we have no difficulty in talking about 'advertising' – to complain about it, or celebrate it, or just to express our indifference – it is much harder to articulate *relationships* to advertising with certainty, for example by establishing patterns of cause and effect, either on individuals or in society. 'Common sense' recognises many questions about advertising: does it manipulate or exploit us? Does it make us buy things we shouldn't buy? Does it misrepresent our lives, and so on? But common sense does not reliably offer convincing or coherent frameworks (or the evidence) with which to answer these questions confidently.

## PUBLIC OPINION

We've been taken over by the advertiser, that's the trouble. We've been brainwashed by packets of detergent. That's a good phrase: 'We-have-been-brainwashed-by-packets-of-detergent.' I'll come out with that down the coffee bar tomorrow night.

(Tony Hancock from *The Succession – Son and Heir* 1961)

As part of their work monitoring the overall reputation of advertising, industry bodies, such as the Advertising Association in the UK, periodically track how often members of the public discuss advertising (Bonello 2000). A UK-based survey conducted in 2000 for the Advertising Association reported that:

advertising is not a hot topic of conversation; only 6 per cent discussed it often, compared with family (48%), violent crime (43%), health (35%) and education (33%).

(Bonello, *Campaign*, 4 August 2000)

A similar recent survey (conducted in 2003) reported that only 2 per cent of respondents felt that advertising was a social concern requiring immediate attention (T.O.M Public attitude to Advertising Survey, *Advertising Statistics Year Book* 2004: 239).

Despite the prominence of advertisements in everyday life, the frequency of advertising issues being in the news, and the interest academics take in advertising, the population (as reported here) does not necessarily privilege it in conversation (relative to other important topics). Nor, according to this survey research, do many respondents class advertising as a serious social problem. Maybe advertising is a topic that interests just the 'chattering classes' – marketers around metropolitan water coolers, lifestyle gurus, Sunday paper columnists and academics.

Perhaps excessive analytic emphasis is given to advertising, overstating its cultural significance and social impact at the expense of *real* issues (Lodziak 2002; Lee 1993; McGuigan 1992), such as the many forms of social injustice. However, a rejoinder to such claims is that our grasp of the facts of social inequality is masked by the normative mythologies of affluence pervading advertising (Schudson 1993) and a tendency encouraged by advertisements to transform general social problems into individuals' consumption dilemmas (Williams 1980), so that indirectly advertising has extensive influence, rendering (by its distractions) some kinds of thinking and action less available than they ought to be – and compounding social problems.

From another perspective Davidson (1992) observes that people will routinely dismiss the 'pretentious' nature of advertising (see also Garfield 2003). However, he disputes the argument that advertising doesn't matter:

> Disdain is only really skin deep, a mantra we are good at reciting but can't possibly believe. (Witness endless arguments about the technical merits of cars those arguing will never be able to afford, or the hankering of ex-pats for Marmite and cornflakes.)
>
> (Davidson 1992: 48)

Davidson suggests that because people consider consumption (and its meanings) to be important, it should follow that advertising (as a chief source of consumer information and ideas) cannot be trivial – even if people say it is. Right or wrong, what Davidson reveals is the inherent difficulty in distinguishing advertising from consumption, and products from the ways in which they are marketed. Advertising has (of its nature) many ways of collapsing boundaries between its imageries and everyday lives. The problem may be this: when advertising is considered, it can be difficult to establish where advertising stops, and *real* things start.

Typically it is hard to take advertising (in the sense of advertisements) seriously as culture, as we might a film, a book or a moral debate. The processes that may or may not bind advertisements to broader and more substantive socioeconomic issues are opaque to casual analysis – and heavily contested in academic accounts. So advertising, because of its dispersed and multidimensional nature, does not readily constitute a 'pure' object of public or critical attention; it becomes a *part* of conversations, which may also (and mainly) be about 'larger' questions such as the economy, family, education, social justice and health. Critical considerations of advertising that may apply to specific controversial product or service sectors, supermarkets, cigarettes, fast food, alcohol and so on are not necessarily relevant to advertising considered 'in general' or in other particular product areas (charities, savings, loans, FMCGs or holidays).

Nevertheless individual advertisements do often lead us to reflections on specific issues: obesity, childhood, the workplace, ethnicity, affluence and poverty, celebrity, health and gender frequently become individual and more collective preoccupations (momentarily) through advertisements' influences. In some such instances individual ads can also become scapegoats, targets upon which to discharge public and private anxieties. This role, as a site of mediated 'public conversation' (Richards *et al.* 2000) and controversy (Cronin 2004a; Winship 2000), is not coherently cultivated by ad-makers, who bear no special responsibility for 'society' or its political and conversational agendas. Nor however is the role inconsistent with a general advertising aim: to generate attention (Davenport and Beck 2001). Benetton's provocative campaigns are exemplary here (see e.g. Falk 1997). If we are to characterise advertising as a kind of conversation then it is probably the case that qua 'conversation' it's a kind of *gossip* – powerful at times, banal at others, artful, elusive, unreliable and unpredictable in outcome, variably interesting, and based in complex intentions, specific instances and locales. Some travel well, some badly. As such, advertising's public presence diverges widely from the kinds of public communications which it is routinely compared to, e.g. religion, education and political or ideological doctrine.

Despite the problems of defining advertising as a specific *issue*, gauging public opinion on advertising has a long history (see O'Donohoe 1995; Barnes 1982; Zanlot 1984). In the UK this tradition goes back to the 1940s and 'Mass Observation'. Mass Observation was an extensive government project begun in 1937 and ending in the early 1950s. The project aimed to capture public opinion across a range of everyday issues (Lukacs 2001: 34ff.). Advertising was one relatively minor topic which respondents were asked to consider, its inclusion perhaps reflecting anxieties building in that period (the 1940s), when political forms of propaganda were very much on the agenda (because of the Second World War). In addition material scarcity and consumers' anxieties were intensified, and consumption habits and related topics moved higher up the public agenda. Political and commercial propaganda techniques began to be considered in the same light.

The responses to advertising collected by the Mass Observation project can be grouped into four basic types, reflecting different positions. The 'resigned' accept that advertising is a necessary evil, which nevertheless serves as a convenient guide to purchase. A second, not dissimilar set of respondents describes actively looking at advertising, 'information seekers' hoping to learn about new products and satisfying curiosity about the availability of goods, at a time when commercial abundance was not the norm, as it is today. This interest was not always related to any direct intention to buy. A third group finds some kind of entertainment in advertisements. Lastly a number of actively resistant respondents show a steadfastly critical relationship with advertising. Box 1.1 sets out these types, with exemplary statements.

**Box 1.1  A CATEGORISED SAMPLE OF MASS OBSERVATION RESPONSES TO ADVERTISING**

**1  Resignation**

. . . It is difficult to estimate – but I choose a 'well-known make' of anything I buy without previous experience, so evidently I have been influenced by advertising and press advertising has probably contributed its share, even though I do not usually read the advertisements through.

**2  Information**

I am most likely to take notice of adverts if they contain fresh information, or are argumentative.

**3  Entertainment**

I don't think I am much influenced by advertisements though I like looking at them. Some of those that amuse me most influence me least – like the Squander bug one of Nat. [ional] Savings. I've no National savings and no money to save and I've never regretted the things I've bought.

**4  Active resistance/critical reflection**

I always endeavour to use my own judgement in appraising the quality of an article, and have a distinct bias against heavily advertised goods. In my opinion it is unnecessary to spend thousands of pounds advertising something which is first class.

And

A Kruschen ad. holding out a feeling of well-being scores over a miserable Doan's backache negative ad. I loathe those ads. which prey on the depressing side of the body e.g. mother, constipated child needs California Syrup of Figs, Pink Pills for Pale People. But press ads have never sold me beer, and by god's grace never will.

And

I am influenced quite a lot by advertising. If I see a thing advertised a lot, I tend to think it must be good. This often happens against the will of my rational self.

(Source: Mass Observation Archive)

The content of these opinions is similar to present day common sense views on advertising – with the important exception that there was less concern expressed (in the 1940s) in terms of issues of culture and representation than current audiences typically convey. Instead respondents' observations concentrated on product representation. These responses also reflected the working understandings of advertising communications predominant in that period (e.g. see Leiss *et al.* 2005; Curti 1967), when it was more often the product features and benefits that were described straightforwardly, as opposed to the more indirect image-based messages of today.

Testimony written in respondents' own words provides a useful counter (despite the title of the Mass Observation project) to analytical arguments based on the 'mass' consumer. The variety and specificity of these responses destabilises the idea of a uniformly stupefied 'mass' readership, common in academic writing at the time (Leavis and Thompson 1964), and subsequently (Packard 1957; Williamson 1978) and attributed in retrospect to past advertising audiences (see McFall 2004 for a critique of such retrospective attributions). Instead we see (partial) evidence of a more nuanced and critical stance guiding the relationship between people and the advertising they saw.

There has been a steady flow of subsequent academic work on attitudes to advertising, with some helpful summary accounts of the many surveys undertaken at various times and in different countries (O'Donohoe 1995; Harker *et al.* 2005; Waller 1999; Wight 1972). Some recent analysis (Brace and Bond 1997; Bond and Griggs 1996; Samuels and Silman 1996), focusing on TV advertising, and drawing on other studies, proposes that audiences can be categorised along the following lines (Box 1.2).

The categorisations presented in Boxes 1.1 and 1.2 are likely to be unstable and permeable. But research of this kind shows a continuing strand in the variability and ambivalence in recorded popular opinions about advertising. That such variability was as evident in the 1940s as it is in the twenty first century indicates that, within the terms of individual research projects, the terms 'contradiction' and 'ambivalence' probably describe the default 'common view'. Perhaps the key difference is that today 'boredom' and various forms of detachment commonly express negative responses to advertising, more than active moral or political resistance to advertising messages.

What research on 'common sense' tends ultimately to reveal is the *absence* of stability and consistency in communities' (or even individuals') responses. In so far as there is popular concern about advertising, when it can be located, it is fragmentary, changeable and unfocused – which is as we might expect from an entity as diverse as 'society' and when (within

---

**Box 1.2  A CONTEMPORARY CATEGORISATION
OF PEOPLE'S CONCEPTIONS OF THEIR
RELATIONSHIP TO ADVERTISING**

**1   Rejecters**
Those who dislike and reject advertising, considering it annoying and devious.

**2   Acceptors**
Those who are entertained and informed by advertising.

**3   Players**
Those who enjoy some ads, engage from time to time, but find some ads devious.

**4   Uninvolved**
Those who find ads boring.

(Source: Brace and Bond 1997)

---

the frameworks of research projects) it contemplates an object as various and multifaceted as 'advertising'.

Currently civil bodies, notably the Independent Television Commission (ITC), take an interest in questions of audience views on broadcasting standards, which includes a large proportion of advertising. In a document entitled 'The Public's View' published in 2001 the ITC reported on a survey of audience views on questions of decency and honesty in advertising, and on issues relating to more general likes and dislikes. The conclusions of the report (Box 1.3), which used quantitative methods (unlike Mass Observation), provide a robust, though limited and generalised, insight into some important everyday questions.

This is an example of how we must always consider 'interest' in views of what 'advertising' is. The report's findings shown in Box 1.3 are not dramatic, nor particularly illuminating. These conclusions and the methods used to chart 'the public view' would meet opposition from some academic perspectives. The motivation driving the production of the report could be questioned by pointing to the institutional affiliation of the report's sponsors, a broadcasting body with an indirect interest in supporting TV advertising – since 'independent' TV is 'independent' of government for funding, but heavily dependent upon advertising revenue.

A further shortcoming of such an empirical statistical method lies in its capacity to grasp only aggregates, and in the reductive treatment of a question, for instance the likes and dislikes of a diverse cultural form like advertising, which (arguably) merits more considered treatment and contextualisation. Such statistical representation of individual expressions of opinion leads, by aggregation, to the production (as opposed to the discovery) of a 'common view'. In the end such an approach is likely to produce findings that support a status quo, producing a view of consensus where, undoubtedly, there should be debate.

Even in its own terms public opinion survey research prompts scepticism (Bourdieu 1979). Problems hidden by the precision of statistical representation can be seen in the example shown in Box 1.4. Three different versions of a basic question yield different responses, which inflect the data finally produced. This comparison demonstrates a well-known phenomenon in social research – that the form of a statement inevitably influences whether or not respondents agree with it. The example here shows that an apparently minor inflection in the research statement draws a radical alteration in response.

Jean Baudrillard, in his 1968 essay on advertising, cites some public opinion research conducted at a time when Germany was divided on political and economic lines between West (which had a capitalist economy and consumer advertising as its outward sign) and East (which was

---

**Box 1.4 SURVEY QUESTIONS AND ANSWERS ON ADVERTISING INFLUENCE**

| | Statement | Agree (%) | Disagree (%) |
|---|---|---|---|
| EEC Survey | Advertising often misleads consumers | 78% | 16 |
| AA Survey | The ads you see are often misleading | 67 | 28 |
| AA Survey | I am frequently misled by the ads I see | 28 | 68 |

(Source: Corlett 1977, cited in MacDonald and King 1996: 244)

---

governed by Soviet socialism with little or no advertising as such).

> We can understand the reaction of the two thousand West Germans polled by the Demoscopic Institute: 60 per cent expressed the view that there was too much advertising, yet when they were asked, 'Would you rather have too much advertising (Western style) or minimal – and only socially useful – advertising (as in the East)?', a majority favoured the first of these options, taking an excess of advertising as indicative not only of affluence but also of freedom – and hence a basic value.
>
> (Baudrillard 1968: 189)

Baudrillard adds to the suspicion that common opinion is questionable by proposing that respondents were necessarily, and at a deep level, ideologically committed to support advertising (as a cultural form) even when day by day they remained sceptical about the value of advertisements they saw.

> Such is the measure of the emotional and ideological collusion that advertising's spectacular mediation creates between the individual and society (whatever the structures of the latter may be).
>
> (Baudrillard 1968: 189)

Such limitations provoke dissatisfaction with the versions of 'the common view' derived from researching public opinion. Having said this, other approaches to advertising and its place in society can hardly succeed if they have no basis in evidence. While 'the public view' as generated by social science or market research should be questioned in terms of its validity and meaningfulness, not to mention Baudrillard's concerns about the capacities of respondents to know their own mind, the alternatives, for example more anecdotal and impressionistic criticism, or dogmatic theoretical generalisations about advertising, have their own pitfalls – some of which will be explored in subsequent chapters. The partial and limiting nature of formal opinions-based research, as well as of more impressionistic and generalising approaches, suggests that there is a value in seeking further and complementary indices of 'the public view'.

## POPULAR CULTURE

Perhaps popular media culture can serve as the place to seek out if not a 'common sense' view of advertising then a snapshot of the current discourse through and about the topics of media-based marketing. Advertising is examined in various popular and journalistic discourses; in newspapers, current affairs and magazine features, and frequently also in popular cultural texts; film, comedy, documentary and of course within advertising itself. Advertisements frequently foreground 'advertising' as a cultural practice in itself, inviting momentary reflection and a kind of critique and analysis of 'advertising' and consumers' relationships with it. For example, this advertisement for French Connection includes (in voice-over) the following critical attack on the genre:

> Where do you think you're going? And who told you to go there? Weren't influenced by the advertising, were you? Big in your face messages like 'buy our denim'. Haven't you had enough of being told what to do, where to go, what to wear? Don't you just hate being influenced? especially by the great big offensive logos at the end?
>
> (French Connection 2004)

There may be evidence to support the view that commercial media represses discussion of advertising (Horowitz 1994, Bogart 2000, Thompson 1913), and there remains a continuing tension between editorial critique of advertising practices and the need to sell media space to advertisers. However, it would be wildly inaccurate to claim that advertising is not (at the same time) subject to almost obsessive scrutiny across popular media.

The media seem to love talking about 'media'. 'Media' influences, personalities, styles and developments are high on the news and current affairs agenda, and advertising – as a nominally glamorous element of media culture – is by no means excluded. One recent indicative development (which possibly counters the view that there is no public interest in the discussion of advertising) is The Advert Channel. Launched in September 2004, 'Britain's first 24 Hour Advert Television Channel' provides a magazine style forum for advertising discussion. Founder Chelsey Baker makes the following bid for viewers:

> Everyone has an opinion on Adverts. You love them, you hate them. They make you laugh, they infuriate you. Old classic ads remind you of days gone by.
>
> (The Advert Channel 694 Launch press release,
> September 2004)

It remains to be seen what impact, if any, this developing channel will have, but it joins an array of broadcasts serious and otherwise in which advertising is discussed, and ads celebrated, ranked and dissected; this alongside a steady flow of analytical pieces in the popular and serious press, such as Delaney's (2007) account of 'the men who made the adverts that changed our lives'. In the US each year the advertising broadcast during the Super Bowl produces speculation and review on a scale matching the launch of a Hollywood blockbuster. Increasingly also advertising and sponsorship surrounding mega events such as the Olympics and the FIFA World Cup is treated as a (controversial) element of the global cultural event.

Advertising can provoke comment and debate because, despite its obvious triviality, it seems to invite analysis at all levels. As sociologists Hennion and Meadel suggest it 'embraces the most persistent metaphysical and religious questions' and also becomes the occasion for 'the most superficial discourse about the consumer society' (Hennion and Meadel 1989). Talk show hosts, philosophers and tabloid journalists, in their very different registers, will turn to advertising in attempts at explaining or exploring particular concerns. Why? Because advertisements are always readily to hand, 'evidence' whenever we want to reflect on the ways in which, as individuals, as families, as a society and as a culture we are managing the relations between people and the things provided to us by social and economic systems. Such conversations help us to think 'collectively' about desire – its elaboration and its management.

For instance when the philosopher and popular broadcaster Alain De Botton produced his critique of a contemporary society, wracked with 'status anxiety', advertising formed an important part of his explanation, so that in a book accompanying the Channel 4 series he observed:

> It is ironic that it should be advertising agents ... themselves who are typically the first to downplay the effectiveness of their own trades. They will insist that the population is independently minded enough not to be affected by ... the siren calls of billboards they have themselves so artfully designed.
>
> (De Botton 2004: 204)

De Botton argues that (despite practitioners' defensive arguments) we are lulled (by advertising's status-based imagery) into a vicious cycle of consumption and dissatisfaction drawing us into the status competitiveness whose attendant anxieties, for De Botton, define contemporary social pathology. De Botton reiterates a critique of advertising most successfully proposed by Packard in two popular analyses published in the UK and the US in the 1960s *The Hidden Persuaders* and *The Status Seekers* (Packard 1957, 1959).

In similar vein, in a 1997 BBC production, psychologist Oliver James examined advertising as part of a broad survey of contemporary Britain, placing the nation 'on the couch'. He worked to expose our collective neuroses, and was led to make a more general point about how advertising damages the national character:

> Defenders of the genre [advertising] sometimes counter attack by citing the evidence that children quickly learn to disbelieve adverts. For example, in one study two-thirds of 126 12- to 14-year-olds believed that adverts 'often or always lie and cheat'. You might conclude from this that they are streetwise and healthily sceptical. But you might also wonder what deeper message they are receiving about lying and cheating: if society accepts and institutionalises mendacity on TV to attempt to trick you into buying goods, then presumably it is not all that wrong to lie, whatever your parents and teachers say.
>
> (James 1997: 109)

There may be some important truths in James's analysis – that advertising degrades standards for truth in public discourse. But in this case, as with De Botton's (2004) argument, advertising appears to serve a further function. As a term within broader social analysis advertising frequently functions rhetorically because as 'evidence' it offers great explanatory power (see also James 2007: 209–37). 'Advertising' personified as a kind of 'folk-devil' (see Appadurai 1986: 53) contributes quite readily to *any* argument, sophisticated, as here, or more simplistic, about why individuals and societies exhibit the various pathologies associated with consumerism (Nava 1997). Blaming 'advertising' rhetorically resolves pressing questions of social conduct and personal health and development about which we might otherwise remain more uncertain – with uncertainty destabilising critical expertise. Advertising becomes a symbolic bad *object*, which can be exposed – a token to be held up in the place of irreducible social and personal *processes* whose complexity might hinder the kinds of dramatic critique favoured in some popular media, as well as many political agendas.

Advertising surfaces as a particular concern at those moments when cultural commentators and individuals are troubled about evident deficits in the functioning of important social and cultural institutions, particularly those supporting religious, educational, familial and political forms of authority. It is argued that these are supplanted when individual action and social life are guided predominantly by advertising messages and the values associated with market-based individual consumption.

In the context of such serious criticism levelled at consumer marketing, there is a danger that advertising (its images in particular), notwithstanding its intention to propagandise on behalf of brands and individual products, nevertheless serves too readily as an object for critical attention. This attention could be distributed more widely and more precisely on any number of the political economic systems, institutional and commercial-brand interfaces and knowledge-systems (Lury 2004) through which consumption is governed.

Recently contemporary conservative philosopher Roger Scruton argued:

> Advertised goods exist in two worlds – one real, the other imaginary. And the second attracts the frustrated emotions which the real world cannot satisfy.
>
> (Scruton 2000: 84)

A number of critics from a variety of political perspectives have proposed similar views, identifying a deceptive gulf between the promise of the advertising image and the functional substance of the advertised product (e.g. Thompson 1943; Williams 1962; Inglis 1971; Williamson 1978, Goldman 1992, Haug 1986). Raymond Williams differs widely from Scruton in his political stance, but like Scruton he is critical of advertising illusion. In 1962 Williams published an important essay on advertising, describing it as a 'magic system'. The function of advertising, Williams says, is to operate continually:

> to preserve the consumption ideal from the criticism inexorably made of it by experience. If the consumption of individual goods leaves that whole area

of human need unsatisfied, the attempt is made, by magic, to associate this consumption with human desires to which it has no real reference.

(Williams [1962] 1980)

The frequency with which this critical stance towards advertising is circulated suggests it represents a key element of everyday understanding. It suggests also that such analysis would inform everyday discussion. Some recent research on children's views of advertising (Myers 2004) supports this assumption. One of Myers's 'tween' respondents, Lotty, aged 10, gives a snapshot of current views of advertising:

Advertising is good otherwise you wouldn't know what to buy. If it is on TV it stands out. *They use attractive words but sometimes they just make it sound good but when you try it is rubbish.* Nike and John Smiths are good ads. Nokia get David Beckham using its picture messaging so you think it is a good thing and so if David Beckham has one, I want one.

(Cited Myers 2004, emphasis added)

Lotty represents a variety of views briefly articulating positions which describe ads as deceptive, entertaining, useful and celebrity-driven. Lotty is able to articulate the acknowledged shortcomings of advertising, in line with James's (1997, 2007) observations, which circulate society in a variety of media. Lotty is clearly bright, but she has no special insight, she is not exceptional in her views. Indeed she speaks simply as one steeped in a culture that finds advertising problematic, and which criticises and ridicules it as a matter of routine. At 10 years of age Lotty is likely to be old enough to have developed a critical stance – much younger children are a source of anxiety in so far as they are exposed early on to advertising and because they appear able to process some advertising information (brand names and so on) while on the other hand seeming not confidently able to distinguish advertising discourse from other forms of information and entertainment (Schor 2004: 177–88), and because, through 'pester power', they place undue pressure on parents struggling to bring up children within a 'consumer culture', while also protecting them (and the family purse) from some of its excesses and costs.

With some important exceptions (children sometimes amongst them) it appears that the public are wise to the advertising promise, at least in so far as opinions expressed to pollsters and in everyday conversations, as well as and when they enjoy joke after joke across the media made at the expense of advertising cliché. Nonetheless pervasive cynicism may not feed any coherent and practical opposition to advertising. A critical disdain for advertising messages is a constitutive element of most consumer advice. Today, a part of the definition of a good and effective consumer worldwide (notwithstanding broader conceptions of personal virtue and some significant regional and cultural variances) is someone demonstrating a capacity to ignore or bypass advertising information, or at the very least to supplement decision-making processes with more reliable sources of consumer knowledge (such as personal recommendations, trying things out, face-to-face exchanges with providers, specialist consumer magazines and websites). And yet mainstream media advertising remains prominent and financially successful and growing globally (*Advertising Statistics Yearbook* 2006).

## THE COHERENCE OF ADVERTISING

Critical opinion developed in more sustained academic analysis contributes more to developed understanding by connecting advertising processes to broader analyses: of industry procedures, cultural, commercial and economic dynamics, generic forms and textual strategies and to an understanding of psychosocial processes. Advertising, and judgements about it, become more meaningful (and more complex) when they link to these broader social and commercial contexts. Advertising is a phase across the movement of objects: from their conception, to manufacture, through presentation, to marketing, retail, and on to consumption and use. Advertising criticism (positive or negative) perhaps makes better and fuller sense if connected to analyses recognising these flows and cycles (and the place of advertising within them), and connecting this further to accounts of social and cultural life. Cronin (2004a) suggests that:

> beliefs in and about advertising ... circulate in the discursive practices of ... distinct groups [and] generate material effects, stabilising and materialising the cultural and economic form that we know as advertising.
>
> (Cronin 2004a: 34)

Thus 'advertising' is substantively made up of the working assumptions and activities of a variety of stakeholders: everyday consumers and audiences; lobbyists for or against advertising in particular product sectors; industry regulators and associations; journalists and popular commentators; academic critics, industry spokespeople, market researchers, creative practitioners, media corporations, agency staff and their clients. Each, in their thinking, practice and conversation, contributes to making up the diversely constituted and complex body of 'advertising'. Each also is likely to carry various more or less tacit understandings of what advertising does, how it achieves its ends, as well as of the impacts advertising has on social and personal life. Advertising does not depend upon the acceptance of any general rationale or consensus to operate: it merely needs a critical mass of institutional and individual activities in society; processes binding consumers, advertisers, agents, media owners, corporate financiers and regulators in complex contracts of commercial and cultural habit; and perhaps paradoxically a certain indifference to advertising from those who (nevertheless) remain fascinated by it.

The following chapter examines one important location in which we might expect to find some more precise accounts and definitions of advertising – the industry itself. Necessarily (it would at first seem) advertising professionals need to develop coherent ways of thinking about (and doing) advertising. So it is useful to begin to examine, in this context, something of what it is that advertising institutions do.

# 2

# ADVERTISING AGENCIES

## Mediation and the
## creative process

Advertising has a number of functions. It is useful to recall the multiple ends attaching to various kinds of advertising. This contributes to establishing the quite broad scope of the genre. This chapter sets out some of these many and specific (and less specific) marketing functions of advertising. It should be remembered that the variation in advertising forms and contents is (to an important extent) tied to the particular aim and circumstance that occasions its production. Academic treatments in the past have been accused of understating the variety (and purposes) of advertising communications (we might say its constitutive sub-genres). Thus, a generalised view of 'advertising' as *always* symbolically rich, information 'lite' or aesthetically ambitious and (thus) (irrationally) persuasive or seductive (in more or less arbitrary ways) has occluded the existence of arrays of less glamorous and more straightforward and functional modes of advertising communications: product-focused ads, event-focused ads (e.g. advising of retail sales), recruitment ads, simple price-based ads, 'boring' ads for everyday marketing. Such mundane 'sub' genres have tended to be forgotten (or side-stepped) in favour of a look at just the aesthetically richer emotional appeals for cars, perfumes and holiday destinations – 'extraneous', 'non-informational', 'pointless' ads – highlighted further within critical analyses of the cultural imagery depicted.

Fine and Leopold (1993) have argued that advertising, like other aspects of consumption, is often misconstrued in the sense that in many analyses, each advertisement (according to this analytical frame) is misidentified as performing (in that instance) essentially the same cultural, economic and marketing tasks as any other (in any other instance), when it is often (also) useful to identify advertisements considering them as specific (and differing) instances of advertising-based marketing and as components in a more narrative-based understanding of the movement of goods through from production and 'along' a specific supply and marketing 'chain'. The advertisement is one moment in that process – a moment specific to the particular context (and conditions) of product sector (clothes, or food, or banking) and the particular advertising task at the time (e.g. brand building, price announcement or product launch) as well as with reference to the wider 'cultural' context.

Willmott (2001) elaborates Hall's (1991) typology which usefully describes four advertising aims that shape (and so also constrain) the generic forms ads typically take.

- *Sales response*: price-based ads aiming to provoke purchases or for people that decide now might be a time to pick up a bargain.
- *Persuasion*: ads that work to persuade consumers of the brand or product's functional superiority, e.g. it 'washes whiter'.
- *Involvement*: ads that aim to highlight and dramatise cultural values-based appeals where the ads aim to get consumers to 'buy into . . . something the consumer wants to be associated with' (Willmott 2001: 94) e.g. manliness, rugged non-conformity or familial warmth.
- *Salience*: ads that aim to get consumers' attention 'not because it performs better, nor because it has complementary values but because it stands out: it is radically different, it is big, it is self assured' (Willmott 2001: 94).

## SELLING THINGS, SELLING IDEAS

Advertising is a part of marketing. Its primary and original rationale, *selling things*, remains the working justification for most advertising expenditure, even when this motive is not immediately clear in the form of some advertisements. More often advertising takes on a wider brief; so we can see it used for selling products, but also in selling *ideas*. Most commonly today ads are engaged in selling *ideas about things*, or even in selling *things as ideas*. 'Idea' in this context should be loosely defined to include facts, figures, functions, feelings, images: the various forms of the cultural and social meanings of things.

A basic advertisement, for example the one shown in Figure 2.1 for rice, will typically work to inform and so perhaps persuade potential consumers to buy a product, as here (mostly) on the basis of its functional properties (product type and other features). At the end of the

**Figure 2.1** Uncle Ben's rice 'For perfect rice, just put the kettle on'.

advertisement an audience does not have rice, but they have the information that it is 'out there' (and in a particular form) to be bought if desired. At its most basic, advertising offers up such information as a way of letting lots of people know about products in the marketplace; alerting to novel or periodically available goods and events, or reasserting and reframing the features of established products.

Not truly an ad for 'rice' *qua* rice, which is a raw commodity, variously refined before coming to the retail marketplace, this Uncle Ben's ad (Figure 2.1) alerts consumers to a particular kind of partially processed rice designed for quick and convenient cooking (by boiling in a bag). The ad explains this product idea by making a visual analogy with tea-making, allowing an association to be made between the process of brewing tea using a tea bag and Uncle Ben's rice-in-a-bag product. However, the analogy with the tea bag contributes to another aim: to normalise the unfamiliar – to domesticate a potentially alienating cookery process. Thus, as well as providing a clear idea of what the product does, the ad also provides the idea that this is (in a way) comparable to daily and more familiar routines, such as tea-making. The ad-makers have taken creative advantage of a practical and functional similarity that links the product to tea-making (kettle, boiling water and a bag). The assertion of similarity is extended so as to imply a comparative degree of cultural normality (one might even say 'morality') across these two distinct activities – boil in the bag rice is presented as being 'just as natural' a practice as making a cup of tea with a bag[1] – an idea we might not otherwise have accepted without this ad's framing of the product. Figure 2.2, a US ad from the 1920s, makes the point even more clearly. The idea of strength and reliability is associated with the services provides by the Prudential with a concrete representation, a sign of the idea of enduring strength. The work of linking, performed automatically by today's readers, is 'spelt' out with the further image of the chain links (see Figure 2.2).

Advertising is able to 'sell' (or at least suggest) quite abstract ideas, from practical product concepts to more abstract cultural values. For instance political ads urge the electorate to vote for this or that political party and ads in many product sectors suggest, variously, that we try to save money, buy authentic goods, try new things or help feed the starving. Advertising's brief thus extends beyond producing the call that we buy a thing, and moves routinely to suggest that we behave differently, in social, personal or political decision making: to be more aware or to think or rethink an issue or a particular consumer object. Products are not forgotten; but selling products as *ideas* is at the heart of the advertising process, so that advertising is a business that depends on a creative transformation. The advertising agency is there (among other things) to turn objects into ideas; framing products in such a way that they are more likely to be intelligible (and acceptable) to consumers' practical and moral sense – not to mention their desire.

Typically the form of an advertisement supports an attempted conjunction – between ideas and product – with the advertisement suggesting a persuasive idea, for example, 'rebuild family ties in everyday dining rituals', or 'eat conveniently', or 'save securely', and suggestively implying that consumers can best approach this end by purchasing the advertised product. The advertising form allows these momentary propositions so

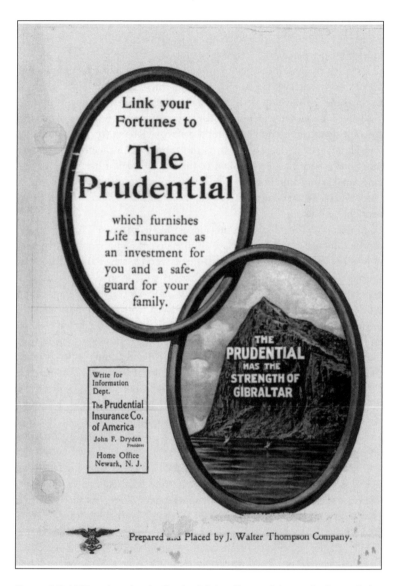

**Figure 2.2** 1920s advert for the Prudential, 'spelling out' the work of associative linking. Courtesy of the J. Walter Thompson archive at the Hartman Center, Duke University.

that a product or activity can become the means to better materialise particular and attractive cultural 'ideas': ideas including but not restricted to those practically or functionally associated with a product's use or properties. The advertising form makes such ideas readily 'graspable' and, in a sense, *purchasable*.

Advertisements' messages are not always set out in the form of logical propositions, such as 'if you buy *this* then you will achieve such and such an outcome, or develop such and such a quality'; instead suggestions are implicit or 'connoted'.[2] The advertisement portrays an image or otherwise conveys significance and feeling for a particular object (or set of objects). Not all advertising clearly presents the product as a means to any clear functional, emotional or social ends. Instead the ad affirms a more or less tangential association between an advertisement 'idea', such as a sense of 'authenticity' or feelings attaching to rebelliousness, and the advertised product.

In everyday life, distinguishing 'ideas' from 'products' in advertising can be difficult. Certainly there is, in the advertising form, an intriguing play between the material product (the occasion for the ad) and the ideas, images and sounds through which the attempt is made to define the product for its potential markets. Thus some advertisements appear to work to make abstract ideas (financial service concepts, ethical debates or lifestyle advice) more concrete for an audience, and so more accessible and immediate, while other advertisements appear to propose ostensibly quite simple objects (a drink or a shoe or chewing gum) and represent them to audiences in terms of complex cultural 'images'. For instance the relatively simple advertisement for Uncle Ben's rice (Figure 2.1), describes some of the basic properties of its rice product while presenting far more complex qualitative ideas and images, pointing to the heritage and cultural meanings of this brand of rice, and requiring a casual re-engagement with a familiar icon.

Most frequently achieved through visual means, the aim of advertising is to associate qualities with objects via (multi-) media representation. There is something *adjectival* about much advertising – as the following (sensually) spoken text from a 2005 TV campaign makes clear.

> This is not just chicken; this is a farm assured naturally fed extra succulent Oakham chicken. This is not just broccoli; these are hand picked spears of young tender stem broccoli. These are not just potatoes; these are pan ready to roast extra crispy King Edward potatoes. This is not just a Chardonnay; this is an exclusive Languedoc gold label Chardonnay. This is not just a pudding; this is a melt in the middle Belgian chocolate pudding served with extra thick channel island crème. This is not just food; this is M&S food.

**Figure 2.3** 'Not just potatoes': Marks & Spencer's TV advertising 2005–6.

A point often made about advertising is that it encourages people not just to buy things but, in doing so, to acknowledge and perhaps take on some of the more complex cultural qualities claimed for the product in its advertising. Brands are important repositories of such ideas.

## BRAND IDEAS

As marketing has developed, an important additional concept has come increasingly to inform marketing practice: branding. Branding is a topic in itself and will be returned to elsewhere in the book (see Chapter 3), as well as being the focus of another book in this series (Danesi 2006). Branding, like marketing, must be understood as an activity to which the various advertising genres are intimately bound, but which extends to include activities that are not strictly advertising. In the context of thinking about advertising's basic aims we should see brands as evolving complexes of powerful cultural ideas (Holt 2004) – ready-made associative chains produced with the intention of both defining the brand and engaging consumers – emotionally, morally and intellectually.

In the example above (Figure 2.1) we know that this rice product is brought to market in the name of 'Uncle Ben', a character who has become a symbol for a variety of rice-based products and who, over many years, has become a commercial cultural icon signifying a number of ideas, including a certain tradition, some notions of family, and the 'authentic' culture of the American south. Thus, as well as the ad providing a practical message about how the product works and the more subtle suggestion –

the normalcy of the boil in the bag process – the ad is redolent with familiar and trustworthy imagery (in the Uncle Ben iconography) and thus in a strong position to achieve a degree of trust. This product might be a new idea – but it is from good old Uncle Ben, so we might try this new way of cooking rice because its novelty is nevertheless rooted in a familiar brand name. Likewise at the end of the M&S ad (Figure 2.3) we seem to 'know' that the food depicted is *qualitatively* different from 'just' ordinary comparable offerings. The ad affirms the brand: the brand underpins the ad and the product.

Brands are supremely adapted to work as complex marketing 'ideas'. A moment's reflection on contemporary culture will reveal the extent to which branded communications and attendant meanings seem to proliferate. The brand image and its established values are important resources for anyone making an advertisement, providing a legacy of significant imagery and recognisable points of reference to draw on or play with.

Advertising is a powerful and contributory element in the work of branding and in the ongoing re-production of brands – in a process that allows numerous complex ideas to attach to a particular *logo*, a logo that is attached in turn to a product (or a service), to packaging, and across the marketing environment. If we choose, we can attach these iconic logos to ourselves – hoping to ensure that our bodies and our environments might reflect some of the ideas (or 'vibes') encapsulated in brand iconographies. Brand logos thus become mobile and powerfully simple forms embodying and carrying on complexes of cultural 'ideas' (including feelings, attitudes and meanings). Enthusiastically or otherwise consumers participate at times in this symbolic activity and advertising plays its own part in the maintenance and circulation of brand meanings.

As a cultural genre, and as part of brand development and communications processes, the form of the advertisement attempts, with appropriate style, to make appeals in which products 'become' good ideas and in which good ideas 'become' products. In an era when branding is an increasing preoccupation for advertisers and consumers, brands become one of these very significant sources of such ideas. Thus advertising has a dual role in relation to brands:

- to attach the brand idea to the advertised product or service in appropriate style;
- to feed and develop the brand idea – with each ad as a contributory iteration of the brand.

Such 'translation' – between ideas and products, and between ideas, products and brands – requires artful processes of meaning-making and symbolic communication. It also requires efficient back-up systems of knowledge management and exchange. While the outcome of this work is revealed in the form of advertising texts (and subsequent chapters on semiotic analysis of texts will explore this further), it is useful also to consider advertising as a broader process of mediation where products are worked through a series of conceptions and re-presentations. This often complex work is performed (or managed) by an advertising agency.

## THE ADVERTISING AGENCY

The advertising industry's central institution, the advertising agency, has developed to help manage and mediate relationships between producers and consumers. Advertising agencies market their services as effective communicators to their potential clients, advertisers, which might include various service providers (like banks or travel agents), brand owners and media companies (for example Nike, Heinz or Disney), retailers (like Tesco or PC World), charities (Such as Oxfam, Amnesty International or PDSA) and manufacturing companies (who make things for sale). These various types of advertiser might seek quite different things through advertising, but the advertising industry works to serve almost everyone who needs to speak to their consumers through the media. Advertisers turn to an advertising agency to find a 'voice' and to find or consolidate an audience of consumers.

Advertisements are the major visible outcomes of the agency's work, a marketing genre designed to serve as instruments or 'devices' (McFall 2004) to help 'intermediate' between production and consumption. Advertising is also a cultural genre which operates by linking producers' products to a version of consumers' 'ideas' – their needs, desires and practical routines – to maintain, establish or re-position the product or the brand as a living part of the consumer culture.

The major role of the advertising agency is to manage and develop processes for the repeated display of goods – usually, but not exclusively, goods for sale. The promised outcome of such work (paid for and performed on behalf of the producer/provider/manufacturer or other interested party) is to provoke consumers' repeated contemplation of goods. The further major intended consequence of provoking such attention promises to bind advertisers' provision of goods and services to potential consumers' existing ideas, their needs and their desires – this in such a way as to increase consumer knowledge and approval of the thing being advertised. The intention is that by increasing knowledge and approval of products, eventually some (increased) expenditure or some other mode of engagement might follow. Thus advertising agencies aim to contribute in an ongoing project producing series of advertisements organised in 'campaigns', which serve as a fundamental part of their various clients' broader marketing strategies.

People working in advertising are often classified among the 'new cultural intermediaries' – those drawn to work outside more traditional professions and who pursue careers which reward their disposition towards creative and symbolic communication. The intermediary role is at the heart of the advertising process (Featherstone 1991; Nixon 1996, 2003; McFall 2004; Hennion and Meadel 1989) and is basic to understanding the work of advertising businesses.

## ADVERTISING: PROVOKING ENGAGEMENT

All producers and distributors of goods and services work to try to establish relationships with consumers (and potential consumers). For marketers, advertising is a 'tool', bought and used to help build and maintain such profitable market relations. More issue-based advertising is a tool for managing 'public relations'. For consumers, objects and ideas come to matter and have meaning in so far as they are culturally intelligible – acknowledged or acknowledgeable as part of their life (or 'lifestyle'). Advertising aims to assist in the production of this intelligibility – with the promise of improving commercial relations and, typically, profitability for advertisers.

Relationships between consumers and products or brands can be classified on a continuum. At one end the relationship may be involved, perhaps emotionally intense or exciting, or more mundane, but ingrained as 'routine'. Some 'everyday' retail brands (such as Tesco, Asda/Walmart or Waitrose) now offer 'product coverage' in almost all areas of life – from food to finance, medicine and travel. They can thus provide a long-standing focus for the 'rituals' of families and individuals, even provoking a sense of belonging. Consumers become heavily involved with such brands, especially when retailers add membership loyalty schemes to encourage frequent shopping visits. Some advertising works to extend consumers' existing engagement, to invite new 'members', and to further consumers' ongoing involvement with the brand or product. Other brands thrive on more sporadic but intense appeals – to consumers' desire for novelty, luxury, excitement or self transformation.

Consumers can become very attached to the objects they buy, such as cars or phones, investing a lot of emotional energy in such items. So mobile phones become a functional and durable symbol of social connectedness, while a car might stand as a symbolic reminder of independence and good taste. In each case a product is not just a thing, but a meaningful thing – an object that matters and which is talked about and valued. Advertising, linked primarily to initial purchase and not to ownership, may not necessarily have a role in such involvement[3] and meaning-making, but as a genre it strives to speak to consumers' disposition to seek and to find meanings in things – alert to consumers' preference for objects that 'make sense'.

It should be remembered that consumption is ordinarily quite prosaic and it would be wrong to overstate consumers' involvement with all goods – there are things that do not inspire much thought or feeling. Consumers' attachments are selective and specific – for some a car or a phone can be (or become) just that; a thing. Just as objects and brands are sometimes involving, so conversely consumers' relationships with products or brands may be fleeting, random and unpredictable, based on little or no emotional or financial investment (for example a packet of Polos or a T-shirt).[4]

It is important to make clear that the capacity of advertisers to set the agenda in regard to meaning-making and product attachment is limited; consumers attribute meanings and attachment to objects which can be more or less entirely unrelated to the meanings intentionally attached to them in persuasive advertising and brand communications. A sense of ownership, practical use and sentiment can each have considerable influence (over time) on the production of the meaning of consumers' objects. It is well known that the product meanings intended by advertisers can rapidly 'wear out' – leaving the object 'empty'. But other, more personal meanings can emerge – with usage, with habit, with wear – or as products circulate as gifts or tokens of esteem.

Advertising professionals are happy when pub goers demand 'a Stella', or 'a Bud', or 'a Grolsch' – because they hear the consumer identifying the object of desire with the name of a branded commodity. However, many consumers specify only the generic; in this instance perhaps asking simply for 'a lager'. Here, as across many product sectors, the consumers' relationship is with the commodity – the thing and not the product name. Thus, for advertisers the aim is to increase the chances that the consumer will be guided to make their choice in terms of a brand name, perhaps by bar staff, or by point of sale brand symbolism, or perhaps because of the success of advertising campaigns past and current. The battle for marketing, using advertising as one key tool, is to transform and cultivate the marketing relationship so that the consumer will at some level recognise and connect with the object *in the guise of its branded name* – and perhaps pay a premium (Pine and Gilmore 1999; Roberts 2004). Thus the aim of advertising, in its contribution to a brand relationship, is threefold. Advertising aims to:

- transform the fleeting and unreliable consumer into the regular buyer;
- secure and deepen consumers' relationship with the brand or product;
- prevent 'infidelity' – that otherwise might lead the consumer to select generic/retail branded commodities or competitor brands.

Involved or uninvolved, enduring or in passing, consumers' relationships with products and services are important, indeed fundamental to the economic process of businesses and society at large, so advertisers know that the communication and the effective representation of products in the culture are of supreme importance for maintaining (or growing) a commercial enterprise. Advertising agencies are there to try and help their clients to achieve more profitable and more predictable relationships with consumers using developed communication skills to better assure the link between producers and consumers transforming objects made for market into products and ideas that make sense.

Producers *need* consumers: their attention and, in particular, their money. And consumers look to producers to provide products (and services) for the satisfaction of needs, wants and desires. But there are some major barriers to achieving the marketing relationship. In marketing-intensive societies consumers can (and do) ignore and withhold attention and interest. They can be distracted and sometimes they switch loyalties, for example to change a mortgage provider, try a new brand of trainers or give to a different charity. Consumers may not be able to access the specific products that producers offer, for reasons of geography or finance; consumers may not be willing or able to spend the time or money required. Consumers may not know, understand or care about what's on offer from a producer. For example, while advertising new cars is an enormous and highly visible enterprise in global markets, there are, equally, millions of non-drivers and non-purchasers who are marginal in the process,[5] and functionally outside an enormous marketing effort – to which, nevertheless, they are routinely exposed. Boredom, ethical decisiveness, fashion or economic constraints – these and numerous other kinds of consumer inertia put a brake on desire and expenditure. Advertising agencies' promise is to help find solutions to improve advertisers' success in these difficult marketplaces.

For the producers' part, they *hope* to provide the products and services that sufficient numbers of people are prepared to consume and at a price that consumers are prepared to pay. Typically they do all they can, within the considerable constraints set by the need to make profits, to encourage consumers' purchases and continued relationship (see Figure 2.4). So producers of goods and providers of services hope to minimise the costs of production, distribution and promotion – while nevertheless remaining

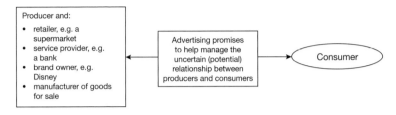

**Figure 2.4** Advertising: between production and consumption.

consumers' preferred choice. This is a difficult balance to strike. Ultimately producers aim to make the biggest and most enduring profits, with the minimum of risk. Advertising takes on a role on behalf of producers and promises to manage part of this risk by ensuring relations between consumers and their clients are maintained and developed effectively.

The advertising industry, primarily ad agencies, exist *on behalf of producers* (and in return for pay) with the promise to help organise, explain and control aspects of producers' relationship with consumers. To do this, agencies must:

- understand the product for sale in detail;
- understand what potential consumers think and might want from the product;
- know how best to reach the audience, to get and keep attention for the product;
- present the product creatively to its market – make the product mean something to potential consumers.

Advertising agencies have various means at their disposal to help with these aims, and are internally organised around those means, namely, account management and planning, research, creativity and media buying. The work of the advertising industry is divided so that attention is given to:

- liaising with the client/and remaining alert to/contributing to brand strategy development;
- researching and understanding consumers;
- planning and buying media space;
- producing creative and effective advertisements.

As Figure 2.5 shows, the media are central to the process, as the media (for advertising) serves as the major means for targeting and reaching audiences of potential consumers. Advertising serves as a link between

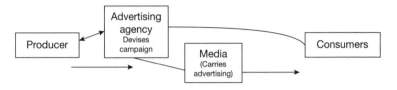

**Figure 2.5** Advertising as a link between products, consumers and producers.

products and consumers via the media, and between consumers and producers via research, creative product presentation and other forms of information.

Given the advertising agency's function to intervene in, guide and 'join-up' relationships between the sphere of production and the world of consumption, the main communications media, press, TV, cinema, radio and outdoor media and now the Internet are integral within all advertising processes. For advertising agencies media serve as tools for linking producers to consumers (White 2000, Yeshin 2006 and see Chapter 3). Contemporary advertising companies have outsourced the media-buying element of the advertising task and so collaborate with media-buying companies in delivering campaigns.

## THE ADVERTISING AGENCY AND THE CLIENT

The thousands of advertisements published or broadcast daily in the major media are the result of collaborative relationships between advertising agencies and their clients. Consider Figure 2.6, an advertisement in *Marie Claire* for a Nokia mobile phone, the 'advertiser' being Nokia. The agency's 'client' is Nokia Plc, whose factories make the phone and who own the Nokia brand. The advertising agency, which managed the process in which the ad campaign, of which this ad is one part, was planned, researched and designed, is Grey Worldwide, a well-established global agency (in turn belonging to the WPP media group). A company called MediaCom bought the media space (in *Marie Claire*). This space would have been bought from the media owners, which in the case of *Marie Claire* is IPC media, a company that owns and sells space in a number of magazines, including *Marie Claire*. The principal and direct commercial beneficiary when ads are placed in their space is the media owner (here IPC). The client, here Nokia (alternatively referred to as an advertiser or brand owner), expects to recoup this expenditure on the advertising campaign, of which this ad is a small part, in the form of a particular commercial advantage, such as increased awareness and understanding of,

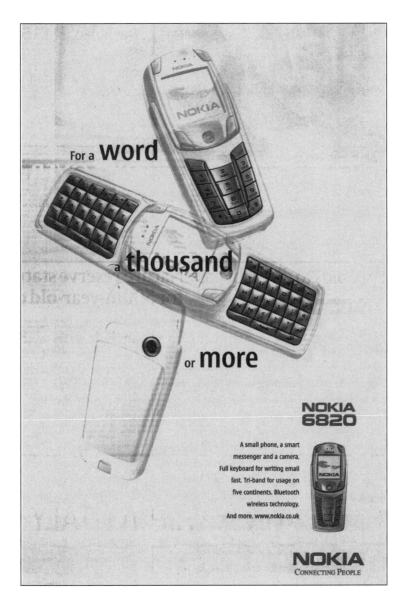

**Figure 2.6** Nokia mobile phones ad: Nokia is the 'advertiser', 'clients' of the agency, Grey Worldwide.

---

**Box 2.1 CLIENTS, THE ADVERTISING AGENCY AND THE MEDIA**

| | |
|---|---|
| **Advertiser/client** | Nokia: Finland-based mobile handset manufacturer |
| **Advertising agency** | Grey Worldwide, an international advertising agency (owned by WPP) |
| **Media buyer** | MediaCom, a media buying and planning company |
| **Media owner** | IPC Media, owns a portfolio of consumer magazines |
| **Media title** | *Marie Claire*, a popular women's magazine |
| **Reader/consumer** | Perhaps you, as well as about 400,000 mostly female ABC1 readers[6] |

---

and esteem and demand for, its products among the 400,000 readers of that issue of *Marie Claire* – see Box 2.1.

Although we know the finished products of advertising agencies very well – the hundreds of thousands of advertisements we have seen throughout our lives – we probably have little interest in the agencies that produced the advertisements. Ads are made on behalf of the client and they belong to the advertiser who has paid for them. It is the client's name that needs to be communicated. Agencies, as a kind of 'middleman', are backstage in the process. For instance, we have heard of Kellogg's Cornflakes, but we don't know much about J. Walter Thompson; we have probably enjoyed advertisements for Levi's jeans, but are unlikely to have heard of the agency Bartle Bogle Heggarty who made them; and, as in the example above, we may well own a Nokia phone, but require no knowledge of Grey Worldwide advertising, or MediaCom. Box 2.2 lists some advertising agencies and the names of well-known clients whose accounts they currently hold.

There are many types of advertising account, as Box 2.2 makes clear. Advertisers come from all product sectors, and some clients are not really engaged in selling products or even services. Potential advertising clients extend from the UK government, which increasingly uses advertising to inform and persuade the public on important issues, to confectionery companies, selling sweets. It is interesting, too, that media companies, such as News International and Channel 4, advertise in order to increase the sales of their media products – for example *The Times* newspaper or (for Channel 4) the viewing figures for various programmes; this is partly

**Box 2.2 SOME WELL-KNOWN ADVERTISERS, THEIR CLIENTS AND THEIR CURRENT ADVERTISING AGENCY 2002/3**

| Advertiser or client | Product sector (indicative) | Agency currently holding the 'account' 2002/3 | Amount advertiser spent on advertising in 2002/3 (£) |
|---|---|---|---|
| Cadbury Trebor Bassett | Sweets, e.g. Jelly Babies | Euro RSCG Wnek Gosper | 17,900,000 |
| NatWest Plc | Banking | M&C Saatchi | 21,000,000 |
| News International Plc | Media, newspapers | TBWA London | 11,610,000 |
| Lunn Poly Ltd | Tourism, holidays | WCRS Ltd | 6,000,000 |
| Diesel | Fashion | Have no agency – they handle it themselves | 1,000,000 |
| COI Communications | Government, public information | Numerous agencies used by different government departments and ministries | 95,000,000 |

Source: *Advertisers Annual* (2004)

to increase the value of the media space that they, in turn, are selling. Some companies such as Diesel do not use an ad agency but handle their design and media work themselves.

In the agency–client relationship, the client, via its marketing group, is in overall charge. 'The client picks the agency, decides the product to be marketed and decides whether or not to use the ideas generated by the agency' (Bivins 2004: 60). The agency can work with varying degrees of autonomy on its clients' accounts, and can be treated as a treasured partner or as a dispensable service.

Advertising executives understand that their clients can review and perhaps terminate contracts with the agency. This happens for various reasons, for instance if current or projected creative strategy appears stale, if the client brand concerned is losing ground somehow, because of moves further up in the agency (with an account following a breakaway team), or even if the people involved just don't see eye to eye. Effectively the agency is 'sacked' and the account (and the attendant income) goes to another, competitor, agency.[7] The UK advertising industry's trade papers are full of news about clients moving accounts between agencies. Industry journal readers (normally advertising and marketing executives) are professionally and personally concerned with which advertisers are ditching which agencies, and which accounts have been 'won' and 'lost'. For instance, of minimal interest to most people, but headline news within the industry, was the announcement late in 2007 that one agency, Miles Calcraft Briginshaw Duffy, had retained the £26m advertising account for Waitrose after the account was placed 'under review' (Nettleton 13 December 2007) while another story (Dutta 3 March 2008) reported that VCCP (Vallance Carruthers Coleman Priest) lost its 'five year hold on' the ING banking account to rival agency BMB (Beattie McGuinness Bungay). Similar moves happen weekly.

## TRANSFORMATION: FROM PRODUCT TO ADVERTISEMENT

When an advertisement finally appears it is usually the expensive crystal-lisation of a labour-intensive process. Advertising demands a combination of bureaucracy and creativity, and a balancing between the interests and priorities of an agency and its client. The client is likely to be preoccupied with the ad's description of the product and its availability, or with maintaining the brand; the agency may hope to give more emphasis to creative ideas which, they will argue, are most important in gaining consumers' attention. The basic structure (Figure 2.7) of the process exhibits the painstaking degree of planning and process that surrounds any final advertisement.

A new client contract typically follows an active sales effort, driven by the agency's new business team, including a competitive 'pitch', in which the agency sets out its credentials and proposes possible creative and campaign strategies. The client talks to the agency through an account handling team, typically via the account manager, who deals with the pragmatics of the client relationship – finance and project management. Working in parallel are account planners, individuals who are assigned special responsibility to manage and administer the agency's overall strategic relationship with particular clients – 'interlocutors' (Hennion and Meadel 1989: 177) or 'creative managers' (Hesmondalgh 2002: 53).

It is important that clients set out the general marketing situation and discuss their initial thoughts about the aims behind the projected advertising. This briefing will be relayed, by the account handling team, to teams in the agency dedicated to specific advertising tasks – research, planning, media or creative staff. The agency needs to know its object as well as the marketing objectives. The product must be understood intimately. Supported by preliminary research, account team members, including creative staff, will get to know the product (as relevant) through use, factory visits and technical briefings. They will also draw on accrued informal knowledge of the product sector and likely consumers.

Media strategists and creative teams will in turn develop campaign plans and concepts, in a process overseen by the account planners. The planner's role is to develop and integrate concepts towards producing the overall campaign with reference to creative and marketing dimensions, and media elements. Crucially a planner, in consultation with the client and researchers, will develop the 'creative brief', a document given to the creative team and used to help to 'translate' clients' abstract marketing objectives into a 'living' creative execution. In the creative brief general objectives and 'buzzwords' are used to spark ideas in the creative team charged with producing the advertisement. Agencies vary in the detail, but typically the brief will set out ideas about: what it is the client is trying to communicate; who the audience is; why the ad is being made; what it is that *must* be included; what tone of voice, 'look' or style the ad needs; what the audience is being asked to believe in, or do; and the general aims for the brand. The creative brief is a 'multiform definition of the product' (Hennion and Meadel 1989: 177). It is the advertising 'idea' in the abstract. It informs the process of drafting and mocking-up, towards the production of possible directions for a final advertisement.

Sometimes work is done, formally or informally, to test embryonic ads with an audience. Important changes of approach or of emphasis can be made at this stage, and the research-based or informal approval from 'guinea pigs' can be an important tool in gaining the client's go-ahead for a campaign idea. An account planner will take responsibility along with the account manager for communicating research findings to the client as they develop. Indeed the client needs to be kept updated on the development of the campaign across the board, and the agency works hard to ensure that the client, usually represented by its marketing team, understands and approves of the initial campaign plans. Ideally a continual process of managed dialogue will be maintained but, specifically, at key points in the development of the campaign, relatively formal presenta-

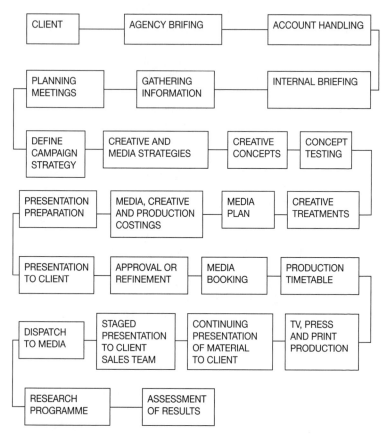

**Figure 2.7** Stages followed by a typical modern advertising agency in
the preparation of an advertising campaign for a client.
From Josling 1995.

tions will be made, setting out creative and (sometimes) media plans.
Client approval will be given and a cost agreed, or, as often happens,
suggested changes will be made. Eventually the clients, account managers,
planners and creative director will resolve any disagreements. Before the
final ad is produced and aired (or printed) all parties, with whatever degree
of compromise, need to be persuaded that the best advertising solution
has been produced.

The model of the advertising process set out in Figure 2.7 is inevitably
a simplification. There are a number of reasons for this. Organisations
that produce advertising today are no longer necessarily constituted in

such a way that all the various functions associated with producing an advertisement – research, media buying, creative work and so on – are housed within the same building, or even part of the same agency. Such organisations, known as 'full service' agencies, have largely been replaced by more flexible clusters that specialise in only one or two of the traditional 'full service' functions, leaving other functions, such as media buying and planning, to other specialist partners. Thus a client could rely on one agency for creative work, commission its research from another company, and have the necessary media buying and planning done by yet another specialist company (see the example of Nokia in Box 2.1). Media-buying companies, such as MediaCom or Mindshare, as relatively higher volume purchasers than a single ad agency, provide better media deals, passing cost savings onto the client (Brierley 2002). This more flexible model has increasingly been adopted to the extent that the full service agency has been pronounced 'dead' (Green 1992): the aggregated 'full service' institution 'unbundled'.

Often at the highest levels of corporate ownership, however, a client, which might be working with various 'unbundled' partners, an advertising agency, say J. Walter Thompson, and a separate buying company, such as Mindshare, are nevertheless working with the same corporation, in the sense that these, and numerous other advertising, media, research, new media, design and entertainment companies, belong to a huge multinational holding company – the WPP group (in this example). The advertising industry is owned by a handful of enormous conglomerates, providing an instance of what Manuel Castells has called 'alliance capitalism' (Castells 1996: 162–4). As Hesmondalgh explains, 'the self sufficient corporation is a thing of the past' (Hesmondalgh 2002: 152). So while 'full service' has been unbundled, at the level of institutions, it is substantially reconstituted at the level of 'networks' requiring yet more competitive self promotion for agencies and other creative and media service providers. This is of particular significance in the globalisation of advertising (and advertising agencies).

As a consequence of such networked and fluid organisation of the industry, a number of new players have been able to enter the broad area of promotional and communications services provision. Management consultants can now give advice on branding, and project-manage a campaign (White 2000). And a company such as Interbrand, which is not an advertising agency, is very successful in providing and supervising expertise in some areas (including brand image, logos and product naming), which before the 1980s were more often the preserve of advertising agencies.

At the macro level 'the advertising agency' is part of a complex series of networks and partnerships; at the micro level, only to a degree and in some instances disarranged by new flexibilities (Law 1999), the advertising process, which passes through the agency, and which appears like a cohesive and integrated flow of purposive work (Figure 2.7), is in reality often fraught, complex and intense (Delaney 2007). It is important to be attentive to this process (advertisements in the making), just as it is valuable to examine the outcome (advertisement texts). The cultural impacts of advertising arise partly from the people who make the ads, and the informal cultures and practices through which they fashion themselves. As Nixon (2003) argues, 'subjective identities and informal cultures of advertising practitioners matter' because

> the informal cultures inhabited by these practitioners will both set limits on and provide resources for the performance of the creative execution in which these practitioners are engaged.
>
> (Nixon 2003: 35)

Advertising creatives do not just deliver an outcome, they put something of themselves into a campaign. This might partly explain the 'reflexive' nature of much advertising (talking about itself), the metropolitan, creative industry preoccupations, as well as the attempts of some campaigns at artistic profundity, often ridiculed by commentators such as Garfield (2003: 101), as well as by audiences and comedians.

The formal advertising agency process is likely to be, at points, compressed or truncated. Some tasks may be drawn out, others elided. A campaign may be developed over weeks and months, yet the key idea emerges in a second. Some individual ads can be conceived and produced (perhaps catching a topical mood) in a matter of days or even hours. Teams are aware that, with volatile clients, the plug can be pulled at any time. Ads are created in a stressful and 'hot blooded' (Malefyt 2003: 139–43) working environment.

The seamless unity of purpose implicit in any schematic model of the advertising agency and its processes (Figure 2.7) belies a reality in which competing agendas may be in play. This is especially the case between those agency staff who are, broadly, more closely associated with clients' priorities of finance, marketing and service provision – selling *the clients' product* – and the creative staff who, typically, are focused on portraying and satisfying a sense of themselves as advertising 'artists', a 'group apart' (Murdock 2003: 32), and who prioritise '*the image*' or creative idea. Advertising professionals 'vacillate between the two terms of [this] contrast' (Hennion and Meadel 1989). As Daniel Miller observes, in any agency project:

> a structural fault [exists] between creatives and account mangers who constantly struggle for relative authority. The former need to claim that it is creative and exciting adverts that sell products, the latter assume it is emphasis on the product itself and brand that ultimately counts.
>
> (Miller 2003: 80)

Frances Royale of London-based agency BBH, demonstrating the conciliatory tone of a creative *manager*, argues that the agency, on behalf of its creative team, works hard to 'get the cut we all want. Equally sometimes the director gets carried away with their vision and loses sight of the product' (Frances Royle, cited in Wilson 2004: 48–9).

As Hennion and Meadel describe it, the underlying tension is quite stark: 'Either products are everything, or else they are nothing. Either men are slaves, or they are mad' (Hennion and Meadel 1989: 175). This rather dramatic description captures something fundamental. What the client brings to the table, via account staff, is a real product; what advertising creatives bring, in varying degrees of moderation, is a capacity for (surreal) or 'magical' apprehensions of products captured via hints, fantasies or a 'vision' – outlandish or tempered to the everyday. The consumer, ultimately, submits or does not submit to the object so conceived and represented. Advertising clients can give such creative ambitions short shrift, as demonstrated in Alan Sugar's (2005) 'no nonsense' view of advertising:

> An advert needs to convey the right message to the market sector that is actually going to purchase the product . . . [but] . . . Advertising is so often a self-indulgence. I get irritated by watching adverts that are meaningless, and so far removed from the product they are selling to convey information. Advertising has become an art form in its own right – and an entertainment. Presumably, companies with big budgets get a return on their investment, but in some instances, frankly, I'd be surprised. In my world we keep it simple: we identify who'll buy the product and we speak to them directly and in a way that informs.
>
> (Sugar 2005: 178)

Sugar's pragmatic view of advertising (as provision of product information) often stands in contrast to the creatives' view, that consumers are bored by information, and require imagination, image, wit and 'art'. Advertising agencies are about containing this tension creatively – binding creative vision to clients' priorities.

An ad agency director who deals daily with the opposing views describes barriers between creatives and management staff in the agency and suggests a middle way:

> I find it better if you get the creative people, the planners and the account men rubbing sparks off each other, on a day-to-day basis. That means the creative work can define the strategy, and the strategy can refine the creative work, and vice versa.
>
> (Respondent, cited in Davis and Scase 2000: 92)

A further strategy that agencies and clients deploy as they work to resolve such tensions is to commission or consult research (an area managed typically by an account planner). In theory, the consumer's view of products and ad concepts, as gleaned, say, from pre-tests, focus groups and more informal methods, is a useful arbiter in deciding where to go with a campaign. However, even here the process is one of negotiation. Creatives argue that such research information, in any case 'suspect' and 'unreliable', serves mainly as a brake on creative expression (and connection with the consumer), and as a necessarily conservative guide (Nava 1997; Winship 2002), reproducing past preferences and opinions as opposed to the all-important innovations needed for good creative advertising – thinking solutions 'off the wall', not 'off the peg'.

Account managers and clients conversely argue that research information is an assurance against failure. Creativity in advertising is risky; research promises a degree of predictability – you should 'look before you leap' (Jones 2004: 141). Research alleviates client teams' commercial and personal anxieties about investing in advertising. Lury and Warde (1997) argue that this is the primary function of consumer research: to convince clients that advertising agencies *know* consumers, via research and other expertise, and so know how best to communicate in the marketplace.

The settlement of advertising strategy debates often depends on the particular quality of the relationship between the client and the agency more broadly. Some clients are very prescriptive and – through an agency's account managers and corporate formulas for advertising, or overly strong brand templates – pull creatives in on a short lead (see Jones 2004: 49–51). Other clients have sufficient faith, or budget, or are sufficiently desperate, to deploy a less strict approach.

Crucial to any campaign is the client's trust in the agency's processes for managing creativity. The maintenance of such trust, held at a high premium, is dependent on the quality of the dialogue and understanding between agency personnel and the client team and on understanding within agency departments. This can go wrong. Advertising creative Tom Carty suggests there is a great deal of meddling, from 'legions' of people working for clients, who have oversight of the final execution:

Clients have the power. They instil a culture of fear and few agencies will stand up to them . . . Ten years ago agencies would have told the client where to get off but now they are too worried about losing accounts.

(Tom Carty, cited in Wilson 2004: 48–9)

It is important that the client can maintain its initial faith in the agency and its work; but the agency cannot simply comply with the client's preconceptions of its brand in the name of preserving concord (and keeping the account) – something must be added. Thus a 'permitted disrespect' of client and the brand tacitly underpins the more or less deliberate cultivation, by some agencies (and by individual creatives), of a 'bad boy' image (Nixon 2003).

The process map set out above (Figure 2.7), and the agency model implicit within it, capture some of the extensive range of tasks, consultative, bureaucratic and practical, on which the ads we finally see rest. What this advertising process aims to secure (as part of a broader marketing and branding effort) is a transformation. Beginning with an unknown or worn-out product or concept, the agency tries to tap its creative resources in order to re-'make' or re-imagine the dull, tired, useless or inert *concept/thing*. The agency hopes (and promises) to produce in its place a symbolic and culturally refreshed or recharged object. The series of compromises, research meetings and client briefings, creative moments of quiet thought, manic brainstorming sessions, voracious information searches and serendipitous insights all aim towards a marketing outcome: to make the product *distributable in the market and welcome to consumers*. This is beyond ordinary distribution, it is not about logistics or geography, it is not even just a question of media exposure, although this is a creative task in itself; advertising is a contribution to the *cultural* distribution of products. The ad campaign allows for the product to *move*, to enter and engage circuits of exchange, commerce and culture. The advertisement symbolically re-presents the product – connects it with living ideas in consumers' lives and minds. Which is to say, as Hennion and Meadel describe it, the agency (working with the client) produces 'a thing, but destined for somebody' (Hennion and Meadel 1989: 175).

The advertising agency is the institution of such processes, 'a laboratory of desire' (Hennion and Meadel 1989). Advertising effects a translation (a modification, a humanisation), binding the brute object, via commercial creativity, to the everyday imagination of consumers. The commodity object, reconceived by advertising, is (maybe) sometimes better able to pass, as if through membranes (of varying permeability), into the consumers' 'world of goods' (Douglas and Isherwood 1978) – a world of cultural ideas about life and lifestyle. This transformative process, animating objects, is sometimes compared with magic (Williams 1980, Williamson 1978; Alperstein 2003). It is also, perhaps, a matter of infiltration. Advertisements, in this sense, are attempts to render the product *passable* against people's variously embedded disposition to *refuse* the objects of the marketplace – to make it admissible and intelligible and viable to the cultural and domestic economic 'Umwelt' – the meaningful and material world surrounding us as we move through daily experience.

As individuals and as a society we are typically alert to advertising as a practice that might contribute to an unwelcome loosening of boundaries between 'purity and danger' (Douglas 2002), good things and junk. Advertising is advocacy, and agencies claim to be the best advocates of their clients' products. It attempts to engage us as we work to discriminate in the marketplace between the authentic and the fake, between the useful and the useless, between the healthy and the unhealthy, and between the esteemed and the derided. Thus, advertising is part of a broad endeavour of promotion and advocacy. The next chapter will consider how such advocacy comes to our attention.

# 3

# MARKETING, MEDIA AND COMMUNICATION

Advertising can be related to activities in marketing under the heading 'distribution'. However, advertising is a special kind of distribution, working in markets, but also in 'culture'. Advertising agencies' creativity serves marketers' attempts to represent products, brands and services in order to make them more readily acceptable and desirable to consumers: consumers who are physically at a distance, and who are not present to consider and compare goods directly. Advertising addresses (potential) consumers who are *at a remove* and who cannot enter, there and then, into direct dialogue about services – or have hands-on contact with products. However this is not just a matter of overcoming physical distances: advertising is also concerned with cultural communication. In this sense advertising works to increase (or maintain) the extent to which particular products, services and brand ideas remain or become *culturally* distributable. Ads make marketed objects more exciting, or perhaps reassure consumers of the acceptability and value of a product, while also reminding or alerting consumers to products' availability, or prompting consumers about an imminent event – a sale or a product launch for example. To effectively manage this type of cultural distribution requires that advertisers have access to advertising agencies to help them:

- represent products, brands and related ideas appropriately and effectively in relevant markets and cultures;
- know and understand consumers (including how they change);
- locate, target and invite potential consumers (distributed in 'time' and 'space', 'society' and 'culture') via media.[1]

Advertising attempts to 'open products up' to consumers' needs, wants and desires. At the same time advertising intends to 'open consumers up' to products and their associated ideas and promises. To help achieve these ends agencies aim to provide various kinds of marketing *intermediation*, for example deploying event or product-specific and informative ads or, in other circumstances, deploying more indirect and symbolically rich modes of communication. Consumers are asked to attend to wide variations in styles and types of advertising, which include appeals variously privileging fact, fantasies or various kinds of consumer 'education'. Such intermediation is advertising's contribution to the distributive labour of getting goods or services to market, variously *moving* both products and consumers. It is useful to think of advertising distribution as simultaneously 'opening up markets' as a tool in practical commerce *and* as a genre in cultural communications.

Boxes 3.1 and 3.2 show a range of possible relationships between products and consumers using the metaphor of open and closed to characterise the relationships. An 'open' product is displayed as desirable and available. A 'closed' product is out of sight – forgotten, unreachable or unheard of: out of the mind of consumers who are 'closed' to it. Open consumers are 'out there' looking for this or that product – for *something*.

Box 3.3 articulates the intermediary role of advertising as it attempts to contribute to the work of opening products up to consumers' desires and opening consumers up to products and their promises.

Advertising targets groups across four main dimensions – demographic, geographic, temporal and cultural:

* *Demographic*: targets by social group (general or specified – age, sex, class stratifications). Note: these are typically approximations.

---

### Box 3.1 RELATIONSHIPS BETWEEN PRODUCTS AND CONSUMERS

Advertising strives to open products up to consumers and to open consumers up to products

| Product closed | Consumer closed | No purchase/recognition |
| --- | --- | --- |
| Product closed | Consumer open | No purchase/recognition |
| Product open | Consumer closed | No purchase/recognition |
| Product open | Consumer open | Dialogue/engagement/ purchase/exchange |

- *Geographic and temporal*: targets audiences (in terms of age, sex and other lifestyle variables), based on *where* they are or *where* they are going (what town, city or region they inhabit or are visiting) and *when* they are (in daily routines, various habitual cycles and in terms of day, time and season, lifecycle); also linked to product and brand lifecycles – long-term versus new users for example.
- *Cultural*: targets in terms of more or less complex cultural identifications, tastes and routines.

Interconnected local, national and global communications systems allow advertising to link its efforts at 'cultural' distribution to the work of geographic and demographic distribution. These constitute 'the media'.

The cultural work of advertising can take place only to the extent that advertisements are effectively dispersed via media: ads *must* be seen or

---

**Box 3.2 INTERMEDIATION: OPENING PRODUCTS TO CONSUMERS AND CONSUMERS TO PRODUCTS**

| | | |
|---|---|---|
| **Product closed:** product is not intelligible to, valued by or desirable for consumers | • Advertising attempts work with producers and marketers to help represent their products to optimise the chances of opening up the product to the consumer – making it practically, emotionally and culturally accessible | **Consumer closed:** consumer rejects, dismisses or does not know about product |
| **Product open:** product is intelligible, desirable and practically or culturally significant or relevant | • Advertising simultaneously attempts to work on consumers by representing the product in such a way that it can be understood to connect more readily with emotional responses (anxieties and desires) and their cultural concerns, including ethical values, practical needs and normative practical concerns | **Consumer open:** consumer feels and understands the function, value and desirability of the product – or is looking for something – perhaps unclear on specifics – but alert to wants/ needs. |

**Box 3.3 RELATIONSHIP BETWEEN PRODUCERS, MEDIATION AND CONSUMERS**

| Producers/providers | Means of mediation | Consumers |
|---|---|---|
| Producers and providers must connect with consumers on a number of levels – advertising attempts to help producers/providers to communicate with reference to consumer:<br><br>• culture (e.g. felt and understood need, desires, dispositions, fashions and lifestyle) | *Cultural distribution*<br>Advertisements attempt to situate brands, products and services in a cultural frame rendering them more intelligible and 'distributable'.<br><br>*Media distribution*<br>Advertisements must be placed in the media and located effectively in media schedules and geographic locations to connect the advertising message with appropriate audiences.<br><br>*Geographic distribution*<br>Takes place through: for goods – global and local networks of transportation, storage and retail and through licensing, franchising and territorial expansion for services. | *Consumer cultures, tastes and lifestyles*<br>'Hearts, minds and culture' – advertising opens consumers up to product- brand- and service- ideas.<br><br>*Media audiences*<br>Consumers are available to advertisers as a consequence of their media usage and can be addressed according to approximations of the size demographic constitution and geographic location.<br><br>*Consumer location and movements*<br>Place is an important variable in consumer decision making and can be targeted as a part of a national, global or local media strategy. Media choices reflect geographic variations/ decisions/market territories. |

**Box 3.3 continued . . .**

| Producers/providers | Means of mediation | Consumers |
|---|---|---|
| • geography (where)<br>• demography (who)<br>• temporality (when)<br><br>The media serve as means for organising these advertising communications across the four dimensions. | *Demographic distribution*<br>Advertisers also need to target groups with reference to who they are – used as an indicator of needs and desires – and based on variables such as age, sex, job type and economic standing. | *Segments/targeting*<br>Media audiences are 'segmented' so that typically media will strive to ensure that a programme or publication brings in particular kinds of audience profiled partly by demographic variables but also by other lifestyle factors. |
| | *Temporal distribution*<br>Goods and services are brought to market in cycles. These cycles can be set by the consumer, or, conversely, the producers can attempt to influence temporal patterns of use – by suggesting (or inventing) new meal times or new annual holidays or by extending the duration of certain holidays – such as Christmas or the school year. A great deal of advertising is linked to events – e.g. to the Olympics or World Cup or Super Bowl or entertainment shows or to retail sales or, for charities and politics, to elections or natural disasters. | *Media time*<br>Is sold in units of time as well as 'space'. Strategies need to consider aspects such as the time of broadcast (daytime/evening), cycle of publication (daily/weekly) as well as seasonality. Combinations of media permit advertising strategists to negotiate the problems of timing and spacing of ads in a campaign – e.g. around 'bursts' and 'drips': i.e. intense high exposure of ads or extended periods of fewer ads – to remind or maintain an idea/product in circulation. |

heard by their intended audiences. Since the 1950s advertising communications have depended on agencies buying space in one or more of
five main media (Box 3.4). As technologies have developed and new media
styles have evolved, advertising has provided economic and strategic
impetus for many changes in the media – broadly speaking increasing the
amount of commercial media available. At the same time other modes of
marketing communication operate alongside media-based advertising
genres.

Print media publishers (magazines and newspapers), commercial TV
companies, commercial radio stations, cinema owners and outdoor
billboard companies sell space available in their media output to
advertisers, providing advertisers with audiences for their advertisements
and earning the media owner the money to fund productions of
programmes and publications; to pay journalists, performers, production
staff, writers, directors and technical staff while also making a profit.
Advertising is a core element of the initiatives media companies take to
produce good attractive media output. The media vary in the extent to
which they depend on advertising revenues or money from direct
consumer purchase. For example, commercial TV and radio have typically,
and until recently, been entirely funded by advertising revenue, while for
cinema the bulk of income comes from ticket sales. Most press-based
media depend on a proportion of their income from both advertising and
selling copies.

Planning and buying media space are the original functions of the
advertising industry and these activities provide the foundation of any
advertising campaign. However, for advertising agencies' clients, media-
based advertising is usually only part of a broader set of marketing
communications processes. Advertising should be understood in this
(sometimes subsidiary) context – as a tool in marketing, and as one
promotional 'genre' among many. In the contemporary media environment traditional advertising is (usually) necessary to, but not sufficient
for, the total task of brand communication. Advertising takes its place
alongside PR, sponsorships, retail marketing and a number of other means
deployed by corporate bodies, in what Wernick has called 'promotional
culture' (Wernick 1991). Main media advertising is increasingly under
pressure to compete with other forms of (non-media-based) marketing
communication.

The advertising industry, hand-in-hand with media providers, produces
the most widely visible fraction of the cumulative marketing effort of the
commercial world. 'Advertising' commonly describes all of this promotional material, but strictly speaking only some items are 'advertising';
others are better described as 'marketing' or 'brand communications'.

## Box 3.4 THE FIVE TRADITIONAL 'MAIN' ADVERTISING MEDIA AND THEIR INDUSTRY REPRESENTATIVES

| Five traditional 'main' advertising media | Industry representative bodies |
|---|---|
| **Print**<br>Newspapers and magazines, including national, international, local, business and specialist consumer publications, e.g. *The Times*, *Vogue*, *The Economist*, *Marie Claire*, *The Grocer*, *Wallpaper*, *Metro*, *The Sun* | e.g. Audit Bureau of Circulation, Newspaper Marketing agency |
| **Television**<br>Commercial TV companies – including digital and analogue, satellite and terrestrial services, e.g. Carlton or Channel 4 in the UK and FOX or NBC in the US | Independent Television Commission |
| **Radio**<br>Commercial radio stations, analogue and digital, e.g. Capital in London or Virgin nationally in the UK – but not including the BBC. Local and national commercial stations | Radio Advertising Bureau |
| **Cinema**<br>Owners of cinema multiplex chains, e.g. Warner, UCI, companies like Pearl and Dean and Carlton | Cinema Advertising Council |
| **Outdoor**<br>Owners of hoardings billboards and other outdoor poster sites; includes some transport spaces, e.g. on tubes, buses and in underground stations. E.g. Maiden, JC Decaux and Viacom Outdoor | Outdoor Advertising Association |

This might be seen as nit-picking, but the classification of the various kinds of communication helps clarify our recognition of the different promotional 'genres' surrounding us – contributing to our evaluations of media content more broadly.

The proper identification of advertising as a communications genre does not depend solely on identifying promotional content in messages. Advertising can also be defined with reference to its modes of dissemination (the five – or six – main media, when we include the Internet) and the kind of communications relationship it can achieve – i.e. between a distant advertiser addressing a group of people specified primarily by their membership of a media audience or readership, and not identified directly as individuals. Both outdoor and some Internet-based advertising offer either more random targeting (outdoor, viral spamming) or more precise (some e-advertising, such as Google's advertising system).

## 'ABOVE THE LINE' AND 'BELOW THE LINE'

> Spending large sums of money on big broadcast messages is sometimes necessary for high level brand image statements, and particularly for those brands that want to reach a large mass of people, but when messages are needed to target individuals, it is very difficult to make a rational case for 'above the line' activity.
>
> (Temporal and Trott 2001: 39)

The orthodox way of thinking about the various kinds of promotional communication has been to draw a distinction between the ways different types of communications materials are distributed and paid for. Advertisements and other promotional advertising materials have been historically classified as either 'above the line' or 'below the line'. When we see an advertisement, for instance on TV or in a magazine, the advertiser/client has had to pay for the media space (the page or timeslot). Getting the ad out is a key point in the advertising process, which is typically managed by an advertising agency or by a nominated media buying company (such as Mindshare or MediaCom). It is this expenditure, on promotional messages placed in paid for media outlets, which (Collins et al. 1986) has been classified as 'above the line' expenditure and can most strictly be defined as 'advertising'. Everything else, however much it resembles advertising, in style or in intention, is classified as 'below the line'. This distinction, as with so much that tries to capture changing advertising industry practices, is conventional and theoretical. It serves to introduce a basic typology provisionally underlying some processes. Necessarily the 'above and below the line' distinction has been subject to revision for some time, with Olins (2003) for instance noting how 'Nike refused to recognize, or at least ignored, the traditional differences between above and below the line' (Olins 2003: 67).

Marketing and promotion of various kinds are basic to the economic system in the modern world. It is quite possible to manage a large company successfully without ever using media-based advertising. Until the early 1990s Marks & Spencer Plc, one of the most successful retail operations in the UK, had almost entirely rejected national 'above the line' brand advertising. The company preferred marketing strategies that concentrated on product innovation and on maximising the advantages of owning an extensive network of retail outlets at prime sites. Promotional methods, for instance in-store displays for new lines (Creer 1994) and 'word of mouth' sufficed. The iconic reputation of Marks & Spencer rested on the spontaneous circulation of good news by satisfied customers, so that, for consumers, Marks & Spencer was sufficiently a natural and accepted cultural 'idea' as well as being a traditional element in UK shopping routines. When the company began to suffer in the 1990s, this non-advertising policy came under review – with above the line advertising proposed as a way of building a new means for brand information to flow; a new way to get the 'good idea' across.

Marks & Spencer's made its first major excursion 'above the line' in a press, poster and TV campaign in 2000; the ads provoked a lot of media attention (*Guardian* 4 September 2000). Unfortunately for Marks & Spencer, by that stage floundering in a competitive market, the advertising strategy received a largely negative reception. Consumers 'hated' it (Bevan 2001: 228). Marks & Spencer has subsequently had more success with advertising, but this instance illustrates that there may have been deeper cultural and market-based forces against which advertising was unable to succeed. While negative criticism pointed at the controversial contents of the ad campaign (a naked size 16 model running over hillsides declaring 'I'm normal'), the failure of the campaign was also attributable to (some) consumers' refusal to relate to Marks & Spencer through main media advertising – identifying its longstanding policy of non-use of media advertising (alongside other institutional practices) as a distinctive and admirable sign of a trustworthy quality brand. More recently advertising has made a highly successful contribution to the re-branding of Marks & Spencer (Pearlman 2005), recent campaigns successfully integrating the brand's universal appeals to 'all kinds of women' within a niche address to younger, trendier shoppers. The high-impact TV campaigns featuring iconic supermodels and celebrities from different eras cleverly articulates the contradictory brand commitments to continuity and iconic style, shared 'looks' and individual variations, as well as to novelty and excitement.

An 'above the line' advertising strategy sometimes *is* the solution to a marketing problem, but often the problem demands other and additional changes to business and marketing strategies. There is far more to the market presence of products and brands than just media-based advertisements, and commercial companies (as well as public information providers, special interest groups and charitable causes) have access to innumerable communications tools to try to build and convey their presence. Marketing agencies have continued developing rapidly since the 1980s, spurred by waves of new technology (including the Internet, telephony and mobile and other digital devices) as well as a plethora of new ways of gathering information about consumers (and the availability of complex geo-demographic data sets). Such 'below the line' activities have gained an increasing share of the companies' marketing budget because of their demonstrable marketing effectiveness and as a response to a perceived disillusionment with traditional advertising formats among advertisers and consumers.

Today's advertisers complement or substitute media-based ads with a raft of additional means at their disposal in the ongoing work of engaging consumers. Some eschew advertising altogether and work through mailboxes, mobile phones and the Internet. They promote in numerous locations across the everyday environment. Thus agencies where service focuses on 'above the line' main media advertising have a number of competitors from among the numerous 'below the line' marketing modes and 'genres'. Contemporary agencies are reconfiguring to bind above and below the line modes – offering integrated marketing solutions.

This situation puts companies whose clients are buying such marketing services in a potentially strong position. Because the range of suppliers of marketing options is extensive, and demand for the advertisers' budget is high, companies wishing to communicate with consumers can drive a hard bargain when they negotiate strategies and prices. However, the enormous market for promotional services and the working assumption that marketing demands expert thinking and skills, and high premium expenditure, means that marketing and (adaptable) advertising companies have largely continued to do well and grow. Marketing and brand managers face bewildering arrays of 'sure fire' marketing and advertising schemes, the sheer volume of which contributes to clutter across media and other marketing environments – not to mention the resultant impact on domestic and public space.

There is a long list of below the line activities which, in their distinction from advertising, offers a sense of the communications relationships (of competition and complementarities) in which above the line media advertising is involved. For instance, the design of packaging and retail displays are important aspects of most marketing strategies. Such work demands some of the combinations of creativity and knowledge about consumer preferences as are employed in the making of advertisements. Ideally such items will co-ordinate with the brand message and icon-ographies communicated by media advertisements. 'Point of sale' display and retail layout make further contributions to the managing of the relationship between the consumer and the products or services they might want. These (and packaging) provide the final link between the physical world of the shop and the imagery and ideas projected elsewhere – especially by media-based advertisements.

Marketing includes informal and semi-formal as well as formal promotional activities: face-to-face greetings, call centre scripts, product placements in films, retail space design, word of mouth driven 'buzz' marketing and 'viral' marketing (Rosen 2000; Lewis and Bridger 2001). People, as matters of chance and of 'art', at work and at leisure, have become 'media', carrying 'advertising' on clothes, uniforms and shopping bags – with controversy now surrounding the advertising use on no-longer-'free' supermarket carriers. Enormous numbers of different brands get exposure in this way, for instance, on T-shirts – French Connection having been the acknowledged masters here, with their 'fcuk' campaigns (Brvicevic and Kay 1998), adding to the flow of brand logos through social spaces of all kinds.[2]

Beyond this the ordinary display and circulation of products in social life is a spur to marketing. The design of products themselves, for instance cars or mobile phones, embodies an aesthetic appeal which is typically conceived by producers as being co-extensive with the broader marketing and branding work of the organisation. Such consumer objects, by virtue of their design, can arguably be seen as incorporations, in themselves, of a promotional and marketing intention. Apple's iPod for instance is frequently cited as an object of consumer desire – with its advertising playing second fiddle to the visceral 'must-have' appeal of the thing in itself.

In the past marketing and advertising were processes appended to the production line, performed after the product had been made. In many product sectors it is more accurate today to think of marketing, branding and advertising as taking place (to an extent) in parallel with production and design: the marketability and image of the product 'invented' along with or even before the product itself, and in anticipatory creations of brands' extensions into new product and service sectors.

## CONSUMERS DIRECT

The direct mail (DM) industry has grown quickly in the past two decades. DM operators send promotional messages by post. Consequently each morning people wake up to a pile of 'carefully targeted' invitations: to get credit cards, to try a new travel destination or a clothing range. As the DM industry has grown, reliance on accurate and well-targeted address-based data has increased – as well as the market value of such information. An upshot of this is the emergence of a market for addresses and collateral lifestyle information about households, occupants and consumer tastes. Comprehensive systems use large volumes of data, based on the national census, to take demographic information down to post-code level. ACORN is one of a number of systems that provide 'geo-demographic' information. It is based on the assumption that the place where people live, overlain with data about incomes and lifestyle, is likely to be a guide to differentiated consumer preferences (Gough-Yates 2003: 63–4; Brierley 2002: 34). Such datasets can help more accurately to target large mail outs, where sending indiscriminately could be much more expensive, and possibly less effective at getting a message across.

Again we see producers using a mediating system (here, a DM agency and the postal service) to connect with consumers. However, this is not strictly advertising as there is no separate carrier medium and the recipient of the message is pre-specified, not as part of a media audience, but as a particular individual; hence, although carried out at a distance, DM is 'direct' marketing and not advertising. This is so even when much DM material might resemble a press or magazine advertisement. The recipient of a direct marketing appeal is typically asked to do something – to send money to a charity, return a form, or buy something (for instance from a catalogue). This call to action gives DM some advantages over media-based advertising, as tracking consumers' response level (and thus the outcome of the marketing expenditure) can be done with a degree of precision often unavailable with poster, magazine or TV advertisements.

Another related growth area is telemarketing, a data-based practice often considered intrusive by consumers. Telemarketing is thriving as a specialised extension to corporations' increasing reliance on the call centre as a general system for managing customer interactions. Superficially like (broadcast) advertising, telemarketing is not strictly advertising as the connection is direct to an individual and not to a media audience. Again there is no primary content. We can only envisage the options video telephony might permit, with its promise of a return to face-to-face selling on a grand scale.

Such technological developments, currently only partly realised, offer the kinds of interactivity and consumer focus that marketing holds at a high premium. As consumers' relationships with businesses become more interactive (the diffusion of technology permitting), digital telecom-based marketing (and associated variants) will take a greater share of marketing budgets away from traditional media-based advertising – as has happened with Internet advertising, notably with classified ads.

Interactivity offers marketers the chance to produce and manage knowledge about their consumers. The desire to *know* consumers is central to many marketing communications strategies, with numerous kinds of research and information collected daily. Marketers track consumers across a number of dimensions, charting basic patterns of purchase behaviour, producing various accounts of consumers' psychology and developing complex kinds of cultural or 'lifestyle' analysis. Tracking place and movement are important both for marketing and for advertisers seeking to optimise the geographic placement of ads and goods – so that in future GPRS technology may allow for the targeting of mobile consumers. Approximations of *where* you are (now) can nowadays be added to 'who' you are among the complex set of lifestyle variables through which producers glimpse and frame potential consumers.

Promotional communication is ongoing within existing marketing relationships. A great deal of promotional work pursues repeat consumers, through non-media channels, revisiting the company's present customer database. Financial services and ex-public utilities (water, gas, telephone and electricity), typically businesses with large numbers of existing and 'involved' consumers, use the existing relationship as a marketing resource – and even sell knowledge about (their) consumers (usually aggregated and anonymous) to other companies as knowledge commodities.

Database marketing allows brands to circulate 'lifestyle' magazines and thus interact more regularly with their customers.[3] The marketing aim is simply to cross-sell their own products: 'You've got a mortgage with us, what about a credit card?' Such brand communications, half journalistic, half advertorial, depict stories of exemplary customers or propose extensions to current service usage to 'educate' readers in getting the most out of their bank, phone, car, etc. The aim is to produce a branded and profitable version of the feeling of membership typically associated with clubs, or other social associations. By producing their own media brands can pursue a targeted process of enculturation alongside more orthodox one-off target marketing. The content of such brand magazines is the brand 'story' retold and reframed many times: the focus is 'not the product . . . but a story' (Jensen 1999: 34–5). The brand keeps 'a channel' to the customer 'open all hours'.[4] Customers tuned in to brands' networks in these ways bypass competition, sending more business down brand owners' income streams.

In many ways such strategies are a step ahead of traditional advertising – a more subtle appeal to which otherwise jaded consumers are more positively responsive. When brands become owners of their own media they change some of the dynamics of marketing communications, as the media where advertising is held is no longer a relatively independent editorially third party, from whom advertising space would normally have been bought. Thus there are magazines and broadcast TV channels where the 'above the line' and 'below the line' distinctions have been blurred: branded content, for example, informing the output of the Audi Channel available to digital subscribers in the UK. Lury (2004) has proposed that brands *are* channels – in that they seek to keep an open flow and exchange of information, goods, services and media between producers and consumers, across multiple cultural and market interfaces – processes co-ordinated and corralled by the cultural pull of the logo. Brands grow and are fed by such processes.

The strategy of cross-selling to current customers is itself a subset of a broader motive, establishing 'brand loyalty'. While advertising is usually (often inaccurately) assumed to be primarily aimed at recruiting new customers, to a very significant degree promotional marketing activity (including advertising) is associated with the aim of maintaining brand loyalty. Loyalty schemes are based on commercial pragmatism. The retention and elaboration of relationships with existing customers leads to sustained profitability.

## 'THROUGH THE LINE'

As traditional media-based advertising strategies have come up against the variety of direct 'below the line' promotional activities, and at a time when advertising agencies' institutional forms, business models and ways of working have been changing, it has become usual to think less about 'an advertising campaign' and more about an 'integrated marketing campaign', or a 'total brand communications strategy'.[5] As a consequence, and under such rubrics, media-based advertising and other marketing activities are treated more readily as constituting one enterprise – however complex and distributed on the ground, so that diverse means and modes of advertising and marketing communication are, at some level, part of a unitary plan, under the joint stewardship of a brand owner, brand managers and contracted communications companies. This development deconstructs the thinking and terminology behind 'above and below the line' advertising. Instead, this integration of direct and media-based marketing has lead to discussion of 'through the line' advertising and brand communications strategies.

As Internet-based marketing matures, the boundaries between above and below the line advertising are becoming even less clear. The Internet, especially boosted by broadband and wireless connectivity, is the technological intervention that most destabilises those communicative territories formed in the late twentieth century and culturally and commercially inhabited throughout that period by mass media advertising. The Internet provides a powerful additional interface between consumers and producers. Websites and email also link consumers to each other, increasing the overall connectivity and flow of ideas and information about products.

Having some of the intermediating properties of a mass medium, while being simultaneously an individualised, interactive (and 'multi') medium, the Internet, and digital technologies of various kinds, now supported through TV, mobile phones and PDAs, as well as PCs, offers the potential for dramatically reconfigured marketing relationships. As Cappo has argued, the Internet has had limited success as an advertising medium:

> The Internet has yet to prove itself as an effective advertising medium . . . marketers . . . have not yet mastered an [Internet] advertising technique. They may one day, but it will take a lot of time and creative effort.
>
> (Cappo 2003: 192–3)

However, a 2004 editorial from the trade paper *Admap* suggests that Internet-based marketing and advertising are becoming increasingly significant, but not directly bound to traditional advertising practices.

> The ultimate digital medium is the newest and most dynamic. Internet advertising has passed 3% of US ad revenues, and is pushing that level in the UK. For many ad agency folk it is still unfamiliar territory, but clients, media agencies and specialised creative shops are forging ahead. There is still little good case study material on how to exploit the Internet for brand-building, though research shows clearly that it can work.
>
> (*Admap* October 2004)

In so far as the Internet is seen as an additional main medium, a kind of extension of press or broadcast advertising where ads can simply be placed to be seen and then acted on subsequently, the Internet has not had as dramatic an impact as was initially predicted in the 1990s (see Barrett 1996: 86–9). However, as Internet-based communications have developed on the interactive capacities made possible by highly sophisticated branded websites (binding branding to its entertainment, retail and information functions) some more significant impacts are evident. As the extent of connectivity increases, in national and global markets, and as the speed and functionality continues to improve (via broadband, wireless and subsequent technologies), marketing and advertising will continue to have to develop, exploit and adapt to new actual and potential market relationships.

Armed with powerful search engines, such as Google, new consumers have new capacities at their disposal. The Internet facilitates and demands innovation from consumers and producers alike. The skilled design of web pages, for commercial purposes, demands a new 'advertising' art. The capacity to be found efficiently by sophisticated search engines (Seda 2004) has become a pressing commercial imperative. As Google and other search engines begin to offer more commercial services, the relations between consumer and producer are re-mediated, potentially cutting out some traditional marketing and advertising genres. Thus Google offers advertisers the chance to 'Find buyers searching for what you sell':

> Google AdWords ads connect you with new customers at the precise moment when they're looking for your products or services. With Google AdWords you create your own ads, choose keywords to help us match your ads to your audience and pay only when someone clicks on them.
>
> (www.volusion.com/google-adwords-promo.asp)

The reconfiguration of marketing relationships as a consequence of the Internet, in some sectors and for some consumers more than others, will require a reconstitution of advertising, part of whose function (to inform and market) is altered. In a period when accurate information is rapidly accessible and searchable, and where markets are at once more remote (global), unmediated (fewer or different 'middlemen') and yet apparently closer at hand – just a click away – the media-based advertising function may become increasingly restricted to producing and maintaining supplementary public cultural currency of and trust in product- and provider-brands. Maintaining trust is not a new function for advertising and, even here, the Internet can serve as a tool and a competitive threat to traditional advertising strategies, by allowing consumers to produce, 'peer to peer', what Howard Rheingold calls 'reputation systems' (Rheingold 2003):

> Today's online reputation systems are computer-based technologies that make it possible to manipulate in new and powerful ways an old and essential human trait. Note the rise of websites like eBay (auctions), Epinions (consumer advice), Amazon (Books, CDs, Electronics), Slashdot (publishing and conversation) built around the contributions of millions of customers,

enhanced by reputation systems that police the quality of the content and transactions exchanged through the sites ... the aggregate opinions of the users provide the measure of trust necessary for transactions and markets to flourish in cyberspace.

(Rheingold 2003: xix)

Social networking sites such as Facebook offer further opportunities for businesses and consumers to share information, to spread and to debunk fashions, as well as becoming a kind of 'advertising' – where individuals use the Internet to promote, to connect to, and to co-ordinate with wider audiences and taste cultures. Facebook, and similar social network sites turn human relations into media content – ads space is sold to run alongside Facebook pages. Such ad space is attractive because it can promise a surrounding media environment where there is a feeling of trust, relevance, personalisation and intimacy – and capturing online those who are leaving TV behind. These are 'gold dust' media qualities for advertising. There is, however, some disquiet about the commercial exploitation of e-friendship networks and more obtrusive advertising than is currently possible will face the familiar charge of clutter and 'media' interruption. Other sites, including for instance You.gov, also offer ways to test and survey sections of the marketplace informally and with great rapidity.

Alongside e-commerce, there is now m-commerce (Frith and Mueller 2003: 284–5; Haig 2002), a set of technologically driven means for connecting consumers to the market via mobile phones. The phone becomes a hybrid currency card, but also a means for rapid information gathering and purchase. Mobile technologies (SMS, picture messages) and wireless networking afford an efficient and novel range of ways to interact with potential or past consumers, especially those drawn to the latest gadgets. Likewise consumers can now shop with the benefit of rapid access to data at their fingertips and stores can beam offers to consumers as they pass. Consultation with others while shopping becomes easy, so friends and family can be consulted on fashion or meal options. Such mobile technologies mean that domestic and consumer space can enter one another efficiently (altering the quality of both). As mobile Internet improves services advertisers and media owners will work to produce systems able to capture the best 'audiences' in time, space and by tailoring media content. Such new conjunctions of course provoke anxieties about technological and commercial 'invasion'. These kinds of network-based communications models do a good deal to further destabilise the traditional communications models underpinning mainstream mass advertising.

As the Internet becomes more widely accessible and efficient, and as trust grows in the Internet as a communications platform, e-commerce and e-promotion will continue to evolve 'advertising' formats; linking producers and consumers, building brands and selling goods. As Jef Richards (2000) states:

> The Internet is much more than just a medium. It is at one time a confluence of all media, a new breed of medium, a mixture of virtually al forms of marketing communication, and even a distribution channel.
>
> (Richards: 2000)

Crucially, and as Richards (2000) adds, the Internet is the first widely used two-way advertising medium. This offers great potentials to advertisers and consumers but also challenges formerly more stable business and consumption patterns. As Anderson (2006) argues, the Internet changes the dynamics of a whole range of markets – including the advertising market – by allowing small-scale producers to bypass diseconomies of small-scale production and hyper-niche product ranges (e.g. rare second hand books) enabling merchants to profitably deal with 'the long tail' of consumers looking for low-demand, quirky, rare or unusual goods. Hitherto it was not profitable to make, advertise or store such goods. With the hyper-efficient search and locate facilities of the Internet, consumer and product can now be united with unprecedented rapidity – opening up new potentials for consumers and commerce (eBay, Amazon and iTunes are among Anderson's exemplars).

It is likely that the advertising genre will continue both in traditional formats while also adapting to the challenges and opportunities posed by evolving Internet, e-commerce and digital technologies.

## ADVERTISING, SPONSORSHIP AND PR

Whitehead (2005) reports on a trend examined widely by industry analysts. An iconic TV advertiser , Heineken (see Delaney 2007) loses faith with traditional ad media and invests 'below the line':

> Heineken is shifting its £6.5m UK advertising budget away from TV to focus on sports sponsorship, blaming the cost of airtime and the cluttered ad environment. In an interview with the Times, managing director Rob Marijnen said that it was becoming tougher to reach the core market of 18- to 26-year-olds in an effective way through TV. 'The enormously cluttered environment in TV ads makes it difficult to make standout ads. It's also very expensive and it's questionable as to its effectiveness,' he told the newspaper.
>
> (Whitehead 2005)

**Figure 3.1** Facebook offers a range of Internet-based services for advertisers – disturbing traditional forms of intermediation.

A further confusion of the boundaries between above and below the line is seen in sponsorship. Corporate sponsorship can be used as an alternative or complement to traditional advertising. A component in the commercialisation of sports and other cultural spectacles, sponsorships have a growing role in supporting activities with narrower appeal, and in funding activities for which there is a significant public need (or desire), but not always adequate economic support from government (or private patrons). Some arts and comedy festivals, concerts, museums, exhibitions and charitable enterprises depend on support from commercial companies; these and numerous other kinds of event have been funded by sponsorship income in a trend that has increased since the early 1980s (a notable example here the Los Angeles Olympics in 1984 (Tomlinson 2004: 147)). Naomi Klein argues that this is partly a consequence of political and economic changes. Governments (in the UK, US, Canada and globally) have been unwilling or unable adequately to fund important public, social and cultural activities (Klein 2000: 30–3), preferring to pursue economic policies based on tax cuts (benefiting individuals), consequently decreasing resources for the support of public services and public culture.

Corporate sponsorship of these kinds is an important addition to, and elaboration of, the marketing process for contemporary advertisers

(Pringle and Thompson 1999). As well as providing subsidies and pragmatic social benefits, to entertainment and cultural activity, sponsorship
provides a means, aside from traditional advertising, in which corporations can get significant local, national or global exposure for their brand
name.

Sponsorship is like advertising in this sense, but it also stands as a
commercial competitor for traditional advertising strategies, sometimes
offering a more focused and integrated element of the 'total brand
message' than, for instance, a traditional double-page spread. For creative
reasons the sponsorship can appeal to audiences who may be put off
by advertising, and from the point of view of targeting, sponsoring can
be tightly focused. For instance, a golf tournament or a hospital wing
sponsored by a pharmaceutical company produces appropriate attention
e.g. from 'hard to reach' industry executives. Moor (2003) describes how
branded music festivals offer instances of highly involved branded
experience – again offering a compelling complement to traditional advertising to a particular cultural group – binding web and live elements to
affirm 'affective bonds' between consumers and brands.

Another alternative to buying traditional media space is to place the
product deliberately *within* the media output, for instance in a programme
or film, or by making the product into a focus for a news story or magazine discussion. At a time when audiences are bored by much advertising
the opportunity to embed a product in a glamorous or otherwise culturally
'credible' setting, such as are provided regularly in film, TV and magazine
features, is an attractive one.

Another marketing method, again media-based, but not paid for
directly, occurs if a company can transform its advertising activity into
'news'. To do this ads will be developed, perhaps deliberately, in order
to make an impact, not so much directly on consumers, but on the
'controversial' news agendas of the day. As one ad executive observes:
'Sex, celebrity and controversy are usually the staple ingredients when
an ad crosses over and becomes a story as much as a campaign' (Martin
Loat, cited in Whitehead, *Brand Republic*, 21 July 2004).

Advertisers and agencies are usually keen to get this kind of coverage,
even when, ostensibly, the news story is negative, with journalists
producing critical readings of the ad or its moral message. When an ad
successfully becomes a story it is celebrated, even statistically ranked, by
the industry as yet more 'news':

According to the Ads That Make News survey, the Smirnoff ad, created by
J Walter Thompson, was the most written about in national broadsheets
and tabloid newspapers, while the government's anti-smoking spot, created

by Abbott Mead Vickers BBDO and showing babies exhaling cigarette smoke, was joint number three.

(Jennifer Whitehead, *Brand Republic*, 21 July 2004)

Making the news agenda is likely to stimulate conversation about deploying creatively daring statement ads that create 'buzz', but as Rosen (2000) warns:

> Everyone in the advertising industry would love to create an ad that gets . . . buzz, but very few become such mega hits . . . there are thousands of commercials that try to make people talk but fail.
>
> (Rosen 2000: 209)

Large companies have recourse to all of these marketing approaches and, via various intermediary agencies and consultants, work tirelessly to maximise coverage across all media. The aim is to attain or maintain prominence in the consumer mind and to bind the product to consumers' cultural sensibilities. The aim is always to build the brand, the product or the idea into the consumers' world – to assure the optimal position of the object within consumers' cultural life and, finally, to try and ensure that the product (or brand idea) comes to mind as consumers pursue everyday practical and cultural activities. Ries and Ries (2002) argue that increasingly such PR activities will be a threat to traditional advertising formats.

## 'ABOVE THE LINE': MEDIA AND ADVERTISING

The marketplace for advertising space is a volatile one. It is complex terrain to negotiate. The media planners and buyers have the job of placing ads strategically and effectively in the hope that target consumers might hand over a fragment of precious attention. At the same time media owners compete for money and attention from those who need to buy space. Different broadcasters compete with one another, as they strive to perfect their programme schedules, maximising niche audiences (with specialist programming) or capturing volume with big hit shows. Publishers compete, too, building portfolios of titles to provide, for instance, a smoothly graduating complementary range of magazines for women of different ages – *17*, *19*, *21*, etc. – hoping to draw advertising income from competing publishing houses while preserving their own publications' share of readership – as far as possible against other competition.

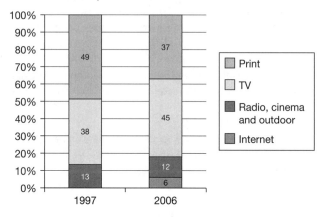

**World expenditure/media mix**

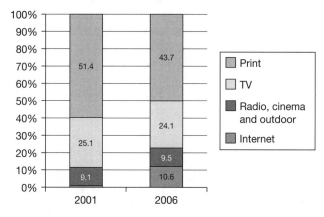

**UK expenditure/media mix**

**Figure 3.2** Expenditure on advertising media (percentage of total advertising expenditure: print, TV, radio, outdoor and cinema, Internet.

Source: World Advertising Statistic Yearbook an Advertising Statistics Yearbook 2007.

The competition between the different media is equally keen. Each media owner represents not just the virtues of its individual media products, but also suggests why *their* particular medium is the most effective for the advertising task in question. Thus radio proclaims its superiority over TV ads and there is also a great deal of rivalry between traditional above the line media advertising and the various modes of below and through the line promotion. PR in particular is a strong competitor for advertisers' budgets.

Advertising space can be bought in five major media: press, TV, radio, cinema and outdoors. Press, the oldest, can be divided into newspapers (nationals but also local) and magazines (consumer and business). Outdoor includes the growing market for space in unusual places: pub toilets, phone boxes, supermarket and airport trolleys, petrol pumps and the longer established market on transport (buses, tubes, taxis and so on). It could be objected that this final category, outdoor and ambient, is not media advertising, as the surrounding environment is not media. Nevertheless paying to place such ads has traditionally been accounted in the same way as in 'true' media spaces. Internet advertising is typically accounted alongside traditional media – and is offering significant competition.

Looked at worldwide, the proportion of the total advertising expenditure is shifting away from print and towards TV and the Internet. In the UK in 2006 the expenditure on Internet advertising represented 11 per cent of the total UK ad-spend. This reflects the relatively high connectivity and affluence of the UK market. It has been suggested that the switch to Internet advertising, largely at the expense of print is a likely continuing trend, with the UK 2006 figure of 11 per cent (from 1.0 per cent in 2001) likely to increase, and with global expenditure to follow. UK expenditure is lower than global expenditure and has gone down slightly since 2001. Total UK ad-spend in 2006 was £19,083,000,000, estimated at 1.09 per cent GDP and which is double the anticipated cost of the 2012 Olympics (*World Advertising Statistics Yearbook* 2007).

## Newspapers and magazines

Print was the first medium for modern advertising. It remains the largest, despite competition from TV and, more recently, the Internet, especially in the area of classified ads (for example in motor and recruitment advertising). The Internet is also a partner to the press, in the sense that many publications produce online versions, with free and paid for content, and including advertising web links. The press and advertising have a complicated relationship, which in many instances could be described as 'symbiotic' (the one cannot live without the other). Without advertising income, much print media would be financially unviable. Some would remain, supported by cover price and subscription, to fulfil the avowed central functions of the press: the circulation of news, analysis, information and entertainment in the public interest. Democratic societies depend upon the free flow of information in order to inform public opinion and debate. Advertising revenue both protects and curtails press freedom. It permits numerous publications to run independently of state control, arguably preserving a space for independent public information. On the

**Table 3.1** Percentage of publications' revenue derived from advertising: regional, national Sundays, national dailies and consumer magazines (%)

|      | Regional including free press | National Sunday papers | National daily papers | Consumer magazines |
|------|-------------------------------|------------------------|-----------------------|--------------------|
| 2004 | 85.3 | 53.3 | 52.8 | 36.6 |
| 2005 | 84.1 | 50.4 | 52.1 | 35.5 |
| 2006 | 83.8 | 49.8 | 51.0 | 35.8 |

Source: *Advertising Statistics Yearbook Press Circulation Update 2007*: 43–5.

other hand, advertisers are typically committed to certain ideas; free markets, deregulation, 'small' government, etc. Historically newspapers committed to alternative models of government or issues such as nuclear disarmament – or to serious high quality critical journalism more generally – have struggled to maintain advertising revenues, and closed or changed editorial stance (Curran 1981; McChesney 2004; Bogart 2000).

The cost of advertising in the press depends on two crucial variables. First, the size of the readership, and, second, the socio-economic and cultural make up of that readership. Other considerations are locality (local newspaper advertising is an important and often forgotten dimension of the advertising market), and the provision, by the newspaper, of special feature sections and supplements. These extra sections support promises of improved readership volume and targeting more specific cultural and consumer groups, for instance to motoring enthusiasts or holidaymakers with car and travel sections as respective examples. Some supplements also offer higher quality photographic reproduction, attractive to elite brands that typically, otherwise, would advertise only in magazines. Media packages highlighting such features are characteristically drawn to the attention of media buyers and planners in a competitive marketplace.

Table 3.1 below allows a brief examination of some of these media market factors. The *Sun* newspaper has the widest readership but cannot command the highest price for its advertising space. This is in part because the disposable income of *Sun* readers tends not to put them in the market for premium goods (with large above the line advertising budgets). More particularly there are better ways to market to everyday FMCGs (fast moving consumer goods, such as baked beans or washing powder) to consumers – e.g. price cutting or buy one get one free. A large audience does not necessarily form a coherent 'target market', as measured by gender, age, geography or other measures of cultural variance.

Relatively, *The Sun* is less dependent on advertising income as, with a healthy level of circulation, it makes significant revenue from its cover price. The opposite case applies with *Metro*, a free sheet. At only half the price of an ad in *The Sun*, *Metro*, a metropolitan-centre-based free sheet, has a circulation of over 700,000 copies daily. The disadvantages of a relatively small readership are, to an extent, minimised because *Metro* has a geographic and sociocultural specificity: primarily London (and other regional cities) commuters on their way to work or college read it each morning.

With only a lower readership, space in the *Financial Times* is nevertheless the most expensive of the examples given. The readership of *The Financial Times* is again geographically concentrated in London (with an important international edition adding yet further value). Culturally the paper is concentrated around the preoccupations associated with 'The City' and *The Financial Times* is able to trade its space at such a high cost, not so much on account of the success it has with circulation but because of targeting success and repute. The FT audience is affluent and otherwise difficult to reach (considered unlikely to watch mainstream commercial TV for example). While the *Sun* may be useful for advertising FMCGs, *The Financial Times* may provide access to readers with a greater relative propensity to take an interest in elite consumer goods and specialist financial services. *The Financial Times* can also offer to play a role in business-to-business advertising, relying on the composition of its readership to include numerous individuals classed as business 'decision makers' and as purchasers of business services. While *The Sun* might argue that its four million readers, many in command of domestic shopping budgets, are 'general shoppers out for a bargain', *The Financial Times* can present a vision of its 400,000 readers as affluent and influential opinion formers, whose views can count in the corporate world, and as executives, with large personal disposable income and an influence on corporate expenditure.

**Table 3.2** Circulation figures and price for advertising space for three newspapers

| Paper | Average circulation January 2008 (daily) | Estimated cost of full page black and white ad for one day |
|---|---|---|
| The Sun | 3,209,776 | £40, 159 |
| The Financial Times | 452,448 | £39,600 |
| Metro (London) | 751,444 | £19,754 |

Source: ABC certificates of circulation.

## LONDON & NATIONAL RATECARD FOR DISPLAY ADVERTISING

This ratecard contains information on running an ad in London only or nationally. If you want to advertise in a particular regional edition of Metro please see the 'Partners' section of the website. If you want London Classified rates please see the 'Classified' section.

### HOW WE PRICE YOUR DISPLAY AD:

- We price advertising on the size of your advert and all of our ad rates are based on SCC (Single Column Centimetre).
- The cost is also dependent on your choice of London only or national and choosing mono or colour.
- Please note our new rates effective from 3 April 2006 to reflect our 11% national and 12% London circulation increase.

| | |
|---|---|
| London Mono | £83 Fixed |
| London Colour | £95.20 Fixed |
| National Mono | £104.30 Fixed |
| National Colour | £131 Fixed |

### WORK OUT HOW MUCH YOUR DISPLAY AD WILL COST:

Metro is 34cms high and 26.8cms wide. Our width is split into 7 columns and each of these columns are different widths.

| | |
|---|---|
| 1 column | 3.5cms |
| 2 columns | 7.3cms |
| 3 columns | 11.2cms |
| 4 columns | 15.1cms |
| 5 columns | 19cms |
| 6 columns | 22.9cms |
| 7 columns | 26.8cms |

- When calculating the cost of any advert, you first need to decide the height and width which is most appropriate for your advert or budget. For example, a credit card size would be roughly 5cms high and 7.3cm wide.
- You must next decide which rate to use, London or national, mono or colour.
- You then multiply it by the area of the ad in SCC. For example, a credit card size ad 5 cms high by 7.3cm wide, has an area of 10 SCC. If you chose to run this ad nationally in mono this would cost £1043 (£104.30 x 10 SCC).

### HOW TO BOOK

TO BOOK A DISPLAY AD OR FOR MORE DETAILS CALL JAMES HOOPER ON 020 7651 5303.

*If you want classified rates for property, jobs, courses, travel etc, please call 020 7938 7751.*

---

Below is a list of all our popular size advertisements which are available and how much they cost, in easy to understand terms.

**5x1** *(5cms high x 3.5cms wide)*
London Mono £415
London Colour £476
National Mono £521.50
National Colour £655

**5x2** *(5cms high x 7.3cms wide)*
London Mono £830
London Colour £952
National Mono £1043
National Colour £1,310

**10x2** *(10cms high x 7.3cms wide)*
London Mono £1,660
London Colour £1,904
National Mono £2,086
National Colour £2,620

**20x2** *(20cms high x 7.3cms wide)*
London Mono £3,320
London Colour £3,808
National Mono £4,172
National Colour £5,240

**20x3/Quarter page** *(20cms high x 11.2cms wide)*
London Mono £4,980
London Colour £5,712
National Mono £6,258
National Colour £7,860

**10x7** *(10cms high x 26.8cms wide)*
London Mono £5,810
London Colour £6,664
National Mono £7,301
National Colour £9,170

**24x4** *(24cms high x 15.1cms wide)*
London Mono £7,968
London Colour £9,139.20
National Mono £10,012.80
National Colour £12,576

**17x7/Half page** *(17cms high x 26.8cms wide)*
London Mono £9,877
London Colour £11,328.80
National Mono £12,411.70
National Colour £15,589

**34x7/Full page** *(34cms high x 26.8cms wide)*
London Mono £19,754
London Colour £22,657.60
National Mono £24,823.40
National Colour £31,178

---

**Figure 3.3** Advertising rate card for Metro

The limiting and constructed nature of these readership typifications can be revealed for example in the fact that many people read both papers. The media space market deals in a mixture of facts (about volumes of readers) and composite readership profiles comprising probabilistic estimations of the financial and cultural make up of 'typical' readers. As individuals we may well not identify with these profiles, although there is a likelihood that our customary choices of newspaper bear some relation to wider cultural and social tastes (as does the decision not to read a newspaper).

The complexity of advertising space prices reflects a number of variables to do with time (days of week), place in publication, feature type, black and white or colour. The rate card from Metro (Figure 3.3) gives an insight into the detailed variances in media costs.

## Classified and directory advertising

In the press there are two main categories or genres of advertising: display and classified. Display is what usually springs to mind when we think of a press ad, set in the main body of the paper surrounded by and surrounding the main features and typically taking up a full, half or quarter page with copy and illustration. Classified advertising appears in a dedicated section with the ads literally 'classified' under headings outlining the types of ad in each subsection: motors, pets, decorating services and so on.

The key distinction here is to do with the implicit mode of attention among potential audiences. While display advertising enters into the field of vision as an unsought by-product of the reading process and comes from any number of possible product sectors, classified advertising implies there will be a more deliberate search on the part of the consumer, seeking out specific information and sometimes inspiration. Uninformed by any explicit intention on the part of the consumer, display rests on a far less direct or purposive relationship than classified.

Another form of advertising, financially important but not considered at length in this current book, is directory advertising. The yellow pages and other similar publications, as well as trade-specific listings and catalogues that detail more specific service and goods providers, form a key source for marketing information. These types of promotion are particularly suited to the transition into Internet provision. The Internet's capacity to provide searchable web-page-based databases online offers advertisers an excellent tool for displaying and describing goods and services and consumers can focus and direct their searches with great efficiency, as well as browsing to gather useful market information. Price comparison websites such as moneysupermarket.com extend this Internet-based marketing function into major product sectors. Likewise estate agents have rapidly adopted Internet advertising, which is especially suited to that market sector.

## Magazines

Usually published monthly or weekly, and generally with a smaller readership than national newspapers, magazines, like newspapers, are subject to the market patterns operating for newspapers – the tension between circulation, cover price and the need to maintain editorial focus and credibility.

As Table 3.3 shows, the rates charged for space in different magazines vary. An advertising or media space buyer when buying space on behalf of clients would want to know crucial facts and figures listing cost, circulation and frequency of publication and, importantly, what kind of people are going to see the advertisement. Media owners are well aware of this crucial extra dimension and, perhaps more intensively than newspaper owners, of the need to promote the qualities and lifestyle of their readership. It is the reliable delivery of readers that guarantees advertising revenue from advertisers (via their agents).

Typically media space is offered at a range of rates, which can be negotiated. Rates vary according to, for instance, the number of issues booked (for example every week for six weeks gets a discount), or nomination of a specific position in the paper or magazine (towards the front, next to a specific feature and so on). So the figures quoted are indicative and subject to variation – as magazines and the media market changes.

**Table 3.3** Circulation figures and price for advertising space for five magazines

| Title | Circulation (2007 second half average) | Colour double spread (£, approx., subject to variation) |
| --- | --- | --- |
| FHM | 315,149 | £39,900 |
| Arena | 25,232 | £13,272 |
| The Economist (UK) | 181,374 | £34,600 |
| Cosmopolitan | 460,276 | £37,900 |
| Hello! | 405,615 | £42,695 |

Source: ABC 2007 and publishers' rate cards.

The shelf-life of magazines depends heavily on the volume of sales and a capacity consistently and regularly to deliver to their 'readership'. The readership is both a numerical and a cultural measure consisting of factors that include age, income, employment type, but also tastes, habits and lifestyle. A good 'readership' corresponds, in terms of demographic profile (and income), to relevant models of 'the desirable consumer' operating in the minds of advertisers (and ad agency media strategists). For example *Arena* markets itself in the following terms:

> *Arena* is aimed at confident, successful men who believe in themselves. These fashion-aware and style conscious individuals have high aspirations, high standards and high levels of disposable income. The *Arena* man is a forward-thinking, original minded individual with an interest in the wider world. Likely to be aged 24–34, he is open minded with a variety of interests which may range from design, fashion, architecture and politics, to sex, sport, music and restaurants.
>
> (Arena Media Information)

The reader profile the magazines promise attempt to serve as a shorthand link between editorial policy (what goes in the magazine) and the media sales pitch. By no means a description of actual readers, this 'character' is a hybrid composed to conjoin commercial imperatives with cultural values; it is a notional space where the advertisers and the consumer are invited to 'meet'.

Magazine editors have a tricky job. The tensions evident in advertising agencies between creative and commercial strategies are reprised in magazines in the form of editorial battles against overly formulaic interpretations of the target readership, and against pressure to clone successful rivals' approaches. Editors perform an intermediary role, a balancing act, as Jackson *et al.* conclude in their (2001) ethnography on men's magazines:

> editors are pulled in several different directions, simultaneously, trying to address men as a group of 'regular guys' while targeting specific market segments; aiming to be the 'reader's friend', while providing advertisers with access to a large market of aspirational consumers.
>
> (Jackson *et al.* 2001: 73)

Promoting the value of its advertising space is a central part of the development of any magazine. Once established, however, magazines can enhance the commercial value of the space they sell by being in a position to promise added value: an aura of 'cool', developed as a magazine becomes the watchword for a cluster of desirable values, ideas and aspirations. A number of magazines have become brands themselves (Gough-Yates 2003: 114–15), as in the case of the very successful and long-running *Cosmopolitan*:

> Cosmo is one of the flagship brands of the National Magazine Company, which claims to be the first publishing house to recognise the importance of magazines as brands. Its philosophy is to create and nurture brands, not just magazines, and to focus on developing and fostering readers' experience of the brand.
>
> ('Cool Brand Leaders' The Brand Council, 2002)

Such publications can then lend some of their brand credibility launching products in their own name. For every successful magazine there is one that falls by the wayside. New magazines have a great difficulty in establishing themselves as they attempt the tense cultural gymnastics and commercial focus required in balancing a repetitive winning formula alongside credible claims for distinction and originality, in a bewilderingly crowded and competitive marketplace where products, to the uninitiated, may appear very similar.

## Television

Press advertising produces the most revenue for the advertising industry but the 'flagship' medium is TV advertising (Cappo 2003). Today's audiences are very familiar with TV advertising formats and broadcast TV advertising has defined the advertising genre for two generations of consumers. As a link binding 'public' display of goods to 'privatised' contemplation, by individuals and households, TV advertising has served as a paramount tool in managing the modern consumer marketplace – dynamically opening up the domestic sphere to commerce.

In the period 1955 to 1980, when (in the UK) there was only one commercial TV channel (in competition with the BBC, which carries no advertising) TV could reliably deliver prime time audiences of around 20 million. Since the early 1980s there has been an increase in the numbers of commercial TV channels carrying advertising – an increase which became an explosion during the 1990s when digital cable and satellite channels became more and more widespread. Today it is in TV that the most radical disruptions and reconfigurations of any of the main advertising media are anticipated.

The increasing number of channels poses one major problem for advertisers. In a multi-channel environment the audience fragments, making it difficult to capture large audiences in one hit, as was possible in the 1970s, when prime time evening TV delivered up sizable audiences nationally. The twenty-first-century evening TV audience is typically distributed across a wide array of channels, a way of viewing encouraged by the availability of TV technology quite cheaply, and consequently the large numbers of TVs in the home (one in the living room, one in the kitchen and one in kids' bedrooms).

The rapid expansion of subscription and pay-per-view digital services may also be a source of anxiety for the traditional TV advertising business model that relied on ad income to pay TV companies in return for delivering access to valuable audiences. While these many hundreds of new channels continue to gain income from showing advertising, many are also part funded from viewers' subscriptions (or, in the case of the numerous shopping channels, by operating as a below the line and telephonic-retail hybrid).The co-existence of different models of TV funding, some advertising supported, others relying on viewers' subscriptions and pay-per-view, alongside the sheer proliferation of channels (and subsequent audience fragmentation and specialisation), provides a significant challenge to the predominance of TV advertising as the major mode of national advertising communication.

**Figure 3.4** An advertisement embedded in a computer game.

The shift to subscription and pay-on-demand TV services is indicative of a new dynamic in the TV media market. Advertising remains the main source of funds for commercial TV companies, but pay-per-view and subscription services mean that the viewer – the 'end user' – of TV output is now paying an increasing proportion of revenue directly to TV companies (Mandese 2004). In such circumstances there is some pressure on the advertising industry to avoid being marginalised in increasingly direct (or dis-intermediated) relationships between media channels or providers and media consumers. TV companies in the future will be faced with a version of the dilemmas long-confronted by magazine publishers, as they seek income both from advertising revenue and from selling copies. This may have knock-on effects on the formats of advertising communications, with creative solutions sought to make advertising effective within reconfigured media relationships. This is evident for instance in DVD-based entertainments and within computer games where advertising remains on our TV screens even though we have tuned out of the broadcast programming.

Time spent online is also increasing. Internet use in leisure time is a significant competitor to TV – even while there are numerous cross-overs between Internet and TV platforms.

Recently developed digital technologies already allow audiences to vary their viewing patterns, as it were, in *time*. No longer simply switching channels within a fragmented but 'concurrent' media environment, properly equipped viewers will pause, record and skip elements of live broadcast content. Such flexible and asynchronous access to broadcast programming will provide yet another problem for the traditional media – advertising – viewer model. Viewers are equipped (if they choose) to filter out advertising messages en masse. While video, remote controls and ordinary inattention have always posed a version of this 'filtering-out' problem for advertising, commercial messages need to work hard to stay in vision as the media consumer develops fuller capacities to become the pro-active editor of his or her media environment.[6] This is part of a more general dynamic in media consumption whereby technology serves to activate and focus media consumers' demand, thus transforming the relationship between media provision and media use. As commentators report:

> More exciting, and more threatening to a variety of business models, is the so-far slow spread of PVRs (TiVo and the like), which both destroy the whole accepted practice of programme scheduling and can severely reduce TV advertising, with consequent impacts on both advertisers and the finances of TV stations.

> (*Admap* October 2004)

The continuing existence of public service broadcasting, the BBC in the UK, is paid for by licence and not from advertising revenue. It offers the most significant source of non-commercial TV (and radio) and as such acts to diminish the size of the commercial TV and radio audiences. Research into the audience of broadcast output, including the regular publication of ratings, is a matter of serious financial concern to commercial media owners and public service broadcasters alike. For the former these figures are a matter of balancing the books, for the latter, of justifying some of the principles behind the public subsidy paid them through the licence fee.

## Radio

The one-dimensional nature of radio (it only has sound) and the lack, until recently, of powerful national commercial broadcasters, consigned radio to a position as an unglamorous media option. Radio continues to be able to attract advertisers by virtue of its close affinity with daily routines (it typically accompanies waking up, breakfast, school run and commuter driving, and increasingly is a backdrop in the growing number of relaxed workplaces). Gradually more mobile phones and portable digital music devices are equipped with radio, suggesting that the capacity of radio to accompany consumers throughout their day will be enhanced.

Perhaps because of the challenging new media environment and the heightened need to compete, advertising creativity on radio has improved. Where in the past 'jingles' would do for an ad on the assumption that 'catchy' and 'repetitive' were the key creative watchwords, now humour, emotion and arresting music take their place (or at least have broadened the creative repertoire). In addition there is a more formal acknowledge-ment of sound as a marketing medium:

> Although not a new phenomenon, sonic branding is becoming an increasingly strong vehicle for conveying a memorable message to targeted consumers. As traditional media grows into non-traditional sectors, today's savvy-eared consumer is accessible anywhere. From non-lyrical soundbites to catchy snippets of tunes, these sonic brands take advantage of one of the brain's most powerful memory senses – sound (Kim Barnet 2001, Sound Finds its voice).

Thus 'sonic branding', via radio, TV and the Internet and interactive objects (such as phones and PCs), is a dimension of advertising suited to radio.

**Box 3.5 RAB YOUTH ADVERTISING**

RAB – YOUTH ADVERTISING
RACC No: 31029/56
16/04/02
60'      'DOCUMENTARY – TV PRODUCER'

CHRIS:   (AS VOICE OVER) As Head of 'Yoof' TV, Piers Taylor-Holland speaks the language of the nation's under 30s. He's also fluent in Italian.
SFX:     OFFICE ATMOSPHERE.
CHRIS:   Piers wh –
PIERS:   Put it there.
CHRIS:   What, oh right . . . (FUMBLED HAND SLAPS, KNOCKS MIC) Like that? Oh I see, fine . . .
PIERS:   Sweet.
CHRIS:   No thanks.
PIERS:   Yo.
CHRIS:   Yo. Piers, why are young people watching less TV and listening to more radio?
PIERS:   Well it's nothing to do with my TV programs, because the kids tell me they're minging – and that's good enough for me.
CHRIS:   Oh right.
PIERS:   It's just the yoof are spending their time skiing the Internet and bigging it up on videotron games know what I mean?
CHRIS:   Y— . . . Actually no.
PIERS:   They're listening to the radio while doing other things.
CHRIS:   Oh I see.
PIERS:   Sweet.
CHRIS:   No I'm fine.
PIERS:   Yo.
CHRIS:   Hm . . . So that explains why about over 90 per cent of 15- to 34-year-olds are now tuning into commercial radio each month.
PIERS:   90 per cent!
CHRIS:   Yes.
PIERS:   That's nearly three quarters.
CHRIS:   Well actu – . . .
PIERS:   But that's . . .
CHRIS:   Masseef.

VOICE OVER:   Radio advertising – The ideal medium when you want to reach a 'growing' audience.

PIERS:   That's quite clever . . .
CHRIS:   I know. Find out more at RAB.co.uk. Are those sweets fruity or minty . . . ?

Box 3.5 gives the script of an ad illustrating the productive cross fertilisation of radio advertising with radio comedy. It is perhaps especially relevant given that much contemporary comedy appeals to hard to reach audiences unimpressed by, or too busy to watch, mainstream TV. A similar argument applies, based on the audience that music-based radio stations (for instance, in the UK, Jazz FM, Classic FM or XFM) can generate around music subcultures. This enhances the capacity of radio to serve as a cost-effective niche marketing advertising medium. Radio offers the further advantage that production is quick and cheap, and media costs are competitive with other media. Digital radio is now available via DAB and as a 'free' extra of TV satellite packages, available also via the Internet, and has a continent wide and global capacity, which, as yet, has not been fully exploited by advertisers. Again convergence with web technologies will improve the advertising capacity of the medium, while also disrupting some traditional formats.

## Cinema

Customers pay to watch films; adverts are a sideshow. Thus the tensions evident in magazines and TV, between creativity and commerce, are less pressing in cinema. Advertising is not a major income stream. Nevertheless cinema has a role for advertisers. Historically cinema advertising is cited as a key contributor (outside the US, where the antecedents of TV ads were in hard sell print) to the creative culture of humorous advertising. Before TV advertising, cinema ads were made with a brief to make the audience laugh: 'When advertising moved to TV, Europe (and particularly Great Britain) already had an entrenched tradition of funny advertising' (Pierce 1999: 189).

More recently (post-1987) cinema advertising has re-emerged from a period 'in the doldrums' (White 2000: 197), during which cinema typically carried ads for local fish shops and car dealers. As a medium, cinema was not considered to be of great value to national advertisers. The development of the cinema multiplex and increasing audiences has revivified cinema as an advertising medium. Cinema has been transformed into the showcase for the best in creative brand advertising. The conditions that support this reputation of the medium are based in the aesthetic potential of the cinematic experience, and various current characterisations of cinema audiences, as young, hard to reach, and relatively well off (White 2000: 196). The environment offered by cinema is superior to the typical home-viewing conditions. The darkness (and sound production) enhance the audience experience. Advertisements, which would pass us by on TV, can be far more impressive and captivating on the big screen.

Ads placed for certified audiences can be more risqué or adult, more culturally and frequently intellectually demanding. While it would be mistaken to assume that the cinema audience is especially 'cultured' or more liberal (they are the same people who watch TV and read the papers after all) the cinematic environment is optimal for screening ads attuned to sophisticated audiences. Critical reception of ads, emerging from a defensive or embarrassed home and family environment, is suspended in the cinema, with the important exception of children's films. Cinema works under a slightly different set of regulatory standards from those applied to advertising on TV. For instance, in 2001, a TV advertisement for clothing chain French Connection was considered unsuitable for TV, even after the 9 pm 'watershed'. Yet the ad was suitable for cinema, a medium that has more rigorous policing of audiences (in terms of age and supervised watching) and, consequently, which enjoys more liberty in what the older audiences can watch. The regulator's ruling was reported in the newspaper:

> The campaign will not appear on British TV, but cinemas will be allowed to show it alongside films with a '15' rating. The Cinema Advertising Association initially offered an '18' certificate, but agreed to downgrade it if TBWA replaced the word 'copulation' with 'collision' and introduced a 'safe sex message'.
>
> (*Media Guardian* 1 March 2001)

The major debates about cinema and advertising tend to emerge around product placement in films. It is here, and not around advertisements that critical voices are raised.

## Outdoor and ambient

The major kind of outdoor advertising (in terms of revenue) occurs via poster sites, ideally placed in traffic congestion spots, or in popular open public spaces. However, as everyday experience makes clear, commercial messages can be communicated outside the various 'private' spaces in numerous other ways. Urban and rural environments are strewn with advertising (Winship 2000 and Costera Meijer 1998). Semi-obsolete in urban locales, phone boxes are now a major outdoor media format, as are taxis, buses, trains (inside and out), beer mats, petrol pumps, mobile poster sites, shopping and airport trolleys, and cup holders and so on. If it moves or if it stands still, it can carry advertising. Branded entertainment events and spaces can serve as promotional media, from music festivals to golf driving ranges. The demand for such novel spaces increases in part as advertisers lose faith in TV as an effective 'catch-all' medium.

The continuing fragmentation of TV has led to reduced broadcast audiences, while outdoor's audience has increased as social change leads to a more mobile population. Why is this important? In the last decade, the number of the top 200 UK advertisers using outdoor has increased from 33% to 90%, increasing outdoor's share of display advertising from 5% to 8%.

(McEvoy 2002)

A futuristic development of affairs is envisioned in the film *Minority Report* (2002). The film portrays the ultimate in interactive, targeted outdoor advertising. As citizens walk by posters and retail displays they are addressed personally, asked about past purchases, and invited to buy more. A 'prototype' is described here:

The washroom media specialist CPA unveiled its 'Talking Poster' which has a light sensitive microchip in its frame. Up to four minutes of dialogue can be recorded and is activated by the arrival of a person at a urinal, for example. Levi's was the first advertiser to use the medium, with creative by Bartle Bogle Hegarty, and included snippets of dialogue such as 'Touch my twisted side seam' in keeping with the 'Twisted' campaign.

The colonisation of public spaces and formerly private spaces by advertising, and by informal modes of visual communication (fly posting, graffiti and various kinds of signage) contributes to the stressful dynamism of the modern urban landscape. Like all kinds of communications, especially when repetitive, uninteresting and unasked for, outdoor and ambient advertising can incite negative and critical responses from individuals, and from individuals and public bodies committed to defending the aesthetic and functional atmosphere of important public spaces and institutions.

Figure 3.5 shows the ways in which consumers are linked to products via marketing. 'Above the line' are the main advertising media. The advertisements are placed here by the advertising agency, which works to co-ordinate with producers (its clients); with consumers (via research); with other marketing initiatives, and with informal cultural trends and fashions. As the diagram shows, it has a pivotal position in the network of communication relations, which crystallise in above the line advertisements.

There are, however, other routes linking production and consumption. These include the various formal and informal below the line activities, such as retail and packaging, informal processes of word of mouth, and 'buzz marketing'. There are various kinds of direct interface and communications-based links, such as direct mail and telemarketing.

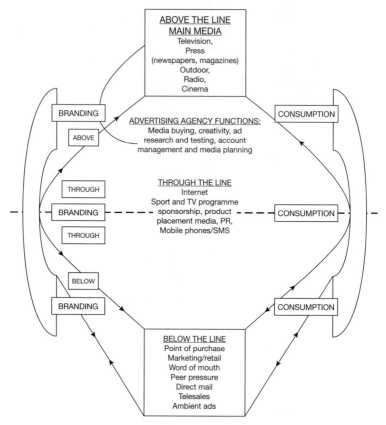

**Figure 3.5** Advertising, branding and the mediation of consumption above, below and through the line.

Finally there are the processes that go through the line – they are based in media, but not in the spots used and paid for in traditional advertising. This includes sponsorship of TV programmes, PR, product placements in film as well as Internet-based marketing (including reputation systems).

Branding, as Figure 3.5 suggests, cuts across these divisions. In integrated communications strategies, advertising, alongside below and through the line approaches, will supplement and enhance the brand and its value. There is a strong tendency towards blurring or even ignoring the 'above', 'below' and 'through' the line distinctions, in favour of ensuring continuities and integrations, as appropriate to brands seeking diverse and sometimes jaded audiences – and fusing commercial, cultural and other intentions across multiple and integrated modes of intermediation.

## CRITICAL RESPONSES TO ADVERTISING AND OTHER MARKETING STRATEGIES

It is notable that much 'below the line' and now 'through the line' marketing activity is, so far, exempted from the critical analyses traditionally aimed at media-based advertising, despite the fact that modern marketing forms of all sorts stand equally as distinguishing features of a consumerist market economy. While marketing activity must share in many of the motivations and techniques driving advertising, a letter through the post offering a loan or a hearing aid rarely incites the same ire in critics as does, for instance, a double-page magazine spread in *Cosmopolitan*, or a 30-second spot during *Coronation Street*. Why this might be the case is an interesting question. One point is that main media advertising typically interrupts something else – a film for example. Direct mail does not do so – though a telesales call will.

The answer in part is to do also with the very real anxiety that the various broadcast and published forms of public art, entertainment, information and debate are potentially compromised by their alliance with (and reliance on) the existence of 'above the line' advertising. An important strand of critical analysis of advertising cites its impact on media provision as a major problem, with the predominance of advertising-reliant media serving effectively to censor the emergence of alternative, critical, editorial and entertainment output. The disruptive capacities of some new, cheaper and more widely available media technologies, offers some potentials in circumventing major media ownership structures. However, ad revenues remain an important ingredient in editorial policy making – with both niche and mass audience appeal continually important guides to media producers.

'Below the line' advertising does not have this significant secondary set of effects on the public communications media (Curran 1981; Curran and Gurevitch 2005). Nevertheless, 'below the line' material can be an irritating distraction. Like advertising, it contributes to the negative feelings that arise in many people, from time to time, feelings prompted by the experience of inhabiting a world characterised by a brash and insistent commercialism. Later chapters will outline these and further criticisms of advertising, considering such concerns in the context of views of advertising as a major genre of cultural mediation in relations between people and things.

# 4

# ANALYSING AND HISTORICISING ADVERTISING

Advertising is a highly visible form of public culture, as conspicuous in its absence – as when advertising is removed from a metro station or a sporting event venue temporarily – as it is in its apparent ever-presence.[1] Without advertising, space is refigured and opens up a glimpse of what feels like a quite different society. Advertising is at once a quite ordinary feature of everyday life, even a reassuring one, while being at the same time a perennially 'alien' communication, *nagging* in the name of particularities (urging this or that product or brand) and in so doing, when we pause for thought, opening up reflection on some of the general features of culture and the market economy. Academic critics have characteristically taken frequent pauses for such thoughts; about adverts one by one, and about what this form of communication does and represents within broader socio-economic and cultural processes.

There are many continuities between everyday working understandings of advertising and arguments set down in some relatively widely-read books and essays (Johnson 1759; Packard 1957; Mayer 1958; Williams 1980; Goffman 1979; Williamson 1978; Klein 2000; Schlosser 2002; Schor 2004 are indicative) helping to define different aspects of the everyday critical agenda around ads. In keeping critical agendas alive and elaborating on more generalised suspicions about ads, such academic resources, along with ideas circulating in a number of other ways, have made a contribution to private and conversational definitions of and expectations in regard to advertising – as well as feeding into public debates around regulation.

An important strand of some academic engagements with advertising is with its history. Advertising, in the various places where it has developed, now globally, has done so within specific and localised processes over time – linked to broader changes within society, economy and culture. Historical perspectives on the emergence of advertising are useful. They remind us that advertising, in its modern form in particular, is a specific product of specific (if grand-scale) economic arrangements (i.e. national and then global market capitalism). As such, advertising is subject to, and is an index of, future transformations. As the characteristic economic and technology-based relationships which depend upon advertisements (and which the advertising industry has depended upon) continue to evolve and develop there will continue to be various strategic adaptations from consumers, advertisers, marketers, regulators and technology providers, not to mention advertising critics. History offers various instances of such adaptations.

Academics' characteristic engagements with advertising variously reveal ambivalence, insight, concern and, sometimes, scorn. The great extent to which advertising inhabits media space and other cultural and public arenas has provoked a proportionate and concerted critical response. The approaches evident in academic critique range from straightforward oppositional condemnation to 'rigorous analysis of the conditions and implications' (Mazzarella 2003a: 55–6) of advertising's institutional prac-tices, as well as focused readings of advertisements (e.g. Cronin 2000; Mort 1996: 109–12; Goldman 1992; Bordo 1990; Goffman 1979; Williamson 1978) and towards broad-based assessments of social and cultural influence. Complementary and important additions include a reinvigorated preoccu-pation with advertising audiences (Leiss *et al.* 2005: 481–518; O'Donohoe 1997; Nava and Nava 1992), and practitioners in the UK (Cronin 2004a; Nixon 2003; Soar 2000; Mort 1996) and globally (Kemper 2003; Mazzarella 2003; Moeran 1996; Tungate 2007). These and other studies have provided focus and specificity in accounts of advertising processes.

Typically academic criticisms have been organised around the following six areas, with the first of these, texts, receiving, as some have argued, a disproportionate degree of attention (Cronin 2004; McFall 2004; Nava 1997):

- texts (advertisements);
- effects (on culture, society and the economy);
- advertising institutions (agency processes, creative subjectivities, new business models);
- media (impact on the press, TV and other media content and communications);
- audiences (readers, viewers and listeners);
- history of advertising (its emergence and impacts in context).

It is helpful initially to consider a term which is central to both academics' and practitioners' understanding of the advertising process: 'the commodity'. Examining the uses of 'commodity' and related words 'commodification', 'commoditisation' and 'commodify' helps us, in turn, to better understand criticisms as well as some commercially oriented reflections on advertising. Everyday objects, when thought about outside the contexts of their ordinary uses and meanings, not to mention their uses in daydreaming (Campbell 1987), are often understood in terms of their nature as 'commodities'. The relationship between advertising analysis and 'the commodity form' is a useful prelude to considering a range of critical approaches, only some of which foreground 'the commodity'.[2]

## THIS IS AND IS NOT A 'COMMODITY': DEFINITIONS

Two statements about the products we consume, one from Robert Goldman (1992) and one from Mary Douglas (1978), show a degree of contradiction in the ways we understand 'things' we consume. On the one hand the products we buy (in an important account of 'commodities') seem to offer an illusory set of social connections – a substitute for real relationships and experiences lost to the economic organisation of our work:

> The commodity form redefines social relations as transactions, severs personal contacts from their social context and offers back to workers, in the form of consumption of images, what has been denied them in the wage contract, namely status, individuality, freedom and sensuality.
>
> (Goldman 1992: 17)

On the other hand commodities – or 'goods' – as Douglas and Isherwood (1978) call some of the objects we consume, seem able, precisely, to assure social relationships:

> It is apparent that . . . goods have another important use: they also make and maintain social relationships
>
> (Douglas and Isherwood 1978: 39)

Advertising is understood as a genre closely involved in processes of commodity consumption. On the one hand (e.g. as Goldman (1992) argues) advertising ensures the completion of a process whereby things become commodities – fictionalising our relationships to social life and to other people. On the other hand, as for instance people within the industry have argued, advertising serves to energise our relations to things, overcoming the dissatisfying and non-descript qualities of commodified mass-produced goods. Advertising is precisely (they argue) a service to offset the dehumanised quality of mass produced goods – as opposed to merely masking abstraction. This debate (and its contradictions) runs through much thinking about advertising and commerce with 'Commodity' a central term in manufacturing, in the marketing and promotional industries and in the critical literature. 'Commodity' is fundamental to many academics' accounts. Critics' and practitioners' analyses tend to use the word with different – sometimes opposite aims. For practitioners (good) advertising stands among the main 'antidotes' to commodification (Roberts 2004). Conversely, for critics, advertising is a communicative genre operating to *extend* commodification into every corner of experience (Goldman 1992: 23–33; Williamson 1978). What is a 'commodity'? and what underlies these contradictory uses of the word 'commodity'?

## ABSTRACT THINGS

A 'commodity' in the most basic sense is something that is useful and therefore valuable to human life. In particular, and emerging from this usage, the term has come to describe the 'form' taken by things when they are produced, mined or cultivated on a large scale, then processed and circulated, especially for market trading. When metals and minerals are refined for trade, when foodstuffs or opportunities to invest in businesses or experiences (such as holidays) are prepared and quantified – re-presented, ready to be priced, traded, packaged and managed – they undergo processes of *commoditisation*. Roughness and impurity, some kinds of qualitative specificity and (where relevant) concrete and material variances, are 'driven out' in favour of abstracting estimates of the grade and (now) more or less predictable properties of the 'commodity unit' (a barrel of oil, a number of shares or a gram of gold, a 'package' holiday and so on).

In this 'form' the good or service (gold, shares, oil or journeys) can be expressed uniformly; every unit is comparable with and exchangeable for an equivalent number (in value terms) of any other. Typically the mediating unit of exchange is monetary, as money provides the ultimate system for permitting and controlling exchange of commodities. This condition of abstract equivalence is the condition of the commodity; it is this condition that allows global markets to move things (and services) 'around', making them available through systems and processes of refinement, logistics and labelling. Most recently the word 'McDonaldisation' (Ritzer 1993) has been used to describe processes of efficient, predictable, consistent and bland organisation of provision, with the famous fast food restaurants suggested as a working model for the reshaping of a variety of other services, from health care to education to banking. McDonald-isation represents a highly ordered and extensive system of commodity provision.

While sameness, rigorous efficiency and predictability are its recipes for success, these features, in theory and opinion, if not always in practice, have also provoked dissatisfaction among consumers confronting a 'dehumanised' process, hence the prominence of McDonalds in anti-consumerist rhetoric and action.[3]

Commodification is how things become purchasable in a rationalised modern marketplace, so the commodification process is at the heart of consumption. It permits vigour and an efficiency in the economy but, and as critics have argued, the scalar differences between corporate and industrial systems of commodity production and provision present disjunctions when set against the labile human-sized world of individuals' consumption and desire.

Even when formed as commodities things maintain their materiality and functionality: you can conveniently prepare and eat ready meals; commodified experiences, fun parks or holiday camps retain impacts and affectivity; likewise services (such as banks or health provision) efficiently progress specific outcomes and processes. Nevertheless the relationship we have with commodities is often felt (somehow) to be lacking.

Canning is a precise and concrete instance of the procedural repro-duction of things (food) in the commodity form. Critiques of 'tinned' food became prevalent in the 1930s. Consumers berated standardised commodity packaging up of 'real' food in tins. Versions of this critical argument frequently re-emerge in different forms today (e.g. against supermarkets, package holidays and education marketing). In all such cases critics essentially deploy a critique of the commodity form. Andy Warhol's work frequently explored the complexities of commodity production and re-presentation (see Figure 4.1) and the crossover between art markets and everyday commodities.

Despite advantages such as cheapness and reliability, commodified goods often risk rejection by consumers. Commodity objects are in a sense *alien*. People want to relate to at least some things as special, as specific and befitting *their* cultural and human needs and *their* desires. This is often true even for the most basic of objects, so that those objects can 'make sense' in use but also in broader cultural systems of meaning, signifying various qualities or combinations of qualities: tradition, intimacy, locality, attractiveness, elegance, belonging, naturalness, authenticity and so on.

**Figure 4.1** Andy Warhol stages the complexities of commodity production and re-presentation: Andy Warhol's Beef Noodle Soup, 1962.

© The Andy Warhol Foundation for the Visual Arts, Inc./DACS, London, 2008. Trademarks Licensed by Campbell Soup Company. All Rights Reserved.

In a system of manufacture and consumption where the consumer and the producer have a social relationship, in a system where sites of production and sites of consumption have a felt connection, in a system where the origin of the thing is acknowledged and understood, such cultural qualities as might be missing from the anonymous i.e. unnamed commodity-product inhere within *this* product (a cake, a meal, a song, a piece of furniture) by virtue of necessarily-associated relations of production and provision. Whether it is a loaf of bread from a favoured baker, banking services from well-known members of the community, a lesson from an admired teacher or a cake baked by your mum, objects and services acquire and carry meanings referring to and across networks of intimacy, trust and sociality. Without a fuss and perhaps only half thought, such things and events have a way of making sense – a sense not felt readily in the presence of (ostensibly) placeless and nameless commodities. A hint of this feeling underlies the commonly expressed preference for old, worn, antique and unique objects (clothes or furniture).

For an object to have acquired a history – a local habitation and a name – is for it to have relinquished a degree of its commodity character. As it ages it comes (back) to life.

The commodity form, as described in classic accounts, has nothing of this 'life', so there is a contradiction at the heart of modern markets: on the one hand they depend (for competitive profitability) on the high-volume production of identical goods in large numbers (mass production, mass provision, globally sourced and assembled of the kind associated with Fordism and post-Fordism) but they also depend on consumers' living desire for goods, for things that they feel will fit and make sense within their worlds of meaning and activity. This is alongside the sense of necessity, which in any case is (to a degree) a part of cultural embeddedness. In at least a part of our consumption (even at its most practical) we require of objects that they connect with the world in our terms – mass produced commodities (alone) risk failing to do so.[4] Consequently sometimes 'gaps' appear between consumers and products and between needs, desires and market provision. Sometimes the various kinds of (mass-) productive efficiency are interpreted, by consumers, as signs of *deficiency*. This leads, as Roberts' dramatic metaphor describes, to the onset of 'business' own *necrotizing fasciitis*, or flesh-eating disease; commodification' (Roberts 2004: 29). Commodities are 'dead': however, as marketers hope, they can be brought to 'life'.

## ADVERTISING AS DE-COMMODIFICATION

Advertising – for commodities – plays upon such tacit preferences, appropriating in the name of the commodity something of the relation we might have to gifts and opposing them to the more perfunctory relations we might have with manufactured goods:

> One day you are sitting on a premium product, enjoying high margins and fighting off consumers. The next your product is being bottom loaded on back shelves or dumped into 'Special' bins.
>
> (Roberts 2004: 29)

Advertising (as a part of marketing) operates quite specifically in this gap, between the dead commodity and the animate 'thing'; its aim is to *de-commodify* objects – to reintroduce into the abstracted materiality of the objects and services delivered by commodity production and provision those 'touching' (Roberts 2004) or 'warm' (Baudrillard [1968] 1996) elements of the human and cultural world that can ignite desire and connection with (formally and formerly) abstracted commodities. The bought object takes on some of the social qualities typically associated with gifts – which is to say they enter into the meaningful circuits of human relating, and perhaps, over time or through deliberate and deliberative acts of appropriation and meaning attribution, the commodity sheds its generic nature and acquires particular qualities: not just any shoes but *my* shoes, the shoes I wore on my first date, or the shoes that someone bought me, and so on. Advertising is perhaps irrelevant to such product-narratives. But, sometimes, advertising tries to feed imaginative thinking – pre-empting personal involvement with attempts to tap desires and anxieties around social connection and belonging – to de-commodify this or that product, perhaps wrapping the object in the relational matrix of brand-based 'membership' and (routinised) intimacies.

Marketing (and advertising has a key role here) works to try to eradicate from the objects that producers and providers can bring to market the commodity-like properties (such as abstraction, deracination, deperson-alisation) that render them overly generic or inert. Marketers seek to suspend the element of the market transaction that feels like a commodity trade and provide instead (in the relevant space) a sense of the relationship between consumer and producer, person and product. Advertising is one of those relevant spaces: among the most flexible and mobile of spaces for re-investing life into the commodity form.

Carl Hamilton's (2000) account of the birth and success of the Absolut vodka brand is an excellent illustration of the transformational impact that advertising can have on a commodity. Starting with the premise that 'all vodkas are created equal' (Hamilton 2000: 116) – i.e. that absolute equivalence is the condition of vodkas, which are a commodity, a clear distillation of alcohol without discernible qualities. 'Absolute pure vodka' was transformed not least by advertising and marketing agencies to become a leading vodka brand, by means of clever packaging (a distinctive bottle), good PR and well-made advertisements. Each slogan simply stated the brand name in conjunction with a specific idea; witty visual puns presenting the bottle as the (absolute) personification of this or that particular quality: attraction, perfection, clarity. And, of course, reflecting the playfulness of the advertising campaign, Andy Warhol joined in and painted the bottle (Hamilton 2000: 144) for an ad with the slogan: ABSOLUT WARHOL.

Advertising binds qualities to commodities striving to convert the generic into the particular, the everyday into the special, the non-event into the special moment, the household routine into the family ritual, the journey into the quest. When advertising is successful, as marketers are often keen to point out, the commodity reacquires its status as a thing, as sensible substance, experiential, a thing including but also extending

ABSOLUT ATTRACTION

ABSOLUT PERFECTION

ABSOLUT CLARITY

ABSOLUT WARHOL

**Figure 4.2** Absolut branding: the commodity becomes 'art'.

functionality – not just any thing but a thing, to cite Hennion and Meadel (1989) 'destined for someone'. Roberts, in his study of branding as de-commodification, cites an anonymous Romanian designer for whom Absolut is anything but a commodity:

> Absolut: It is smart, funny, trendy. It always has a different story for us – inviting us to discover 'what's the story this time?' It can be anything it wants, transforming any object, situation or issue. I don't even drink Vodka, but I love the Absolut brand.
>
> (Roberts 2004: 180)

Advocates for (good) advertising claim that, as a cultural form, advertising makes a significant contribution: affirming connection, trust and meaning-making in a world of inert commodities. It should be said, however, that advertising is often, but not *always*, necessary in this process. Advertising is never a sufficient cause in the production and reproduction of a powerful branded range of products, but it is often a headline player in a concerted performance of elements of branding that run through the organisations that conceive, produce, design, distribute and assure the 'good'. The sustainability of a 'good' brand depends upon keeping overwhelming routinisation and abstraction out of the consumer experience so that the consumer continues to trust the brand across numerous exchanges he or she might have with it over a period.

## COMMODITY-SIGNS

This end – (re-)*substantiation* of the commodity form – is achieved by using signification to re-present the objects of mass production in ways that render them transmissible into, as meaning-full within, the 'semiotic' flows of conventional communication and association, flows whereby culture and human relations are articulated and realised through things. As Douglas and Isherwood make clear, commodities serve such purposes in every culture. Neither advertising nor consumerism has invented the significance of objects:

> Forget that commodities are good for eating, clothing and shelter; forget their usefulness and try instead the idea that commodities are good for thinking; treat them as a nonverbal medium for the human creative faculty.
>
> (1978: 40–1)

This 'thinking' in modes flavoured by, for example, fantasy, pragmatism, calculation and social sensing, is doubtless ongoing in consumer cultures worldwide. What continues to trouble advertising criticism, however, is the risk that such thought processes are too often scripted; inflected by commercially-produced advertisements, rather than by 'natural' cultural processes. Asking what 'natural' cultural processes might *be* is a helpful question – even when ready answers may not necessarily be at hand. Typically, advertising critics have suggested that the image-based links made between people and commodities through advertising have included an element of confusion – an element of fantasising (Williams 1980) not suited to optimising daily capacities for making meaningfully creative or practical decisions in the context of social, personal and environmental factors.

In understanding the relationships between people and things emerging in consumer cultures where advertising plays a highly visible role, critical academic perspectives have had a long-standing tendency to view the advertising work of reanimation as a central problem. Thus advertising is not a process to counter-commodification but an extension of the commodity process into culture; one whereby the work of abstraction reaches out of the systems of production, management and industrial processing and marketing and right into the very stuff of life: culture. Commodities within this regime are not so much for thinking (as the concretion, elaboration, affirmation and objectification of social relationships) as for fanciful thoughtlessness. They are associated with a narcissistic individualism (Lasch 1979) where relating and thinking are to be denied, and with a wilful forgetfulness in regard to the labour on which the provision of (often) cheap goods depends (Klein 2000), not to mention the profitability supported by a market system configured towards increased consumption and towards increased material efficiencies in production and in the distribution of products and producers.

## REVISITING ACADEMIC PERSPECTIVES

Critiques of advertising and consumerism by academics and by others, in these terms at least, are typically not taken to heart by the advertising industry. The industry tends to ignore such critiques on the grounds that such arguments are aimed at capitalism and the global economic system as a whole and not – in a focused way – at advertising as a particular social and economic practice. In return it is difficult to find examples (outside marketing) of academics' uncomplicated 'celebration' of advertising – partly on the grounds that the industry is well-equipped to promote itself and partly due to long-standing differences between value systems operating in commercial and educational settings (Leavis and Thompson 1964; Whitehead 1964). However, a substantial field of study has developed – throughout the twentieth century – around advertising as part of a preoccupation with the problems of culture in the contexts of commodity production and consumption – a field of work (e.g. Klein 2000) connected also in some ways (lately) to significant incidences of popular protest, with demonstrations often attacking brands as a component of activism operating under the banners of anti-globalisation.

At the same time, and notably since the 1980s, academics have produced ongoing and detailed reflections on the terms of reference, assumptions, methods and conclusions of previous critical analyses (e.g. Cronin 2004a; McFall 2004; Nava 1997; Fowles 1996: 52–76; Fine and Leopold 1993: 194–217; Fiske 1991; Mattelart 1991: 201–17; Schudson 1981). Partly as a consequence of such work, refinements and revisions continue to be made to those formerly well-established critical positions that had unambiguously and uniformly identified advertising negatively: as a powerfully manipulative image machine (Williamson 1978), as resolutely 'anti-culture' and anti-human (Henry 1966), as infantilising (Baudrillard [1968] 1996) and as systematically productive of social misrecognition and false and variously 'abstracted' desires (Galbraith 1977; Baudrillard [1968] 1996; Packard 1957; Leavis and Thompson 1964). Today the picture academics paint of advertising is more detailed, more complex and perhaps less clear-cut – with advertising being 'framed' and reframed (Nava 1997) according to an array of broader preoccupations, many of them captured in Williams's phrase 'problems in materialism and culture'.

Critical approaches to advertising have come from across academic disciplines, in particular in literary studies (Leavis and Thompson 1964), linguistics (Tanaka 1999; Myers 1994; Leech 1966) and philosophy (Scruton 2000), as well as media studies, cultural studies, economics and sociology (Cronin 2004; Schudson 1993; Nava and Nava 1992; Williams 1980; Williamson 1978; Galbraith 1977), including valuable examinations of the history and development of advertising (Odih 2007; Tungate 2007; Delaney 2007; Leiss et al. 2005; McFall 2004; Lears 1994; Laird 1993; Marchand 1985; Pope 1983; Nevett 1982; Williams 1980; Ewen 1976; Presbrey 1929).

Searching accounts have emerged from diverse and often opposing political positions – advertising has provided a common enemy for the political-academic left and right. Particularly emphatic critiques energised by various, (sometimes) compelling socialist, feminist and liberal arguments remain relevant (e.g. Odih 2007; Winship 2000; Goldman 1992; Williams 1980; Williamson 1978; Goffman 1979; Adorno 1991; Baudrillard [1968] 1996), and continue to provoke debate. Sometimes criticism of advertising has been driven by more culturally conservative sensibilities (e.g. Scruton 2000: 55–67; Thompson 1943) and this work continues to resonate with those concerned to defend particular 'traditional' cultural and aesthetic values.

More psychologically oriented work has provided useful and detailed accounts emphasising the states of mind, body and culture associated with inhabiting a society where advertising is a prevalent means of cultural communication (e.g. James 2007; Richards *et al.* 2000; Haineault and Roy 1993; Richards 1994: 102–4; Orbach 1993: 56–7; Lasch 1979: 72–9). This is in tune with the widening popularity (and relevance) of various kind of therapeutic discourses (notably psychoanalysis) in academic and social analysis.

It should be of no surprise that advertising has spawned such a vast critical literature. After all, the advertising industry continues to be prolific in its own ways – obviously in the production and circulation of advertisements, but also in its own reflective and promotional accounts of its practice, with innumerable working papers, best-practice papers, textual analyses, competitive awards and broader philosophical accounts of the industry. Since the early days of the industry advertising professionals have continued to work reflexively, to adapt (often largely within their own terms) to an expanding and unpredictable array of promotional tasks, new product sectors, new territories, new technologies, new media, new audiences, new regulations and new professional and cultural values.

Dynamic change has characterised political, cultural and economic and techno-media environments since the war, nationally and globally, with each decade, from the 1960s and through the 1970s, 1980s and 1990s, as well as in the new millennium cited as pivotal for the advertising industry (Himpe 2006; Springer 2007; Cappo 2003; Nixon 2003; Frank 1997; Mort 1996; Wight 1972; Delaney 2007). The study of advertising has been alert to such changes at the micro level, responding to advertising's cultural and institutional transformations and, at the macro level, attempting to make sense of advertising in the contexts of some of these unfolding sociocultural and global narratives. Advertising criticism has become increasingly relevant as academics have striven to engage with and understand changing contemporary cultures and attendant questions about consumption, materiality (and materialism), meaning-making, representation, identity, citizenship, social communication and the politics of ethnicity and gender. Under academic scrutiny advertising, apparently so trivial and incidental, has on occasion been cast as a significant and contributory part in wider social, economic and cultural movements.[5]

## CULTURE AND CREATIVITY

Academic critics tend to question industry claims to 'progressive' creativity and innovation and have frequently drawn attention to advertising's 'pseudo' creativity and 'superficiality' (Adorno and Horkheimer 1979), or to the ways advertising misrepresents life and misdirects desire (Williamson 1978), repetitively offering up a variety of limiting visions of social 'virtue' in ways regarded as partial and (incrementally) damaging. Critics have sought to alert their readers to the tendency for advertising, as a cultural genre, to usurp or mime other, more substantial, forms of social communication, promoting apparently quite complex ideas in the name of an 'empty', mercantile and ultimately unsatisfying materialism (Thoman 2002; Wilson 1968; Thomson 1943). This includes an identification of the well-established strategy whereby advertising works to co-opt emancipatory discourses – for example around gender politics, ethnicity and representation, environmentalism, alternative health, reflexive media and advertising criticism and so on (Frank 1997; Horowitz 1994: 135–42; Goldman 1992; Ewen 1988; Myers 1986). Such advertisements, it is supposed, work to attach the critical sensibilities they provoke to consumers' sense of particular products and services, as well as disarming jaded audiences' sometimes deep-seated negativity toward advertising communications (held in general) – thus (in intent) pre-empting critical negation of this or that particular advertisement's appeals. The recent French Connection ad cited above (see Chapter 1, and see also Chapter 7) is exemplary here, but examples of advertising co-opting critical discourse can be traced, for example, back to the 1960s when Packard's critical ideas about 'hidden persuasion' and 'status seeking' (Packard 1959, 1957) were routinely played on in advertisements (Horowitz 1994: 135–42).

Academic criticism is alert to advertising's purported influence on cultural life – on its interventions in the relations between people (how we see and value each other (Winship 2000; Cortese 1999; Goffman 1979; Millum 1975 for instance)), and between people and things – how we use, value and relate to objects/objectives (Cronin 2004a; Richards et al. 2000; Leiss et al. 2005; Berger 1973; Marcuse 1973; Inglis 1971; Baudrillard [1968] 1996; Williams 1980). Critics recognise an important aim guiding much advertising: the desire to re-present objects (or services) produced and made available en masse for the marketplace, as objects continuous with, and thus belonging to, consumers' lives, interests and culture; material objects carrying, circulating and thus better enabling (some) cultural meanings and so inflecting everyday action and desire (Zukin 2004: 258–9; McCracken 1990). It is this – advertising's cultural 'project' – that has provoked most criticism (see Ewen 2000; Lears 1994; Leiss *et al.* 2005; Inglis 1971). As Schudson (1993) proposes, advertising requires analysis because:

> whether or not it sells cars or chocolate, [Advertising] surrounds us and enters into us, so that when we speak we may speak in or with reference to the language of advertising and when we see we may see through schemata that advertising has made salient for us . . . as symbol, the power of advertising may be considerable.
>
> (Schudson 1993: 210)

Advertising (its critics argue) declaims an insistent set of arguments loudly yet furtively, appealing to and furthering questionable motives (Key 1974, 1989, 1992; Packard 1957). As we walk the streets, or sit in our homes, we must contend with a series of 'mirages'. Many of these, in some way, seem to tempt us out of the relatively solid relationships (Twitchell 1999) (to principles, futures, people and things and their uses) that (should) sustain us, in favour of market-based imagistic invitations, to a series of what might be called active submissions to the objects, experiences, relationships and futures available (symbolically) and apparently most conveniently via market-based consuming. Available, that is, to individuals, more or less, in proportion to their power in the marketplace – their wealth, creditworthiness or their 'pecuniary strength' (Henry 1966). The point is that advertising encourages a belief system (and supports a 'culture') where individuals' market power (their affluence and consuming activity) can become evermore emphatic markers of social and cultural virtue. To venture confidently outside this consumerist world (critics argue) becomes routinely 'unthinkable'.

While there is clearly no coherent doctrine about 'how to live' discernible within the hundreds and thousands of advertisements we might see or hear in any given period (a significant flaw in the analogy with religion), critics have proposed that, as an aggregate, there are recurrent themes and assumptions which are affirmed, again and again, to naturalise and, to an extent, reinforce certain values and ideas about living at the expense of others (Ewen 2000; Leiss *et al.* 1990; Goffman 1979; Baudrillard [1968] 1999).

Underlying such critiques are concerns about the sources of such ideas about 'the good life'. In whose interests is it to promote individual consumption, personal affluence and market choice as key markers of a good society? In so far as it is acknowledged that advertising manipulation is fundamental to the workings of global, national and some local market systems, it is held to account as a tool exerting excessive power on behalf of, either:

- a damaging and out-of-control national and (lately) global economic system organised to circulate commodities in the interests of corporate profitability;
- philistine business leaders who 'know the price of everything and the value of nothing'; or
- agents of a free market liberalism committed (in the name of competitive individualism and 'equality' of opportunity and choice) to maintaining a status quo which systematically disadvantages the economically weak and the socially and culturally excluded.

All this is at the expense of a range of alternative visions: of environmental responsibility, of more collective and co-operative organisation of social production and consumption, of more collective social and political decision-making, and of more direct political regulation of public and media communications – broadly, the range of political priorities of socialist economic policy.

In recent decades academic arguments against advertising have been subjected to certain important and detailed revisions and elaborations (Nava and Nava 1997; Fowles 1996; Davidson 1992; Richards 1994), notably on the topic of the advertising audience (Cronin 2004a; O'Donohoe 1997; Nava 1992): nevertheless, it would be fair to say that the academic view of advertising remains largely negative, in part amplifying some more widespread popular dislike of over-insistent marketing communications, but also extending critique in more particular investigations, considering broader and deeper sociocultural impacts around materialism, culture, subjectivity, gender and politics. The aim of this and subsequent chapters is to examine and to begin to set out some of the perspectives that academic theories provide to help put advertising in context.

## MEDIA AND ADVERTISING: CRITICAL PERSPECTIVES

There is a long-standing anxiety among academic critics about the impact advertising has on the media output it funds, and indeed on the very structure of the media industries (Curran 2002; Bogart 2000; Baker 1995; Williams 1969). Academic critics have looked in some detail at advertising's relationship to media (McChesney 2004: 138–74; Curran 2002, 1981; Bogart 2000; Moeran 1996: 169–275; Williams 1969) as well as, from slightly different angles, at media producers' relationships with advertising (see e.g. Gough-Yates 2003: 132–58; Jackson et al. 2001:

62–6). A unique feature of (above the line) advertising, as a media genre, is its peculiar relationship with its 'host' media. While advertising is typically classified as peripheral to 'real' media content (e.g. news, features, editorial, TV programmes and films) by many media professionals as they report the news, criticise a product or direct a script, advertising is nevertheless basic to the commercial processes supporting print and broadcast media organisations (Gough-Yates 2003: 132–58; Jackson *et al.* 2001: 62–6; Bogart 2000; Nixon 1996; Tunstall 1993), to the extent that it provides the financial conditions that make most contemporary media activity possible, and is thus of considerable relevance to corporations' strategic and operational management (see Chapter 3). As we have seen, there is a resultant tension underlying the production of media output, sometimes posed as a tension between professionals' editorial or artistic integrity and the commercial pragmatism of media managers. The complexities of such relationships have provided grounds for much academic debate, as well as being a source of ongoing tension and anxiety within the advertising institutions and between different stakeholders (clients, creatives, media editors and so on) in the advertising production and dissemination process.

The function of the media extends beyond entertainment and into political life, so the debate about advertising likewise moves from everyday concerns about 'dumbing down', 'comic' newspapers and TV trash, to include concerns about democratic processes. For citizens to participate confidently and enthusiastically in political and community processes (voting in elections or attending local public meetings, for instance) they need to be informed about what is at issue. They need to be furnished with information on which to base their judgement and actions (such as votes). In the absence of such information, and a media context (ideally) in lively political debate (written or spoken), it can become difficult for citizens (locally, or nationally, not to mention globally) to make and act on formal political decisions, to find politics relevant, or, ultimately, to articulate a political voice.

Given the importance of an independent, robust and informative media system in the maintenance of a healthy democratic culture and society, any 'institution', like advertising, which appears to wield power over the form and contents of (at least some) media output, requires constant scrutiny. Thus analysts have worked to track the impacts ads have had on media content (as well as observing the more complex influence advertising has had on the formats of other media and communications genres) with public information broadcasts, election addresses and some elements of print media coming to take on the 'look' and 'feel' of promotional advertising. This has happened to such an extent that advertising has come to define the style of a great deal of contemporary cultural output (Adorno and Horkheimer 1979: 162).

A common criticism made of academics' approaches to advertising is that they tend, perhaps naïvely, to treat the advertising industry as a total, integrated and concerted system seamlessly implementing its marketing function.

The revisions to the many critiques which routinely treat advertising as a 'monolithic' institution extend across other dimensions of analysis. For example, while advertising is commonly understood to be a unified practice regardless of the product sector or the particular advertising task it is performing, some accounts have encouraged thinking about the varied and specific nature of advertising as embedded within a longer chain or narrative about relations between supply and demand (Fine and Leopold 1993: 20–35).

Different product sectors use advertising (or do not use it) according to different market logics, and in the service of very different kinds of consumer relations (one-off purchases, 'brand building', repeat purchase, extensions of use and so on). As we have seen, ads have many functions. As Fine argues in regard to consumption, so too, when thinking about academic critiques of advertising,

> this posits each commodity as the creation of an interdependent system of production, distribution, and retailing and of specific cultural determinants including, where appropriate, advertising. Recognising that the origins of and linkages between, each of these factors will be different for each commodity makes it possible to explain the changing extent and nature of advertising rather than simply interpreting it at the visible end of each of these chains.
> (Fine and Leopold 1993: 195)

What Fine and Leopold establish is that within different systems of commodity provision and acquisition, be it cars, chocolate, higher education, legal services or cotton wool, organisation of production, retailing, after-care and advertising will differ in important respects from one commodity/product sector to another. The corollary is that critiques emerging from and validated in relation to an analysis of a Jack Daniel's, a Gucci or a Mercedes ad, might have less general applicability beyond the immediate marketing situation out of which they emerged than we would assume. They cannot provide the basis for a general critique of advertising and consumption because the advertisements are serving varied marketing functions in starkly different marketing situations.

It can also be misleading to posit 'advertising' as a unitary and never-changing practice across another dimension – the historical one. It is clear that advertising has not always been as prominent a part of cultural and economic life, and not always performing the same various functions. Advertising is changing. It is useful to consider contemporary changes alongside an account outlining some of the origins and emergences identified in the history of advertising – as a way of historicising both practice and critique. The next section looks at some of these transitions to better help locate contemporary advertising as genre and practice.

## ADVERTISING: GENRES AND HISTORY

Advertising is a genre and an institution largely to do with relationships, and their mediation, between manufacturers, agriculturalists, wholesalers, retailers and shoppers; between sellers and buyers, producers and consumers.[6] It allows for a specific mode of address and for the pursuit of the (fleeting) communications relationships typically necessary to large and widely- (nationally-, globally- and regionally-) distributed markets. Historically and with a wide-angle view there are enormous changes to consider across the four centuries of advertising:[7] these can be traced only cursorily here.

The history of the emergence of advertising is also about the forms of the modern advertising *industry* taking shape, and concomitantly the stabilisation (and lately the more emphasised de-stabilisation) of role relationships between producers and consumers, clients and agencies, media buyers and media owners, regulators, audiences, researchers and planners – all those served by advertising's (evolving) institutional frameworks.

So advertisements constitute a genre with a history in certain market and institutional relationships. To map something of this it is helpful to have some period 'headings' under which to sketch the development of the advertising. There is no claim that this is a definitive historical schema in any way. Instead it is one that aims to suggest a sequential development in advertising to order a vast and open ended field; in the finer grain of advertising's development many stops and starts, forerunners and throwbacks are evident. That said, the headings are:

- proto-modern advertising 1600–1780;
- early-modern advertising 1780–1880;
- modern advertising 1880–1950;
- late-modern advertising 1950–90.

As Braudel (1982) argues of market society, so it is true of advertising: there can be 'no linear history' of its emergence (Braudel 1982, cited in Slater and Tonkiss 2001: 13). Nevertheless Sandage (1961), referring to the period before the Industrial Revolution – around the mid eighteenth to mid-nineteenth centuries – briefly charts a progressive transition. It is not clear that there ever was a 'leap' from 'word of mouth' to a modern advertising system, but instead complex series of social, economic and cultural developments took place (emergent advertising among them).

## Proto-modern advertising 1600–1780

> If one have pearls to sell he should say, I seek to sell some pearls; and another, I seek to buy some pearls . . . Such a one seeketh for a master, another a workman; Some this, some that, everyone as he needeth; and it seemeth that this means of enter-warning one another would bring no small commodity into common commerce and society.
>
> (Montaigne 1594, cited in Presbrey 1929: 35)

The French essayist Montaigne, writing in 1594, describes the need for a space where those that have something to sell, for example pearls, should be able to communicate with those who might want to buy – pearls or whatever else happens to be for sale. It would be, he argues, 'no small commodity' ('commodity' in this instance meant benefit) to enable such communications to take place routinely.

A 'means of enter-warning' described as 'no small commodity' stands plausibly as a precursor for today's advertising services. The 'commodity' now is larger but the principle is the same, providing *means* to better ensure that (unknown and distant) buyers and sellers 'meet' asynchronously, in print or other media.

Montaigne uses the collocation 'enter-warning' as an approximate synonym for 'advertising'. 'Advertising' contains in its etymology a link (via Latin: *advertere* – literally, to turn towards) to the idea of warning – 'watch out!' – hence the opposite: 'inadvertent'. Both warning and persuasion have been long-standing features of commercial communications with '*caveat emptor*'[8] as applicable to advertising as to retail transactions.

'Advertising', although the word itself was not then used in all the senses it has today, began in the early seventeenth century out of the various attempts to provide means for announcing the availability of goods. This need emerged fast in cities like London and Paris, where commercial trading between anonymous buyers and sellers, and between remote (national and colonial) trading centres, had begun to develop. Presbrey (1929) and Nevett (1980) have provided useful accounts of the (at first) gradual, and then quite explosive early growth in advertising communications in the period 1650–1700.

By the late eighteenth century, advertising was a major component of the early modern media (via pamphlets, public notices and early newspapers). Low levels of literacy, localised circulation and considerably fewer media forms and titles meant that while advertising was a 'common', not to say 'despised' feature of everyday London life (Johnson 1759) it was not the 'all pervasive' genre described and experienced today. Nevertheless Johnson was able to observe:

> every man now knows a ready method of informing the publick of all that he desires to buy or sell, whether his wares be material or intellectual; whether he makes clothes, or teaches the mathematicks; whether he is a tutor that wants a pupil, or a pupil that wants a tutor.
>
> (Johnson *The Idler*, 20 January 1759)

On the evidence presented by Presbrey (1929) and others (Nevett 1980; McFall 2004) there were significant developments to move to this point; here some broad brush strokes can be drawn.

Advertising followed, and then, at points and in certain sectors, like patent medicines, supported some of the expansion of commercial life in the sixteenth to eighteenth centuries. The first advertisement in Europe appeared in a (German) pamphlet of 1525; in London the first 'advertisement' or 'advice' is recorded in 1625, with a second in London only in 1647, and then subsequently a rapid expansion in various formats including newspapers in the seventeenth and particularly the eighteenth centuries (Presbrey 1929: 35–73).

Advertising's initial development traces through, and is traced by, the many developments associated with early modernity in Europe and, later, in the US (Presbrey 1929: 40–62, 113–40). Colonial trade; early industrialisation; improving literacy; embryonic media; various technological improvements in printing and transport methods; growth in populations, migrations and concomitant growth of metropolitan centres; the move to wage labour and increased affluence. All were implicated in, and no doubt partly stimulated by (to varying degrees) the developments of markets and commercial promotion, including advertising.

## Proto-advertisements (new relationships)

Regarding this early history, just one aspect, the *kind* of communications genre that emerged, is a useful focus.[9] The earliest ads in the seventeenth century typically (and with noted exceptions) made use only of written text announcing events and describing products and some attention-grabbing printer's marks such as '!!' and '**'.

Presbrey (1929), records a key forerunner of today's advertising in seventeenth- and eighteenth-century London. He presents examples from the publication *Whitson's Merchants' Weekly Remembrancer of the Present Money Prices of Their Goods Ashoar* [sic.] *in London* (Presbrey 1929: 56). This pamphlet, published first in 1681, provided inventories of trade goods landed in London's docks from developing overseas trading. The publication included prototypical text-only 'advertisements', written by a publisher, John Houghton (Presbrey 1929: 56). These examples are for, respectively, (medicinal) sulphur and 'perukes', the then-fashionable wigs.

> For a friend I can now sell very good flower of brimstone, etc., as cheap or cheaper than any in town does; and I'll sell any good fir [sic.] any man of repute if desired.
>
> (Cited Presbrey 1929: 57)

> I know a peruke [i.e. wig] maker that pretends to make perukes extraordinarily fashionable and will sell good pennyworths; I can direct to him.
>
> (Cited Presbrey 1929: 58)

Houghton gradually refined such early 'advertisements' by adding advertisers' names and then addresses. This step established an important change. The intermediary was *depersonalised*, and the advertisement served to connect producer to consumer, with no *named* person in between. In itself minor, this detail nevertheless represents a key transition in the structure of dissemination of commercial information from 'word of mouth' to prototypical paid-for mediated advertising. As Judith Williamson (1978) suggests, a key feature of the advertising genre is that while of course people do make ads,[10] it is 'not their speech'; it is the speech on behalf of the advertiser, i.e. she or he who seeks to advertise. In an embryonic way it is this link to consumers via anonymous commercial advocacy that Houghton sets in train. Some basic one-line ads (below) are indicative; Presbrey suggests that Houghton here has learned the value of adding in the supplier's name to the ad (Presbrey 1929: 59) and de-emphasising his own.

> Last week was imported:
> Bacon by Mr. Edwards
> Cheese by Mr. Francis
> Corral beads by Mr. Paggen
> Crab's eyes by Mr. Harvey

Horse hair by Mr. Becens
Joynted babies[11] by Mr. Harrison
Mapps by Mr. Thompson
Orange flower water by Mr. Bellamy
Prospective glasses by Mr. Mason
Saffron by Mr. Western
Sturgeon by Mr. Kett.

These 'ads' point to the beginnings of the primary advertising relationship (advertiser, a *paid* agent and an audience) as well as to a crude kind of 'branding' in the sense that a *name* is attached to a supplier of a good so that stock is distinguished by that supplier's name. The next step would be to mark goods on the docks to ensure that stock belonging to the different traders was correctly designated; this was a further small step towards a world of brands, which via maker's marks, accreditation 'by royal appointment', patron's crests and the trademark moved us towards the logos and labels of the nineteenth, twentieth and twenty-first centuries. Branding as we know it did not begin to develop until the nineteenth century (Danesi 2006) but Presbrey suggests that Houghton was the 'father of publication *advertising*' (emphasis added) and that his 'enterprising methods, emulated and developed by others, resulted in a wide extension of trade uses of publicity' (Presbrey 1929: 60).

Such embryonic ads seem basic to the contemporary eye. However, it should be borne in mind that in a world where the range of ostensibly 'novel' objects was so much more limited than it is today, the mere announcement of a new or rare commodity (coffee or tobacco, silk or spice) might have been more 'spectacular' or affecting (Barnard 1995) than the old advertisement texts (as seen now) would suggest.

To draw direct comparisons between contemporary and past media environments seems beside the point. After all Samuel Johnson is famous for suggesting that advertising developments had reached a high plateau in the eighteenth century; he described advertising as an art 'so near to perfection that it is not easy to propose any improvement' (Johnson 1759, cited in Presbrey 1929: 72). He may have been right in his terms; technology aside, early rhetorical technique was at times quite sophisticated (Barnard 1995; McFall 2004).

As McFall has suggested, with clear evidence[12] (McFall 2004; see also McKendrick 1982), creative advertising and promotional tactics were used liberally from the early eighteenth century onwards. Not only were there straightforward announcements and extravagant proclamations about the health-giving properties of 'tobacco' (Presbrey 1929: 49) and the 'cure all' coffee (Nevett 1980), but there were also instances of the kinds of emotional appeal more often associated with modern advertising and research-inspired[13] 'hidden persuasion' (McFall 2004: 82–3).

As publication techniques improved and the wider distribution of newspapers became possible, through coffee houses and public reading rooms, advertising became the evermore widespread and artful practice critically evaluated by Johnson (1779, cited in Presbrey 1929) complementing the more basic and direct forms of commercial communications such as handbills, hawkers, callers and shop signs which marked the space of the growing city. At the same time important developments (concurrent with all stages of the emergence and development of advertising) included improvements in literacy and distribution networks, both for goods and for media.

Prototypically there was, by the middle of the eighteenth century:

- a genre of communications linking producers or providers with consumers, sometimes via paid intermediaries;
- an emerging 'art' of rudimentary design and persuasive commercial writing;
- a media system gaining revenue from placing advertisements in its pages (while also charging its readers);
- a developing public critical discourse about advertising expressing general irritation and more deep-seated concerns.

## Early-modern advertising 1780–1880

Addison (1710) and Johnson (1779) in the eighteenth century could offer critical evaluations of the rhetorical and commercial tactics of advertising; early in the twentieth century, H.G. Wells[14] could rely (in 1909) on an audience familiar enough with advertising and its methods to write a (retrospective) satirical account of the genre. Set in the 1880s the novel *Tono-Bungay* (Wells 2005 [1909]), named after the patent medicine marketed by the protagonist's family's growing business, offers a picture of advertising and marketing techniques towards the end of the Victorian era. This excerpt from a chapter in the novel entitled *How we made Tono-Bungay Hum*, reveals Wells's jaded familiarity with a maturing communicative genre:

> my uncle . . . wrote every advertisement; some of them even he sketched. You must remember that his were the days before the *Time* took to enterprise and the vociferous hawking of that antiquated Encyclopaedia. That alluring, button-holing, let-me-just-tell-you-quite-soberly-something-you-ought-to-know style of newspaper advertisement, with every now and then a convulsive

jump of some attractive phrase into capitals, was then almost a novelty. 'Many people who are MODERATELY well think they are QUITE well', was one of his early efforts. The jerks in capitals were, 'DO NOT NEED DRUGS OR MEDICINE', and 'SIMPLY A PROPER REGIMEN TO GET YOU IN TONE'. One was warned against the chemist or druggist who pushed 'much-advertised nostrums' on one's attention. That trash did more harm than good. The thing needed was regimen – and Tono-Bungay!

(Wells [1909] 2005: 145)

Olins (2003: 48–9) suggests that Wells's fictional and satirical account is a 'largely accurate' portrayal of a late Victorian company that 'embraced every modern branding principle'[15] including 'thinking global and acting local', and 'brand extension' (Olins 2003: 48).

In the 1780s, over a hundred years before *Tono-Bungay*, Josiah Wedgwood's pottery firm had established itself nationally (and internationally) using advertising among the 'familiar forms of modern marketing' which, as Wernick (1991) argues, have been 'integral, from the very beginnings of industrial capitalism, to the mass production of consumer goods' (Wernick 1991: 12). Wernick provides an insight into a complex media and advertising environment in operation at the time of the French Revolution – with Wedgwood (in the 1780s) engaged in selective 'media planning':

While he [Wedgwood] eschewed handbills as too down-market, and for the same reason was reluctant to use paid advertising in the newspaper press (alongside ads by medical quacks and the like), he did encourage 'puffs' and even placed paid notices in both British and European publications drawing attention to new lines of ware.

(Wernick 1991: 14)

Such evidence of a thriving and sophisticated (if sector-specific) advertising and promotional culture before the nineteenth century in Britain is also reported by McKendrick *et al.* (1982) who describe the commercialisation of English society in the eighteenth century. In the US, Presbrey (1929: 181–205) and Laird (1998: 16–22) provide evidence of similar developments from the 1820s onwards. In his account of the famous impresario and entrepreneur Phineas T. Barnum (1810–1891), Lears (1994) provides an early American promotional pioneer to set alongside the UK's Wedgwood.

Mid-ninetenth-century inhabitants of major metropolitan centres were routinely acclimatised to advertisements. As Hindley and Hindley (1972) state, 'it is known that there were several hundred advertising agents operating in London alone by the end of the nineteenth century'. To back this claim they are able to identify 73 advertising agents by name with founding dates from the 1830s to the 1890s (Hindley and Hindley 1972: 203). They also reproduce numerous examples of Victorian ads, pictorial evidence of a rich nineteenth-century advertising environment (see also De Vries 1968).

Despite such developments Williams (1980) is able to argue that the prominence and centrality of advertising as image and persuasion was in some respects undeveloped in the mid nineteenth century:[16]

> By the 1850s . . . and with Britain already an industrial nation, the advertising pages of the newspapers, whether *The Times* or the *News of the World*, were still basically similar to those in eighteenth-century journals.
>
> (Williams 1980: 173)

In 1880 most advertising agencies were typically working primarily in the provision of what is now understood as media buying and selling (see, for example, Figure 4.4). As Presbrey (1929) makes clear:

> At the beginning of the twentieth century most of the English advertising agencies were still of the type representing a list of newspapers and periodicals with which the contractor had a special relationship.
>
> (Presbrey 1929)

In the US this was also the case, with developments in the 1880s onwards (Walker Laird 1998; Ohmann 1996). This activity was called 'space broking' – or 'farming'.

In a relationship the means of mediation become a valuable asset. Once something is acknowledged as valuable, it is likely an attempt will be made to realise the value – to turn it into a commodity for profitable sale. As manufacturing volumes increased the need to communicate with national markets became a condition for the distribution of large volumes of goods. Those who could 'deliver' media space at a good price were able to command considerable payment for their services. Space broking (or 'farming') emerged as a new 'profession'.

Commodities both presuppose and create markets, and markets presuppose and create traders. The birth of modern advertising lay in the interaction between:

- producers' *need* for national communications;
- (potential) *availability* of the means for national communications;
- *desire* of newspapers for extra income;
- entrepreneurial *will*, among traders, to bring these compatible desires together for mutual profit.

**Figure 4.3** J. Walter Thompson ad for Thompson's battery. Courtesy of the J. Walter Thompson archive at the Hartman Center, Duke University.

**Figure 4.4** J. Walter Thompson ad. Courtesy of the J. Walter Thompson archive at the Hartman Center, Duke University.

So advertising was born out of the emergent market for a new commodity: media space.

Figures 4.3 and 4.4 show advertisements from J. Walter Thompson, one of the first and for many years the biggest advertising agencies in the US, then the UK and worldwide. These ads were aimed at potential advertisers, offering space in the media.

> Any Advertiser who will supply me with the requisite powder I will provide with such shot and shell that when fired into the Public they will surrender at once.
>
> ('Thompson's battery', JWT ad 1889)

What is interesting here (aside from the military metaphor, which indicates something of the way early advertising professionals positioned their services) is the requirement that the advertiser provide 'requisite powder' – the DIY content of the advertising message. Overwhelmingly media space was on offer. No extras.

## Advertising institutions: patchy but intensive development

A demonstrable transition in the type, scope and scale of advertising was taking place as the beginning of the twentieth century approached. That such a transition was uneven and with regional and national variations should be taken as read. Some product sectors used advertising a lot in the nineteenth century: patent medicines, books and non-perishable foods, entertainments, soaps and cosmetics, cigarettes and various inventions – such as Dr Scott's electric hairbrush and everlasting 'electricpatent' socks (Hindley and Hindley 1972). Others, those with localised markets or for whom advertising was considered 'downmarket' or illegal (for example law firms and services such as banking) did not use it.

Meanwhile certain other restrictions (some self-imposed) on the media, notably paper tax and the right to use illustrations, forestalled (to some degree) the pervasive development of many of the features recognisable in twentieth-century advertising. The preparation of copy and design was carried out by manufacturers themselves or by newspaper printers as much as by specialist 'creatives'.

Those advertising agents that existed at this stage were often effectively subordinated to either a client or media publishers, subdivisions of media or manufacture. But some acted as go-betweens, being paid by both parties. In this 'early modern' period 'advertising agencies' such as those described by Presbrey (1929 in the US and UK) and by Hindley and Hindley (1972) were enterprises operating with many and quite differing business models.

Early to mid-nineteenth-century advertising did not routinely have the advertisement formats and the organisational structures of modern advertising, forms which imply and affirm roles: advertiser, advertising agent, creative, researcher, consumer, commercial media publisher and so on. By the 1880s these were developing. At the same time, a certain organisation and stability for some of these social, economic and commercial relationships – for example linking consumers to producers directly (through advertised brand names) and thus 'cutting out' at least some of retailers' control of the relationship with consumers (Brierley 2002; Norris 1981) – was taking place, with large agencies like J. Walter Thompson leading the strategy.

Situating advertising *between* supply and demand depends on the mode of division of supply from demand, that is, kinds of separation between producer owners and consumers emerging with industrial manufacturing and global trading. Without division and separation there can be no 'relationship' to negotiate. It is the character and history of its forms of division and separation that define the terms, experience and organisation of any relationship. This is certainly the case with advertising. As part of an attempt to control the types of commercial relationship that developed at the end of the nineteenth century, advertising can best be thought of as part of a history that describes the emergence of changing modes of production and changing characteristics of 'the consumer' – divergences and re-articulations of relations between spheres of production and consumption.

There are a number of inter-related developments and perspectives to consider. Primarily, modern advertising is tied to the emergence of a geo-graphically distributed, urbanising, mass-producing and mass-consuming economy (Falk 1994; Lears 1994; Leiss *et al.* 2005; Williams 1980; Ewen 1976), one where people are paid wages in return for their work in quite specific and narrow 'alienating' jobs. Alongside the other marketing pro-cesses, advertising contributed to the management of relationships between the supply side of the economy (the things made) and demand (the aggregated needs and wants of consumers). Its roles – to inform demand and to inform consumers' choices between competitors – were also about 'making consumers'. In this sense, advertising completed the production process. Not unlike packaging and distribution, advertising became a 'vehicle' designed into the process of getting the goods from the factory gate and, in exchange for money (as much as possible), into the consumers' shopping basket. This rather domineering sense of advertising no doubt informs the military imagery shown in Figure 4.3 (from 1880).

A modification of this simple model of advertising as production of demand sees it as a *regulator* of demand, and, explicitly, as a regulator of the anxiety attached to being in possession of a large quantity of stock and the means to produce more, yet with no cast iron guarantee that what has been produced will be sold. Thus advertising, from the producer's point of view, is seen as insurance, protecting capital investment in factories and labour costs from the risk that the output of these investments will yield inadequate returns. Walter Bagehot, writing in 1873, and echoing something of Montaigne's suggestion made in 1594 (above), described the imperatives facing manufacturers wanting to trade. Two factors were important:

> First. That as goods are produced to be exchanged, it is good that they should be exchanged as quickly as possible. Secondly. That as every producer is mainly occupied in producing what others want, and not what he wants him-self, it is desirable that he should always be able to find, without effort, without delay, and without uncertainty, others who want what he can produce.
>
> (Bagehot 1873)

**Figure 4.5** 'Experience and knowledge will light you to success', JWT ad (1902). Courtesy of the J. Walter Thompson archive at the Hartman Center, Duke University.

Advertising agencies were able to offer a baulk against such uncertainties. One advertising agency explicitly took up this conception of the role of the industry. Figure 4.5 (from 1902) asserts the power of advertising to relieve manufacturers' 'worry'.

In the twentieth century the larger advertising agents (such as JWT) began to position themselves as expert intermediaries easing the uncertainty of the manufacturer. Advertising was an ally to help national manufacturers establish powerful positions in relation to other market intermediaries, notably retailers and wholesalers.

## Modern advertising 1880–1920

Ohmann (1996) notes a clear change in advertising styles in US magazines around the last decades of the nineteenth century. He contrasts a page of ads from 1880:

> OLD: Display is minimal, visual representation almost absent. Lines of agate type speak in mainly sedate, declarative sentences or fragments about qualities of the product. Reading the ads, except for their abbreviations and ellipses and the strain on ones eyes is much like reading any other text in the magazine.

with an ad from 1900:

> NEW: Display is compelling: visual representation is photographically exact though surrealistic. Three different type sizes and two different faces render a slogan, an imperative, and a terse bundle of information about the product.
>
> (Ohmann 1996: 176)

Ohmann's characterisations capture significant snapshots of moments in a transition. There was of course no such clear 'before and after'; no watershed. But as Leiss *et al.* (2005) have convincingly shown, there are clear phases and changes in advertisements and these can be mapped on to wider contexts, in culture perhaps, but certainly in the organisation and management of commercial communications.

The move from plain to elaborated ads, not to mention the growth in size and numbers of advertising pages (Ohmann 1996: 176) in these decades, was partly to do with a change in what advertising agents were doing:

> The social and institutional setting in which advertising exists today has been present since the beginning of this [twentieth] century: mass-produced goods, a mass market reached through mass publications whose single most important source of revenue is advertising, and a professional advertising trade handling all major advertising accounts.
>
> (Vestergaard and Schroeder 1985: 4)

Both in the US and in the UK, modern advertising's organisational forms and practices began to take shape in a concerted way as the nineteenth century became the twentieth. As Laird (1993) points out with reference to the US, in '1890 no advertising agency could provide the assortment of services that were standard by 1910' (Laird 1993: 16). Presbrey (1929) notes the (for him recent) development of 'full service' and concerted international operations in advertising in the early decades of the twentieth century:

> There were, however, even then agencies which gave full service . . . agencies like that of T B Browne do an international business, with offices in continental, colonial and American centers and set copy in most languages of the earth.
>
> (Presbrey 1929: 107)

'Full service' meant providing both media buying and creative work. The development of an autonomous advertising industry and the specific form of a 'full service' agency, independent of both client and media provider, was a crucial step. For large manufacturers developing into national markets there were four main motivations underlying the establishment of a distinct and institutionally autonomous advertising system. As Laird (1993; 1998) explains (summary points 1–4), these were:

(1)   The shift from owner operation to corporate management in leading manufacturing and merchandising firms.

As large founding owners and their families brought in professional managers to run their businesses, for example following flotation on the stock exchanges, there was a tendency for professional managers (who now ran large corporations at an operational level) to employ the services of other professionals – the burgeoning ranks of advertising agents – effectively 'outsourcing' cultural and communications aspects of the consumer relationship. Hence:

(2)   The growing recognition of the importance of controlling marketing channels by promoting trademarks directly to consumers.

Goods were sold at a distance and in generic forms. For example shoppers would typically not buy a branded packet of biscuits but instead purchase biscuits by weight (in a brown paper bag). This posed problems for manufacturers who were unable to ensure that consumers knew, recognised, appreciated and distinguished one maker's (their) products from another's. The move to trade marking (the precursor of branding) was a spur to maintaining a link (via insignia on product or packaging) between producers and consumers in such a way that retailers could discriminate between competitor manufacturers' goods, and so that manufacturers could ensure (through advertising and quality provision) that their brand would be reordered wholesale as a recognised and recognisable named good which consumers could know, distinguish and purchase repeatedly.

Consumers could then further be engaged (by advertising price information) into consistent *manufacturer*-controlled marketing – pricing mechanisms (cuts and increases) – so preventing retailers from marking products up or down too much. Advertising required trade marking (later 'branding'). It rarely sells 'biscuits' or 'bread' or 'mustard', but 'McVitie's', 'Coleman's' or 'Hovis'. Advertising gradually became a key tool in the work of establishing trademarks and elaborating and defining the significances of brands and logos, supplemented by:

(3) The development of a national marketplace mediated by magazines and newspapers.

The expanding and diversifying media and a willingness to accept advertising were crucial to the emergence of the industry. The circulation of magazines increased (Pope 1983: 8–9) and the number of new titles went up consistently throughout the century – as has the proportion of press dedicated to advertising. Advertising revenue has been fundamental to the development of consumer and lifestyle magazines (and journalism). As Curran (1981; Curran and Gurevitch 2005) argues with reference to newspapers, however, historically, while advertising revenues have supported newspapers, they have tended to favour certain titles over others, meaning, for example, that papers taking a consistently left-wing view have not succeeded in competition to attract advertising against more market-friendly papers. An adjunct of this was as shown in point (4):

(4) The responses by advertising specialists to these changes, with new perspectives on the functions of advertisements and their own function as professionals.

Advertising professionals began to work to codify and disseminate their practice so that they were in a strong position to persuade manufacturers that it was the advertising interface, above and beyond other potential marketing methods, that could most efficiently ensure demand for products. New services (creativity and research) were added and enhanced and trade journals, for example *Printers Ink*, and books such as Walter Dill Scott's *The Psychology of Advertising* (1910) and Claude Hopkin's *Scientific Advertising* (1966) claimed that advertising had the status of a science.

The long association with patent medicines, 'miraculous' potions typically with no actual effects or with ill effects, continued to mark early advertising as a disreputable business (Laird 1998; Lears 1994; Turner 1952: 168–9), and media publishers and other advertisers sometimes worked together to expose blatantly fraudulent claims. Thus the *Ladies Home Journal* in the US exposed a number of appeals made to women readers, and in the UK the *Daily Mail* ran a notable campaign against dishonest advertising of a 'medicine' called Yadil (Turner 1952: 186), putting a large and successful manufacturer out of business.[17] An advertising executive successfully sued an electric comb maker whose ads had promised, as it turned out falsely, that the product would turn grey hair black in ten days 'or £500 guaranteed' (Turner 1952: 199–200).

This alliance of press and 'respectable' advertisers was not disinterested. By sidelining the blatant advertising *lie*, the media and advertising industries built credibility for 'legitimate' advertisements – purifying and thereby increasing the value of media space while pre-empting consumers' and politicians' most indisputable critiques. Today self-regulation (for example by the Advertising Standards Authority) is based on a similar, now formal, alliance: it balances the interests of advertisers and the media, and serves (a version of) 'the public interest', working at the same time to sustain a broad degree of consumer trust – operating continually to legitimate advertising communications. As Offer writes:

> Advertising seeks the attention of a jaded and wary consumer. In order to persuade, it needs to be credible. It needs to establish trust. Credibility, however, is not easy: few products or services are remarkably superior to the competition. So there is a temptation to stray from the literal truth, which makes the achievement of credibility more difficult. Now the more credible advertising becomes overall, the higher its standards of truthfulness, the more tempting it is for individual advertisers to mislead. In formal terms, the dominant strategy for an individual advertiser is to mislead. But if everyone follows this strategy, credibility is seriously undermined. Discourse becomes less truthful than anyone individually would want. Such situations give rise to a form of market failure known as 'the tragedy of the commons': every grazier believes that one additional cow on the common will hardly be noticed. When each of them releases just one more cow, the common is soon trampled into mud. The 'commons' in this case are credibility and trust. We end up with less than we would like. Hence advertising becomes less beneficial than it might be, for the public of course, but also for those who commission it.
>
> (Offer 1996: 213)

The early decades of the twentieth century saw advertising working out the rules of these 'commons'. Arguably the metaphor of 'the commons' is unfortunate, as Williams (1980) and other have striven to make clear: it is precisely because advertising marks 'public' space, which is not held 'in common' but is instead owned, bought and paid for by private interests, that more deep-seated criticisms have emerged. That said, part of the institutional project of modern advertising has been to develop the scope and to establish professional standards, to improve reputation, to codify practice and to respect consumers' views. These aims have been pursued as a means to enhance the profitability of the industry but also sometimes as ends in themselves. It is partly for these reasons, setting aside a steady supply of 'shocking' exceptions, that advertising today has been purged of basic fraudulence, at least at the level that semiotics calls 'denotative' – in the describable matters of fact. Box 4.1 shows some of the ways in which advertising has developed in the twentieth century.

The 'full service' agencies were routinely offering an additional service: copywriting. This was a way of enhancing the value of the media space brokered. Offered, as a free service, copywriting and other creative designing became an important incentive to advertisers. For agencies it was an attempt to ensure that space could be sold and the commission earned, existing clients retained and new clients attracted. Creative work, the most prominent aspect of advertising today, began as a sideline, a free gift in the major package – the media space.

The JWT house ad copy shown in Box 4.2 shows the text of an address to potential advertisers describing the value of their experience in creative advertising copy. At first advertising creativity consisted solely in writing copy.[18] Later it became more usual to use illustrations for advertising imagery. The development of creative services is apparent, apart from the evidence of numerous early century examples (Ohmann 1996; Leiss *et al.* 2005), from some later 'house' ads from J. Walter Thompson. The first (Box 4.2) describes the power of copy, the second (Figure 4.6) the power of images. Agencies' creative departments rapidly provided opportunities for illustrators, writers and later photographers to earn money in an area in some sense adjacent to artistic or literary production. No doubt many of these were the earliest incarnations of a 'creative class' (Florida 2002), what Featherstone (1991), drawing on Bourdieu (1984), has identified as the 'new cultural intermediaries':[19] those seeking to bypass traditional middle- and lower-middle-class identifications and so becoming adept in the expressive symbolism of novelty and the trans-formative ethos of consumerism, blending 'bohemian' ideals (Campbell 1987) with commercial ones. In the post-War era and certainly by the 1960s advertising was established as a glamorous and creative profession, with its roots in, and it co-extensive linkage to, sales and marketing substantially disavowed.

## Box 4.1 SOME INGREDIENTS SUPPORTING AND ACCOMPANYING THE EMERGENCE AND DEVELOPMENT OF ADVERTISING THROUGH THE TWENTIETH CENTURY

| Production and supply | Media | Consumption and demand |
|---|---|---|
| Industrial manufacture of large volumes of goods in large centralised factories | National and large circulation local media | Sufficient levels of accessible potential consumers |
| Extended networks for distribution including canals, railways, roads and international ports Shipping and air travel National and global logistics networks | Government has to provide a framework of regulation allowing media and advertising to develop | An emergent propensity to consume The spread of culturally-based sense of the value, legitimacy and necessity of varied types of consumption Acceptance of planned debt |
| Retail outlets for customers Department stores growing; supermarkets; malls | Media growing, extending the networks of connection between supply and demand | Relative affluence and increased disposable income Flexible credit systems operating across product sectors |
| Flow of investment seeking opportunities to make profits, including international investment | As new technologies develop, for instance TV and commercial radio, advertising extends its reach and develops its forms e.g. colour photography, digital channels | Social and personal mobility Consumption linked to status Leisure, travel, novelty and trying new things as a burgeoning ethos Reactions against periods of austerity |
| Reduction in will and means for self-sufficient local and domestic modes of production | Diversification and specification of media outlets: not 10 magazines, but 110, then 1000; not three TV channels but 300 Reliable data on audience size and, later, demographic types | Consumption as part of projects of identity and belonging; in the face of recessive and/or oppressive traditional structures of support and identification New markets, new sectors: teens, independent women etc. |

Creativity reinforced the professional image of advertising, as well as adding some glamour to what was essentially a brokering profession. Trying to ensure effectiveness was the logical and practical end in this development. However, as Leiss *et al.* (2005), Lears (1994), Marchand (1985) and Ewen (1976) show, the more elaborate creative and persuasive elements of advertising were quickly mobilised by advocates for the advertising industry, not just in praise of commercial effectiveness, but in arguments that advertising was a contribution to a civilising process – effectively, as they saw it, 'educating' consumers in the arts

**Figure 4.6** Copy and image: Woodbury soap.

and manners of consumerism – a new ethic for changing times. At the same time the persuasive and artful nature of creative advertising re-alerted commercialism's critics[20] to the genre's now more assertively *cultural* influence. They added these deep-seated concerns (about cultural decay) to some of the economics-based arguments set out against the growing industry in the UK and commentators such as Sidney Webb (1914), who complained about advertising in terms of the competitive power it gave large firms over small ones. In the coming years the arguably pragmatic motivations for developing advertising's creativity were quickly tied to wider debates about changing cultures and changing economic conditions.

The emerging model of the full service advertising agency came to include yet another important element: research. Research supporting the advertising industry can be divided into three broad types:

- research and audit of media circulation and use;
- researching consumers;
- research in advertising effects and copy testing.

## Research

Audience and circulation research had two purposes. The first was purely financial. Once advertising rates were established for circulation figures it became important to have certified agreement about what the circulation was. With, initially, relatively simple equations between circulation volume and the cost of space in any particular publication, it was necessary that claimed circulation tallied with real circulation.

This research was financial in its terms of reference, a check that advertisers, and the agencies who served them, were getting what they paid for in terms of newspapers' circulations (that is, the size of audience it reached). This accounting-based research is evident in the name of the body set up to ratify the figures. The Audit Bureau of Circulations (ABC) was set up in 1931 in the UK and its equivalent in the US (also ABC) had been running since 1914. A joint venture between media and advertising institutions, it sought to establish (by audit) credibility in the rates and circulations of newspapers and magazines. Copy testing began in the 1930s (Turner 1952: 232) with some rudimentary methods of assessing the readability of ads. Early and more elaborate research methods in advertising were cut short in the late 1930s by World War II.

The JWT house ad shown in Figure 4.6 delineates the roles that research plays. It positions the agency as a link to understanding consumer preferences. It is the user who knows, and the agency can use this

NATION'S BUSINESS for May, 1931 103

MAKER ☆ ☆ ☆ ☆ USER

*which one knew?*

Three directors of a large manufacturing company were in a friendly but exceedingly vigorous disagreement.

What did women consider the most important value in the article that this corporation manufactured? What characteristic of the product appealed *most* to women, users of the product?

One director championed the decorative value of the product. Another director defended a convenience value. The third director smilingly but aggressively backed still another convenience value.

• • •

The J. Walter Thompson Company was placed in charge of advertising for this corporation. In order to seize upon the most effective theme for an advertising campaign it was necessary to know which of the directors was right.

There was just one way to find out, of course. The J. Walter Thompson Company proceeded to ask the women themselves.

A majority of the 2,000 women who were interviewed said that all of the values named by the directors were important. But even more important was one which none of the directors had named . . . a certain performance value.

That became the foundation of a successful advertising campaign.

• • •

In an increasing number of instances it is now possible to determine just what it is that women *do* think about a given product in the market. Not always what they say, but what they *really think*.

The J. Walter Thompson Company pioneered in the effort to learn the real interests of the actual buyers of eighty-five per cent of all advertised products . . . *women* . . . and to address advertising directly to them.

Today the selfsame principle of seeking out the very heart of a problem, in no matter what field, makes this company an acknowledged leader in those products which are most dependent on advertising . . . products in the highly competitive fields . . . in the United States and throughout the world.

•

New York • Chicago • St. Louis • Boston • Cincinnati • San Francisco • Los Angeles • • Montreal • Toronto • • London • Paris • Madrid • Berlin • Stockholm • Copenhagen • Antwerp • • Alexandria • Port Elizabeth • • Buenos Aires • Sao Paulo • • Bombay • • Melbourne • Sydney • • Batavia • • Wellington • • Osaka

J. WALT[illegible]ANY

Nation's Business - May, 1931

Figure 4.7 'Maker . . . user': which one knew?

### Box 4.3 EMERGENT MODES OF ADVERTISING INTERMEDIATION

| Supply or production | | Demand or consumption |
|---|---|---|
| The advertiser | **Space trading**<br>Linking supply and demand by disseminating advertising messages through the growing media | The consumer or audience segments |
| | **Copywriting and creativity**<br>Enhancing the value and cost of space by offering attractive and effective creative executions as part of the advertising service; building agency and industry reputations for craft; employing culturally 'tuned in' artists and writers. More broadly, 'education', informing, or inculcating a 'consumerist ethic'. Note: the degree to which advertising can be held to perform this function is disputed. | Lifestyle segments |
| | **Research**<br>Adding value, credibility and reliability to the advertising process by:<br>1 securing data about the quantity and distribution of readerships (media research); enhancing trust in circulation figures and thereby trust in the advertising process; Audit Bureau of Circulation<br>2 offering an understanding of the detailed needs and desires of potential audiences as part of the advertising package (consumer research)<br>3 trying to establish the effectiveness of the advertisement pre- and post-publication/broadcast, again establishing trust in the advertising process. | |
| | **Planning: communication and integration of formally discrete functions**<br>Managing daily processes bringing together advertising intermediation functions. Strategic planning campaign and brand development. | |

knowledge to convince the maker that it has the secret of successful selling. In summary, then, Box 4.3 identifies the emergent modes of advertising intermediation.

## Later modern advertising 1950–90

If we pick up an ad from before World War II it is quickly apparent that we are holding a historical document. Indeed old advertisements, for instance Guinness campaigns and London Underground posters, are celebrated and reframed as artistic popular culture (Timmers 1998; Davies 1998). The general account of advertising in the present given by this book contrasts with previous epochs of advertising. We can see in later modern advertising the development of some crucial distinguishing features in the sphere of research, media, and in the integration of advertising as genre and institution into cultural, social and economic life.

Integrating the functions of account management and planning quickly became an expertise of its own in later modern advertising. While advertising demanded the work of specialist skilled personnel to perform the discrete tasks of creativity, research and media buying, there was equally a need for staff to take an overview of the advertising campaign across all its dimensions, and, crucially, to liaise with the client. In order to ensure that client relations (and account payments) were properly managed, the account manager role extended beyond its purely financial administration to include general co-ordination and client liaison. These developments were central to the industry's attempts to better establish credibility and professional status for its work. As Nixon points out, in relation to London agencies in the 1950s and 1960s (Nixon 2000) professionalism was a powerful script guiding agencies and industry bodies towards ensuring that advertising was a 'responsible' industry – in a period when fears about propaganda and manipulation were rife. This reframing of ad agency organisation was both client-facing and consumer-facing. It served clients because it allowed agencies to present a more professional face in financial and daily client liaison work. The planner role enabled agencies to better co-ordinate its research-based and other links to the consumer (through research in particular). This was important in the post war period, and as the 1960s, a decade of unprecedented change in consumer affluence, moralities and expectations, unfolded. Advertising began to take on an important role, promising producers means to 'control' unpredictable demand, as well as developing creative work that could engage new consumer sensibilities – with new 'markets', teenagers, affluent singles and, gradually, greater numbers of professional women emerging. Primarily then, in the 1960s the role of the planner emerged

## Box 4.4 CHARACTERISTICS OF CLASSIC AND INTEGRATED COMMUNICATIONS

| Classic communications | Integrated communications |
| --- | --- |
| Aimed at acquisition (of customers) | Aimed at retention and relationship management |
| Mass communications | Selective communications |
| Monologue | Dialogue |
| Effect through repetition | Effect through relevance |
| Hard sell | Soft sell |
| Transaction oriented | Relationship oriented |
| Modern, linear massive | Post-modern cyclical, fragmented |
| | (Adapted from Van Raaij 1998) |

as a link to the consumer through research, but also as a link to the client and between clients, research and the creative team. Leiss *et al.* (2005) make clear the listening function of the planner role; similarly, Lury (2004) has established the fundamental function of feedback in branding. Planners serve as the major carriers of advertising's intermediary functions.

Indeed, these developments can be discerned in advertising's texts. Some important insights into advertising and social history have been developed through examination of changes evident within the (aggregated) texts of advertising (Leiss *et al.* 2005; Richards *et al.* 2000) and there is clear and ample evidence for changes in advertising, in terms of content, form and function, which can be collated from looking at advertisements sampled at different periods in modern history.

It is important not to understate the impacts of new media technologies on advertising practice – extending advertising into radio, then, in the 1950s, television. In 1954 CBS, an American TV corporation, became the largest advertising medium in the world. The 1960s is notable for its 'creative revolutions' in popular music and across culture. Advertising was not insulated from such transformations, with New York agency Doyle Dane Bernbach credited with turning the advertising genre upside-down with its now classic modern ads for Volkswagen, Chivas Regal (whisky) and Canada Dry (soft drinks) providing new and potent templates for more minimalist and witty ads emerging from 'creative teams'. This creative double-act system – a copy writer and an art director working in sometimes long-lasting partnerships compared to marriages (Nixon 2003) – has become normal practice in the decades since the 1960s. Delaney (2007) identifies the contribution such creative teams made to popular ad-culture in the 1970s, charting also the increasing traffic between advertising agencies, creative industries (notably film), city-finance and political life.

A defining feature of advertising in this period is the extension and expansion of advertising globally. This was largely undertaken by the extension of large agencies' networks opening offices in large and capital cities worldwide (Tungate 2007) to match up with client and media networks, and to service and bid successfully for the new multi-national clients – in line with the concurrent global expansion of national corporations – initially supporting and supported by political expansion and colonial trade in preceding centuries from US and UK, Europe and Japan. The emergence of large advertising and media conglomerates, such as WPP Group and Publicis, Omnicom, Havas and Dentsu, expanding through series of mergers, acquisitions, take-overs and buy-outs between the 1970s and the present has consolidated the global nature of advertising, while also affirming its convergence with other media and communications industries.

By the end of the 1990s advertising, a genre that was 'despised' in the eighteenth century, somewhat marginal and frowned upon in the nineteenth century, and treated with growing suspicion (as it grew with unprecedented rapidity) in the twentieth century, was accepted as a component part of the cultural and social establishment as the twenty-first century approached – and as a major component of the economic fabric of market-consumerist societies globally.

This chequered history has, naturally, left a legacy of critique and analysis. Just as it is important to locate 'advertising' historically (it is after all, in many respects, a quite different activity today than it was in the 1700s), so, too, it is useful to bear in mind that the reception of 'advertising' – including the academic, critical understanding that has always surrounded advertising practices – is a significant component of the genre, contributing to the overall character of advertising in its various contexts and in term of it functions, impacts and likely future evolutions.

# 5

# ADVERTISING AND CULTURE

*To His Coy Mistress*

Had we but World enough, and Time,
This coyness Lady were no crime.
We would sit down, and think which way
To walk, and pass our long Loves [sic] Day . . .

An hundred years would go to praise
Thine Eyes, and on they [sic] forehead Gaze.
Two hundred to adore each breast:
But thirty thousand to the rest.

An Age at least to every part,
And the last Age should show your Heart.
For Lady you deserve this State;
Nor would I love at lower rate.

(Andrew Marvell 1681, cited in and
abridged by Citroën 1993)

An old-fashioned poem? Yes; at least part of one. But it is also something else. These lines have been taken from an advertisement for a range of Citroën cars (see Figure 5.1). The words themselves are from the love poem 'To His Coy Mistress', first published in 1681 and written, as the advertisement tells us, by Andrew Marvell. The ad copy that follows invites the reader to link sentiments expressed in that poem with their latest product range – as Citroën suggests:

Writing in the 1600s, the metaphysical poet Andrew Marvell captured for all time the inspiration of beauty. Consider now, the stunning new Citroën range of cars . . .

(Advertisement text)

The creative team in the advertising agency have found a way to convey the idea that the Citroën range is beautiful; that, in some sense, a person could fall in love with these cars. Just as the section of the poem suggests how the lover will spend time carefully cherishing every part of the woman he desires: eyes, breasts, forehead, and 'the rest', the advertisement's images offers up the car's body for closer consideration; headlights, windscreen and a curvaceous boot. The analogy is clear and the proposition simple: the Citroën range of cars deserves all the adoration given by a loving poet to his beautiful mistress – the relationship to a thing (a car) is reconceived as a relationship between people, and the metaphor car-as-woman is given another airing (see, for example, Dichter 1960; MacRury 1997; McLuhan 1951).

Adapting a love poem (one of the most celebrated love poems in the English language) is a clever way of condensing and communicating a number of ideas. In particular this approach, and its elaborate reference to a literary heritage, intends to position the Citroën product range, the brand and its consumers, potential and actual, as elegant, artistic, as prestigious or as 'cultured'. This last word is important. It brings to mind the aim of much advertising, which, as symbolic mediation, attempts to get audiences to engage more fully with the quasi-inert objects produced by factories and technology and then to connect us with them in elaborated cultural terms, to help tie products into shared meanings and 'living' value systems. As we have seen, advertising aims to animate, to make things meaningful and valuable, to encourage potential consumers to find commodities interesting, variously to enrich the abstracted; connecting everyday or exotic experiences with social values, relationships and affective life.

Many readers seeing this advertisement might point out that far from allowing them to engage with the Citroën cars, the love poem is an irrelevant and off-putting distraction. Ad agencies try to persuade clients (Hennion and Meadel 1989, and see Chapter 2 this volume) that it is worth taking the risk of provoking such responses. A research-based calculation or belief in creatives' intuition convinces the client that a particular creative strategy (such as this one), while alienating or absurd in the minds of some, is creatively 'right' for the target audience, as conceived at the time, and for the projection or elaboration of the brand (Lury and Warde

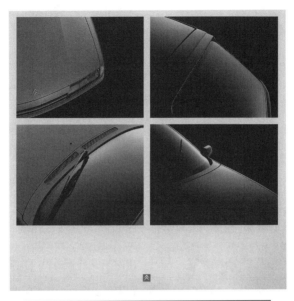

**Figure 5.1** Plates from insert-advertisement for Citroën cars: with thanks to Citroën Corporation.

1997; Cronin 2000: 43–4). McCracken provides a helpful account of a process of cultural meaning 'transfer':

> Advertising works as a potential method of meaning transfer by bringing the consumer good and a representation of the culturally constituted world together within the frame of a particular advertisement. The creative director of an agency seeks to conjoin these two elements in such a way that the viewer/reader glimpses an essential similarity between them.
>
> (McCracken 1990: 77)

It would be a straightforward task to locate this advertisement in an account of target audiences' tastes, and an agency's creativity deployed to enliven a commodity, marketing communications in pursuit of a specific 'positioning' strategy (Trout 1969; Ries and Trout 1981; Lury 2004: 88). But this ad (and advertising as a cultural genre), and the account of metaphoric transformation of the product that such advertising representations attempt, raises questions about the advertising genre beyond the perspectives of a pure business-based marketing outlook. It invites different analytic and critical vocabularies: the vocabularies of cultural and 'literary' analysis.

As part of an influential and longstanding way of considering advertising as cultural communication critics have drawn on some of the perspectives provided by literary criticism (see e.g. Stern 1989). One particular and significant examination of advertising emerged from a group associated with the journal *Scrutiny*.[1] The underlying critical ethos of the mid-twentieth-century journal was 'humanist': an assertion and definition of 'human' culture and experience against the encroachments of techno-logical, commercial and utilitarian modernity.[2]

From *Scrutiny*'s primarily literary perspective on culture two major 'offences' leap out immediately on looking closely at the text of the Citroën advertisement (Figure 5.1 and see the text quoted at the start of this chapter). First there is misspelling in the poem citation; second, the poem has undergone an extensive and significant edit. When 'Literature' is deemed a precious resource for preserving and passing on a valued culture – as for *Scrutiny* critics it was – it is usual to find a heightened sensitivity to linguistic accuracy. One could expect to hear disdain in the voice of a literary critic confronted with an advertisement like this, which, misspelled 'thy' (stanza two, line two) and did not correctly punctuate the possessive ('loves' printed, where it is 'love's' in the original). These slips would perhaps support the accusation, expressed for instance by Thompson, that 'admen' are 'uniformly illiterate'

(Thompson 1932: 242) and 'slovenly' (Gifford 1934: 168).[3] The critics' concern with language goes deeper, however. A more substantial argument (against advertising) proposes that fancy *words* should have no place in the presentation of functional *things*. E.B. White summarises an important position in advertising criticism: 'The kind of work on goods that profits the consumer is not done with words, but with tools and instruments, and by the aid of calculation' (E. B. White, cited in Thompson 1943: 43) Advertising is identified as a genre that systematically misuses language and which confuses the connection between words (and indeed other kinds of symbolic expression) and material objects and ideas that, in advertising, they are used to represent (see e.g. Leavis and Thompson 1964; Thompson 1943; Orwell 1954; Adorno and Horkheimer 1979 amongst many examples of criticism of advertisers' language).[4]

A literary critical approach to this particular advertisement (Figure 5.1) might be preoccupied initially with exposing something that is not (immediately) obvious from the way the poem has been presented – that most of the original text of the poem is missing. This absence is emblematic of a broader lack – a more general absence often identified (more or less explicitly) in discussion of the characteristic representational strategies of advertisements. 'What has been excluded? And why?' are sometimes helpful questions to ask of advertising, of individual ads and of the genre more widely.

In this example the missing elements open up some broader considerations about advertising as a cultural genre and point towards some of the general anxieties at the heart of Leavisite and other modes of advertising criticism. To explore this absence, some further lines from the end of the original and complete poem, on which an important sense of Marvell's 'To His Coy Mistress' depends, are useful:

But at my back I always hear
Time's winged chariot hurrying near;
And yonder all before us lie
Deserts of vast eternity.
Thy beauty shall no more be found,
Nor, in thy marble vault, shall sound
My echoing song; then worms shall try
That long preserved virginity,
And your quaint honour turn to dust,
And into ashes all my lust:
The grave's a fine and private place,
But none, I think, do there embrace.

Far from being a courtly poem about the 'timeless' nature of beauty, as the copywriter's gloss suggests, 'To His Coy Mistress' is an argument designed to persuade the mistress to give up her 'coyness' and to sleep with the poet. The argument counters the flirtatious promises of endless (and platonic) praise, reminding instead of the inevitability of time passing, of bodily decay and death. 'To His Coy Mistress' (Marvell's original) performed a vigorous critique of the empty idealism traditional to some love poetry. By no means a poem about 'the inspiration of timeless beauty' (as Citroën has it), Marvell's poem argues that, given (and properly accepting) the shortness of life, and the finality of death, the woman ought to stop playing hard to get and express life and bodily desire in the process.

The advertisement's editing betrays the distinction between the world conceived typically in the advertising genre and a less complacent philosophy. Citroën's 1993 'editing-job' on the poem exemplifies the deceitful sleight of hand that *Scrutiny*-inspired criticism sought to expose in advertising. The principles of selection shaping advertisements favour a partial and limited sensibility; here is a case in point. The advertisement wants to pretend that it has evoked the spirit of 'love', but the difficulty is that the version of 'love' offered up – the 'philosophy' of the advertisement – is saccharine and thoughtless. The poem proper, Marvell's original, argues that 'love' is meaningful in a *human* context, where bodily desire and time – and their corollaries, death, loss and suffering – are acknowledged. Otherwise love is an empty, fanciful and 'inhuman' concept, unconnected with any proper apprehension of human experience – not 'love' as a (true) person would know it. Such a critique returns the argument to advertising's role as a genre mediating in the cultural and commercial relations between people and things.

As Cronin argues (from another but illuminating perspective), drawing on Foucault:

> Death discursively stabilizes or substantialises the category of 'the person' as an individuated subject and as distinct from the category 'thing'. One way this is secured is by drawing a distinction between the finite social life of a human and the potentially infinite social life of a thing.
>
> (Cronin 2004a: 90)

The advertisement, in wilfully ignoring the elements of Marvell's poem (and its understanding of human relations), which fully acknowledges and examines death, loss, love and the passing of time (in all their connections), invites instead a relationship to the commodity (the car) in which persons (as it were) cross over from the 'human' world into the 'commodity' world – 'timeless' and 'ever-young'.

Identifying such textual dynamics (of abstraction as well as censorship) is at the heart of the many advertising critiques that cite advertising as a genre typically wedded to an overriding misconception, one which misrepresents the world (commodity by commodity) as full and endless, as ever-replaceable and so ever-present and thus in a sense 'eternal' – meaning in fact *ahistorical*.

The consumer diminishes his or her humanity in so far as, overrun and bypassed, through seduction or desire, he or she becomes complicit with the commodity world – and (over)invests his or her sense of subjectivity in the advertising image. Such complicity sacrifices subjective connection with history, tradition, biography, narrative, experiential complexity and acknowledgement of relatedness, and all in favour of a momentarily gratifying but superficial fantasy life – bottled or packaged and for sale. Leavis and other literary and cultural critics were committed to the view that the thinking and feeling encouraged by poetry (such as Marvell's) is *better* than the thinking supported by the advertisement's promises about consuming this car.

Advertising attempts to mediate and thereby re-order people's relationships with things (Leiss *et al.* 2005; Cronin 2004a). 'Love', for Citroën, and contrary to Marvell's more complex grasp, is seen as a relationship of possession, almost proprietary (and, of course, here, gendered). Such a conception of 'love' is to do with the re-orientation of the poem, the attempt to equate human love with 'love', consummated in the act of purchase and ownership, for a thing: a car. The main problem, which a moral or humanist critic might highlight, is a misdirection of human feeling brought about by the advertisements' errant mediation of the relationship between people and things.

The relationship between people and things so mediated is culturally insufficient. Such arguments have been basic to Leavis's and many others' critical analyses of advertising. A pervading anxiety has been that advertising is an inferior genre diminishing public apprehension of, and engagement with people, things and cultural wisdom.

Leavisite and other kinds of critical writing on advertising seek to affirm 'real human life' as a crucial counterfoil against the fake animation of commodified things and advertising representations. Mortality and loss and their acknowledgement serve critics as the counterpoint to advertising's glimpsed promises of a world of (mere) things and its (illusory) promises of infinite plenitude. Thus, as Leavis and others argued, the re-ordering of human relations under the templates of market relations – the advertising genre being a major instrument of that process – provides deep cause for concern because such a transition amounts to a disordering of the category 'humanity' in favour of the commodity system and a too-mechanical ordering of production and provision over what Leavis and others celebrated as irreducibly human 'life'. As Thompson's elegiac criticisms affirm and reaffirm: 'humanity is uprooted and atrophied in an unprecedented way and on an unprecedented scale' (Thompson 1932: 9).

Leavis was, however, wrong in insisting so dogmatically that the scope and space of such pleasure lay so narrowly within the ambit of a minority that shared his own outlook and that of his (middle)-class, (white English) race and (male) gender, and his contribution to the criticism of advertising has been bypassed as a consequence of this limited understanding of culture and society. In addition, and from a perspective alert to the impacts of digital and other new technologies for production and provision of goods, anxiety about a 'mechanical' undermining of human life draws a perhaps too absolute distinction between an essentially 'human' culture and non-human spheres of 'industrial' or, rather, *post*-industrial productivities. Leavis's approach, while compelling in its passionate disappointment at the world, falls down because, as Williams writes, 'Literary criticism was offered as . . . the central activity in all human judgement' (Williams 1983: 184–5). It is not.

## ADVERTISING, LANGUAGE AND CULTURE

Schudson usefully illustrates the link between everyday speech forms and advertising (critiqued as a particular type of speech) in a way that indicates some of the underlying grounds for critical approaches to advertising communications in their broader social contexts:

> Think of a smaller social system, a two-person social system, a marriage. Imagine it to be a good marriage, where love is expressed daily in a vast array of shared experiences, shared dreams, shared tasks and moments. In this ideal marriage, the couple continually make and remake their love. Then why, in this marriage, would anything be amiss if the two people did not say to each other, 'I love you'? Why, in a relationship of such obviously enacted love, should it seem necessary to add out loud, 'I love you'?
>
> Because, I think, making the present audible and making the implicit explicit is necessary to engage and renew a whole train of commitments, responsibilities and possibilities. 'I love you' does not create what is not present. Nor does it seal what is present. But it must be spoken and re-spoken. It is necessary speech because people need to see in pictures or hear in words what they already know as deeply as they know anything. Words are actions.
>
> This is also true in large social systems. Advertising is capitalism's way of saying I love you to itself.
>
> (Schudson 1993: 231–2)

This extended analogy is useful in helping to think about the idea that language, and other communicative media, used repetitively and as a constitutive element in maintaining, performing and experiencing social and personal life, is a 'cultural asset' worthy of protection from misuse – creating, contesting and affirming ways of thinking and living.

There is an extended tradition of critical writing which highlights (usually to condemn it) a 'contagion' of art and language by commerce and advertising. Anxiety about such uses of culture is not confined to Leavis, or his era. John Berger catalogued the similarities and differences between classical realist art and advertising composition (Berger 1973). Williamson (1986) highlighted the common propensity of advertisements to allude to modern art (especially surrealism). Moody (2000) points to Typhoo's tea advertising based on Shakespeare in part of her analysis of the UK advertising industry's complicity in processes of 'the invention of tradition' in the 1980s and 1990s, further pointing out that advertising not only misrepresents goods when (by association) it appropriates cultures, it misconstrues cultures, by associating them with goods.

What underpins the distinction between art and commerce and purity and impurity? A detailed argument comes from philosopher Roger Scruton, who continues to represent much in the Leavisite tradition of criticism in contemporary debates. It is 'important', suggests Scruton, 'to make a crucial distinction, without which the history of modern culture cannot be properly understood: that between the aesthetic object and the advert' (Scruton 2000: 83–4). Scruton argues that however much advertising resembles art, on closer (and proper) inspection the advertisement is art in reverse:

> The advert is similar to the aesthetic object, but crucially different in this: that it must neutralize the critical faculty, and arrest the process whereby the actual is compared with its ideal and the ideal with the actual. The work of art endows its subject with intrinsic value, and therefore upholds the distinction between things with a value and things with a price. The advert erodes that distinction; it creates a fantasy world in which value can be purchased, so that price and value are one and the same.
>
> (Scruton 2000: 84)

Scruton outlines a fundamental tenet for the cultural critique of advertising – an account of the genre in which he attempts to secure a fine but absolute distinction between two modes of communication: art and advertising. The former is sacred, the latter profane. Art (and authentic culture) supports the operation and development of discrimination, judgement and a proper apprehension of experience – what is best in humanity.

Advertising (on the contrary) supports and indeed feeds our capacity to evade thought, thereby diminishing capacities for a more profound connection with experience (of self and others). If we accept Scruton's position and such humanistic critique more generally, we must repeat the Leavisite conclusion that, trivial as they may appear, advertisements degrade humanity.

Some critical analysis defends specific cultures and their genres of mediation because (in symbolic expression and instituted forms) 'cultures' can (seemingly) capture and epitomise an essence – what is basic to an identity, to a way of being and to a community – at least for a passage of time. 'Cultures' are identified as (and identified with) acquired resources for symbolic articulation of the self, providing channels for desire, enlivening objects and objectives, and binding individuals to others in common practices and 'structures of feeling' (Williams 1987). Cultures provide a way of seeing and a way of being seen – the various youth cultures, numerous 'black' cultures, national popular cultures, 'working-class' cultures, Asian cultures, or a distinctly feminine culture. 'Culture' in this sense governs (multiple) conceptions of the world, in which, in all forms of social action (including consumption) 'being' is pursued and (partly) achieved as opposed merely to 'having' or to 'doing' (Fromm 1976). In this way cultures provide the principle support for identity and identification: a route (or 'root' (Fornas 1995)) linking experience to a feeling (or narrative) of authenticity, meaning and purpose; more or less shared, more or less tacit, perhaps escaping reductive summaries, perhaps intelligible only in performance.

Given such understanding of cultures (and the analyses of cultural appropriations above) three things should be clear:

- advertising continues to be cited frequently as an antithesis of 'culture', its mediations a disruption of the processes of cultural being identification and authentic human experience;
- advertising nevertheless strives very hard, in its work of mediations, to perform 'cultural' roles, in linking and defining the desirable relations between subjects and objects/people and things;
- in a 'consumer society' in which commercial relations comprise a significant portion of social relations, any clear distinctions between culture and commerce become increasingly elusive.

The assertion of a clear line between commercial and cultural symbolic realms has increasingly been understood as a problematic project. It is a problem in terms of thinking about 'high' aesthetic cultures, but also in the contexts of understanding the complexity and provisional nature of the modern and post-modern communications – where the staged contravention of boundaries and distinctions of many kinds have become routinely integral to symbolic cultures across many genres – with the advertising industry often disseminating popular examples of such mix-and-match aesthetics.

## REPRESENTING A CULTURAL WORLD: ADVERTISING WELL-BEING

Advertising is a discourse that seeks, more often than not, to present the world as whole, when it is more commonly experienced as fragmentary. The following is a further example of the appropriation of a cultural text and a coextensive occlusion of complexity in experience – a complexity where an apprehension of 'loss' might (otherwise) be encountered (in experience of the original text and music). But instead feelings of loss are evaded in the advertisement's selective appropriation.

*Text:* Müller Vitality: 'Ain't got no/I got life'

I got my hair, I got my head
I got my brains, I got my ears
I got my eyes, I got my nose
I got my mouth, I got my smile
I got my tongue, I got my chin
I got my neck, I got my boobs

I got my heart, I got my soul
I got my back, I got my sex
I got my arms, I got my hands
I got my fingers, I got my legs
I got my feet, I got my toes
I got my liver, I got my blood

I've got life, I've got my freedom
I've got the life.

These lyrics and the accompanying tune, first sung by Nina Simone in 1968, have recently been made famous in an advertising campaign for Müller yoghurt products. The ads in the series depict multicultural montages[5] of active dancing people enjoying life; vitality; 'Müller vitality'. The montage cuts are bound musically to each other, giving the brand a vibrant presence on our screens and in our ears. The celebratory music and Simone's voice affirm the connection between 'life', 'Müller', 'vitality' and a feeling of activity and celebration, made available (and this is the marketing intention) through the consumption of Müller's products. It is a celebration of ownership, but not the acquisitive ownership condemned by popular anti-consumerist sentiment. The ad, like a long running campaign for MasterCard, celebrates the fact that 'the best things in life are free'.

The ad's tone, musicality and feel are eminently suited to energising the idea of 'vitality', Müller's brand 'ethos'. We might even predict that this sensibility evokes the kind of 'intimacy' and affective appeal described under the idea of 'lovemarks' following Roberts (2004). But the song (in itself and in its appropriation by the advertiser), as well as being a potent and well-crafted celebration of 'life', is a cultural text with a history; one whose resonance opens up a wider perspective than the advert qua advert can reach into. The Müller advert, and its often repeated melody, casts not so much a penumbra but an echo. For it is through its music (lyrics and 'the grain' of Nina Simone's 'voice' (Barthes 1997: 179–89)) that a 'reading' can be traced against the ostensible and uncomplicated health and well-being message of the ad. Simone's song is clearly celebratory of *something*: but clearly also, as we recall its original context, it is not yoghurt.

One opportunity advertising criticism offers is to examine the associative residues of texts to help think about the wider contexts of advertising mediations. Blake (1997) offers an acute reading of British advertising in the 1990s proposing that while the ordinary social participation of black and minority ethnic people was, at that time, only beginning to be registered and reflected in marketing *imagery* (Blake 1997: 224–5) the trend for advertising to draw heavily on *audible* cultural texts, i.e. music, and especially popular music and jazz, meant that the relative invisibility of black faces (in UK advertising) was (paradoxically) contradicted in the enthusiastic readiness on the part of advertisers to use black music, black voices and black performance to express brand presence. So while the multicultural and post-colonial cultural history of Britain was not readily evident in the visual registers of UK advertising, that history was present if *listened* for (Blake 1997). A decade on Müller's life enhancing 'lid-licking' celebration of universal well-being occludes a significant history.

It is useful, again, to ask questions: what is missing, what editorial decisions have been made following the formal and cultural rubrics of the advertising genre to form the Müller text thus? The lyrics cited below, cut out from the original song, for advertising-based reasons of timing, message content and genre format, reframe the lyrics that the 'complete' twenty-first-century advertisement text preserves and circulates. The missing words set out an inventory of absence; a litany, performed with a hint of mourning more fully realised in other black soul and blues performances. In its original the song is an instance of what Paul Gilroy has described as 'slave sublime' (Gilroy 1993, cited in Blake 1997: 229).

> Ain't got no home, ain't got no shoes
> Ain't got no money, ain't got no class
> Ain't got no skirts ain't got no sweater
> Ain't got no perfume ain't got no bed
> Ain't got no mind
>
> Ain't got no mother, ain't got no culture
> Ain't got no friends, ain't got no schooling
> Ain't got no love, ain't got no name
> Ain't got no ticket, ain't got no token
> Ain't got no love.

The advert (in common with many advertisements) works by using intertextual[6] reference. It trades on a cultural valorisation of anti-consumerist and anti-market sentiments. It can be summed up as, in song, the celebratory assertion of freedom and the body in the *absence* of possessions, and *despite* possessions; the body as inalienably different from material 'possessions'. Reclamation of the self from the relations of the market is a curious but familiar advertising 'message': for what advertising often does (paradoxically) is to propose a world to us celebrating ideals about non-mercantile relations to objects: the healthy body as a 'gift' and not a commodity – the advertisement's song indexing a celebration of gratitude rather than shopping. As Offer (1996) suggests: 'What advertising attempts to do, is to simulate the gift relationship in the market economy' (Offer 1996: 225).

In this case the song lyrics mark a double (and triumphant) refusal – a refusal not just of a consuming materialism that finds itself in 'shoes', 'perfume' and 'beer' but also a refusal to anymore be bound to a 'market system' that institutionally deprived subjects of aspects of 'selfhood': a name, a home, a mother, class, culture and education. Which is to say the song (in its original conception) presents a refusal of slavery, an institution whose history remains a contributory component to inequality, racism and loss. Various aspects of black cultural legacy are selectively mobilised and recycled as part of contemporary cultures – precisely because of the potency and alterity conveyed within cultural expressions felt to deliver impact up and against relatively more mainstream cultural representations. Advertising is foremost amongst the mainstream popular genres trading on such impact potential – seeking de-commodifying and authenticating sounds and imagery to position products.

This is not to say that this particular advertisement campaign (and its act of intertextual appropriation) is in any straightforward sense especially 'bad' – and requiring some ritual or rhetorical act of condemnation. Cultural texts cannot readily be placed 'off limits' to commercial communications – and in some ways they thrive on recirculation and recontextualisation. However, the inevitable selectivity of advertising as it packages up imagery, but also sounds and ideas, within its necessary and inevitable generic forms tends (as in the Marvell/Citroën example above) to accentuate a conception of the world where ideals – 'life', fullness, goodness, or 'presence', 'self possession' and 'freedom' – appear to exist as a matter of course and not, as is normally the case, and as more complex representations acknowledge, as contingencies predicated upon more painful and difficult contextual biographical and historical narratives – e.g. of loss, of labour, of conflict and of pain.

Advertising is a genre which has typically understated or ignored an important strain in cultural production, and so also misapprehended an important sense of the relations between subjectivity and objects, a sense which works – through cultural texts and aesthetic representations – to render, process and *think and apprehend* such states and histories of 'loss' absence and abandon: states which assert and acknowledge non-identity, labour, fragmentation and otherness as amongst the necessary supplements to ideals circulating within a promotional culture predicated upon a social life where the daily pursuit of commodity-based well-being, thorough the marketplace and via competitive consumption, promises – but does not reliably deliver – adequate resources for various and developmental identifications.

## REPRESENTING PEOPLE AND CULTURE

Alongside such critiques of advertising as a limiting mode of cultural communication, there is a separate set of anxieties about advertisements' idealisations, occlusions and exaggerations. These concerns have contributed a good deal to ongoing and wider critical interrogations of advertising and its characteristic modes of representation. The volume and intensity of advertising communication, its emblematic cultural position as a signifier of contemporary living, its assertive visibility; all taken together with its implicit role in the theatrics of self-identity and cultural identification, have provoked frequent examination.

There is particular concern with the 'unintended consequences' (Pollay 1987) of advertising representations. This is not so much to do with 'marketing manipulation', and not, directly, to do with the economic processes that bring products and services into the shops.[7] Instead, concern alights on how advertisements represent the world; how they show 'us' living and how, as they seem to imply, they suggest we *should* live.

Analyses alert to such concerns emphasise ways that advertising might be seen to airbrush-out various identifications and lifestyles, at the same time normalising-in lifestyles via reiterative depictions which are unattainable, unsustainable, delimiting or exclusionary. Such representations are at once (by intention) inviting while also becoming at times uncannily censorious, inducing, for instance, self-criticism and anxieties about personal appearance or social success.

In this conception of advertising, an institution designed to manage commercial processes – selling goods – ends up taking on an (unwarranted) wider role: contributing to and affirming societies' repertoires of normative representations and proposing definitions of social 'virtue' (Marchand 1985), 'well-being' (Leiss *et al.* 2005) and 'the good life' (Falk 1994).

Voiced or unvoiced discomfort sometimes emerges in particular as we confront the advertising *image*, both in the individual instance and in our sense of advertising as cumulative and 'shared' discourse. This is most clear around advertising representing *people*. Advertising's stock in trade[8] representations of smiling faces, beautiful bodies, traditional familial structures and roles, romance, and, until lately, the genre's habituated default to ethnic 'whiteness', as well as, typically, a generalised affluence – together have constituted a 'look'. Schudson (1993) has described as advertising's 'capitalist realism', meaning that ads have tended to show a credible but nevertheless illusory sense of the lives and experiences un/available to us or to others, through consumption. This 'look' has regularly been critiqued (Friedan 1963; Millum 1975; O'Barr 1994; Cortese 1999; Ramamurthy 2003; Kilbourne 1999; Kilbourne *et al.* 2005) with the extended metaphoric conception of advertising as a 'mirror' (Williamson 1978; Pollay 1987; Fox 1984) continually troubling critics and consumers alike.

In particular the question of representing men and women has been a concern with many academic studies focusing on gender in ads (Seely 1994; Nixon 1996; MacDonald 1995; Winship 1981, 2000; Moog 1990). In a different tone reflective practitioners within the industry have been keen to offset complaint, critique and ridicule from audiences around gender depiction (Clifton 1995; White 2003, 2005). The globalisation of advertising has inevitably provoked analyses highlighting representational issues regarding cross-cultural imageries. US and UK-based advertising conventions and ideals have tended to disseminate influence trans-culturally (O'Barr 1994; Tjernlund and Wiles 1991; Lawson and Brahma 2006; Cronin 2000; Frith and Mueller 2003: 118–19) amplifying anxieties about economic globalisation by pointing out the risks of cultural homo-genisation of identities delivered through complementary vectors: mega-brands and the advertising image (Klein 2000). Clichéd and stereotypical conventions for representation – of women in particular – have become a kind of genre-defining feature in popular, academic and journalistic characterisations of advertising (Kilbourne *et al.* 2005; Courtney & Whipple 1983) and a source of frequent critical as well as parodic reflec-tions on advertising – in mainstream popular comedy as well as, since the 1980s, in advertising self-parody (Goldman 1992).

One defining approach in the debate on gender and advertising came in Goffman's *Gender Advertisements*, written in the 1970s. Goffman (1979) provides numerous examples of the gendered conventions governing the typical depictions of men and women in advertising. His sample of ads came from US magazines and newspapers – but the conventions employed are more or less familiar in other advertising representations of the time, and into the present (Kang 1997). For instance Goffman presents detailed examples of the ways that ads often depict men in a 'parental' role while women adopt seemingly dependent or indulged positions – as child-like figures 'protected' by a male. Women, models posing in the ads Goffman looked at, could frequently be shown to be holding postures suggesting they were at a remove from the reality of the situation at hand. Such detachment affirms protected childlike status. If a male is present he is the one in control, indulgently protecting space for the woman/child's playful intransitivity; the man ensuring difficult or 'adult' objects, objec-tives, technologies and responsibilities, are at a remove. *She* is precious – adorning product and scene – but *He* manages and directs contact with action (technology and the 'adult' world). *He* has precedence.

Goffman argued that advertising is a genre that amplifies and affirms patterns of behaviour which are structured into daily habit and ritual – part of everyday life's rituals of self-presentation. Advertising images, he suggested, show an extreme 'hyper-ritualised' form of the gender-relational dynamics typical of the societies where they appear.[9] In the 1970s Berger's (1973) observation rang especially true: 'Men act and women appear' (1973: 47) This summarises an analysis of gender-based power structures in social relations – sometimes labelled 'patriarchy' – wherein males were typically enabled and encouraged to take up more active and prominent roles wielding public political and economic power – in whatever sphere of influence – and with females placed in relatively subordinate social positions and holding sway in restricted areas of the domestic sphere, e.g. 'home economics', and (typically) facing sociocultural obstacles in establishing (for example) senior positions in the workplace. Advertising representations of the period (and with some continuities in today's ads) typically stood as visual affirmations of Berger's (1972) act/appear gender distinction.

In a more recent gender-oriented analysis of advertising Coltrane and Messineo (2000) point out, with reference to numerous content analyses involving large numbers of ads, that:

> Research consistently documents how TV commercials present conventional gender stereotypes, with women shown as young, thin, sexy, smiling, acquiescent, provocative, and available. Men characters, in contrast, tend to be shown as knowledgeable, independent, powerful, successful, and tough.
>
> (Coltrane and Messineo 2000: 363)

At the same time there have been considerable efforts to update gender representations in advertising – new feminisms and femininities entering the frame of the advertising image. As a consequence there have been detailed efforts at rethinking some aspects of advertising critique in this area – reflecting this growing repertoire of gender representations in advertising – and related shifts in social and market power. O'Donohoe (2006) has talked about 'yummy mummies' as object and audience in advertising, challenging stereotypes of domesticated femininity (as de-sexualised and unglamorous). Winship (2000) has examined series of ads where women are depicted in 'castrating' roles – partly disturbing typical patriarchal depictions in earlier ads and (publicly) articulating complex shifts in both femininity and feminism. Lewis and Rolley (1997: 306) have talked about 'woman-centred pleasures offered to both heterosexual and lesbian women' – presenting imagery which, on close examination, challenges routine assumptions about advertising depictions and the range of femininities they describe.

Gender relations and representations have become a keynote across both cultural conversation and advertising practice; an almost permanent agenda item. Advertising has been prolific in imagining and re-imagining women and men in ways which cut across, undermine, repackage and fuse ideas from previous feminisms. Advertising practice has developed in a number of ways producing imagery spiced with a degree of con-sumerist individualism and scripting masculinities and femininities which play at and with gender roles. 'Advertising' has not acted in any coherent way in the face of 'genderquake'[10] (Wolf 1993). We might identity three strategies and readily find evidence in support of each across TV, magazines and the Internet.

1   Advertising has reacted: addressing some untenable gender-representational practices.
2   Advertising has parodied and played: turning mockery of 'old' advertising gender stereotypes to the advantage of currently advertised products.
3   Advertising has carried on regardless: an ongoing commitment to traditional codes of gender representation is apparent across advertising and in many sectors.

Here as elsewhere, it is useful to remember that 'advertising' is not a unitary practice or cultural programme, as if its constituent agencies flock around, producing ads in line with this or that shift or trend. Transitions in 'ethos' and in representational styles are reflexive, contested, complex; variegated across, within and outside the industry – anticipating, missing, catalysing, bucking and tracking wide cultural trends.

Retrospectively it is clear, however, that advertising has been slow to respond to critical concerns about its gender representational assumptions – partly a consequence of a proto 'lad' culture within the industry, described by Delaney (2007) and examined in detail by Cronin (2000) and Nixon (2003). It is also the case, however, that increasingly audiences have been vocally and actively opposed to sexist cliché (Myers 1986; Winship 2002; MacDonald 1995; Gough-Yates 2003).

Significant sections of the audience have been turned off by ads considered to be patronising. This has no doubt contributed to a climate today where Goffman's 1970s ads appear out-dated in terms of implicit gender politics – even while many representational habits continue (Kang 1997).

In a quite understated way, in Figure 5.2 we can see an example of the continuation of some of these gender codes. Tissot's recent campaign presents high-profile contemporary celebrity figures alongside different products.

It is useful to recognise that hyper-ritualised codes of gender – used 'straight' or in pastiche form, as they have been in recent ads for insurance company Sheila's Wheels (Odih 2007: 195). This depends upon some continuity with everyday ritual and presentational performance. Critics of advertising gender representations are typically concerned at the narrowness and idealisation of imagery – relative to other genres, such as film and literature – where characterisation and representation can elaborate more readily (broadly within the terms of their particular generic

This ad is for a multi-functional Tissot watch. It features footballer Michael Owen. He is focused determinedly on the technology and depicted as in action and in control with the aid of a stylish but hi-tech watch. This is a classic advertising gender image of masculinity which amplified Owen's status as a football hero and picks up on his image as a focused and accomplished sportsman. Arguably it also plays on an archetypal transition: from boy to man.

This may be in line with both the image making for the watch (toy or timepiece?), and the celebrity image developing (prodigy or superstar?).

This ad, for another product in the same campaign, features Indy racing car celebrity Danica Patrick. She is a powerful role model challenging some traditional stereotypes with a career driving fast cars competitively. However as mediated through the gender conventions of advertising we might note, and in contrast to Michael Owen, that she is passive – looking into the middle distance and, as Goffman (1979) pointed out, at a remove. For viewers who identify with Danica Patrick the ad poses an attractive counterpoint between traditional femininity alongside this celebrity's image as a post-feminist icon – a counterpoint that at the same time re-inscribes the celebrity identity and the codes of femininity.

**Figure 5.2** Gender codes mediate advertising's representational styles, amplifying or cutting across celebrity images.

codes). It is useful to remember that advertising is but one source for the representation – and apparent affirmation – of identities. Nor, even within its limited representational repertoire, could it be said that advertising does not (on occasion) offer up eye-catching dramas and characterisations. BT (British Telecom) ads, focusing on familial 'communication' as a meta-issue, have worked often, with a recent extended soap format showing post-divorce complexities within contemporary family life. In the past the OXO family was similarly credited with offering a meaningful gloss on the evolving dynamics of the family – reflecting and affirming stabilities but also, minimally, some key transitions.

Advertising is a genre understood as alluding to fantasy as much as to 'real life', and one operating alongside numerous other sources for imaging and scripting gender – pop-videos, film, TV drama, peer cultures and family traditions – many of these equally or more compelling than advertisements in their own terms. Its status means that the public predominance and undoubted impact of advertising's gender images should not be too readily confused with an un-attenuated capacity to 'construct' identity or determine behaviours.

Nonetheless, and perhaps (in some instances) in proportion to the fragility of other sociocultural resources for both private and public affirmation of identity – in transitions between age and life-stage, between home, school, work and between place and place – the prominent identifications some advertising offers up (in the name of marketing) can disorient and distract in the name of promissory identifications and 'fullness' (Williamson 1978).

## ADVERTISING AND REPRESENTATION: EXAMPLES, EXEMPLARS AND IDEALS

The 'tyranny of typologies in marketing and communication' (Clifton 1995) underpins long-instituted representational practices and the conceptions surrounding them. This can be traced from the early history of advertising 'technique'. The stylistic emphasis in advertising moved, in the early twentieth century, from a primarily media-based marketing technique, providing information and circulating trademarks, towards more deliberative and culturally-attuned copy and images. With general improvements in the technologies of representation and a widening of advertising's aesthetic scope, the depiction of people gradually became a useful creative tool.[11] Primarily these early images presented instructional demonstrations of what the advertised thing was for, as imagistic examples alongside new gadgets or other products (Leiss et al. 2005: 240). People depicted in ads provided quasi-diagrammatic surrogates for the salesman. Other imagery dwelt on the factories where the product was made. By the 1920s these approaches had been largely abandoned (Leiss *et al.* 2005; Ohmann 1996). People became central to advertising's deeper project to *humanise and moralise* goods.

From the early years of the twentieth century, advertising began more often to illustrate people not just as demonstrators of things in use, but as variously symbolising and thus animating products. These people were located in rigidly conceived class, ethnic and gender specific milieus and relationships. Advertising began evoking the social usage and significance of things, enlivening products' roles as props in 'the theatre of consumption' (Leiss *et al.* 2005: 197). Ads assertively attempted to secure meanings for goods, easing their adoption into the everyday (Marchand 1985). This representational practice continued to develop alongside further more and more startling gestures in advertising display throughout the twentieth century. A cultural and educative role for advertising invoked images of persons as part of an emergent rhetoric of soft-sell marketing (Webb Young 1954). This has developed – in line with broader cultural changes – into a convention, a genre and an industry routinely collocating glamour, seductiveness and physical idealisation within the marketing process.

Practical, professional and philosophical legitimation emerged from two sources. Hopkins's (1966) classic *Scientific Advertising* was cautious about imagery, but suggested it had a function if tested and trailed. An early advocate of advertising-psychology as 'science' also – like Hopkins – committed to asserting a new professionalism in advertising practice, was Dill Scott (1910), who developed an influential account of techniques in the depiction of 'persons' in advertisements and provided a simple outline of the thinking behind advertising representation, a way of thinking that endures both in industry practice and in casual critique. For Dill Scott advertising was most effective when the people depicted in it could incite 'sympathy'. An advertisement was likely to be effective if the people shown were 'like us', or like 'our ideal'. He explained:

> I have a certain amount of sympathy for all humanity, but I sympathize most with those of my own set or clique, with those who think the same thoughts that I think and who are in every way most like myself.
>
> (Dill Scott 1910: 34)

Advertisers, it followed, should try to appeal to their consumers by depicting people in advertisements *like* those consumers, or resembling the ideals that consumers aspired towards. There is in this something of the mentality of an equation: balancing accounts, grouping markets with their cultural representation, matching 'like' for 'like', as Dill Scott made clear:

> If I desire to be prosperous, I feel keen sympathy with the man who appears to be prosperous ... if I desire to attain a certain station in life, I feel sympathetic with those who appear to have attained my ambition.
>
> (Dill Scott 1910: 34)

To illustrate this principle Dill Scott presented examples. One advertisement, showing a couple 'who are not "of my class"', produced no sympathy and no positive advertising effect. Another ad, in the same product sector, depicted 'approximately my ideals'. This ad does provoke sympathy, and so, Dill Scott says, it produced a positive advertising effect in him and (he presumed), in others like him (Dill Scott 1910: 35–7).

Dill Scott's argument provided a foundational rationale for the professional rule of thumb, and the public common sense, which together, even today, govern discourse about the production and consumption of advertising imagery. To work well advertising imagery needs to produce 'sympathy' (in Dill Scott's sense) in its viewers. Advertisements are thought to show people like the audience, and like the target market as conceived by the advertiser, in terms of physical and social similarity (class, age, gender, ethnicity and so on). Agencies' deliberations about casting and the work of directing for advertisements are part of the creative work delivering necessary translations, moving from a marketing brief on target audiences to a suitable iconic sign: a face, a body, a temperament or a gesture, to optimally capture and captivate audiences' anticipated 'sympathy'. If you are promoting a 'family' car, show a 'family man'. Marketing 'sophisticated' chocolates? Present them at an ambassadorial party. Engaging the youth market? Try a hip hop celebrity.

It would be possible to think about people in ads differently, and indeed there are many other ways of using people in ads quite other than as ideals and exemplars. People might be there to enliven the 'personality' of the brand (Mr Muscle, Ronald McDonald, Peter Kay for John Smith's beer); people could be there representing (no doubt inaccurately) the sites and processes of *making* the goods. Advertisers have been known to place *themselves* in the ad: Victor 'I bought the company' Kyam for Remington and more recently George Foreman for grills, Paul Newman for salad dressing and celebrity film critic Barry Norman for pickled onions – binding traditional modes of endorsement, celebrity branding and corporate branding – or in the case of Barry Norman, micro-marketing. More broadly celebrities, while sometimes offering an invitation to sympathy and emulation (Kerry Katona for Iceland; Kate Moss for

Rimmel; Jason McAteer for Head & Shoulders), may personify certain values without being precisely a 'model' or like-for-like embodiment. Indeed it is in their extremity and difference – or their variously-relayed 'off set' ordinariness that increasingly many celebrities grab attention. Fantasy-based emulation is here only part of appeals which when more fully understood can be seen to mobilise the capacity of celebrity-models to traverse 'real' and 'imaginary' milieus – binding branded and unbranded environments – at once glamorising *and* authenticating in various measures and as differentiated from blank typological modelling from anonymous exemplars familiar from non-celebrity ad formats.

Nevertheless, and notwithstanding increasing numbers of exceptions, there is a working assumption among some practitioners, critics and consumers, and in relation to some product sectors more than others – especially perfumes, household goods and cars – that, in advertising representation, the faces, bodies and by extension the lifestyles shown should be 'like' the ideals of 'consumers': that is, us. This underpins the perplexing hybrids of realism and idealisation which produce the utopian banalisations of everyday life so often shown in ads.

The criticism, prominent from the 1960s onwards has been that the illustrations cued as everyday examples were in fact (impossible and limiting) exemplars and ideals. Representations suggesting simple correspondence to social and gender type became injunctions suggesting – and even, in some arguments coercing – correspondence to an ideal. Numerous advertising 'revolutions' (Wight 1971; Dobrow 1984) have been led by an impulse away from such cliché. Nevertheless, the marketing conception of advertising 'people' has retained its capacity to influence genre codes. Thus, overall, the industry does little to ward off such criticisms, interpreting the psychology of sympathy and correspondence in particular ways and implemented them accordingly. To sum up:

1   The emphasis in showing people in ads has leant towards the ideal and the aspirational rather than 'real'.
2   The emphasis is towards typification and away from specification. Thus resemblance means correspondence to an ideal type approximating 'the majority' or 'average' consumer rather than pointing up to variety and difference.
3   These have become established as normative representational strategies for advertising, with deviations used primarily:
    • for comic effect;
    • in before/after or with/without formats;
    • in the case of ethnic diversity, to assert exoticism or progressive distinction and 'novelty'/cosmopolitan chic.

In practical terms this assumption of approximate correspondence to market-oriented typifications – in idealised mode – had a particular consequence, recently and to a degree addressed within the industry regarding the representation of minority ethnicities. The advertising aim, to link audiences to products by depicting generalised representations (stereotypes) of large (majority) demographic groups – women in their 30s, men aged 25–40 and so on, or to personify a product or brand for 'youth', maturity or the young at heart – demands a peculiar blankness in models and actors (Schudson 1993: 210–12). Media targeting is complemented by cultural targeting. This feature of advertising, in many ways specific to the genre and its peculiar mode of de-characterisation, directing actors towards generic typologies or universals – 'young busy mother', 'dull father', 'temptress' and so on – has posed a problem for ethnic minority performers inhibiting commonplace 'visibility' of ethnic identities in advertising. However adept an ethnic-minority actor might be in this technique of advertising 'anti-acting' (Schudson 1993: 212), i.e. of appearing without a 'story', pulling back other specified or particularising qualities, nevertheless visible ethnicity, for example the 'quality' of blackness or Asianness, cannot be 'pulled back'. For a period extending well beyond the fact of a multi-ethnic demographic make up (in the US and the UK), the perceived inability of black, Asian and Hispanic faces to provoke 'sympathy' in predominantly 'white' national markets provided advertising with a 'technical' rationale for what critics and consumers suspected to have been a more institutionally-grounded exclusion of black, Asian and Hispanic faces from advertising in the US and UK but also, in various ways, globally (Cortese 1999).

This produced a knock-on effect in audiences: members of various social groups, some more than others, were prone to ask of advertising, from time to time: 'Where am *I* in this picture?' Such exclusions, which have been by no means uniform or comprehensive, have nevertheless been all the more significant as, throughout the twentieth century, advertising has been taking its place as a powerful cultural genre locating and identifying the 'good life'. A discourse of the virtues of products took on some of the properties of a discourse about virtue. Exclusion from this discourse marked an exclusion that extended, by inference, beyond marketing. Advertising has responded to the increased complexity and diversity in the marketplace by an incremental admission into the frame of the ad of diversity, identity-hybridity, specificity and difference.

# STEREOTYPES

The generic use of stereotypes in ads provides one commonly discussed mechanism through which difference and diversity are managed in the representational frame of the advertisement.

Criticisms of alternate glamour and banality portrayed in the life of 'advert people' often refer to the idea of stereotypes. Stereotypes in themselves and as a topic can be something of a blind alley. There is no disputing the existence of ads' tendency towards narrow and limiting depictions of people, but this doesn't necessarily take us anywhere we have not been before. 'Stereotype', routinely invoked in media studies, takes its meaning from its use by an eighteenth-century French printer who needed to describe the plates cast for his printing machine. Modern usage inherits the word in the sense that a 'stereotype', like cast and re-printed visual figures, are formed through and for repetition: simple, intelligible and mechanically efficient – shorthand rather than nuanced context-bound representations.

Advertising representations, taken, by way of a sample, as a 'representational universe', deviates from 'the real world'. Exclusions, stereotypes and selective misconstructions are readily evident in advertising viewed in this way. Often such deviations are tracked over time and set against real social histories, real populations, real lives and bodies. Evidence-based calls have been made for an increased frequency of black faces in advertisements to redress a deficit deduced from comparison between the advertising universe and the social world (or a segment of it). Detailed studies link workplace inequalities regularly experienced, along the lines of gender and ethnicity, to the absence of women and minorities in senior positions when advertising portrays the world of employment. Or it is proposed that models on display, in particular when they are female, be heavier, older – less 'perfected'.

More broadly, where advertising shows families it is suggested that, in line with demographics, family households be shown as less 'nuclear' – with single parents, ethnically mixed – and so more in line with real experience, and also that family life should appear less harmonious. When advertisements show different nations, critical analysis recommends that more accurate portrayals of socio-political, cultural and architectural detail be employed – the real China or Scotland or Egypt are not in evidence and the 'character' of the Chinese, the Scots and Egyptians has been travestied. The reality that some advertising critics want returned in advertising representations is a kind of social realism. They seem to want advertising to depict a society either more like society *is*, or, and here, often, is a source of confusion, they want ads to depict the world (critically and ideally) as they would like it to be – i.e. different from the

As Winship (1981) observed advertising often depicts femininities through different types of hands. Here a traditional domestic role is both affirmed and played with – the oven gloves presumably unnecessary for this convenience-based domesticity.

A man links adventure and traditional power through the 'lens' of product – and for us – through the lens of the advertisement – a contemporary fantasy of post-colonial masculinity.

The classic poses of feminine seduction and passivity are a genres defining script in advertising of all eras.

The quasi-surrealism and sensuality combine in this ad which subtly encodes the black model as exotic 'forbidden fruit' – possessed of or by heightened sexuality.

**Figure 5.3** Advertising relies on stereotypical themes – binding glamour to routinised postures and settings.

typical ad-vision of middle-class consumerist paradise. It is unclear if advertisers react directly to such critique. However, consumer opinion about advertising (and not academic opinion) tends to hold more sway with the industry.

The tensions between realisms and utopias as guiding principles for critique of stereotyped ads are often shared, in different ways, by advertisers seeking to balance credibility against fantasy-based seductions. For both critics and advertisers (for different reasons) the enemy is abstraction and dehumanisation – through over-convention and through the absence of qualities – to localise, humanise, realise and energise advertising communications. Tensions between such 'aesthetic' concerns and marketing typifications run through advertising critiques.

There is a perception, on the part of producers and viewers of advertising, that representation of ethnicity and other 'specifying' qualities, such as accent, in some way disrupt the plane of attention, that inclusion of specifying differences will disturb the aesthetic or marketing balance that advertisements typically try to maintain between individual engagement and (market) generalisation. A UK report entitled 'Include me in', examining ethnicity in advertising, makes this point clearly:

> Characterisation of minorities is seen as weak. Audiences have a strong sense that minority representation is there to make a point, to propose an issue, rather than as an integral part of the plot. Minority characters are presented as problems rather than as persons. There remains a 'burden of representation', whereby non-White actors have to 'act their skin colour'.
>
> (Broadcasting Standards Authority 1999: 3)

One Asian child cited in the report pointed out that:

> You know when it comes to an ad, like when you see a yogurt ad or something, you see attractive little kids, you know, going on their bikes and things like that. But when it comes to Asians, they do it funny.
>
> (Young Asian respondent, Broadcasting
> Standards Commission 1999)

His sense that advertising 'does' Asian ethnicity 'funny' captures the idea that, often, ethnic actors appear in advertising for a 'reason'. We could transpose here part of Goffman's analysis of women in advertising. He noted that while male actors appear to be 'naturally doing the things that they are depicted as doing in an adverts; going to work, catching a train, playing golf and so on – women actors (for example posing as executives or soldiers) always seem to be "pretending", to be playing at the role' (Goffman 1979: 51).

Issues around representation, whether of ethnicity, gender, class, sexuality, age or disability, have predominated in advertising studies. However, in the emergent era of media and audience fragmentation the complex dynamics of the audience (now a prominent preoccupation of the industry) makes for an additional important dimension. As media audiences fragment and minority interests develop, broadcasting and press can better engage with and address audiences across major dimensions of sociocultural difference and hybridity. Certainly it can no longer be convincingly argued in relation to UK or US advertising that multi-ethnic society is invisible – even while underlying genre conventions seem to dictate the look of many ads.

While gender and ethnicity have provided the main areas of critical analysis of stereotyping in advertising studies, it is important to note also that there are a number of other important dimensions of inclusion / exclusion and visibility/invisibility in advertising representations. There is a tendency to privilege youth and health over age and disability. The consumer either is young, or aspires to youth. While some ads have played with this set of presumptions, typically advertising has persisted, in line with its broader ethic / aesthetic of 'timeless' and placeless consumption, to locate 'life' and 'virtue' in the places and spaces of the young, and, as products determine, youthful or ageless consumers. If age is often indeterminate, then social class is also largely under-expressed – in terms of very strong accents or other visible markers associated with care-worn or 'hard' lives. The 'before' pictures of, for instance loan or beauty products will admit these realities – the product magically effacing the outward signs of worry or loss, debt or injury: a face cream or a low-rate loan seemingly alleviating the situation. This tendency replicates the critiques laid out at the beginning of the chapter – about advertising as a genre averse to grasping loss and narrative and repeating slot by slot an ahistorical present – necessarily privileging the 'new', 'now on' and seemingly holding time at bay.

As Frosch (2004) argues, with reference to the stock image catalogues from which many advertisements are made, there is a tendency to normalise the romantic couplings of heterosexual relationships. While sexual orientation is not a 'visible' source of identity differentiation, it is only in recent decades that outwardly homosexual imagery (same-sex couples kissing for instance) has been in evidence. As Lewis and Rolley (1997) and Cortese (1999) have argued, ambiguous sexualities have a powerful appeal in certain product sectors – notably around fashion and where 'metrosexual' lifestyle aspirations are likely to translate into a positive advertising appeal.

Advertising representation issues invite consideration the workings of the industry, not only in terms of who is employed in advertising (an industry which tends to have quite a young and middle-class workforce, with creative decisions often lying with male staff). Cronin, in part of her (2000) analysis of advertising makes some further valuable points that regarding the way 'the advertising industries operate in targeting particular gendered, racialised and classed markets', points out that:

> neatly segmented markets do not exist as social facts to be discovered and manipulated by advertising agencies. In targeting groups of consumers, advertising campaigns actively generate them as categories and create subject positions which are refracted through gender, 'race', class and ethnicity.
>
> (Cronin 2000: 7)

This argument about the ways advertising imagery is 'encoded' (Soar 2000) in agency practice and in the media creative industry networks that support and distribute advertising gives an accurate but 'broad brush' characterisation. There are notable instances of progressive agencies and imaginative practice to offset overly sweeping condemnation of the industry as a whole:

Representation necessarily leads us to consider texuality. Some elements of criticisms based on 'images of' people in advertising do not fully engage with accounts of signification and the composition of advertisements – how meanings are put together and how they emerge in ads. This is a matter of signs and signification – and it is useful to be alert to a media culture in which advertising representations are understood in a context where signifying processes can shift and disturb basic assumption about identity and identification.

## ADVERTISING AND A CULTURE OF SIGNS

Contemporary advertising is defined in part by a history it shares with many media genres. The twentieth century witnessed rapid developments and enhancements in technologies for the production, circulation and consumption of cultural *signs*. Between the mid-nineteenth century and the present day, advertising has become integral to media experience: from printed national newspapers to colour magazines, on to radio, TV and film and, lately, including digital TV and the Internet (Nevett 1982; Springer 2007). In this period arrays of new aesthetic, representational and sign-making techniques, within advertising and across media, have worked, variously, to disrupt, represent and reproduce human cultural life. Media-based signification processes lie at the centre of contemporary cultural experience, preoccupying both casual reflection and academic analysis (Giddens 1991; Jameson 1991). The advertising industry has given direct and indirect stimulus to what Goldman and Papson (1994) call a culture of 'hyper-signification'. Such a proliferation of sign-making has provoked a concomitant interest in academic critique (Williamson 1978; Goldman and Papson 1996; Danesi 2006; Cronin 2000; Lury 2004; Cronin 2000) and industry techniques (White 2005) towards better understanding complex, mediated, cultural and sign-based communication processes – such as advertising.

In the next chapter we will look at semiotics – the study of signs – which provides approaches that have proven useful in attempts to more closely grasp how advertising operates as a part of, and across, culture, society and commerce – conceptualising the ways signs work. Adverts offer numerous potently visible (Rose 2001) and audible (Van Leeuwen 1998) texts; sources for the study of commercial-cultural signification.

Advertising is only one of any number of significant semiotic arenas – with each and (almost) every aspect of life understood, from semioticians' variously nuanced perspectives, as constituted in the processes of *signs and signification*. Sebeok (2001a; 2001b) outlines an ever-widening range of objects for semiotic analysis – from human cultural practices (for example walking, haircuts and tattoos) and extending into biology and the natural sciences. Semiotics is 'a technique for studying anything that produces signs' (Sebeok 2001a: 5) [12] and advertising campaigns, for producers, as for consumers, are extended, reiterative and compounded sequences of tightly orchestrated and often widely distributed semiotic activity – ongoing attempts to focus desire and build the brand (Lury 2004: 74–97).

Given the non-stop centrality of semiotic activity in all areas of life it is mistaken to set advertising up as a uniquely privileged category of objects (or texts) for semiotic analysis. As indicated briefly above, semioticians have developed a view that *everything*, not just ads or, say, films or magazines, should be understood as *semiosis*. Advertisements, while to a degree framed, by commercial intentionality, as intently and intensively *significant*, and so cut off from and cutting up the everyday flows of cultural signification, are also, inevitably, and at the same time, just a contributory part of these flows – not discreet from but intertwined in media cultures and clutters. This is the case both as we apprehend advertisements intermixed within media and in 'outdoor' spatial contexts (for example, respectively, on TV, or on billboards). Such media-entertainment-advertising syntheses bring about cross-fertilisations and confusions that permeate everyday life. These are equally prevalent in the sense of the inevitable 'mental' intermingling of advertising signs. Ideas and associations, products and faces; vivid, from moment to moment, or recalled, cut across new experiences, associations and apprehensions, with further ideas and images evolving, reframed by and reframing time, place, objects and culture. The allusive or *intertextual* character of advertising signs – musical snippets, celebrities and brand names circulating-incessantly encourages such association. The 'always on' promotional nature of media entertainment, public and cultural spaces – and the movements of celebrity faces between such highly permeable realms of signification – ensures a significant semiotic churn. The promotional-media-entertainment culture interplays refresh brands that advertising alone might not reach.

In 1964 Roland Barthes, in an attempt to emphasise the importance of studying signs, made the following observation:

> In a single day, how many really non-signifying fields do we cross? Very few, sometimes none. Here I am, before the sea; it is true that it bears no message. But on the beach, what material for semiology! Flags, slogans, signals, sign-boards, clothes, sun-tan even, which are so many messages to me.
>
> (Barthes 1977a: 112n)

However, in a multiply mediated world of hyper-signification, even the sea is an object for the study by semiotics, as the Sony ad (Figure 5.4) implies. Indeed *semiotics*, as opposed to Barthes term 'semiology', would certainly extend to count the sea as a semiotic object – a component of the distinction between the two terms extends semiotics to encompass e.g. non-human signs and unintended signification: as Cobley (2001) writes: 'communicative acts and intentionality are only a small part of the universal semiosic repertoire' (Cobley 2001: 260).

If we look at Figure 5.4 it is immediately the case that the sea, as imaged in the ad, may well stand for something to us – and as such it constitutes a *sign*. The meaning processes, or 'semiosis' attaching to such signs is the focus of the following chapter, providing closer insight into the specifics of advertising textuality.

**Figure 5.4** Sony advertisement: technology for the signification of intimacies, global and local.

# 6

# SIGNS AND
# TEXTUALITIES

The beating heart of an ultrasound foetus selling a Volvo car (Taylor 1993), a patient caught at the moment of his death to promote Benetton clothes (Falk 1997); long 'dead', immortalised celebrities seemingly resurrected to sell the latest DM boots (Pfanner 2007). Sensational signs: and it is not least through advertisements that we have become well used to the representational field opening up perception and curiosity to the startling, as well as the seductive and the artful. Photography, telephony, micros-copy, radio, x-ray, film, TV, the Internet; myriad devices for image and sound reproduction, as well as, most lately, many highly mobile digital media platforms. All of these contribute to an environment where irrefutably both manufacture and the reception of signification lie at the heart of the everyday: representation, action and experience.

Signification is the essence of all cultural experience – past and present. Contemporary institutions, individuals and today's media systems engage us proactively through cultures of signification – intensive, reflec-tive, technophillic, and, often, with a seeming default to the 'promotional' (Wernick 1991). Advertising is a major component of this culture, a firmly-established genre shaping eye-catching communications routinely visible and audible in many places – collapsing private preoccupations into public spaces and global imagery into local worlds. Advertising supports templates influencing developments in other communications; notably in the presentation of Politics (Mayhew 1997; Scammell 2007; Kline 1997) and across entertainment cultures (Donaton 2004) in film and pop videos. Advertising provides major financial incentives to sustaining high volumes of sign productivity and dissemination and furnishes a ready generative 'grammar' for multi-media promotions.[1]

Contemporary city dwellers, and that is most of us, globally, experience and contribute to the 'sharp discontinuity in the grasp of a single glance' identified by Simmel ([1903] 1950) as the hallmark of the (today extended) metropolis. Recent media technologies counter and amplify long-established proto-advertising practices: street criers and sandwich-board carriers, shop window displays and handbills. City and suburb offer up promotional sign upon sign (Winship 2002; Costera Meijer and Van Zoonen 2002: 327); 'new' information readily at our finger tips, sound-tracks shuffling, billboards and echoes round every corner. Such 'ambient' advertising signs define but also deface and de-territorialise city-spaces (Abaitua 2006; Cronin 2006; Williams 1980; Stallabrass 1996).

So, contemporary culture involves a degree of habituation to moving[2] from instance to instance, reading, and hearing, processing and producing signs. Faces, texts, voices, bodies, stories, looks, skin – as well as the products we buy and use, all, potentially, become enhanced instruments of – and objects for – the communication and display of signs. Paradoxically, we are both accommodated in and disoriented by such *semiotic* productivity, and we strive to cope and contribute within the cultural environment – in whatever ways society affords us. Sony's advertisement above suggests, 'go create' (Figure 5.4); urging us to signify, globally and locally using (their) new communications technologies – to produce, receive and interact widely and intimately with and within the *semiosphere*[3] (Lotman 1990). An important complementary aspect to such processes of creating signs is in the analysis of how signs and signification operate. This chapter will develop some concepts around signs and texts in specific relation to advertisements.

Amongst so much significant clutter – and constituting a good deal of it – advertising signs seek to establish product-recognition and to support continuity in product-identification. Ads introduce disruption and novelty in consumers' relationships with 'systems of provision' (Fine and Leopold 1993) and in the cultural 'meaning of things' (Csikszentmihalyi and Rochberg-Halton 1981; Slater 1997). At times they persuade us to 'try or buy' this, or that: an Internet wine service (as with Figure 6.1), and so on, across the market. Sometimes signification reframes a familiar product, amending or renewing its significance in the marketplace. Figure 6.9 shows an ad re-presenting Galaxy chocolate as a late-night sensual indulgence rather than an everyday snack – its former image.

## ENGAGING ENVIRONMENTS OF SIGNS

Advertising signs, one by one and all together, claim prominent places in real and virtual space. Advertising is placed, and places itself, at the heart of the promotional-cultural semiosphere.[4] Contemporary cultures – experiences of the street, and the magazine, not to mention the (mobilising) Internet – assertively furnish sites and times where the production and interpretation of signs is not so much something we do, but, and in a particular sense, something we *are*.

A culture so readily characterised in terms of prolific (and perhaps profligate) production and consumption of promotional signs is one where signification or semiosis (Sebeok 2002), invites attention. Placing signification at the heart of human culture (and, therefore also, nature[5]) is in particular a project for 'semiotics' – the study of signs. Many semioticians – those who use the terms and techniques of semiotics – have paid particular attention to advertising, both to critique from various political-economic positions 'outside' advertising (notably Barthes 1964, 1988; Williamson 1978; Baudrillard 1996; Goldman 1992; Harvey 1989; Jameson 1991; Goldman and Papson 1994; Odih 2007) and, in other modes of intra-industry criticality, to try, from within, to enable industry practitioners to better understand processes of cultural signification (Beasley and Danesi 2002; Beasley *et al.* 2000; Levy 1999; Valentine 2007) or as part of a broader projects of social-semiotic analysis (Mick 1986; Lury 2004: 74–97; Hodge and Kress 1988: 8–12; Van Leeuwen 2005: 6–14). What does semiotics bring to the advertising debate? This can be considered with reference to some examples and by setting down some of the major conceptual tools used in semiotics.

## ADVERTISING AND SEMIOTICS

Purple grapes and green leaves; a laptop computer and a glass of wine; what links these elements together? Not an idyllic fantasy of leisured writing, but an advertisement found on the Internet (see Figure 6.1). And a further question: what, if anything, links them to *you*? One answer, to both questions, is straightforward and correct. An advertiser wants to sell some wine. There is no trouble seeing that this is the intent of what might, in another setting, seem like a random list of things to find in a single picture. However, this text is quite easily understood (simply and instantly) as yet one more 'take it or leave it' invitation to a market exchange, one more instance of the advertising genre; here, as mediated in the browse and click networks of e-commerce.

Contemporary advertising audiences are well used to imagery far more incongruous than in this[6] example, which might stand as a conventional 'still life'[7] for the contemporary and mobile 'wireless' citizen – consumer. The meanings we might find in this ad, in the conjunction of elements

**Figure 6.1** A simple passion we like to share: web ad for e-vineyard.com.

composed for us by an advertising agency's creative team, are quite obvious. The makers of the ad are working to relatively familiar genre rules, *codes* guiding the format and character of advertising signification, codes which also support our particular manner of reading or browsing such an ad as this, found on the Internet. The ordinary 'decoding' of an advertisement[8] should not be thought of, primarily, as extracting or uncovering a 'hidden' or secret meaning as in a crossword puzzle – though some ads invite such decipherment. 'Code' here should be understood predominantly in its senses allied to general rules or protocol, 'codes of behaviour', rather than the familiar sense of puzzle or espionage. The meaningfulness of advertisements – such as it is – is more a matter of context and negotiating relevance than of decipherment. The codes governing reading ads and the textual material that we perceive *circumscribe* rather than pre- or pro-scribe sense-making.

Slightly differing codes might inflect the composition and experience of an outdoor poster version of the ad if we walked past one – perhaps with even less attention from both *sender* (i.e. the advertiser) and *receiver* (i.e. us) paid to informative content in the text. Pedestrians and Internet users browse differently. A large part of advertising creativity today depends upon selecting the right media mix, placing texts to optimise consumers' engagements within the advertising meaning-making system, and within its various specialist and converging communicative modes: Internet, TV, radio, press, cinema, outdoor and ambient.

The product type contributes to decisions about how and to what extent, for example, detailed information, humour or sexual imagery is presented or *encoded* (Hall 1990; see Soar 2000; and note preceding points about 'codes' and 'decoding') in the ad, as well as inflecting varying degrees and modes of attention from readers. The look or tone of an ad will be designed so as to best ensure that it gets the message across appropriately – in the right *register*. Financial services ads, ads for quick-cook sausages and ads for nail polish, typically operate within partly differing semiotic codes. As we will see in Chapters 7 and 8, a good number of contemporary advertisements seek to make an impression by destabilising codes, registers – and expectations.

Beyond simply seeing – perceiving – the advertisement, meaning-making requires a further act: we might say of *getting*[9] the message as opposed to (merely) receiving it. We rapidly process the collocations of signs set out before us in the advertising text. The likely process, in this instance, reading this ad, seems more or less automatic; but it is a process that is also, more or less, 'involved', i.e. involving our making sense of the sign-based movements of text and culture – and perhaps tapping preoccupations of our own. The text is a composite sign, made up of both visual and verbal signifying elements: grapes, leaves and blocks of written text in Figure 6.1. We engage if and as the ad engages us. We can describe our engagement with the advertisement as a 'semiotic' process – to do with signs and meaning. Semiotics is relevant to advertising like this because:

- advertisements are texts where signs, typically, words and images and brand logos are interlinked within carefully orchestrated processes of textual signification to convey a marketing or other promotional message;

so that:

- advertisements engage target audiences – and others – via media communication and textual signification;
- audiences connect with advertisements through interpretive and affective processes of semiotic engagement or semiosis;
- the advertisement sign contributes to evolving meanings and experiences of the product and/or brand for consumers and across the culture at hand;
- semiotics attempts to model some of these processes – offering insights not just to *what* ads mean, but proposing *how* they mean.

Typically semioticians have taken a primary interest in *what* signs and texts might mean, especially by giving emphasis examining *how* meanings are made and processed. Semiotic analysis also pays some attention to relevant social and communicative contexts. Semiotic analysis of an advertisement such as Figure 6.1 should give some consideration to *when*, *where* and *why* the text might have been produced, transmitted and consumed – and by and for *whom*. These questions provide a preliminary framing for any close analytic reading of advertising.

## Semiotic concepts

Semiotic terms are abstract and quite complex. The conceptual laboriousness of semiotic analyses and the elaborate nature of semiotic concepts emerges largely from the complexity of the processes being described: the movements of representation, perception and interpretation. However, the sense of linguistic complexity – and 'jargon' (White 2005) – emerges partly also from the unfamiliar challenge of articulating the nature and processes inherent in everyday signs; an advert, a traffic light or a stranger's smile.[10] Analysis of ordinary sign dynamics requires an effort of theorisation in reflective strategies of de-familiarisation. Semioticians' combinations of neologism, revivified terms from classical rhetoric and linguistics jargon – producing various conceptual outlines – deliver just this sense of 'un-familiarity in the ordinary' in a manner well suited to a 'de-familiarising' engagement with the most everyday signs – such as advertisements. Semiotics is in fact a 'meta-semiotic' discourse, as its referents are semiotic processes themselves – an attempt to step back from normal relationships with everyday cultural signs. The remainder of this chapter sets out some further terms and approaches from semiotics to better explain something of audiences' engagements with advertising texts – understood as signs – and providing some basic examples of semiotic analysis of advertising textualities.

# MODELLING ADVERTISING SIGNS

In semiotics, from the work of ancient medics of nearly 3,000 years ago, interpreting the signs and symptoms of illness, until Charles Sanders Peirce[11] formulated a more elaborate account in the nineteenth century, the sign was generally conceived as comprising two levels. On one level was the entity that made a sign a sign, for example a sound, image or sensation; on the other level was the entity signified by the sign i.e. a meaning, or conceptual sense. In analyses of signification inspired by Ferdinand de Saussure,[12] sometimes identified as 'semiology' to distinguish it from 'semiotics' (the more prevalent term today and with a Peircean influence), these sign elements are tagged 'signifier' and 'signified' respectively. Saussure's term 'signifier', for him, initially meaning the sound pattern of a word, was extended by some theorists (primarily Barthes 1964; 1977a) as part of a developing understanding of some *non-verbal* forms of communication.[13] 'Signifier' has subsequently gained a good degree of currency in semiotics more broadly (Danesi 2002: 31: Chandler 2002: 36), with 'the signifier' the preferred[14] term in social, cultural and media theory in many detailed examinations of cultural signification (e.g. Jameson 1991; Baudrillard 1996; Harvey 1989).

There are then two influential models of the sign. One account divides the sign into two constituent and co-extensive elements, called 'the signifier' and 'the signified' (Figure 6.2). Another more elaborate account divides the sign into three elements: the sign (or 'representamen'), its 'object' and its 'interpretant' (see Figures 6.3, 6.4 and 6.5).

## Saussure's language-based model of the Sign

The two-part model (see Figure 6.2) derives from Saussurean linguistics,[15] and is based on the analysis of linguistic signs. It has subsequently been more widely applied to other signifying systems, notably fashion, food and cars, for instance by Barthes (Barthes 1957; 1964), and specifically to advertising, and in variously developed ways (e.g. by Williamson 1978; Barthes 1964; Leymore 1975; Goldman 1992; Odih 2007). 'Semiology' (as opposed to semiotics) is effectively an approach which draws a more or less direct analogy between verbal systems and other systems of meaning.

The signifier calls up, by virtue of its inseparability from it, a concept, the 'signified', which, along with the signifier, fulfils the 'sign'. Signifiers (in one conception) perform this task purely by a process of the movement of differences. Signifiers are understood, in Saussurean terms, to signify

This is often represented diagrammatically. The sign, primarily understood as a linguistic entity, is composed of two co-extensive elements: the signifier and the signified.

For example:

**Saussure's SIGN**

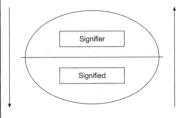

Signifiers become bound to signifiers and are understood in a context of interpretation, and with reference to the code in operation at the time. Together they constitute the SIGN.

**Signifier**
A sound pattern in the mind and/or the verbal expression that produces it.

**Signified**
The concept to which the signifier refers.

**The relationship between signifier and signified is understood (in this model) to be arbitrary and conventional.**

This is to say that there are 'unmotivated' relationships between signifier and signified meaning that the relationship between signifier and signified is 'arbitrary'. This means that there is nothing in e.g. the sounds producing the word, and the related sense impression in a hearer – of 'cat', that suits 'cat' for better or worse, as a fitting signifying partner to its signified – i.e. the cat-concept that for us, 'cat' brings to mind. This is to say that in other conditions or other languages, other signifiers would do just as well.

The signifying association is a contingent matter – of history and culture – the linguistic **convention**, observed by a large language community, i.e. English speakers, and that has secured 'cat' in its expected meanings and uses.

Sebeok (2001) writes:

> The English word *cat*, for example, is an example of a particular kind of human sign – known as *verbal* – which stands for a referent that can be described as a 'carnivorous mammal with a tail, whiskers and retractile claws' (2001: 3).

Chandler (2002) gives the following further example, emphasising context:

> 'The word "open" (when it is invested with meaning by someone who encounters it on a shop doorway) is a sign consisting of:
>
> - a signifier, the word "open";
> - a signified concept: that the shop is open for business' (2002: 19).

**Figure 6.2** Saussure's model of the sign.

by virtue of their differences within the system at hand. Thus a yellow ball on a snooker table takes on its value (two points) only in relation to the values of other different coloured balls, and only by virtue of not being any of the other colours; this in combination with a working convention that secures the signified point value(s) within the game. Put it on a chess table or a grass verge and its (former) meaning is left behind (save by a memorial process of reconstruction). It remains a sign, however, and solicits further interpretations – or, perhaps, stands as a clue, a signifier in search of (reconstructive) resolution.

The signifier 'balloon' attains its meaning by virtue of not being 'ball' or 'saloon', 'balloon' marking its reference and meaning by virtue of not being any other verbal signifier. This is to say that language, and the signifying systems that Saussurean semiology models on language, are understood to work primarily as relational systems of differential signifiers, whose terms have no meaning outside their code. Meaning is released within the context of the code by virtue of relational movement of distinctions realised, at the level of signification, within the code. This is an important starting point for understanding the principle of arbitrariness discussed below. This description of sign operation applies primarily to the kind of media semiotics that grew out of Saussurean sign theory rather than the mainstream of semiotics. Such accounts are limited and limiting in their tendency to misrepresent signification (as a whole) by equating sign processes too closely with dynamics modelled primarily on *linguistic* signification – at the expense of a wider understanding of context-bound sign processes.

Such analyses of advertising signs (Williamson 1978; Goldman 1992) emphasise how contemporary advertisements' signification is more or less free from reference to, or direct description of, specific product properties, but often including or suggesting a product or brand name in the ad text alongside other cultural imagery related only by a tenuous logic. The highly orchestrated text becomes itself a composite signifier producing an overall impression, 'meaning' or concept – a 'signified'.

In advertising, as understood within this model, signifiers – combined within texts and communicated via the media – operate to convey an advertising representation.

The sights, sounds and surfaces of advertisements' composite arrangements of signifiers are circulated in advertising texts promoting banking, holidays, perfume, charities, potatoes, good health or international tourism and so on: advertising signifiers working variously to make arresting marketing appeals within globally- and locally-distributed media-based marketplaces, just as town centre market stall holders shout and display the prices and availability of goods to passers-by. Modern media-based advertising attempts to fulfil the communications needs of producers in a spatially-distributed market system. Creative, well-orchestrated signification is considered an element in market competitiveness – along with price and functionality. Signification is a matter of setting out one's stall.

Semiotic analyses working with this model of the sign concentrate on the ways that advertising works as a persuasive form using various methods to produce a (false) equation and a transfer in the mind of potential consumers – between the concept or image signified by the ad and the advertised product available in the shops. It is an application of this model of sign processes that enables Williamson (1978), for instance, to argue that advertising is a genre committed to deflecting attention from the reality of the product (e.g. away from its functionality, its real value and the costs and processes of its production) and towards a serial misperception of the value and meanings of the product advertised for sale.

Typically analysis operating within this framework assumes a degree of compliance amongst readers in what Williamson (1978) called the 'advertising-work'; a routinised transfer of signified meaning onto the advertised product. Readers (seemingly) allow arbitrary imagery (signifiers) orchestrated through advertising textuality and repetitive advertising and effectively establish new cultural product-signs linking up cultural ideas to commodities, and producing commodity-signs evoking seductive but unwarranted 'signifieds'. Products then serve speciously as signifiers evoking, for example, sophisticated beauty, or feminine assertiveness, ecological responsibility, rugged masculinity or familial togetherness.

The 'signified' as used in media semiotics' analysis of advertising is often said to be the product. It is clearer to say that the signified of an advertisement is the 'product-sign', a conceptual mental object, perhaps to be equated with the real product-object, and produced by the (encoded) arrangement and interaction of signifiers. Not a thing so much as the idea of the thing, an idea which, in turn, is reframed in connection to other ideas associated in the mind of the reader or viewer. This conception has been reframed with Peircean concepts preferred in capturing the subtlety of referential and interpretive processes.

## Peirce's triadic model

A triadic (three-part) model of the sign comes from Peirce (see Figures 6.3, 6.4 and 6.5 as illustrative outline depictions of the Peircean sign). For Peirce the sign incorporates: the representamen, the form of the sign (sometimes still tagged as the 'signifier'); an object to which the sign refers, in the mind or in the world; and an interpretant. An interpretant is not an interpreter (it is not a person), but the bringing together of object and representamen to constitute a sign. Necessarily in fulfilling the sign, in a dynamic called 'semiosis', the sign, in its processing, brings about the generation of a further sign, engendering a flow of sign-based associative activity. A major and further difference from the Saussurean-inspired semiology model of the sign identifies different modes of relationship between the sign and its referent, allowing for a helpful conception of the signifier–referent relation – an important and differentiating feature of this model – escaping the linguistics-based semiological presumption of arbitrariness.

## ADVERTISING SEMIOSIS

The Peircean model allows a richer conception of sign-processes embedded in contextual and embodied thought processes – as well as in symbolic cultural ones. We are not (just) *reading* signs – decoding specious collocations of signifiers in ads – but living them, linking signs to context and experience through calculation, evaluation and desire. Meaning-making happens not just in the interconnection of signifiers (i.e. the level of the representamen) but instead signs emerge in a way that both traces and constitutes experience in concurrencies of symbolic, practical and embodied reference: in advertising industry jargon these link to ideas of consumers' product-involvement and ads' salience and relevance. We decode signs, advertisements included, but we also align ourselves and our worlds around them. Even in the seemingly trivial world of product-based propositions (baked beans or holiday choices) ad signs can touch us, provoking embodied and emotional responses – affiliation and disaffiliation – thinking grounded in feeling, working meanings through as much as working meanings out.

Merrell (2001) provides a helpful reflective and illustrative account of Peircean semiotics focusing on an engagement with an advertisement. The emphasis on context, feeling and embodiment is notable. This differentiates his analysis from the decoding approaches emerging from a linguistics-based conception of the sign. The sense of embeddedness and interrelatedness of signification, body and context is far more available to

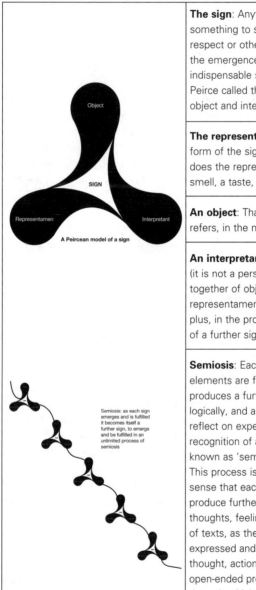

**The sign**: Anything that stands for something to someone in some respect or other. It is constituted in the emergence of three indispensable semiotic components. Peirce called these representamen, object and interpretant.

**The representamen**: This is the form of the sign, it is the thing that does the representing – a sound, a smell, a taste, an image, etc.

**An object**: That to which the sign refers, in the mind or in the world.

**An interpretant**: Not an interpreter (it is not a person), but the bringing together of object and representamen to constitute a sign, plus, in the process, the generation of a further sign.

**Semiosis**: Each sign, as the three elements are fulfilled, necessarily produces a further sign. This leads, logically, and as is evident, as we reflect on experience, to the recognition of an unfolding process known as 'semiosis'.

This process is unlimited, in the sense that each sign will, necessarily produce further signs – gestures, thoughts, feelings, words, elements of texts, as they are apprehended expressed and experienced, in thought, action, and perception: an open-ended process ad infinitum through which we engage, open up and navigate the world and our experience of it.

**Figure 6.3** Peirce's model of the sign: semiosis.

|  |  |  |
|---|---|---|
| **ICON**<br>Iconic signs refer in the mode of resemblance – sharing the look, feel or other qualities of whatever it stands for. | **INDEX**<br>Indexical signs refer in the mode of natural or causal connection. Smoke refers to fire because the former causes the latter. An arrow pointing up, down, or left or right refers to real conjunctions and relations of place to place. | **SYMBOL**<br>Symbolic signs refer because we have learned a signifying link – between roses and romance, black and death, the word 'cat' and the feline animal, tartan and Scottish-ness, white hats, black hats and 'goodies'/ 'baddies' in Cowboy films, etc. |
|  |  |  |
| The couple as in the ad are iconic signs. They resemble likely customers, even while in an unlikely setting, here on a symbolic journey representing homeownership. | The phone number functions in the text is an indexical sign – composed of symbolic signs. It connects, causally, with its object – the Abbey call centre. Other indexical signs include an ('index') finger pointing at something 'there', or the smell of roses. | The sky – with storm clouds – functions, in the Abbey advertisement, as a symbolic sign, of threat and danger looming, as well as of hope – with the sunshine peaking through. |

**Figure 6.4** There are three main types of sign in Peirce's model: icon, index and symbol. They are distinguished in the mode of reference.

|  |  |  |
|---|---|---|
| **ICON** | **INDEX** | **SYMBOL** |
| The grapes in the advertisement (Figure 6.1) function as an iconic sign. They resemble grapes – they look like what they depict – fresh, juicy and from the vine. | The grapes in the advertisement (Figure 6.1) also function as an indexical sign. They point to, and have a natural relationship with, vineyards, wine and the service advertised. | The grapes in the advertisement (Figure 6.1) function as symbolic signs – perhaps borrowing something from the iconic grape sign – of freshness and 'rawness'; they also stand, conventionally, for conviviality, pleasure and celebration. |

**Figure 6.5** The same sign can operate in differing referential modes: grapes as icon, index or symbol.

the Peircean approach, its sign modelling offering a more grounded 'social' and experiential account of subject and sign in dialogue:

> You are pumping iron in your basement while the TV blares out an athletic event. Then a commercial disturbs your concentration on your weights. You hear 'Coke is it!' Ah, yes. You're sweating, panting, and ready for a break. You head for the refrigerator upstairs. But wait a minute, 'Coke' is what? There was nothing actually said in the commercial about quenching your thirst. In fact you weren't even watching [the TV]. You were only listening to it . . . So where's the bite to the sign? The bite is in that sound 'Coke!', that you have heard hundreds of times. It is nothing more than a syllable, a simple representamen. But you have become so familiar with it, like millions of other people throughout the world, that it immediately translates you into a feel for its semiotic object, a bottle or can of the cold, brown, effervescent stuff. Your tongue feels a little drier, your body a little hotter and sweatier, your muscles a bit more weary. You come in tune with the proper interpretant,

with hardly any need consciously or conscientiously to think or say it. Soon, with a can of 'Coke' in hand and once more at the bench and contemplating your iron, your previous semiotic object has become a representamen, its own semiotic object is the contented cool feeling in your stomach and gut, and the interpretant is the pause which relaxes . . . . signs evoke and provoke more signs, without end.

(Merrell 2001: 30)

## LEVELS OF THE SIGN: DENOTATION AND CONNOTATION

For a semiotician any absolute notion of 'simple' use (or perception and action and meaning) of, upon or through an object unmediated by signification is a misconstruction. It mistakes the character of the relationships and interactions between people and things. Even 'simple', obvious meanings – of an object or in representation, e.g. of a bottle of wine in Figure 6.1 – remains a matter of signification: a sign serving the function of 'denotation'. *Denotation* describes instances of signification where a direct and stable relationship between the signifier and what is signified is held in mind – positing a notional, functional and natural-seeming correspondence between signifier and signified.

Even in 'simple' or routine use, e.g. of wine, money or chocolate, and especially in the anticipations and fantasies of acquisition, consumption, service and magical transformation sometimes provoked by advertising, products are operating in some sense as 'signs', standing for something, to us, i.e. to actual or potential consumers, as, if and whenever we watch, listen and engage, moment to moment. Advertising signification, or 'semiosis', can fascinate consumers – or, rather, semiosis (partially) *constitutes* our fascination; producing thoughts, engaging activity and interest and evolving ideas and preoccupations. Such attention and involvement – perhaps tipping us selectively towards a re-evaluation of an advertised product or service – is the stuff of advertising. It provides the rationale for most advertising activity and expenditure – not to mention a good deal of the mystique and glamour around ads' 'creativity'.

Advertising creatives aim to induce fascination by asserting or elaborating likely or possible significances attaching to the advertised product or brand in an imagined or presumed audience. The detailed product-sign portrayal is finalised sometimes after pre-testing, where responses and significant associations – or connotations – are traced, and, if necessary, and as far as possible, moderated and managed for the final execution of the advertisement text. Advertising aims to organise and orchestrate positive connotations in the service of the campaign aim – to sell the product or build the brand, for instance. It is the most subtle but also chaotic aspect of advertising 'art' – with advertisers' intentions confronting the instability and unpredictability of cultural meaning-making. The sustainable 'production' of a brand image depends on the successful association of suitable connotations to the product or corporation.

This can be thought of in term of ads' integrating levels of meaning – what the ad *tells* directly and what the ad more subtly *says* to us (Barthes 1988). In Saussurean and Barthesian approaches a sign is often spoken of as having two levels of meaning. It tells its readers, directly, literally, one message. At the same time, and in the same space, it says something else, something further – it *denotes* grapes but also *connotes* romance or passion by inciting conventional associations to the imaged fruit. The first level is called the denotative. It 'speaks' the literal element of the signified. The second level is the connotative, the sign's opening up associated ideas, not by the direct reference – to (e.g. Figure 6.1) wine, grapes or direct verbal meaning, but by reference to the cultural associations the sign carries – qualities such as passion, freshness or tradition.

Following elements of Barthes' work in *Mythologies* (Barthes 1972) Danesi (2006) argues that connotation, even though it is 'second-order', generally happens initially in signs. Connotations or associations are so strong because they draw on the power of deeply-held social and cultural ideas. Denotation 'naturalises' connotative associations into intelligible configurations of meaning. Those connotations might border on the 'outlandish' or 'surreal' but become credible by virtue of being part of an intelligible 'system of denotation'.

The process by which meanings are linked to other meanings, of course, is not an insight of Barthes alone. It is a key component of semiotics as a whole. Saussure notes this in his concept of the 'associative' dimension and it is evident in Peirce's idea of 'unlimited semiosis' (Eco 1976) by which an interpretant has the power to constantly transform into a new representamen – and so on.

## ADVERTISING SYNTAXES AND PARADIGMS AND FRAMING: ORGANISING SIGNS

Processes of semiosis, as we have seen, can be both arresting, but also quite random – as signs engender thoughts and preoccupations at odds with, or quite unrelated to the initial signs that may have set a particular train of thought on track. Thoughts and feelings meander. Advertising signification aims to track and trace back common patterns of thinking and feeling; representations figuring established chains of thought in text, image and sound to evoke and re-evoke cultural meanings and to manage two potentially conflicting ends:

- holding attention to the marketing proposition – through relevancy and aesthetic or other impacts;
- keeping the product or brand ideas/proposition *credibly* in the audience's mind.

In many ways advertising operates like any and every cultural genre: it uses cultural signs to communicate meanings – in more or less affecting and exploratory ways – to pose and repose propositions, to compose and recompose feeling. A distinctive feature of ads, however, is that as they play on, rattling (or rather jingling) the associative chains of significant cultural meaning, their aim is that further links (associations) can be inserted, securing a product idea more firmly within significant associative matrices – cultural repertoires of significant association. Advertising sign-play is then, also, in its intentionality at least, a purposive kind of play in the service of marketing ends. In some instances this can result in ads as extended product and deal descriptions. In other cases the marketing intention is evident only in the form of a barely noticeable logo – tied to cultural signification and only elliptically related to sales. The balance can be variously struck.

One useful way of thinking about this is to see how ads combine signs to affirm cultural association – between brand or product idea and significant cultural ideas. Semiotics offers some useful concepts for thinking about this: *syntax* and *paradigm*. Paradigms and syntaxes are opposing and complementary types of list – extant virtually and notionally in the 'ether' of cultural meaning, and actually in the concrete practices and histories of personal and cultural signification. They furnish rules of association telling us what properly goes with what according to the culture and context at hand – conventions and logics exercised and enacted through signs and signification. Table 6.1 gives some random examples of para-digms – what Jakobson (1960: 368) called the 'axis of selection' – the 'place' from which signifying elements and choices are taken or emerge. The paradigms listed show different instances of the same thing – variations within a set – that might be selected from a notional array. Such lists can be used to think in an indicative way about symbolic resources for qualita-tive specification of variation and difference between potential signs in the process of ad composition or encoding.

An art director selecting a model for a scene in an ad, flicking through portfolios or picture archives and holding in mind the hoped-for look and

**Table 6.1** Random paradigms: signifiers or objects from within a category showing similarity and variance: axis of selection

| Spoons ▶ | Persons ▶ | Balls ▶ | Computer ▶ | Model-type (female) ▶ | Celebrity ▶ | Cityscape ▶ | Fruit ▶ |
|---|---|---|---|---|---|---|---|
| Soup spoon | You | Rugby ball | PDA | Blonde and skinny | Paris Hilton | London | Oranges |
| Salt spoon | He/she/it | Squash ball | Apple Mac | Boyish and tall | John Wayne | Beijing | Grapes |
| Ladle | We | Red snooker ball | Desktop | Mixed race, Afro-Caribbean | Fergie | Houston | Mangoes |
| Wooden spoon | You (plural) | Cricket ball | Notebook | Redheaded, curls | Britney Spears | Paris | Apples |
| Teaspoon | They | Golf ball | Tablet PC | Sophisticated, sleek, older | Albert Einstein | Warsaw | Kumquats |
| Dessert spoon | Nobody | Football | iPhone | Brunette, curvaceous | An 'ordinary' person | Managua | Kiwis |

feel of the campaign, is selecting from within 'paradigms' seeking (for example) a face to serve as a sign to embody certain qualities in the overall text. Likewise a creative team suggesting a new celebrity endorser might, without thinking explicitly in such terms, consider paradigmatic variances – in look, attitude, age and so on, across a fine-grained profile seeking a sign conveying the right qualities in the overall ad – as a prelude to deciding whose face would slot into the campaign. Likewise for settings, props and so on. Selection is a matter of orchestrating signs (in complex detailed combinations) towards the developing campaign product-sign-image.

Such acts of selection are more or less intuitive; they operationalise acute cultural sensibilities about the meanings and impacts that particular signs (iconic, symbolic, indexical) in combination (e.g. a person, a word, a cityscape, a fruit, the curve of an eyebrow, age, stance, melody or typeface and so on) might solicit in the overall frame of the advertisement. They may be accompanied by the agonistics of creatives' certainties and doubts, clients' preferences or practical constraints, and then once assembled, anxiously tested and researched. Will the sign-components convey what we intend them to mean? The semiotic work of encoding – of appropriate meaning-making – is the half-conscious and half-spontaneous work of selection: adjusting, refining, editing, accepting, rejecting, and discriminating between signifiers across innumerable cultural 'paradigms' to the dictates of a creative brief and as modulated through the selected sensibilities and intuitions of the creative team operating, as far as possible, to an agreed brand and cultural 'vision' or style – and tailored to the constraints of half a page or 30 seconds of advertisement.

Equally important is how the selected signifier fits into the ad alongside all the other selected elements. Syntagm describes the 'axis of combination' (the complementary opposite of the paradigm (Jacobson's (1960: 368) 'axis of selection') We might know the related word syntax, which is a linguistic term used in computing languages; for example you get a 'syntax error' when there is a term out of place in a coded instruction to the computer. Syntagm is another kind of series in which elements are placed in order. However, the syntagmatic series requires that we place different elements according to type. Jacobson (1960) calls syntagm the 'axis of combination'. For example a simple sentence structure of Subject–Verb–Object combines words selected from three separate paradigms in a grammatically-correct syntactic order (Subject/Verb/Object). Examples don't have to be language-based, however. For instance a conventional outfit might include shoes, trousers, jacket and shirt – elements *selected* from possible choices of shirts, shoes and trousers (paradigms) and *combined* to 'match' and fulfil expected *syntactic* conventions.

**Table 6.2** Examples of syntagm: axis of combination

| Axis of selection ▼ | Paradigm: people who do things ▼ | Paradigm: actions or verbs/things people do ▼ | Paradigm: objects on which actions are taken ▼ |
|---|---|---|---|
| Linguistic paradigms | I | THROW | THE BALL |
| | YOU | KICK | THE TOMATO |
| | WE | SQUASH | THE BEE |
| | CHILDREN | EAT | BACTERIA |
| | WE | SHARE | WINE |
| Non-linguistic paradigms | Paradigm: Shoes | Paradigm: Trousers | Paradigm: Shirts |
| | Trainers | Jeans | T-shirt |
| | Brogues | Chinos | Formal shirt |
| ◄——————————— Syntagm ———————————► | | | |
| Axis of combination | | | |

These examples (Table 6.2) of grammatical syntax are (symbolic) signifiers, words from the English language. It is important to understand that we don't just speak in syntaxes composed of paradigmatic elements. We inhabit cultural convention through the intersection of selection and combination – clothes for example. Box 6.1 offers examples of basic syntactic relations, taken from the world of objects, arrangements selected from objects/ideas which we know 'go together' in accepted syntactic patterns.

It should be possible to see from these examples that a syntagm is a mode of serial organisation that typically provides a narrative format; it is in any case connective. Syntaxes are the unspoken rules stating what 'agrees' with what in series, and what comes before or after what – in combination. The first example shows a syntagm defined by the conventional order of eating utensils – even cutlery can be seen as 'syntactic' in the conventional arrangement and combination of elements.

Likewise the advertisement genre has established basic generative and combinatory forms which allow for syntagmatic organisation of elements from differing paradigms in a way that readers are able to find acceptable, when, in other situations, such combinations might represent a 'syntax error' – a combination of different elements selected from paradigms which may formerly and formally not be allowed by sense or convention to readily compose a comprehensible relationship.

## Box 6.1 EXAMPLES OF BASIC SYNTACTIC RELATIONS

| Syntactic combinations of paradigmatic elements | Explication and elaboration |
|---|---|
| Knife, fork, spoon | These utensils are selected from the three paradigms knives, forks and spoons on the basis of an organising principle which specifies eating utensils and cultural conventions around consumption of food. |
| January, February, March, April, May, June, July, August, September, October, November, December | Both a paradigm – twelve months – and a syntactic series – an expected sequential order. The association between products and natural cycles of seasons and holidays (Christmas in particular) is central to a good deal of advertising activity. |
| Slippers, pyjamas, book, stairs, bed | The advertising example Figure 6.9 shows inserts Galaxy chocolate into a syntax around bedtime ritual – the product inserted to 'complete' the series – an attempt to bind the product to everyday routines. |
| Purple grapes and green leaves, a laptop computer, a glass of wine | The advertisement example in Figure 6.1 shows a montage arrangement of visual signs brought together in a spatial syntax by the formal genre expectations of the reader, the text and the layout on the page. The syntax that is naturalised in the ad ties iconic, indexical and symbolic signs to bind fresh authentic ingredients, to vineyard manufacture, to Internet purchase, and to culturally legitimated social-enjoyment and acceptance of the service proposition – e-vineyard.com (Figure 6.1). |

It should be clear that some syntagmatic arrangements of paradigmatic elements are more acceptable than others – but also that disruptions of syntax are often noticeable. They jar and startle. 'Knife, fork, bucket' makes us think twice. 'Knife, fork, spoon' makes a good syntagm – especially if we are used to inhabiting a culture where this is the normative array of utensils expected for eating (as in many but not all cultures). A person deeply bound to a more formal ethic of eating might see this as a basic listing; a person committed to informality might see it as overly elaborate: surely just a fork would do! Conversely a moral statement about deviance might be directed at someone who insisted on eating all meals (and all courses) with only a spoon, flouting the 'natural' order of things. Advertisers of Müller yoghurt have presented an ad in which a cutlery-less man, desiring to eat yoghurt, improvises a spoon from a photograph of a long-lost love. The intent is to show appetite unbounded by constraints of custom, an effect easily achieved by disrupting established syntactic and paradigmatic patterns in the conventional organisation of rituals around eating. The ad signifies the product (yoghurt) into a 'special' position in relation to 'normal foods' (eaten normally), while also depicting an urgent new relation between eater and the advertised yoghurt – under the slogan heading 'Müller love' – implying an equation between Müller-branded products and conventional romantic passion.

Kelloggs' Crunchy Nut cornflakes are routinely advertised by displaying such aberrant performances, in one recent instance collapsing the temporal narrative syntax – pour flakes in bowl, add milk, pick up spoon, take food, put in mouth and so on – by showing the milk poured directly into the cereal box, and then the mixture being 'drunk' from the box by a manically hungry man. Kellogg's thereby syntactically encodes the person–thing relation for Crunchy Nut cornflakes as not ordinary but *mad*. The product then sits, relative to others, as a marker of a mode of mock-eccentric everyday hedonism, thereby re-presenting a banal cereal – perhaps a semi-routine purchase – as a signifier whose consumers' 'passionate non-conformity' signifies a way of investing 'excitement' and 'disturbance' into breakfast routines

The Bertolli ad (Figure 6.6) plays with the verbal text, inserting a sign of the product 'nibble' tying it, jokingly, within a syntactic arrangement connected to 'natural' advertising codes of romance and mythical conceptions of Italians' reputations as lovers, and lovers of food. The ad text is a space where hitherto unrelated qualities (love and bread-bite nibbles) are selectively bound to one another in the syntactic frame of the advertising text. Innocent smoothie advertising integrates its product array into the cycle of the year, drawing on the syntactic narrative ordering

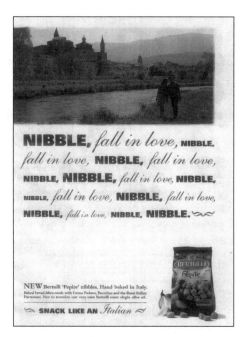

**Figure 6.6** Bertolli Pepite plays with syntax in the copy, inserting a sign of the product, 'Nibble', into a repetitive cultural narrative.

**Figure 6.7** Innocent integrates its product array into the syntactic cycle of the year.

**Figure 6.8** An initially uncongenial syntagm 'Children eat bacteria' is explained, secured and naturalised throughout Yakult's ad campaigns.

**Figure 6.9** Galaxy: the product is placed as a plausible component of a bedtime ritual.

of month by month change, and associated their drinks with the cultural and natural cycles of the calendar.

In Table 6.2 (above) the syntax or narrative 'children eat bacteria' might stand out as one of the less acceptable syntactic arrangements in a culture where bacteria are seen as primarily contaminants. However this syntactic conjunction has been effectively naturalised by advertisers of 'pro-biotic' products such as Yakult, thus transforming an unacceptable proposition, linking something culturally 'dangerous' with something nurtured ('good' bacteria and children, respectively) into an acceptable one – naturalising bacteria consumption as a daily practice associated with fun and health. In anthropological terms, danger is transformed into purity (Douglas 1966). The image Figure 6.8 is a visual sign affirming this conjunction for us.

The advertisement for Galaxy (Figure 6.9) is able to situate the product in a narrative arrangement attempting to secure an association between the chocolate bar and relaxation. One has only to imagine a different selection from the paradigms 'clothes' and 'things people take to bed' to envisage a viable ad that positions the chocolate bar differently. The product is placed in syntagmatic and narrative relations with selected signs from the paradigms, footwear, bed wear and 'things to take to bed'.

## FRAMING: ADVERTISING LAYOUT

While the syntagmatic relations provided appear as serial and narrative, it is a further feature of the advertising genre that it allows, in its juxtaposition of images, words and sounds, the forging of acceptable syntagmatic relationships by asserting formal *spatial* relationships between signifiers within the signifying field of the text, or by linking sign elements by colour-coding. So although narrative is a key tool in advertising, various techniques of montage, colour-coding, layout and counterpoint are also used – always, however, with the generic pur-pose of producing in the space of the text a credible conjunction of signs binding products to eye-catching series of cultural signs.

This aspect of advertising textuality that co-ordinates signs and significa-tion in space is the work of framing. Just as unrelated paradigmatic signifiers, connoting disparate values and outlandish settings are made sensible by the assertion of familiar narrative and syntactic orderings and by denotative depictions, so the conventional layout of the to-be-combined signifying elements is used to try to better assure that the audience makes proper sense – and sensibility – entertaining the advert's intended play of associa-tive signs. It is the spatial and syntactic structures of layout that best assure the intended equations between product and connoted significations.

Goldman (1992) describes (in this instance with reference to an ad showing a model advertising perfume) a basic ad's generic patterning working to encourage:

> readers to see the model's perceived attributes (the signified) embodied in the bottle, so that she might hope to appropriate, upon purchase, the promise of the sign inscribed on the bottle.
>
> (Goldman 1992: 27)

This happens because we have become used to linking up the discreet 'frames' in an advertising text – slogan to logo to imagery to product shot. This is evident in print ads. But readers are habituated to equivalent pattering operations in TV and radio ads.

Van Leeuwen (2005; Kress and Van Leeuwen 1996) describe the ways texts and spaces utilise framing. Van Leeuwen (2005) offers insightful semiotic accounts of spatial and temporal organisation across a number of genres and other areas of activity – including ads, but also office space, village layouts and music. The underlying point is that semiotics can

---

**Box 6.2 VAN LEEUWEN'S TYPOLOGY OF AD TEXT LAYOUT: SEMIOTIC CONNECTIONS AND SEPARATIONS WITHIN PRINT ADVERTISEMENTS**

- Segregation: two or more elements are separated by empty space, and this indicates that they should be seen as belonging to different orders
- Separation: two or more elements occupy entirely different territories, and suggests that they should be seen as similar in some respects and different in others
- Integration: text and picture occupy the same space – either the text is integrated in (e.g., superimposed on) the pictorial space, or the picture in the textual space
- Overlap: frames may be porous – for example, part of the picture may break through the frame or letters may be half in the pictorial space and half in the textual space
- Rhyme: two elements, although separate, have a quality in common – what that quality is depends on the common feature (for example, a colour, a feature of form such as angularity or roundness, etc).
- Contrast: two elements differ in terms of a quality (as realised by a colour, or by formal features, etc).

(Source: Van Leeuwen 2005: 13)

register patterning of connection and disconnection, association and disassociation.

Such dynamics can be usefully traced in advertising textual organisation. Van Leeuwen outlines the following types of connection and disconnection derived from his analysis of a sample of advertisements.

To sum up then: advertising texts operate in contexts of culture and situation. Advertising representations strive to integrate product and imagery through conjunctions of component signs, product details, logo and brand ideas. The hoped-for associative integrations that the ad texts invite and affirm aim to credibly bind sign and product in three main ways:

- connotation is naturalised in denotation – unexpected conjunctions rendered acceptable and normative within the genre codes;
- paradigmatic qualities are selected and bound to products by advertisements' syntactic patterning via appropriated cultural narratives, myths, stories and ritual ordering;
- framing and colour coding formally link elements to underscore associations between the signs projected upon and through the overall frame of the ad text.

## TEXTUAL ANALYSIS

The following analysis of Figure 6.1 attempts to explicate some of these processes. As with any textual reading of this kind the analysis can be neither exhaustive nor definitive. The analytic reading operates, just like much advertising signification, primarily in registers of suggestion and allusion.

### eVineyard.com analysis: a simple passion we like to share

Selling wine on the Internet poses a tricky advertising problem as it is a traditional and relatively elite product, popular with older consumers, who may retain some mistrust of e-commerce, in general, and for selling wine in particular. A recent analysis of problems facing wine sellers gives some sense of the 'culture' around wine consumption, and of marketing conceptions of consumers:

> Market researchers have come up with the concept of 'Chardonnay girl', an 18–24 working-class woman who has a 'wide drinks repertoire', with wine

slotted in as an early evening drink. There is also the 'Adventurer', a man (or sometimes woman) from the professional and managerial classes, who does not know a lot about wine but who likes to experiment. What advertising campaign could possibly convince both? Do you make it sexy? Emphasise how easy it is to drink? Sweeten the wines and slap on cheeky labels? Associate it with sex and sand? Can the 18–24s be weaned away from beer and spirits?

(Burk 2003)

This excerpt from a brief analysis of the wine marketplace is a useful preamble to thinking about the semiotics of the ad, in a cultural, marketing and product-focused context.

Glancing at the images the advertisement Figure 6.1 shows a bunch of grapes and a laptop with a glass of wine on its screen – in the bottom right corner. Perhaps it is the grapes that stand out – a purple 'juicy' patch of freshness and colour – grasping our attention as it becomes intelligible – drawing us into the ad. There are three blocks of text, a headline slogan 'It's a Simple Passion We Like to Share', and a longer body of text, describing the website, its wine-selling service and something of the ethic of the company (or its brand). Finally, at the bottom of the page, 'eVineyard.com' and a tag line, 'wine anyone?'

Closer inspection reveals this as an advertisement for a service, rather than for a product. Still closer attention confirms that the advertisement is proposing we visit a website. The text allows us, at the denotative level, to link up the signifiers and (in so doing) develop a concept – a signified, which includes the idea – the proposition – that if we want some wine, as we might, then we can buy wine from eVineyard.com, a website offering a range of wines from different countries. The advertiser eVineyard.com is an Internet wine company. While a number of product sectors do very well on the Internet each product sector presents its specific problems. Internet advertisements attempt to manage these. The ad text – found on the Internet – offers a relatively simple communication, with one dominant image, a bunch of grapes, at the centre of the ad. Looking more closely, the written language poses no problems provided we can read English.

'eVineyard.com' may make us look twice. Still discernibly English, this 'word', or perhaps better 'brand-signature', signifies an Internet address, and names the company, both basic symbolic-linguistic significations. But, and at the same time 'eVineyard.com' offers up a connotative sense; bringing to mind and affirming a certain up-to-date-ness (and 'precision' and 'immateriality') of specifically Internet-based commerce – in opposition to brands such as, say, Oddbins, Victoria Wine or a local supermarket.

These connotations overlay a second and opposing sense. The 'Vineyard', compressed between 'e' and 'com', brings to mind a verbal sign referring to traditions of rusticity and direct wine purchase, 'from the land'. In addition, perhaps, it suggests further signs, French-ness, 'a year in Provence', establishing feelings of authenticity referencing a mythic French countryside, culturally to hand for a target market who might make an (intertextual) link to TV or tourist-based knowledge of vineyards – and especially as juxtaposed – an intra-textual cross reference back – to the iconic sign: the grapes image.

The modern suffix and prefix ('e-' and '.com' respectively) offer a satisfyingly discrepant code within which to bracket connoted tradition: 'vineyard'. This minor rhetorical gesture illustrates a key semiotic idea: that the juxtaposition of codes from formally distinct areas of life produces 'texture'. Here the brand-signature balances abstraction against authenticity – this is part of the semiosis afforded by the ad.

The key word in the advertisement is 'passion'; the ambiguity in the word releases potential associations, is a minor pun. The first is the general sense of 'passion', which enlivens the advertisement, humanises the space of the sign (and thus the transaction it is trying to promote). The link between 'passion', the purple of the grapes and their fullness, injects the sign, makes it 'juicy' – invites, if we bypass cliché, a feeling into the experience. But all is understated; there is nothing *too* exciting going on in this ad.

A second sense of 'a . . . passion' is available concurrently; more disciplined semiosis might connect (qua interpretant) to the symbolic sign 'passion' in the paradigm of 'passions' understood as cultural pursuits or enthusiasms: golf, gardening, various kinds of collecting . . . wine. An ad not strongly coded by gender, this connotation peculiarly suggests the manifestation of a *male* sense of 'passion', in the sense of hobbies/enthusiasms. Feminine 'passion' in advertising, most often, has a different connotation (romantic and sexual). 'Simple' bypasses 'passion' as 'passionate' and seems to settle the ad in favour of passion as 'enthusiasm'.

More generally the text invites imaginings set in a world of togetherness. The words have been selected to emphasise the sociable and simple nature of drinking wine, binding, with a classical three-part list, the virtues of 'good friends', 'good times' and 'good wine'. This written text serves to ward off unwanted associations of snobbery, still mythically associated with wine, a residue from its social uses before its democratisation (via supermarkets and journalism) in the 1970s, but also of excess, a taboo attaching to alcohol, however loosely, as a licensed product. The ad text grounds the proposed act of consumption, invoking a balanced communalism, neither excessive social restraint (snobbism or coterie) nor hedonistic excess (binge, bar room or lone drinking).

More particularly, the *commercial* (and impersonal) nature of participation in this service – ordering wine online – is suppressed in favour of a communalism evoked by 'sharing'. This is a two-fold strategy. First it performs the age-old advertising manoeuvre that offers commercial relations in the form of quasi-membership of a 'group', here suitably non-exclusive yet also legitimated by a gesture towards the rhetoric of cultural education 'we'll introduce you . . .'. Importantly this de-commercialisation, performed at the level of the text, serves (also)to allay any potential mistrust attached to the Internet as a location of financial exchange.

'Sharing' occludes the reality of a transaction that will, of course, be both commercial and electronic, both abstract and distant, facts that will remain whether or not the overall experience is educational, friendly or retains any of the other connotative qualities – associated signs – momentarily 'liberated' and in mind via the textures of signification. The ad text channels any negative ideas – dispatches them – by the counteractive mobilisation of less alienating connotations: friends, vineyard, sharing, real fruit, amiable, serious but lightly held connoisseurship, culture, etc.

The written text functions as 'anchorage', a role Barthes describes as 'elucidation', but also as a control, 'bearing responsibility – in the face of the projective power of pictures – for the use of the message' (Barthes 1977b: 40). The text performs a particular function here, acting as a 'counter taboo', perhaps warding off 'bad' semiosis (e.g. associations with technophobia, residual puritanical anxieties around indulgence, fear of commercialism, insecurity about wine buying, distrust of Internet commerce, anti-marketing, tasteless abstraction (i.e. absent product, e-clinical-ness) and corralling signifying ingredients towards 'good' semiosis (juiciness, camaraderie, sharing, seriousness, casualness, learning and so on). The work the text does – to corral and accumulate positive signification, and to undermine or counteract bad associations is unlikely to be binding or total.

There are two distinct visual signs set out on the page (within the total sign of the advertisement). First, and most prominent, is the bunch of grapes, fringed by green leaves. Less prominent (by size), an image of a laptop computer is given emphasis because it occupies the bottom right corner of the page. This position is the conventional location for tag lines, logos and artist's signatures – so has accrued special importance in (westerners') visual 'grammar' of the page. The laptop screen displays a glass of red wine – red chosen over white – *perhaps* encoding, connoisseurship, with red wine (arguably) a more 'serious' drink than white – and perhaps more 'adventurer' than 'Chardonnay girl' (Burk 2003, cited above).

A frequent motif in advertising is a reference to the medium in which it is being viewed. This incidence of self-reference is not entirely analogous with, for instance, TV advertisements which show viewers watching TV, because in this case the medium, the laptop computer, and by implication the Internet constitutes part of the message. The 'product' is, in part, just this Internet link. Nevertheless here (again with an eye on significance) a (paradigmatic) *selection* has been made (and encoded). A laptop has very different connotations from a desktop – mostly associated with 'mobility' – which is both a practical and a social 'virtue' (to do with an opposition between 'home and work' and between individualism, independence and family 'connectedness'), one primarily asserting citizenship in the world of 'information' – business and 'white-collar' working.

The iconic sign of the grapes appears there by virtue of an act of careful selection, even the 'casual' is posed in advertising. Just any old bunch of grapes will not do. Along with the green tinges, offsetting the deep burgundy colour of the bunch, the retention of leaves announces 'nature' and in particular a certain rawness: the leaves distinguish these grapes from those cultivated (and prepared) for eating, securing (by this distinction) the thoughts of grapes picked fresh from a vineyard and destined for processing: the raw grapes as an indexical sign of a process that ends with 'cooked' wine.

The grapes form an iconic sign, which also has an indexical relationship with 'wine', a constituent (but not exhaustive) element of the sign that completes the advertising sign, and which is *not* arbitrary. There is a certain logical relationship between grapes and wine, indexical, in Peirce's sense, which can be further described as 'metonymy' – a rhetorical figure where the part comes to represent the whole. In a similar example Barthes suggests a further refinement, 'asyndeton', to describe the rhetorical strategy of depicting, serially, coffee bean, coffee as powder and coffee in a cup (Barthes 1977b: 50). This rhetorical figure performs narrative by omission, with montage and juxtaposition of signs provoking a tacit 'filling in' thought process composed in web-browsing semiosis – sign, interpretant, object, representamen, sign and so on: a more or less perfunctory, more or less restrained dialogic engagement of textuality.

The grapes, the laptop, the glass of wine appear (at a glance) as 'so many scattered blocks', discontinuous and unconnected by any obvious logic or the extensive associations that might emerge. The composition helps ground the syntax and binds the signs together. In the space of the advertisement signs are 'mounted' and 'set' in a syntagm that is 'not theirs and which is that of the denotation'. Barthes continues:

discontinuous connotators are connected, actualised and spoken through the syntagm of the denotation, the discontinuous connotators as though into a lustral bath of innocence. The discontinuous world of symbols plunges into the story of the denoted scene.

(Barthes 1977b: 51)

Ads work by a fusion of a syntagmatic order of denoted signification with a paradigmatic order of sign/interpretant. Thus, in the space of the ad, scattered iconic, symbolic and indexical signs, drawn into the space of display and interpretation, gain associations (feelings and ideas) from disparate (hinted and glimpsed) cultural, personal and bodily sources (technology, neighbourliness, nature, pleasure, longing, loneliness, thirst) and can coalesce and inhabit a (montage) 'story' – in the conventionally ordered visual plane of the ad text – with a kind of 'logic', an *implicature*, that links them together – intelligibly, and perhaps (momentarily) indexing desire, affect and even action.

Put another way, the generic form of the ad, the basic components that are easily understood and placed in conventional order as we gauge and collate the contents of (latent, but understood) advertising frames (body copy, main image, pack shot, slogan, etc.) invite with them secondary components (new signs brought to mind) that (might) suddenly appear more acceptable by virtue of inhabiting representation in the sensible space of the accepted form of the total sign – the advertisement. The product-sign (in semiosis) breaches our horizon of cultural meaningfulness: we might buy or buy into the sign in the form of its proxy 'presence'; as product, service or brand idea.

The following chapters look at the ways that many of the genre conventions operating in advertising have come under pressure. Audiences' stock critiques and apathy in the face of ad formulae, cultural shifts in modes and means of representation and media dissemination and changing advertising and branding priorities registered within the industry have together reframed the routinised generic conventions of text and reception. Advertising continues to change in interesting ways, even while, in many other ways it retaining longstanding, well-established characteristics and semiotic gestures.

# 7

# NEW FORMS AND INTIMACIES

## RHETORICAL ADVERTISING

Advertising, as Wernick (1991) says, is a form of rhetoric. Rhetorical skill is part of what advertising agencies are hiring out to their clients, and rhetorical aims – to persuade, inform and impress – have typically governed the form of advertisements. 'Rhetoric' usually describes the spoken and written arts. Because it has been associated with classical culture and with verbal communication, rhetoric is considered to describe a language of 'the past'. However, classic rhetorical methods and intents have continuities within today's technologically sophisticated and semiotically enriched media-based advertising, in terms of function (e.g. to persuade), and in terms of some of its forms or figures (McQuarrie and Mick 1996). Voice-over artists (informal or grave) and copywriters (straightforward or 'purple') are exercising versions of the ancient arts of rhetoric, as are sales people, celebrity endorsers, telemarketers and party political broadcasters; even art directors and editors, as they cut an ad to achieve a dramatic crescendo or when they lay out a page, deploy a 'rhetoric' of sorts.

Contemporary advertising is a semiotically-charged multiply-mediated form of public speaking (advertising is after all governed in the US under laws of free *speech*). As a rhetorical art advertising has developed its various characteristic mannerisms – the generic features alluded to in a number of ways so far. As the media and consumer environments are becoming more complex, and as consumers' sensibilities are changing – in no small part as a result of the ever-uneasy experiences of consumer culture – it is evident that rhetorical styles and manners are also all the while changing, even breaking down, or, as some might see it, breaking *out*, so that the advertising genre diversifies – with Internet and digital media providing particular pressures on old forms and outlets for new ones.

## CHANGING ADVERTISING

Tried and tested forms of advertising address continue to be used unreflectively today but consumers are understood increasingly to ignore or ridicule 'lazy', patronising or outmoded advertising. The advertising industry confronted by this state of affairs sometimes appears to be at a loss, even exhausted. Berger (2001) offers a to-the-point version of what has become something of an industry mantra:

> Almost everyone, including advertising's most dedicated practitioners, freely acknowledges that the vast majority of it is banal, unimaginative and mind-numbing. We've all winced at those hyperactive car commercials heralding a 'sale-a-bration!' at the local dealership . . . and the detergent ads in which stains on shirts disappear for the hundredth time . . . We've flipped through endless fashion-magazines' ads so posed and lifeless they seem to bore even the models appearing in them.
>
> (Berger 2001: 9)

'Cliché' is the default critical response to poor advertising inside and outside the industry. However *this* ad, or *that* campaign, *this* creative team or *that* agency is the 'exception', so that, as Berger and others are able to show, there are a lot of ads which people like, which win awards and which are treated as a valued part of everyday 'culture' (Alperstein 2003; O'Donohoe 1997; Fowles 1996; Nava and Nava 1992); and lots of ads (evidently) that clients are persuaded to pay for. However, less celebrated ads should be remembered when defining and evaluating the genre. The 'vast majority' of industry output described by Berger (2001) as 'banal' must have nevertheless been *made*, presumably despite the seemingly laborious and censorious processes of pitching, testing and hot-house creativity that preface publication or broadcast.

Among the many generalisations to be avoided around advertising are those which posit either 'artistic creativity' or 'mechanical dullness' as *the* exclusive condition (including the 'next' or the 'past' condition) of the advertising genre; not particularly in the name of discriminating sensibility (ethical or aesthetic), but because, to reiterate, such sweeping statements imply a unitary and common purpose, a shared modality across the millions of daily instances of advertising communications. Advertising texts are momentary crystallisations inflected by competing agendas from local or global marketers, from research, from creative ambitions, from competitors, from changes within the product sector, from regulatory interpretations, from convenience, serendipity and opportunity. As such, advertisements do not readily constitute particulars upon which an account of the 'general' condition of advertising should be too readily based.

This is just to be borne in mind as a preamble to thinking about illustrations and examples which seem contrariwise to suggest a general transition into a 'new' advertising; one which is quite legitimately (see Larson 2003; Nixon 2003; Mort 1997; Dobrow 1984) regularly announced and re-announced. So while undoubtedly there are new developments, any narrative of obsolescence and renewal needs to be tempered with the acknowledgement that continuities in tastes, formats, styles and purposes are as much a part of the contemporary advertising genre as genuine novelty. Phases, cycles, contradiction and retrospection rather than plain progress or phased transition describe the true dynamics of change when 'advertising' is considered in shorthand and as a 'whole'.

## DISARMING ADVERTISEMENTS

Advertising (since the 1970s, and indeed before) often appears anxiously conscious of itself and its tools. As even a cursory glance will confirm, contemporary advertisements do not uniformly or automatically follow basic formats to deliver the product message, an aspirational 'lifestyle image' or the latest USP.[1] A conspicuous fraction of contemporary advertisements (in all media) do not simply extol various expected 'virtues' or even set the product up as a prop in a desirable milieu. Williams' magic system seems to be changing. Advertising creative Hal Riney, in a 2002 article in the American advertising trade press expressed the widely held view that 'after at least two generations of TV bombardment in the US, the magic of traditional advertising is no longer magic' (Riney, cited in Cappo 2003: 85). This conclusion holds across the main advertising media.

In terms of 'values', ads do not now always (just) routinely 'add a bit of glamour' or promise success with the opposite sex, at work, or in parenting and so on. In terms of form, basic or outright low production values are celebrated (in the UK Phones4U, Ocean Finance and McDonald's have recently shown ads with a 'home-made' feel) and 'bad' scripts become cults (Ferrero Rocher continuing to 'spoil us' throughout the 1990s). These sit alongside self-consciously artful opulence (Chanel No. 5, Jaguar) aiming to stand out by overstating advertising's alleged 'flaws' (moral materialism, glamour and unreality). Elsewhere 'risky' human themes – 'bad' mothering (Müller yoghurt); awkward parenting in non-nuclear families (BT); selfish greed (Terry's Chocolate Oranges); 'geek-ishness'(Yakult); immaturity (Carling, WKD) – each and all is admitted. Such culturally 'iconoclastic' ads perform a challenge to imaginary cultural 'boundaries' – boundaries that have long been bypassed in other genres and between the ad breaks, but which strive to provoke some feeling and engagement, some flicker of the unexpected, a jolt in the train of thought and a nudge and a wink to the audience: 'we're in this together'.

In short much contemporary advertising (especially in markets where advertising has a lengthy and prolific history) has long since ceased to rely (exclusively) on its stock of formulaic imagery, rhetoric and technique.[2] Ad-makers have striven to design a more 'human' element into the genre, and consequently ad watchers have frequently noted a retreat from advertising as a genre claiming to represent a quasi-religious socially sanctioned consumerism – status driven materialism and its attendant ethos – and towards more fragmentary and contradictory communications and gestures.

## HEROIC TO COMIC

If ads ever tended mostly to be *heroic* (in ethos and narrative) they are now as often as not *comic* – not merely in the sense of joking (ads have always made people laugh), but in the identifications and relationships they invite. Today's advertising (in some instances) more readily admits (a sense of) the all too human: a compromised and imperfect world view associated with comedic sensibilities – a more embodied sense of relationships between people and products – more material than ideal. Almost always and at the same time flanked by the expected ideal bodies, faces and places (inside and outside the ad text), there are ads that seek engagement at more 'human' scale. Figure 7.1 shows a recent TV ad for a cranberry juice drink.

Clearly this ad serves to disturb the ordinary expectations of viewers presented with bikini-clad models in an ad for a food product. The ad makes use of the familiar voice of comedian Kathy Burke (popular in the UK in a variety of 'down to earth' character roles) and produces a comedic intimacy in the space of the ad – traditional identification may be invited by sleek models, but, more likely, viewers will engage with (advertising's version of) a critical realism about the advertising promise. The ad asserts a reversal of the 'typical' advertising work (of conjunction between product and idealised image) and, with mild humorous effect, produces an opportunity for a more intimate identification – with (Burke's) critical sensibility – that quashes the expected promise.

VOICE-OVER: 'Ocean Spray may be full of New England cranberries, antioxidants and Vitamin C but don't kid yourself that will make you look like them. They were born that way, lucky cows.'

**Figure 7.1** Ocean Spray cranberry – authenticity as an ideal and as a performative (meta-) communicative event.

This is not critical realism in the academic sense. A marketing message (or perhaps better a marketing *moment*) is achieved. For a start we hear the selling propositions (New England cranberries, antioxidants and Vitamin C) but in particular the voice-over provokes a moment of 'meta-communication' (Bateson 1972) intending both to startle and charm jaded consumers – just as the 'over the top' hazy beauty of the scene hints at parody. It is in such metacommunication that new intimacies are forged, and this is where much contemporary advertising works – paradoxically attempting to continue to assure marketing relationships in a genre that increasingly must trade in signs attesting to and resonant with audiences' avowed critical sensibility *against* consumerism, commodities and market relations.

The slogan framed by the Cranberry commodity in its natural, pure and abundant state 'real goodness from a real place' asserts an iconic sign producing a vivid essence for the total product sign. The final frame underlines and is underlined by the ad's appeal to and performance of 'authenticity'. This alongside the 'intimate' joking form of the ad achieves a consistency with the marketing brief; to assert the authenticity of the product. This is done not (just) by relaying the ideal of authenticity (through traditional advertising signification) so much as *by a textual performance of authenticity* (in tone of voice and in the humorous subversion of genre expectations).

This very basic ad for elephant motor insurance (Figure 7.2) is one of a series in which, again with a comedic effect, ordinary acts of communication are shown to break down mid flow. The ad deliberately parodies a commonplace motif in ads[3] (the cards originally used by Bob Dylan) is 'sampled' in numerous advertisements. Any precise link to the significance of the original performance disappears in such re-contextualisation.

VOICE-OVER : Are you finding your car insurance a bit of a handful?
Well with elephant.co.uk you can get a quote in minutes and we can save
you money. Why? Because elephant.co.uk is direct online, which means
lower costs so you can save even more money on your car insurance
so if you want to get your hands on even cheaper car insurance check
out elephant.co.uk we really could save you money it's easy it's fast it's
elephant.co.uk check it out.

**Figure 7.2** Ad for elephant.co.uk.

In the elephant.co.uk campaign the process of ad-making and filming
is pulled into the frame of the ad, just as in post-modern restaurants, the
kitchen is in full view of the eating space – a certain 'illusion' is foregone
and 'production processes' are exposed in the name of intimacy:
Authenticity asserted by the 'frank' exposure of artifice.

The Dylan cue card technique has been copied by numerous ad and pop
promo makers. It is now a cliché in itself and the elephant.co.uk ad trades
on the incongruity of the mascot (another ad cliché) and the cue cards.
We see the ad falling apart in the making.

There is nothing, in the voice-over, to distinguish this ad from a
thousand hard sell clichés characteristic of this product sector. Low cost
motor insurance is not that easy to advertise, since, typically, it is a product
where the price and details of the insurance policy provide clear grounds
for discrimination. Insurance, as a financial service, is an area where image-
based advertising is hard to swallow; a consideration doubtless prominent
in the minds of the ad creatives. Instead the campaign rests on depicting
the constant 'on set' failures of the cast, crew and mascot to make the

advert 'properly'. This 'behind the scenes on stage' and reality into comedy–drama hybrids approach correlates in many contemporary popular arts – for instance the American sitcoms *The Larry Sanders Show* or *Curb Your Enthusiasm*.

## 'REAL' STORIES: PSEUDO 'DIVINE' TO 'ALL TOO HUMAN'

This repudiation of past advertising cliché (advertising cannibalising its forms and canons) includes a (partial and occasional) repudiation of *some* consumerist ideals. Ads do not show the world 'warts 'n' all', an aspiration outside the advertising remit and beyond even more sophisticated communicative genres' attempts at 'honest' representation. However, the forms and representational strategies apparent on our pages and screens are heavily inflected by the techno-aesthetic gestures circulating across pop culture, the sensibilities and formats of reality TV, alternative comedy, pop art and its performance variants as well as cinema. In the 1950s and 1960s the most ambitious advertising resembled Hollywood writ small; just now (on occasion) it seems, instead, to present *The Office* writ large.[4] The success of reality TV and its parodies, such as *The Office*, is part of a wider trend central to advertising and bound to a renewed consciousness of and pleasure in the artifice (in terms of creative production and in terms of credibility) of media communications. Advertising is a genre saturated in this self-consciousness – with authentication of the communication the underlying goal (Leiss *et al.* 2005; Gilmore and Pine 2007; Lewis and Bridger 2001).

For instance ads continue to use celebrities to do 'testimonials', but these celebrities are not always selected as straightforwardly heroic or admirable figures.[5] Instead they can be self-consciously chosen to challenge a (latent) and nostalgic conception of the standard celebrity role model ad (and its attendant cultural tenor – materialist consumerist conformity). Acknowledged 'faults' as much as virtues are traded. Famously the 'human' failings of 'disgraced' Kate Moss cost her a job in one campaign (H&M), but enhanced her worth in others – e.g. Rimmel and Virgin.

Sometimes 'real' people are used, corporate staff or 'satisfied and authentic-looking customers', a deliberate foil to celebrity glossiness and a ritually repudiated 'typical advertising' – a stepping back from the anonymous exemplars: perfected models, remote pseudo ideals. The successes of reality-TV-related formats have clearly inflected the advertising genre. Advertisement styles feed and feed on the fashion patterns of the surrounding media; all adjusting and re-adjusting across multiple and shared contexts of production and consumption.

## AD-MAKERS AND RENEWAL

The 'arts' and 'sciences' of advertising are always dying and being reborn; with every new breakaway agency, with every manifesto, with each new media technology advertising re-adapts. At the same time 'unwritten' rules, wise 'back to basics' maxims and 'classic' examples circulate in journals and in conversations, forming a permanent foil to ceaseless innovation (for instance Lance and Woll 2006).

Looking back on the 1990s, as Mort (1996) had on the 1980s, Nixon (2003) finds examples of young creatives who revile the clichés of the industry: another 'new era' for advertising. Perhaps *this* is the source of the rhetorical unease apparent in contemporary advertising. It may be the case that the experimental self-consciousness that seems at times to characterise some (but by no means all) advertising is simply a manifestation of the industry working, continually, to reflect on its practices: creatives working to integrate competing agendas. Thus it is a manifestation of the ongoing battle, ongoing from agency to agency, and from campaign to campaign, between clients' conventional insistence on advertising as a marketing form, and creative agencies' desire for aesthetic licence. Similarly it may simply represent a perverse displacement, from art to commerce, of the dialectical tension identified in the history of culture, between what T.S. Eliot (1920) called 'tradition and the individual talent' and which Harold Bloom (1973) described as producing 'the anxiety of influence', one generation's generic rules ceremonially rejected by 'new kids on the block'.

## SPEEDING UP

There is one area where change is clearly manifest. The genre is speeding up. Every surface of the TV ad world is moving faster. This change leaks into the genre from the quickening evident across culture – some have suggested the MTV generation is best attuned to the anti-narrative montage-cutting of pop videos. Fast action movies similarly work at a higher pace and quick-fire sitcom scripts have left more pedestrian delivery behind. Ads have picked up the same dynamism, one also apparent (in a different register) in the very processes of the economy – the volumes and rates of production and consumption of goods, services and experiences. Numerous writers (Jameson 1991; Harvey 1989) have found significance in the foreshortening of the sheer speed at which signs are processed and communicated. Lewis and Bridger (2000) identify a fundamental change to 'the soul of the new consumer':

> The acceptance of developing screen technologies . . . has reorganised our mental experience of space and time, no less than the high speed train and the aeroplane previously transformed our physical experience.
>
> (Holland, cited in Lewis and Bridger 2000: 153)

Specifically, this 'speeding up' of advertising has contributed towards a general movement in media communications towards rapidity.[6] The 'normal' pace of TV advertising (measured here in average shot length in seconds and average number of shots during an average 30-second advertisement increased from 8.9 to 13.2 and on average the shots became shorter (from 3.4 per second down to 2.3); see Table 7.1. A significant adjustment in audiences' engagements with advertising texts is suggested by MacLachlan and Logan (1993) and their study has been picked up by subsequent analysts (Lewis and Bridger 2001: 155–9; Chandler and Griffiths 2000). Advertising provides ample evidence of speedy and sometimes disorienting editorial cutting styles[7] associated with post-modern aesthetics (Jameson 1991; Postman 1986). Playing with traditional 'cutting tones' and camera angles (Goldman 1992) are examples of the 'experiments' advertising creatives engage with in the continual struggle to develop the genre and be commercially and (if possible) 'artistically' successful. As a consequence, today's audiences are ever more attuned to such strategies – developing 'advertising literacy' (O'Donohoe and Tynan 1998) but also apathy (Lewis and Bridger 2000: 9) towards commercial communications.

While it is not obvious what, if anything, such a speeding up indicates taken as a whole, it is clear that the faster-paced message is consistent with the analysis of a genre (contemporary TV advertising) operating (as an aggregate) in a register which is 'beyond' information delivery and (with many exceptions) moving more often towards sensory impact – such ads reward an alert sensory engagement, but not necessarily a (cognitive) search after meaningful information. This might make sense if considered in the light of the availability to advertisers (and consumers) of ever more accessible sources of information in press advertising, via websites and in consumer magazines. Thus, and as Richards *et al*. (2000) propose, with detailed evidence, it would be wrong to conclude that advertising as a whole is less information-rich: it is (instead) the case that *televisual* ads are increasingly relieved of the burden of information communication – and freed up to engage consumers in registers less suited to the delivery of facts or clear concepts. Advertising's 'informatic' function does not dis-appear, however; it is carried elsewhere – distributed across the numerous information sources in the integrated brand interface. There are further

**Table 7.1** Average shot length and average number of camera shots for 30-second TV commercials from a sample of 240 ads, 1980–91

| Year | Average shot length in seconds | Average number of shots |
|------|------|------|
| 1980 | 3.4 | 8.9 |
| 1982 | 3.9 | 7.6 |
| 1984 | 3.9 | 7.7 |
| 1986 | 2.9 | 10.3 |
| 1988 | 2.6 | 11.5 |
| 1989 | 2.3 | 12.9 |
| 1991 | 2.3 | 13.2 |

Source: MacLachlan and Logan (1993); Lewis and Bridger (2001); Chandler and Griffiths (2000).

changes in the advertising 'landscape', such that the genre is expanding and distorting in the face of new consumers and new competition.

## 'GENREQUAKE'

When Naomi Wolf identified a 'gender quake' (1991) people instinctively knew what she was referring to: a ground shift in relations between men and women, with knock-on effects across numerous fields of action and representation. It would be fair to say that contemporary advertising is facing what might be called a 'genrequake' of similar order, this driven in part by a shift in relations between consumers and producers, but also as a consequence of the exhausted uncertainty of established advertising forms. More prevalent in some media and product sectors than in others, advertisements, or rather the promotional imperatives that advertisements have succinctly and repetitively delivered, are now being redrawn through and across a variety of other media spaces and genres, blurring the boundaries between traditional media and traditional advertising. Most recently the Internet has, at times, been both a stimulus to and a locus for such changes – digital technologies providing further mechanisms towards a refiguring of advertising and its attendant communications-relations.

Donaton (2004) gives an indicative example, describing short films circulated on the Internet on behalf of BMW cars (also broadcast as films and released as a DVD in a series under the title 'The Hire'. *Powder Keg* is one in the series of five):

This movie, *Powder Keg*, was beautifully shot – on location in the United States and Mexico – and featured high production values, a haunting soundtrack, and solid acting performances. It was directed by the acclaimed filmmaker Alejandro Gonzalez-Inarritu. The driver was played by the handsome British actor Clive Owens. But the film didn't win any Academy awards – not for its screenplay, its direction, its acting, its music, or its cinematography.

In fact it wasn't even nominated.

In fact it wasn't even a movie.

It was an ad, a 10-minute commercial designed to show off the speed, handling, braking power of BMW's X5 sport utility vehicle.

(Donaton 2004: 97)

These hybrid 'adfilms' attest to a movement in promotional culture where genre boundaries are being moved, redrawn around film, TV formats and other kinds of cultural output. The line between ad as appendix to the body of culture is yielding (in some instances) to an attempted integration. The media-as-host and advertisement-as-parasite relationship identified by critics (e.g. Thompson 1932), or the ad-media symbiosis accepted as the default for commercial media, is being challenged by new media-advertising hybrid genres – such that critiques of parasitism on the media will give way to critiques of advertisers cloning media output. This produces a new order of anxiety for critics. Advertisers using this approach risk heightening the very cynicism in audiences that they are attempting to circumvent by deploying these new modes of address (such as the hybrid ad-film or the 'supermarket sponsored' cookery show). Legislation in Europe around product placement (Laitner 2007) will make it easier to broadcast such films on TV. The anticipated struggles of traditional advertising service providers in the face of a new media environment have been cited as legitimation for softening previous regulatory schemas about TV-based product placement (*The Economist*, 1 November 2007) indicating that such adaptations have institutional support.

The availability of the Internet as a form for the exchange and circulation of short films – e.g. via Facebook or YouTube – has quickly come to appeal to advertisers seeking the kudos of a so called 'underground', 'hip' and hence 'authentic' media space for brand communications – this especially as there is a sense that mainstream media are being rejected by a significant minority of creative and culturally alert audience members, audiences whose attention and esteem is highly valuable to brand owners. As mobile TV / MP3 technologies come on-stream and converge further with telephone and computing technologies it is through entertainment-rich (and hard-sell-marketing-lite) promotions such as these that the hi-tech-savvy

---

**Box 7.1 CHANEL No. 5 TURNS TO HOLLYWOOD**

The fashion house hopes *Moulin Rouge*'s star can inject some pizzazz into its 83-year-old scent.

It is the ultimate media placement. Viewers of the terrestrial TV premiere of the film *Moulin Rouge*, starring Nicole Kidman, on Channel 4 this Saturday, will also see the full three-minute version of a new campaign for Chanel No. 5 in its first break. The ad, like *Moulin Rouge*, is directed by Baz Luhrmann and features Kidman reprising her role from the movie.

Five months ago Chanel, working with Luhrmann's agent, approached Channel 4 suggesting the programme/ad deal. The agreement neatly dodges any regulatory issues, as ASA codes aimed at maintaining the separation of programming from ads do not apply to films. Arguably it also achieves the dream media buy – an almost seamless join between programme and ad.

Similarly, Chanel's media agency Mediaedge:cia, together with cinema sales house Pearl & Dean, has negotiated with cinema owners for the execution to be shown as part of the run of film trailers, rather than with the other ads.

(Claire Murphy *Marketing*, 17 November 2004)

---

audience fractions will be engaged – while this should not be overstated (as main media advertising will continue prominently in the routines and spaces of everyday life) it is undoubtedly the case that advertising will continue to adapt to and adopt new technologies and new media relationships.

Future advertising is a genre where audiences will increasingly and actively opt in (or out). This has not been lost on contemporary ad-makers, who, as a consequence, must try all the harder to make ad-communications that will stand on their own two feet – the primary and not the secondary element in media communications. This is a challenge advertising will need to go a long way to meet. Murphy's (2004) trade press account of Luhrman's three-minute Chanel No. 5 ad (see Box 7.1) brings up some key issues about the changing genre.

1    The relations between new-format ads and the host media: new ad formats disturb media, risking their integrity and popularity. They potentially steal limelight from other advertisers and disturb the main content – here the film *Moulin Rouge*. On the other hand

they can enhance the package, offering entertainment and curiosity value.

2   The relationship with regulation. Here the three-minute ad escapes ASA scrutiny. Concerns might be raised that such an exclusion could allow advertisers to effectively outflank the regulatory system by developing unregulated formats for material that could infringe codes.

3   The merger between programme and ad is secured adding value to the promotional and cultural impact and credibility of the extended spot.

4   The ad has 'passed' as a film trailer in cinema, thus allowing it to receive a different and perhaps more desirable kind of attention from the cinema audience.

5   The ad is an event, reported in the press and cast as entertainment rather than marketing – creating valuable buzz.

## GENRE BOUNDARIES: LIFE, DEATH AND BODIES

Among the many criticisms of advertising discourse, and as demonstrated in Chapter 5, is that 'serious' issues such as loss and death are routinely occluded from the 'world view' of advertising. While this remains generally the case, in the genre's quest for moments of authenticity, and in terms of the genres' self-conscious, auto-critique, this occlusion is occasionally breached. For instance a 2005 Reebok ad, subsequently banned after complaints about its imagery, used a controversial hard-hitting quote from hip hop star 50 Cent, famous to his fans for having been shot. An icon of hip hop culture, 50 Cent's celebrity embodiment of black street culture permitted a repackaging of the sport-shoe advertiser's 'carpe diem' message to be laced into the 'authentic' signifiers of race and criminality. The ad attempted an arresting counterpoint to advertisers' abstracted 'vanilla' presentations of affluent middle-class youth lifestyle, which silently speak of what Schudson (1993) called 'capitalist realism'.

As Falk (1994; 1997) suggests, there has been an increasing tendency to incorporate 'dangerous' or risky forms and themes. Thus Benetton famously depicted a dying AIDS patient in one ad, as well as producing numerous campaigns confronting the audience with the fact of racial difference – an advertising strategy predicated on a complex understanding of cultural meaning and communicative impacts, and upon the 'buzz' value of polemic. Figure 7.3 shows one example of Benetton's controversial series. In each case, the Benetton ads strive to reframe advertising – proposing it as a genre suitable to carry material relevant to public debate.

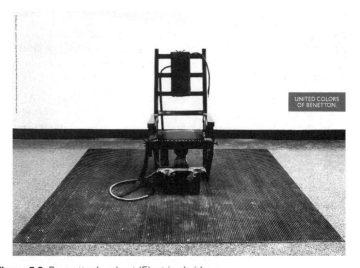

**Figure 7.3** Bennetton's advert 'Electric chair'.
Source: © Copyright 1992 Benetton Group S.p.A. Photo: Lucinda Devlin. Concept: Oliviero Toscani.

Their logic is perhaps that in the sheer triviality of its concerns traditional advertising can no longer credibly claim to marshal attention – not in a world where the most ordinary news item can touch profound feelings and engage debate – and in a world where nevertheless audiences seem oblivious even to the most pressing issues of news.

In Figure 7.3 Benetton grabs attention not with the promise of an ideal lifestyle but with a shocking assertion of one of the many ways is which death is present to us in life and society. There is no appeal to sympathy (in the sense of emulation) but instead there is an appeal to pathos – to feeling. There is a reformulation of the basic advertising aim 'pay attention' but without the depicted promise of a good life – the 'pay off' is not idle fantasy but (perhaps) a moment's thought – not necessarily about the issue ostensibly at hand (capital punishment) but about the ethics and aesthetic of such an advertising appeal.

The acceptance of advertising as a discourse entitled to carry more serious themes is related to secularisation. As official public discourse has become both more rational (and as religion has ceased to dominate cultural and symbolic life in the way it once did) and more emotive and sensational, there is a space in the pseudo public sphere created and inhabited by advertising to touch on a wider range of themes – including anxiety provoking areas at the boundaries of life and death, purity and danger, the ordinary, the exotic and the cosmopolitan.

## HUMOUR

Often, however, when advertising does flirt with the more serious aspects of life it more often than not manages the associated anxieties through humour; thus advertising operates in a way that is consistent with many other discursive modes – mobilising humour as a technique for exploring and managing difficult ideas and feelings and the contradictory nature of experiences.

Humour has a special ability to open up new intimacies and relationships. Advertising is a mode of representation that can easily come between an audience and a product, the implicit market relation as much an indication of alienating separation *from* as connection *to* a product or brand. Humour allows a contrary emphasis, simulating or perhaps stimulating a felt connection – closeness and not distance – an echo of what Bergson (1911) identified as the laughter of belonging.

If we can laugh along with an advertisement we have (momentarily) admitted it into the 'human' world of living culture. When we cannot laugh we experience, or allow only the mechanical marketing relation – an inhuman communication which, because it seems not to recognise us, goes unrecognised in turn. In such a circumstance we are unlikely to be open to the ad proposition. Humour is now fundamental to much brand communication, as brands struggle to mimic aspects of the intimacies of human relationships – brand owners' hoped-for affirmations of relationship and belonging.

The allusive quality of contemporary advertising is well-acknowledged. It is often used in a humorous way. Amongst the most powerful resources for cultural signification available to advertisers are the back catalogues of a century of previous media communications; digital technologies and databases of images, sounds and scenes. These ensure the fingertip availability of texts to interweave, one into another and around a brand proposition or a product advertisement. Such advertising has lead the way in the development of communications made up from the potent reassembly of past media moments; from history, from film, from celebrated biographies. The 'history' to which contemporary advertising refers is a media archive – an archive whose power to evoke nostalgia energises contemporary communications, the present re-mediated to us through the revived text and imagery of the digital 'past in the present'. Marketing content seems to play second fiddle to the experience of surprising juxtaposition, the *effort* of allusion – connecting the half-forgotten face, object or riff to its new context in a contemporary advertisement. This sustains the all important audience attention. The ingredients list for such ads includes:

- *celebrities*: dead or alive, they appear in ads as a matter of course, often reprising half-forgotten roles or amplifying current fame (and gossip);
- *music*: backing tracks allude to the nostalgia of older generations or pick up circulating retro trends and fashions;
- *parody*: allusions to other ads, past ads or other media genres. This works also to link audience and marketer in pseudo-intimate disdain for the market relation. Montages juxtapose film clips or old reels. Virgin trains has built an ad around footage of scenes from Hollywood classics, while One 2 One mobile phones (now T-Mobile) made a famous campaign in which current celebrities have one-to-one conversations with great celebrities from the past.

The ad shown in Figure 7.4 (broadcast in 2004) uses a past UK TV personality, Valerie Singleton, in a mock up of a fictional 'future in the past' promotional film 'made in 1979' by McCain.

> VOICE-OVER : In 25 years time the people of Britain will look back and say 'Ah, yes that was the year that changed our world forever!' Their world will be very different from ours of course, they'll probably have mobile telephones and watch movies on shiny little space aged discs and a Russian billionaire will probably have brought Chelsea. But in their kitchens and in their hearts they'll still have McCain oven chips with less than 5% fat. I see a happy future viewers don't you? Chin up Britain.

The McCain ad uses digital techniques to re-create a fake past in 'back to the future' mode. The audience is alerted to the way that history is often experienced today in televisual mode – with impacts partly gained from the discrepancy between old and new codes of televisual representation. The ad plays on the comic potential of the televisual cliché: 'Who would have thought it?' It picks up on themes of nostalgia, it parodies old TV news item formats, it draws on the power of a past celebrity – an increasingly common strategy based in the affective power of familiar objects, sounds and people forgotten and then suddenly recollected.

The ad playfully invents a heritage for the brand – and marks the movement of oven chip 'technology' from its position (for one generation) as novelty, to its position now as familiar and routine. This strategy is partly informed by the market risk that oven chips might (today) be seen as modern and fake and be set negatively against older, more laborious but also more 'authentic' ways of cooking and consuming potatoes – an effect of food-health agendas and the now mature product's place in its

**Figure 7.4** McCain 'Future in the past' ad.

lifecycle. The ad works to build intimacy for a product which was previously sold as a hyper modern 'never before seen' innovation. McCain attempts to build and deconstruct product heritage – and does so by plundering fragments from popular cultural history, recombining them in the intimate interplay of the shared joke. Advertising has a strong affinity with humour, as the frequency of amusing ads attests. One explanation for this might be found in Mikhail Bakhtin's (1981) suggestion that laughter brings objects 'closer':

> comical creativity works in the zone of maximal proximity . . . laughter demolishes fear and piety before an object, . . . making it an object of familiar contact and thus clearing the ground for an absolutely free investigation of it.
>
> (Bakhtin 1981: 23)

The unfamiliarity of novel commercial objects and contemporary suspicion about the grandiose ad-claim are engaged by humorous ads hoping to produce an intimacy valuable to marketing and branding. Such intimacy, between subject and object is assured by and dependent upon humorous signification which seeks after a sense of 'sharing'. Ads borrow from humour a ritual 'building up and knocking down' self-deprecation. Products are less often presented to provoke awe and admiration: instead ads disarm us against the marketing appeal – with the charm of humorous intimacy.

Humorous communication rests in a sense of 'belonging'. Laughter arises within – and as a way of enacting membership of – a living group.

It helps to constitute a meaningful sense of shared values (even in isolation). This sense of grouping, real or virtual, around a funny ad, explains the high value placed upon humorous advertising, by both advertisers and audiences. A central aspiration of advertising is to serve as in some way *affiliative* in the name of product or brand. This aspiration is supported by humour's capacity to test and affirm audiences' attunement. A funny, tuned-in ad delivers up a cultural kick on behalf of the product, one that may elude clichéd appeals to status, identity and other less visceral symbols of group connection. Humour is, paradoxically, both more elusive and more palpable as a marker of engaged 'belonging'. Brands want to be laughed *with*, and not *at*. Humour is an instance of advertising asserting cultural modes of exchange in the space of and to ease commercial exchange. The affiliative capacities of humorous advertising become a particular asset to cultural dissemination of brand or product ideas in the face of cultural environments where other 'shared' resources may be relatively less in evidence. Contemporary cultures have a particular hunger for new resources for affiliation; a hunger born, paradoxically, of the fragmentation and differentiation that is characteristic of much post-modern media-based experience. Contemporary (humorous) advertising strives to perform affiliative work in this 'space' and in the service of sponsoring brands, aiming to short-circuit viewers' tendencies to disaffiliation and cynicism. It is difficult in this contemporary moment to accept the validity of some of the early injunctions against humour in advertising from founding thinkers such as Hopkins (1966) who famously argued that 'people don't buy from clowns'. Nevertheless bad ads based on poor jokes provide the very worst instances of cultural and commercial communications: like a comedian on stage, bad ads can 'die' in the face of an unwelcoming audience.

## GESTURE AND MOVEMENT

Advertising variously appropriates, circulates, invigorates and corrupts languages of all kind, gestures included. The Phones4U ad (Figure 7.5) is an example of the way in which ads work to try to invent or inhabit gestures and movements for the brand. This use of bodily communication helps truncated communications (such as a poster) and in multilingual markets, where verbal language can lose some of its power, so advertising is increasingly employing gesture at the heart of campaigns. Gestures serve in situations where verbal communication is inhibited by language (as well as by situation). Lack of time, or brevity of attention span, provide further reasons why (for advertising) a quick gesture is a good way to embody and convey an advertising message or even a living 'logo'. Gestures are

**Figure 7.5** Phones4U ad.

not always mobile across cultures and languages, as a recent campaign examining global/local misunderstandings for HSBC makes clear. Nevertheless there is increasing interest in producing ads for brands, which can be globally portable. Slogans do not always travel or translate well. A gesture might work instead. We can see from a number of examples that ad-makers are now building gestures into the semiotic architecture of brands. Thus PC World is known for its stamping foot, Asda for a prudent pat on the back pocket, Tic Tac has devised a shake of the box and its attendant sound as a courtship gesture and Phones4U has made a satirical jab at the overuse of gestures in their spoof-like ads (Figure 7.5).

## ASOCIAL MOVEMENTS

As well as the significant formal gesture, advertising deploys the body in another mode. Adopting new cinematic technologies, such as those produced by Bartle Bogle Heggarty for Levis's 'twisted' campaign, ads sometimes evoke a conception of bodily movement characterised by distortion and disconnection, a digital body, fluid with sensuality as opposed to an analogue (and social body) identified to represent everyday interpersonal relations – or the traditional postures of heroism and seduction. Advertisers intuit that what preoccupies the youth audience is likely not to be so much any social milieu, or any predictable lifestyle representation, but a conception of fluidity and movement. In one ad a girl detaches her head, and her limbs are bent impossibly; in another a couple run through brick walls in a stylised and controlled process, half-flying, half-falling. The ad does not convey a scene inviting identification as such but mobilises texture and movement, hardness and softness, morphological flexibility. Obliquely but effectively, and in the name of the brand, these ads appropriate not a sociological meaning but a more subtle sense of materiality and movement – one to be attributed to the product, but without passing overtly through the codes of social recognition (of status and identity) on which much advertising has appeared, often, to depend – for instance in Goffman's (1979) accounts of bodily posture and social ranking of gender.

This is one of a number of ways that ads capture a zeitgeist where the accent is placed heavily on the flexibility and fluidity of identification and even on the (paradoxical) identification with 'non-identity'. In advertising this occurs in part because the genre straddles two moments: a modern one where ads were understood as a focus for identification, and a 'post'-modern one where the boundaries and possibilities for meaningful identification are perpetually in question and as such provide a marketing resource – audience attention.

Advertising textualities have certainly shifted away from a number of the genre clichés of the 1970s and 1980s. Amongst the drivers of such change has been a concomitant set of shifts in audience expectations. Indeed, it is partly a matter of broader shifts in audience tastes, as well as in the advertising industry's evolving conceptions of who, where and what their audiences might be like, that has driven and legitimated the changes registered under the heading the 'post-modern' advertising text – ads that raise expectation – and eyebrows. The next chapter looks in more detail at audiences – an important piece in the advertising jigsaw.

# 8

# AUDIENCES AND
# PSYCHOLOGY

In the previous two chapters we have looked primarily at advertisement *texts*. There has been a tendency in academic advertising studies to privilege texts as the main focus of analysis – a tendency emerging from scholars sharing in the assumptions, methods and approaches of other cultural, literary and media-oriented work. Text-focused semiotic analyses are not entirely blind to the moments of reading and reception (Van Leeuwen 2005: 3–14), and a good deal of textual analysis does attempt to build readers and contexts into the picture (e.g. McQuarrie and Mick 1992; MacRury 1997; Stern 2000; Van Leeuwen 2005). Nevertheless there is some value in taking reading, viewing and audiences more prominently as starting points in thinking about advertising: decentring the advertisement-text, seeing it as a restraint upon as opposed to a determinant of meaning-making and the terms of engagement in commercially-oriented communications. A number of valuable approaches have emerged from such a perspective, using various sociological and psychologically-based methods: social psychology, ethnography and psychoanalysis.

Readers of advertisements feature in some way in all thinking about advertising. Common sense, critical sense and commercial sense recognise, in their various ways, that readers (not forgetting listeners and viewers) are the *point* of advertising communications processes. The most self-absorbed ad creative will acknowledge that advertisements are made to be seen and/or heard, even if, as may be the case, the audience she or he might have in mind is a judging panel at the advertising awards, other creatives' professional opinions or an overbearing client, rather than a supermarket shopper in his or her living room (Nixon 2003). Other agency staff, planners for example, will represent the audience informally or via research as the proper 'target' of any creative output (Hackley 2003), often suggesting amendments to the final composition. The advertiser will typically pay for campaign media on the basis of a system predicated on the registered size and type of its audience, costs weighted by the frequency with which people might have an 'opportunity to see' (OTS) the advertisement. Certified Audit Bureau of Circulation (ABC) figures chart the composition of audiences in some detail, profiling readership along lines of class, gender and age. Audience numbers provide a major 'currency' traded between media space buyers and sellers – with 'the attention economy' (Davenport and Beck 2001), target audiences and campaign 'reach' structuring preoccupations and decisions daily across media and advertising industries. Campaign effectiveness research is based on audience surveys in checks of exposure, recall and attitude changes (Green 2005).

Psychologically-based studies point to the ways advertisements stimulate consumer (and non-consumer) behaviours, or provoke various other effects. Social psychological concepts have been elaborated and applied to advertising via marketing psychology, tracing perception and memory: 'cognitive dissonance' (O'Shaughnessy and O'Shaughnessy 2003: 150–2), brand recall (Keller 1993; Mick 1992), likeability (Neijens et al. 2006), sex roles and ad impacts (Jaffe and Berger 1994) and evaluating audiences' 'propensity to buy' advertised products (Scriven and Ehrenburg 1997).

Recently neuroscience-related technologies have begun to permit attempts to record advertising effects on the brain. Efforts are made to harness developments in neuroscience for the benefit of marketing agendas and knowledge development (du Plessis 2005a; 2005b), in a set of initiatives tagged as 'neuro-marketing' (The Economist, 10 June 2004). For some, such developments re-ignite anxieties about advertising research adopting scientific 'mind control' techniques first explored, for instance, in various mid-twentieth-century science fiction novels and in other critical commentary (Williams 1951; Huxley 1932a; 1932b; 1959; Orwell 1949; Packard 1957; Key 1974; 1989; 1992). For others 'neuro-marketing' raises questions about the appropriate usage of scientific resources and expertise.

Scratching the surface of such hi-tech neuropsychological advertising research approaches typically reveals more doubt than certainty about specific applicability. Antonio Rangel, echoing sceptical dismissals of subliminal advertising in the 1960s, suggests: 'If you define neuro-marketing as the use of neuro-technologies to improve the effectiveness of advertisements or sales, I have not yet seen a single instance of success' (Rangel, cited in Mitchell (5 January 2007)).

Socio-political and cultural analysis is also *always* based on an understanding of the audience. Classic political, economic and culturally-focused analyses have implicitly and explicitly been concerned with the audience. Even while describing 'the masses' or the abstract 'subject', critics (Thompson 1943; Adorno 1991; Packard 1957; Williamson 1978; Ewen 2000) are ultimately concerned with how people (mis)read and (mis)understand advertising imagery; criticism aiming to disturb the power advertisers seem to gain and exploit in manipulating or corrupting the audience – en masse or in segments.

Regulators, such as the Advertising Standards Authority (ASA), lobby-ists and politicians have depended on their understanding of (anticipated or presumed) audience response and effects, for instance on children's eating habits (Ofcom 2004) or adolescent smoking (Pollay 1993; Klitzner *et al.* 1991; Fischer 1993). Interest in such ad responses is sometimes a prelude to legislation or deregulation. Industry authorities and government adapt rules and principles for industry self-regulation for different categories of audience in line with working conceptions of (different) audiences' vulnerabilities and expectations and with reference to particular 'dangerous' advertising sectors (Cronin 2004a). Elsewhere the ASA's regulatory work is partly driven by complaints from audience members.

Advertising industry research is dedicated to understanding advertising and its consumers intimately; testing ads and investigating potential strategies campaign by campaign (Hopkins 1966; Lance and Woll 2006; Hackley 2003) and in relation the wider cultural questions facing the industry (MacDonald 1997; MacDonald and King 1996, 19–28, 77–83; Obermiller and Spangenberg 1998).

Despite these varied and sometimes unconnected kinds of attention to audiences there are parallel concerns that 'the reader' or 'the audience' is always at risk of being forgotten. Creative practitioners might become too absorbed in professional ambition – and their 'art' – or clients insist on tried and tested methods, neglecting audiences' shifting tastes. Presump-tuous academics at times place audiences at arm's length as abstracted critical-theoretical constructs. Regulators police 'invented' standards of social taste. Neurological scans do not show 'the consumer mind', just traces of excited brain activity – with little decipherability or predicative power. Target audiences are probabilistic estimates; real people do not watch or read or listen to order.

Such objections are rooted within deep-seated inter- and intra-disciplinary debates, and in local professional arguments. 'Advertising audiences' are attended to, yes; but like children in a messy divorce, they can be obsessively fought over and so, nevertheless, at times, 'neglected'. Thus to say that advertising experts and institutions 'forget' the audience is not quite right. More convincing is the argument that says audiences (and the various individuals and groups that comprise them) are not routinely given the *right* kinds of attention; so that they can at times be misconceived, misunderstood and, therefore, effectively missed out in orthodox and instituted understandings of the advertising process – even amongst the plethora of data and profiling that crosses media and marketing executives' desks. Consumers discovered by market research are in some senses 'imaginary' (Lury and Warde 1997), created as much as explored (Arvidsson 2004; Hackley 2002) – artefacts of 'administrative research' (Adorno 1978).

In addition to misunderstanding audiences' consumption habits, frequently it is the case that there is a lack of contextual comprehension of 'reading' (or viewing or listening) habits and events. Among these elusive moments of ad-interaction are those to do with audience gratification. The pleasures afforded, from time to time, in watching or sharing this or that funny, sexy, or artful ad are readily dismissed or condemned by critics (Postman 1986). The industry measures the 'likeability' of ad campaigns in a limited way, as part of attempts to square the circle of creativity and effectiveness. However, this offers a limited account of 'the pleasures of the text'.

O'Donohoe (1995), drawing on a number of studies in the heritage of so-called 'uses and gratifications' research (Katz *et al.* 1973; Katz *et al.* 1975), as well as some primary research with young audiences (O'Donohoe 1997), outlines some of the kinds of gratifications advertising audiences have reported. These are outlined in Table 8.1 with some additional illustrative points. Alperstein (2003) is also alert to various elements of advertising consumption: the genre's contribution to the social, cultural and dream life of audiences – excavating some of the introspection invisible in, but a constituent part of, everyday advertising experiences.

In some ways, far from subverting accounts of advertising as manipulation, or dismissals of advertising as trivia, such uses and gratifications might well amplify critics' concerns about engagements with and within ad culture. However, respondents' articulations of activity and 'reward'-seeking provide counterpoints to assumptions about passivity and some hints towards thinking about the complex semiotic, affective, informational and social processes that underscore aspects of advertising reception. Uses and gratification studies do underline some of the enjoyable nature of ad watching, pleasures also suggested in the popularity of many programmes dedicated to laughing at or with 'the world's funniest ads' and such like.

**Table 8.1** Advertising use/gratification

| Categories | Specification |
|---|---|
| Marketing uses | • Information (ads tell us things we might need or wish to know)<br>• Choice, competition and convenience (we save time finding out about market information by using ads)<br>• Quality assurance/reassurance (good ads serve as a a mark of the stability of the advertiser)<br>• Consumption stimulation (persuading self/others about a purchase/investment/donation)<br>• Vicarious consumption (enjoying a 'what if' moment – of planning or fantasy)<br>• Added value (product reputation enhanced by ads can enhance value to consumers).<br><br>        (O'Donohoe 1995) |
| Structuring time | • That is, breaking up the flow of TV watching, punctuating concentration spans.<br><br>        (Alperstein 2003) |
| Enjoyment | • Entertainment (humour, sentimentality etc.)<br>• Diversion (from watching programmes, reading or other activities)<br>• Escapism (various kinds of consumerist fantasising)<br>• Play (textual play). |
| Scanning the environment | • Surveillance (keeping informed about consumer cultures)<br>• Familiarity (seeing reassuring brands and objects)<br>• Sexual voyeurism (checking out attractive models and celebrities)<br>• Education (learning about products, causes and issues)<br>• Social interaction    Family relationships (living room laughter/consideration of ads)<br>• Peer relationships (with friends/acquaintances – on- or off-line). |
| Self-affirmation/transformation | • Reinforcement of attitudes and values (ads open up miscellaneous cultural and political issues)<br>• Ego enhancement (imaginary confirmation of self-identity/ideals)<br>• Aspirations and role models. |
| Extension to O'Donohoe's (1995) schema accounting for significant post-1995 Internet developments | • Digital storage and retrieval technologies have ensured ads are amongst the numerous digitised cultural texts circulating within professional and informal groups. It is now far easier to retrieve, store and circulate ads – in the service of numerous of the uses identified by O'Donohoe's (1995; 1997) young respondents.<br>• Web-based facilities such as YouTube have enabled ads to be consumed and shared more readily. This has enhanced 'viral' marketing – as funny or shocking ads circumnavigate the globe via web links and mails. The expansion of e-based social networking has stimulated the sharing and discussion of ads peer to peer on websites such as Facebook and MySpace with ads offering a component of various types of cultural affiliation and display and providing a new target media destination for ad creatives and brand marketers seeking buzz and credibility amongst the youth audience. This is especially true of humorous ads (Kasapi 2007). |

Source: Adapted from O'Donohoe 1995.

The pleasure in advertising parody mobilised in many contemporary ads to disarm critique (see Chapter 7) is indicative of an ongoing love/hate play of desire and frustration in the face of consumer culture. This is elaborated effectively by campaigning critics using digital technologies – readily-available means for producing high-quality 'culture-jamming' media output cheaply and quickly. This has allowed activists connected to, for example, *Adbusters* (see Danesi 2006: 128–9) to provide creditable 'spoofs' of advertisements, turning the textual style of advertising back on itself and using modified ad posters as part of an entertaining critique of corporate capitalism. Such 'adbusting' activities extend a long tradition of politico-comedic engagement with advertising and can be considered alongside feminist and other activists' ad-oriented art and graffiti popular in the 1980s, which, with some success, raised consciousness about clichéd representations of women[1] and other political issues (Winship 2000; Myers 1986: 83–107; Stallabrass 1996). Contemporary audiences also enjoy the self-parodic gestures often present in commercial advertisements (Savan 1994: 289; Goldman 1992). The propagandising power of such spoof ads however insightful and creative they are, and however like the ads they parody, should not however be overstated, as Cronin (2004: 91–3) has usefully pointed out.

Whatever uses and gratifications advertising might afford audiences, audiences are liable to report (at the same time) stubbornly refusing to engage with some or even any advertising. This contributes to numerous pressures (Saatchi 2006; Zyman 2004) on traditional advertising and is as much a matter audiences' indifference as their registering any active resistance or 'appropriation'.

## ENTERTAINMENT AND POPULAR CULTURE

The technological change in TV audiences' viewing habits over the last 40 years has contributed to the ways in which advertising and promotion are designed into different media. The availability of Tivo and Digi-box recordable digital TV, alongside more established TV viewing management technologies – VCR, DVD, pay-per-view, various Internet and digital computing-based platforms and, last but by no means least, the remote control, together with audiences' ever cited boredom with ads – has meant that advertisers continue to fear being squeezed out of reconfiguring audience-media-technology-programming environments. Donaton (2004) and others (Leiss *et al.* 2005; Roberts 2004; Davenport and Beck 2001; Lewis and Bridger 2001; Dawson and Hall 2005) have argued that advertising must compete more directly with other sources of entertainment, with competitor ads, other promotional modes[2] and also with media content – off and online.

Indeed, if promotional communications cannot beat the competition to the audience (and they often cannot) then, as they seem to be doing (Alperstein 2003: 141; Donaton 2004; Langer 2003: 249), advertisers must join with the competition – film, programs, websites, magazines and radio merging with promotion. Such convergences are redoubled and refracted by the convergence of technologies. As your mobile phone becomes your TV and your pop video becomes your advertisement, as your iPod becomes your GPRS PDA and your direct mail becomes a mobile reminder, to talk about ad '*breaks*' will become an act of nostalgia. Scenarios touting the 'everywhere and nowhere' future of advertising provoke (different) anxieties for advertising agencies and in critically-minded consumers. It is likely that ad avoidance will continue as a powerful appeal in promoting future media technologies while opting into advertising exposure will be a frequent payment option in new and old media. Commercial promotion is rarely long-avoided: as we have seen, ads are just displaced, for instance into product placement (Fuller 1997) and 'non-spot' ads, sponsorship of TV programmes, sports, video games and so on.

Audiences will continue to experience the line between advertising and entertainment blurring and dissolving, with the one genre (advertising) collapsing and morphing into the spaces and flows of others: film, drama, news, concerts, exhibitions, seminars, websites and broadcast 'chat'. Donaton (2004: 39–47) points out that, as Wernick's (1991) descriptions of Wedgwood's promotional methods in the nineteenth century suggest, such convergence is not exactly 'new'; and see also Olins' (2003) discussion of *Tono-Bungay* (Wells [1909] 2005) cited in Chapter 4 above. Promotion, culture and commerce have become integrated spheres of activity over a long period, with the ever more fragmentary audience the final destination of such media-promotional-cultural convergence.

## READING INTERTEXTUALITY: DISPERSAL AND INTEGRATION

Advertising's convergence with broadcast entertainment and other kinds of popular culture (festivals, long form advertorials, games-spaces, product placements in TV and films) formalises outwardly a 'merging' reception researchers have been alert to for some time. O'Donohoe (1997) demonstrates intertextual 'leaky boundaries' between advertising texts and the popular cultures of young people; Alperstein (2003) provides numerous examples of the integration of advertising snippets in daily conversations, private 'stream of consciousness' moments, of ad segments in dream-like introspection, and of audience's alertness to the intertextual moments (Alperstein 2003). Noting and mobilising allusions is part of 'advertising literacy' (Myers 1999: 203; O'Donohoe and Tynan 1998) and intertextuality the condition of contemporary promotion (MacRury 1997: 242). To be advertising literate is to engage, apprehend and comprehend the flows and significances from screen and page, of brands, celebrities, products, sounds and styles.

Fowles (1996: 188–91) offers a useful account of watching ad breaks during an episode of *Roseanne*. His narration highlights continuities between themes and tones within advertisements, touching on ideas around familial separation, maturation, 'femaleness in modern life', romance, illness, the programme content and his responses to the sitcom episode. For instance, an ad for L'Oréal 'would seem to fit with the show's exploration of the passage of years'. He continues:

> Viewers who feel a kinship with Roseanne's plight, as the character experiences the departure of her daughter, may also feel a kinship with Plenitude Advanced Wrinkle Defense Cream from L'Oréal. For those who are feeling deplenished, there is Plenitude; for those who feel themselves aging, there is wrinkle defence cream.
>
> (Fowles 1996: 190)

His point, clear also in O'Donohoe (1997) and Alperstein (2003), and touching on the notion of reception as 'unlimited semiosis' (Eco 1976; Merrell 2001) and see the account of experiencing a Coke ad in Chapter 6 above), is that the viewer necessarily brings together the 'symbol domains' of advertising and popular culture in a flow of personal association, intertextual allusion and musing. The (intended or unintended) tie-ins between pop culture (as legitimate resource for reflection) and advertising as marketing do not trouble Fowles. Such integrations indicate consumers' active participation selectively binding the flow of symbolic goods, via pop culture to personal memory and desire (see also Alperstein 2003: 5–7). Others might find this admixture insidious (Scruton 2000: 55–67) and it is at such points that the intactness of cultures, genres and other domains are most violently reasserted by critics defending the 'purity' of art against the danger of 'commercialism'. Fowles, on the contrary and more optimistically, sums up his half hour of TV watching – 'around and around the references have flown' (Fowles 1996: 193) – and he concludes:

> What an individual viewer selects from the congenial advertising popular culture mix will depend on the particular meanings the individual is in need of at a given point in time . . . The spectator seeks out particular imagery that

invokes and draws out the spectator's own harboured and snarled feelings . . . For the creation and maintenance of self identity, the spectator looks for those special personalities that can be imaginatively emulated or interacted with. The spectator is also looking for those products whose symbolic overtones suit the meanings the spectator wishes to elicit in oneself or in others.

(Fowles 1996: 195)

Fowles's account of ad watching reveals a risk, however. The invocation of too-abstracted figures, 'the spectator' or 'the reader', permits the kind of unwarranted and speculative theorising that some reader response work (such as ethnography and uses and gratifications) had sought to redress. The trade-off is between the nuanced and connective richness of imaginative narratives of reading (such as Fowles's) versus less intimate and more abstracted accounts and measures from specific, methodically sampled, readers.

The 'active media literacy' described by such approaches might be seen as neither 'literate' nor 'active' by cultural critics such as Scruton (2000; also Leavis and Thompson 1962), for whom reading is a qualitatively different activity than ad-consuming, and based in a specific account of imaginative engagement with 'special' aesthetic texts. Active readers of ads describe (mere) fantasising (Britton 1998: 109). Nor is such mind-wandering engagement with ads deemed valuable when set against the more exacting standards of inductive or deductive reasoning – readers testing evidence or principles against the product proposition at hand. The disciplined forms of rational engagement with ad texts are typically demanded by critical perspectives on advertising (Thompson 1990: 208–12).

The advertising 'audience' continues to provoke controversy around issues of 'advertising literacy'. Lodziak (2002) argues against the over-valuing of ad-media-literacy 'achievements'. He suggests that such valorisations depend on an account of human agency and identity based too heavily on ephemeral symbolic consumption – occluding more 'solid' identity resources: work, family and peer groups:

In its rush to excavate the play of meaning (and the play of identity) in viewing TV, and the pleasures experienced from viewing, it fails to ask the audience a fundamental question: How significant to you, in the total order of things, are the meanings and pleasures you claim to derive from TV entertainment?

(Lodziak 2002: 107)

Lodziak argues that, if asked, respondents would be likely to reply that everyday media pleasures are minimal and relatively not particularly meaningful. He suggests that the problem with some audience research is that those who conduct and interpret such studies 'have attributed significance to what audiences consider to be insignificant' (Lodziak 2002: 107). Those seeking to defend time spent watching ads – actively or passively – as a component of worthwhile cultural consumption have perhaps to work harder to distinguish the derived watching-pleasures from escapism, and continuing engagement from inertia. Some analyses of the advertising audience have attempted to reframe uses and gratifications in a narrative about culture and change.

## CHANGING AUDIENCES/CHANGING CULTURES

In recent decades interest in the advertising audience has come in particular from feminist scholars (such as O'Donohoe 1997; 2001; 2000; Stern 2000; Nava and Nava 1992) who have articulated a double-pronged attack on advertising, but also on some of the assumptions, values and methods informing advertising criticism (Nava 1997). Traditions of ad critique have routinely cast advertising as eroding the public's capacity for rational discourse in general (Mayhew 1997; Williams 1980) and consumers' individual capacities for reasonable decision-making in particular (Key 1989, 1973; Packard 1957; Thompson 1943). Within this tradition there has been a tendency to posit Stepford-like *wives*, 'babes in consumer-land' (Packard 1957: 92–5), as especially vulnerable to advertisers' claims. Masculinity has been associated with production: femininity with consumption (and reproduction) notwithstanding radical shifts in gender relationships, responsibilities and experiences. Advertising, it has been assumed, manipulates audiences in general, but women in particular.

Feminist critics have asserted that such critiques are complicit with a gendered set of (de-) valuations of 'masculine/feminine' (Fuat Firat and Dholakia 1998: 76) implicitly marking 'the feminine'. 'The consumer', coded as feminine, is regarded as less capable of judgement and more prone to the irrational impulse. *She* is the subject/victim of ad culture and a key vector for the cultural success of consumerism (Cross 2000: 45–6; 184–6)

Dissatisfaction with a generalising and gendered positioning of advertisers' passive victims and coupled with the post-modernist tendency to challenge ordered hierarchies of cultural value (Dunn 1991) drew researchers to return to the 'real' audience, part of a growing preoccupation with, and revalorisation of, the concrete and particular instance, over and above abstracting or systematic generalisation in methods of audience inquiry (Ostergaard and Jantzen 2000). Real readers' engagements with advertising were explored, not via survey, not via conjecture, and not via market research on ad effects, but by talking to readers directly about experiences of advertising. Talking to real readers offered an opportunity to 'mind the gap' between real readers' responses recounted from the micro-cultures of living rooms in interviews, and text-centred analyses of macro cultural-economic interactions.[3]

At the same time, as Gough-Yates reports (2003: 72–3), a series of studies of women ad readers appeared in industry publications *Marketing* and *Campaign* (Hodson 1985; Rawsthorn 1984; O'Reilly 1983). Gough-Yates notes, these studies revealed a significant generational differences in responses to and feelings about advertising:

> Women aged between thirty-five and fifty-five ... saw advertising as a 'hidden persuader' of which they had to be wary. These women also tended to be unsophisticated in their understanding of 'how ads work', showing relatively little awareness of the various codes and conventions deployed in the construction of brand image. In contrast younger respondents – who had grown up with media as an integral part of their lives – were found to be more confident and discriminating in their judgements about advertising and had less fear of its 'effects'.
>
> (Gough-Yates 2003: 72–3)

It is clear that industry and academic researchers have become increasingly concerned that some of their working assumptions were faulty. The various returns, to readers, and to audiences as 'actual' consumers, marked a transition away from a confident vision and method that, at base, pretended to *know* the audience. There was emphasis instead (by talking to readers) on more flexible, dispersed and uncertain approaches more willing to accept the incomplete, provisional, particularised and contingent nature of cultural consumption – of texts, of ads and of goods.

In the industry the growth of qualitative and ethnographic research methods in the 1980s and 1990s was partly a product of this new vision. In academia the work was largely successful in contesting those arguments which had routinely posited textual and ideological domination, jettisoning notions of readers as individuated 'islands of cognitive and affective response, unconnected to a social world, detached from culture, removed from history and biography' (Buttle 1991: 97).

## CREATIVE DECONSTRUCTION: AD READERS AND POSTMODERNISM

Specifically preoccupied with questions of cultural consumption, Nava and Nava (1992) explored readers' aesthetic experiences and critical reflections

(Nava and Nava 1992; Nava 1997) on the outputs of the advertising industry. In particular this study opened up interesting suggestions about how some creatively ambitious advertising might change culture: ads working not exactly 'against the grain' (in the manner of *Adbusters*) but nevertheless having discernible (cultural) impacts beyond the typical intentions of marketers. General audience activity aside, the study's focus was on the potential for specifically 'creative' engagements with ad texts leading to a proposed re-evaluation of the cultural-aesthetic value of contemporary advertising. The main interest is not primarily the question of the ad genre's cultural legitimacy (Is it Art?), in the Leavisite sense (Scruton 2000; Leavis and Thompson 1964; and see Chapter 5). Instead at issue is the capacity some aesthetically creative advertising might have in disturbing entrenched discourses and power relations embodied in representational regimes of Fordist modernity.[4] This argument articulates a direct opposition to Williamson's ([1978] 1982) suggestion, echoed by McGuigan (1992: 122) and in extended detail by Goldman (1992) and Lee (1993), that, more or less, the increased 'semiotic refinement' of advertisements 'has not made the least difference to their basic function' (Williamson [1978] 1982 : 2) – which is to say that (in the final analysis) arty ads are no more and no less culturally interesting than basic before and after washing powder commercials.

Nava and Nava (1992), by talking to and working with young people, examined the proposal that advertising literacy might constitute a kind of 'cultural capital' – a developmental resource or creative capacity. The study emphasises some similarities between advertising and other quasi-legitimate popular cultural media arts – especially film and pop music. Rather than working to define or defend a distinction between art and advertising (as for example Scruton (2000) see Chapter 5 above) the analysis traces its ad-reading participants' line, one that allows no absolute discontinuity between advertising and more legitimate cultural forms:

> The very fact of excluding advertising from the sphere of art forms and identifying it as other, as defined predominantly by its material concerns, serves not only to differentiate and cleanse other forms, it also obscures the material determinants which operate across all of them.
>
> (Nava and Nava 1992: 174)

Art, entertainment, and cultural production of many kinds are necessarily implicated in the contemporary commercial system. To classify advertisements as inescapably of a wholly and distinctively non-cultural and non-aesthetic genre even into and beyond moments of consumption and circulation fails to acknowledge crossovers, commonalities and links evident at the levels of production and texuality between ads and popular media. As a recent Baz Lehrman ad for Chanel No. 5 perfume makes clear (Murphy 2004), and as BMW films described by Donaton (2004) indicate, the creative community celebrated for making films (like *Moulin Rouge*) or aesthetically ambitious pop videos are often the same people deploying and (arguably) conveying (largely) similar sensibilities, crew and techniques in making ads as are on show in cinemas and modern photo-art galleries. Delaney (2007) charts the numerous crossovers between advertising and cinema in the UK since the 1970s in some detail, citing luminaries such as David Putnam and Ridley Scott as having worked across both industries – and suggesting that there has been some cross fertilisation between genres.

The self-consciously arty ads under discussion in the study were of the kind typically aimed at the young 'media savvy' audience. The study reports how ad-connoisseurs critically assess the latest offerings, demonstrating readerly 'agency', developing decoding skills and pop-culture capital. Teen audiences take pleasure in some ads and are 'discriminating' – i.e. not 'dupes' (Nava and Nava 1992). Advertising reception is not a matter of docile interpretation and consumerist assent; it becomes an event for consumer/proto-producers who 'watch and rewatch the commercials' sharing a developing expertise. Cultural 'comparisons and connections will be made' (Nava and Nava 1992: 173), interactive intertextual exchanges as part of sociable everyday exercises in critical-cultural expression and engagement.

One question relevant here, and echoing Lodziak's (2002) arguments above: 'so what?' is, 'What does it matter if young people find ads enjoyable and challenging?'. The reply offered by Nava and Nava (1992) posed a challenge to a series of long-established assumptions and conclusions about advertising and its cultural place. The critical engagement brought to advertising by some young audiences does have a consequence, Nava and Nava suggest. Audiences gradually influence an (insecure) advertising industry because creative practitioners seek the critical approval from savyy audiences. Pressure from (youth) audiences and sharing values and discussions with and within such discriminating groups, encourages creatives to work to 'produce ever more subtle and sophisticated advertisements'. These in turn generate 'more discriminating audiences' (Nava and Nava 1992) developing an informal iterative process of ad production–consumption–critique–ad production which becomes cyclical and dynamic.

Audiences watch the latest ads, apparently not acknowledging the advertised products; indeed, as part of their appropriation of anti-consumerist sensibilities, many ads (in a somewhat complex contradiction) might feed anti-market sentiment as much as advocating consumerism. The result, in aggregate and incrementally, is that cultural and creative elements of advertising 'art' become detached from the avowed (commercial) function of the advertising genre. This is in part (merely) an extension of a well-worn observation about ads offering more than the programmes they surround (e.g. Enright 1988: 48–50; McGuigan 1992: 120) But Nava and Nava (1992), drawing on Frederick Jameson (1998, 1991), pose this question:

> To what extent can post-modern forms be considered oppositional or progressive? Is there a way in which they can resist and contest the logic of consumer capitalism?
>
> (Nava and Nava 1992)

Detached (at the point of consumption) from commercial intentions, advertising is theorised here, in the context of evidence from reader-respondents, as possessing a surplus semiotic resource. Ads provide a 24-hour aesthetic playground, a nursery-like enclave, in which adolescents (of all ages) can develop and rehearse, not precisely media literacy, but a portable critical perceptual apparatus, inheriting an 'elite . . . type of engagement' (Whitely 1994: 135) that is anti-realist and anti-authoritarian, ostensibly even anti- or post-consumerist. The casually emergent sensibility is, however, neither elitist or exclusionary because it remains connected to, and indeed dependent upon, the sites, rhythms and fashions of popular youth and other oppositional cultures. This argument tentatively offers up the possibility of advertisements contributing not just pleasure and escapist gratifications, but lining up amongst the occasions for disruptive and exciting moments of cultural engagement and challenge – on a relatively wide scale. Jameson poses a connected question, but cannot resolve it:

> We have seen that there is a way in which postmodernism replicates or reproduces – reinforces – the logic of consumer capitalism; the more significant question is whether there is also a way in which it resists that logic. But that is a question we must leave open.
>
> (Jameson 1998: 20)

The question remains open, notably around the apparent capacity of advertising to commune with, absorb, embody and mobilise (elements of) the sounds, images and critical stances of contemporary culture (Lopiano-Misdom and Luca 1997; Nicholson 1997). This feature of the ad genre produces an ad aesthetic ostensibly in opposition to established consumerisms and ad styles. Some ads come to resemble and feel like 'independent', 'de-commodified' cultural products contributing to an audience-driven flow which destabilises advertising's institutional forms and textualities: deconstructive moments disturbing the 'literature of consumption' (Scott 1994), interrupting the 'hyper-rituals' of Goffman's (1979) 'commercial realism' and ironising 'the 'capitalist realism' (Schudson 1993) characteristic of 'the official art of capitalist society' (Williams 1980). This optimistic reading of advertising disturbs the tradition of ad critique and proposes an image of audience and industry operating sporadically in dialogue – through emergent taste cultures – to shift advertising to develop a surplus cultural function (in some instances and markets) becoming, paradoxically, and in pursuit of particular marketing successes, a semiotic resource for the developmental rehearsal of anti-marketing sensibilities.

The counter-argument remains, however: for Goldman (1992), as with Williamson ([1978] 2002), Lee (1993) McGuigan (1992), and Odih (2007) – and in terms similar to Lodziak (2002) – potential moments of popular creativity dissipate in the processes of absorption into the advertising system. The logo cannot provide a legitimate *aesthetic* signature, no matter what brand advocates and enthusiastic audiences intend or pretend to claim. Advertising is a genre that *simulates* cultural experience and stimulates nothing but marketing intentions.

This debate indicates in outline that there is little commensurability between approaches looking at readers as creative agents, and those critiquing advertising as a 'magic system'. As Jameson's (1998) irresolution suggests, and as Schor (2007) puts it: 'the agents versus dupes framing has been a theoretical cul-de-sac'. Schor (2007) provides a useful reminder of the need to rethink wide angle and long view approaches to advertising, *alongside* continued close-up consideration of consumer/audiences' daily readings and rituals. Schor (2007) points out some of the difficulties of linking micro-analysis of reader-consumers to macro critiques of consumerism and the economic system. In doing so however, she (parenthetically) hints at the continued validity of criticisms anxious about academics' occasional tendency to patronise audiences:

> In its simplistic formulation of agents versus dupes, the agentic view is clearly preferable. After all, it is hard to do good social science from the assumption that people are idiots. (On the other hand, it is also important not to overstake the case for the agentic consumer. For every hip indy music connoisseur, there is most likely a bleached-blond, Coach carrying, North Face-jacketed

college student with a Tiffany heart bracelet around her wrist who is inarticulate about her consumer choices.

(Schor 2007: 24)

The 'advertising audiences' debate has moved on – or been played out – with ads, critics, audiences and industry re-engaging across other political, media and cultural terrains. Consideration of consumerism, advertising and branding takes place within wider debates about globalisation (Klein 2000; Micheletti and Stolle 2007) in relation to over-consumption and environmental issues (Shah *et al.* 2007; Klein 2000; Micheletti and Stolle 2007) or by examining specific areas of provision; fast food (Schlosser 2002), retail power (Blythman 2004) or specific audiences, particularly children (Schor 2004) and teens (Quart 2003). Leiss *et al.* (2005) are, however, able to provide an extensive study which is alert both to change within specific audiences, detailing the 'negotiated messaging' emerging in advertising made for 'Generation X' (2005: 481–518), while also locating this analysis in a historicised discussion of changing textualities.

It is in techno-aesthetic new media networks and in the real and virtual relations that they foster that the most palpable disturbances to the traditional dynamics of media, advertising, culture and consumption are in evidence. Contemporary media audiences, 'Generation Xers' (as identified in Leiss *et al.* (2005)) brought up to the creative revolutions of the 1960s, and not to mention the children of the 1980s and 1990s who have followed on, energised by waves of new technology, are in many ways discriminating, demanding, critical and exacting in their engagements with advertisements and with popular culture more generally. This, along with an equally important strand of audience response, i.e. indifference, and alongside a number of wider institutional pressures, produces 'feedback' informing ongoing and reflective refiguring of advertising practice.

Some of the loss of confidence in the creative and marketing force of traditional main media ad formats (Zyman 2004; Saatchi 2006) that began in the late 1980s (Mort 1996; Langer 2003) certainly engendered new forms and textual approaches explored in Chapter 7. At the same time audiences, whether apathetic, anomic or alienated, have nevertheless continued to fuel a global expansion in consumer-goods centred culture (Lewis and Bridger 2000; Gilmore and Pine 2007; Alperstein 2003; Miles *et al.* 2002) Outside the living rooms of TV teens, wired housewives and switched-off thirtysomethings, advertising remains a key signature – defining the look and feel of the real and 'hyper-real' market environments – of cities, streets and shopping malls.

# INSIDE OUTSIDE: DYNAMIC AND STATIC AUDIENCES

Two recent analyses add something important to thinking about the relations between the reader and advertising text. A sense of the places and times in which texts are read and access to readers' narrative account broadens the notion of the audience. Costa Merja and Van Zoonen (2002) describe an instance in which a poster is viewed at a bus stop:

> It is eight o'clock on a cold winter morning. I am waiting for the bus to the city-centre, hardly awake and shivering. The bus stop is lit by a huge billboard just behind me. On it is Jennifer Lopez . . . flaunting her luscious body and beautiful hair for the international cosmetics firm L'Oréal . . . an old man is leaning on the billboard, his head leaning against her shapely buttocks. A young man comes along and catches the picture of the old man in a paradisal position. He winks at me, as if we both see a common meaning in the scene. I start to feel uncomfortable. It's a bit much for the early morning: the obtrusive presence of the Latin star Lopez and her impeccably made-up face and body, the conspiratorial invitation of the young man to share in the voyeuristic irony created by the picture in the bus stop.
>
> (Costera Meijer and Van Zoonen 2002: 327)

The various framings and re-framings in the ad, brought out by an idle yet dynamic engagement and disengagement, might be read back as a metaphor to set against the account of the transfixed reader. Janice Winship's (2002) paper on 'Women outdoors' connects with both discomfort and debate. In it she looks at magazine- and poster-based campaigns, and argues that contexts of reception (magazine/private versus poster/public) are crucial. She observes a scene where a famous Wonderbra advert is set next to a poster ad which engages it in some intertextual banter:

> Whilst motorized transport offers a safe cocoon from which to enjoy this billboard humour for the pedestrian passer-by caught in the imagined exchange, the site – at a junction on a ring road in Sheffield – more shockingly throws into relief the private and intimate made public. Especially for women, the alienating urban environment and potentially unsafe subway resonate with the memory of nineteenth century patriarchal precedents – ideas about public women as out of place, fallen women, the street walker, the prostitute (Wilson 1994). 'Hello boys' becomes a provocative invitation to sexual advance if not attack. The poster goads onlookers. Indeed someone – workmen, boys just

having a laugh, or could it be feminists? – has thrown cement to bespatter the danger zone of the breasts.

(Winship 2002)

These ways of looking at ads are alert to the context of reception. This is not however to warrant celebration of unfettered interpretive 'play'. Ads induce anxiety; disturbance as well as humour. But, instance by instance a picture can be built up of the potentialities the genre opens up for debate, as well as the narrowing it seems at times to usher in. Van Zoonen and Meijer (2002), Winship (2001 and see Meijer 1998) present readers as mobile, their engagements with advertising by no means necessarily positive, but preserving, before the advertisement, a space for distancing and criticism, dismissal as well as engagement – a space potentially available to each and every reader.

Cronin (2004), emphasising the dynamic 'rhythmical' patterns of city time/(s)pace, and advertising's role in ordering and refreshing the city-scapes, suggests that the notion of mobility in textual engagements 'can capture the uniqueness of those moments of travel, thought, and embodied experience whether they mesh completely with the commodity time-space' of advertising 'whether they ignore, refract or resist those structuring elements' (Cronin 2004).

For some approaches the dynamics of the 'cityscape' and advertising's intervention in its rhythms and flows find a parallel in the 'interior world' of the consumer. Marketing psychology predominates in the industry's conception of consumer behaviour and advertising reception – instituted in media planning and buying models – upon long-standing models of ad stimulus and audience response, image exposure, recall, attitude change, etc. However, even within the industry there is some acceptance of the mechanistic redundancy in some of its working psychological assumptions – a realisation that has underpinned a number of appropriations from, collaborations with and allusions to cultural theory (Boutlis 2000), semiotics (Valentine 2007) and, as we will now discuss psychoanalysis (Dichter 1960; Martineau 1957; Stern 2002; Gordon 2006).

## ADVERTISING AND PSYCHOANALYSIS

If the close reading of advertisements, through semiotics and other kinds of textual analysis are critical acts whose emphases (primarily) open up the spaces of the object and the text, then psychoanalysis and its various accounts of consuming and experiencing advertisements, in line with aspects of other types of reader-oriented study, attempts to open up the spaces of the subject and desire. It is with the subject, free associating about dreams on the proverbial couch, that psychoanalysis starts. Advertising (so it is supposed) typically starts with its objects: products, brands and target markets. It is probably better to say that relations between subjects and objects are usually on the agenda in both advertising and psychoanalysis; and in the criticisms they inspire and provoke.

The most famous and best-selling book about advertising, Vance Packard's (1957) *The Hidden Persuaders*, was a 'sensationalist' (Horowitz 1994; Davidson 1992: 1–2) account of the coming together of a form of psychoanalytic exploration called 'motivation research' (see Richards *et al.* 2000: 23–4; Dichter 1960) and the advertising industry. The relationships between the two fields of activity are more complex than the title of one of Packard's magazine articles, 'The Ad and the Id', (Packard 1957) suggests. Psychoanalysis is *not* a tool of commercial mind control. However, an understanding of psychoanalytic concepts can certainly assist in thinking about advertising, even while these remain two quite distinct topics.

So psychoanalysis and advertising are divided, if not by any common language, then by common preoccupations. Frankfurt school critics have described the culture industries in general as 'psychoanalysis in reverse' (Adorno, cited in Leppert 2002: 32). This provides a particularly fitting slogan for the advertising industry if its work is understood to confuse and undermine subjects thinking and desire, or, more dramatically, to keep them in 'psychic bondage' to delusional engagements with commodities. This is the antithesis of psychoanalysis, which offers, in some sense, to free the subject from the extremities of fetishism and fantasy, and to reintegrate experience within 'proper' boundaries – although this claim does not go undisputed (Frosch 1997: 156–9). Psychoanalysis aims to be transformative in the long-term – working to restore the patients' sense of 'goodness' and his or her capacities for relating to the world, its objects and other people. Advertising, instance by instance, appears to offer shorter-term 'solutions' typically related to consumption of available goods. Britton (1999) speaks about truth-seeking and truth-evading genres and states of mind. Advertising has largely deserved its place in the latter category, even while being *in toto* and at times a powerful (if elliptical) reminder of the truth value and importance of desire and its objects.

Advertising and psychoanalysis are both discourses concerned, in their distinct ways, with conceptualising and addressing questions of 'desire', 'greed', 'motivation', 'the unconscious', 'symbolic communication' and 'suggestion'. At some level both discourses are concerned too, with social questions, for example around familial attachment, gender, generation, status, identity, bodies, belonging, pleasure, leisure and duty. Necessarily consumption (and non- or anti- consumption) reflect many of these areas of questioning, and advertising indirectly shares, through its imagery and via research, in culture-wide conversations about these topics. An unintended but prominent consequence of advertising communications, PR and lifestyle discourses more broadly, is the maintenance of more arenas where questions and conclusions about 'consuming issues' are posed and re-posed – potentially inducing fetishism and insecurities – around food, looks, belonging and so on.

Psychoanalysis, as discipline and activity, connects with consumption quite directly. It considers patients' self-image and eating disorders as well as disorder made manifest in various kinds of obsessive consumer behaviours: addictions and phobias (Orbach 1993). Observation by one early pioneer in applying psychoanalysis to culture reveals a now almost commonsensical psychoanalytic take on consumption, as substitute gratification; the commonsensical quality is testimony to the enormous and partly unacknowledged influence and currency psychoanalytic ideas have in popular culture.[5] Thus Horney wrote: 'A feeling of being loved, for instance, may suddenly reduce the strength of a compulsive wish to buy' (Horney 1937: 125–6). A more developed treatment of this theme is found in Fromm's (1976) To Have or To Be. These authors, like Adorno, are in some ways associated with the Frankfurt school and outline a critique of advertising and commodification based partly on psychoanalytic concepts.

Seventy years on, one current philosophy of branding, 'lovemarks' (Roberts 2004 and see Chapter 5), attempts, in making consumers 'fall in love', 'irrationally' with brands, to conjoin symptom and cure, with consumption of these ('living' and loveable) brands set as a cure for malaises associated with consuming those, 'bad', generic commodified ones. The too ready equation of human relations and market relations is a perennial concern within psychoanalytic accounts of contemporary culture, and in treating some contemporary patients: Just as it has been in thinking about advertising, from semiotic, cultural and political-economic perspectives. However, psychoanalysis, with its subtle and varying approaches to the subject, body, desire and anxiety, is not uniformly a 'stick' with which to beat advertising (Falk 1994; Richards 1994; Richards et al. 2000), although it would be fair to say it has been used for that purpose on many occasions (Williamson 1978; Haineault and Roy 1993; Lasch 1979: 71–7).

# ADVERTISING: ARTICULATING AND RESOLVING CONFLICT

A major psychoanalytic insight is that people live in conflict, not just with others (as politics, economics and sociology principally describe it), but also within themselves. Such conflicts are constitutive of all human action and emerge in developmental processes (of separation and individuation), notably during and after breast-feeding (perhaps the first material act of consumption), and also as part of what Freud described as the 'Oedipus complex', named after the hero of a Greek tragedy who killed his father and slept with his mother. The involved and involving early passages of the infant's life and as the child develops become the stage for a traumatic play of early fantasies and anxieties, to be suffered, enjoyed and managed within the culturally and semiotically mediated and mediating family. Progress, good or bad, will engender residues (unthinkable desires and anxieties) in the psyche-soma (mind/body) to subsequently shape and lend tone to adult narratives and experiences of desire and restraint, social connection and disconnection. The developmental process tempers engagement with and within semio-cultural resources – capacities for language and communication, meaning, gesture and object relating. Advertising (in this culture) as one such frequently-encountered socio-semiotic resource becomes one important area of experience where anxiety and desire play out.

Ongoing adolescents and adults develop capacities to acknowledge, learn from and manage anxious conflict. Cultural resources are beneficial in spurring thinking and enlivening experience. Internal conflict can also leave a person paralysed and inhibited with guilt or fear, or lend his or her actions and thinking processes the character of symptoms: obsessive, narrow, manic and unrealistic – perhaps over-investing in the advertising promise or violently rejecting engagement with 'tainted' goods (e.g. food or fashions) and the social relations they appear to embody or enact.

Cursorily, the resultant character structure emerging from the developmental experience described by psychoanalysis is one where conflict (and pain) are inherent in the healthy person: *present* but *coped with*. The art of life becomes the ability to integrate and manage conflict and loss creatively and productively in, as Freud suggested, 'love and work',[6] but also, and increasingly as modern wisdom suggests, in 'good' – i.e. personally regulated, sustainable, satisfying and meaningful – consumption. Of course determining the 'good' is a matter of conflict and it is not always clear what role advertising has in helping consumers towards 'good' consumption – though, as Dichter (1960) and others have proposed, non- or curtailed consumption out of excessive guilt or other inhibition is socially debilitating – just as much as greed. Advertising does provide some legitimation for pleasure and engagement, to set against culturally-affirmed Puritanism.

For the unhealthy person conflict and loss are not managed. Various damaging compensations, substitutions and evasions prevent thriving: addiction, greed, delusion and narcissism. Advertising has been implicated as contributory in each of these – often in the generalising diagnoses of broader cultural critique (e.g. Lasch 1979).

The divided conception of 'the self' is not unique to psychoanalysis (Fukuyama 2002: 118). Ordinary experience supports the view that we have contradictory wishes. It follows that we cannot always fully understand ourselves, our motives and choices, or relate well to others. If we do not acknowledge our conflicted constitution and the conflicted underpinnings of action and motivation our outward actions, and our attached rationalised accounts of motivation, may not, indeed cannot, adequately reference the unacknowledged impulses that precede, shadow and materialise in manifest decision and action. Psychoanalysis is often thought of in these terms; as a 'key' to understanding and dealing with such complex hidden or 'unconscious' conflict and motivation.

Undoubtedly a good deal is lost in translation between the consulting room and consumer motivation or advertising research report. Never-theless, market-based actions – choosing a car or a pair of shoes – are often based on quite dramatic compromises between different 'interior' impulses: a creative effort or a struggle to condense and resolve numerous competing impulses in manifest and symbolic action – to behave well, to be loved, to 'defeat an enemy', to make amends, to be noticed, to show restraint and so on. Advertising makes it easier to think goods into experiences and the conflicting narratives that structure the self in action. Minsky (1998) has suggested:

> Advertisers have been able to define the particular commercial forms our unconscious wishes might take so that cars or beer, Coca Cola or a pair of Nike trainers may come to represent, for example, sexual wishes, power, status, security, comfort or a sense of belonging.
>
> (Minsky 1998: 185)

These narratives are connected to a subject constituted in conflict. That the self psychoanalysis describes is conflicted should be clear when the relatively familiar concepts of 'id', 'ego' and 'superego' are considered. The notion of communications articulating and managing conflict has been used to look at advertising quite directly – though it should be said that a good deal of the subtlety and richness of psychoanalytic thinking – in

**Table 8.2** Id, ego and superego: schema applied to advertising appeals and responses

| 'Principle' | Pleasure | Reality | 'Principles' |
|---|---|---|---|
| Freudian term | Id | Ego | Superego |
| Subjective mode | Impulse | Reason | Conscience |
| Typical appeal | 'Do it now' | Wait | 'Don't do it' |
| Aim | Satisfaction of appetite | Balance | Moral precepts |
| Main preoccupation | Energy discharge | Survival | Guilt |
| Main consideration | Desire | Wallet | Fear of debt |
| Action | Buy it | Limited funds | Do without |
| Evidentiary support drawn from . . . | Advertisement | Budget plan | Bank statement |

Source: Adapted from Ads, Fads and Consumer Culture, Arthur Asa Berger (Berger 2000: 112).

particular the embodied nature of psychoanalytic transactions – is stripped away in some applications.

Nevertheless Arthur Asa Berger (2000) (see also Richards *et al.* 2000) has examined advertising using frameworks derived from Freudian psychoanalytic conceptions of the subject. For instance Berger transcribes qualities associated with each of the psychoanalytic 'principles' into a table in which he also includes characteristic types of advertising appeal. Table 8.2 offers a slightly extended version of his table.

While advertising is normally cast as an appeal to the id, and so to fantasising, acquisitive and perhaps greedy parts of humanity, examined closely it is clear that advertisements, in different instances, attempt – indeed to a degree *must* – at times address *all modes* of subject–object engagement (Brown and Richards 1998). For example, ads combine appeals to appetite and rule breaking (id) with prudent calculation (ego) and evocations of tradition (superego). Notionally an advert for 'scrumptious apple pies: big, cheap and made like grandma's' 'speaks' (to) all three motivational 'principles'. There is no part of our subjectivity which advertisements do not attempt to prod in the ongoing effort to win over 'hearts and minds', and few consumers consider products thinking exclusively either about basic cost, or of promised gratification in isolation. Nor will someone, out of loyalty, buy British or from Marks & Spencer if the appeal and the price do not work. The three principles operate in concert and it is the function of the ego to manage the tensions emerging from discrepant urges (e.g. guilt v lust). Consumers typically weigh such things up – at some level. Irresolution and inaction in the marketplace emerging from the non-integration of the three modes (id, ego and superego) might be symptomatic of a distorted engagement with consumption – as much as from the failures of the market to provide an acceptable options in acceptable conditions. Nor would a brand succeed long if indexing a limited array of consumer motives – brute rationality or pure hedonism.

Lasswell (1932) provides an early version for this type of 'triple appeal', one developed later in market research and various conceptions of the consumer operating implicity in the advertising industry (Tadajewski 2006). Lasswell (1932) proposes:

> If the personality system is divided into reaction patterns assignable to impulse, conscience and reason, it follows that the meaning of any social object to any particular person is to be interpreted in terms of its appeal to one or more of these main divisions.
>
> (Lasswell 1932: 524–5)

When advertising is looked at in this way it becomes apparent that different advertisements, brands, product sectors and campaigns variously balance their appeal to the id, the ego and the superego. The 'character' of a product, a campaign, a brand, or even a culture might be helpfully rendered by a close look at the relative weight and prominence (in the semiotic mix) of one or other of the appeals, so that some brands might be characterised in terms of their propensity to evoke 'id' impulses (e.g. Ferrari or Terry's chocolate), with others giving relatively more voice to 'superego' values (e.g. Volvo or Green and Black's chocolate, Figure 8.3) and with some (perhaps including still a mix of appeals) highlighting a straightforward appeal to pragmatic ego values (see Richards et al. 2000).

Figures 8.1 and 8.2, both show ads for chocolate. The ads subtly distinguish one product from another with the first, for Snickers, appealing to id impulsiveness, and the Minstrels ad pitched at a more disciplined mood.

The Snickers ad (Figure 8.1) positions Snickers as a rough and ready snack. Gratification is not to be deferred. The Minstrels ad (Figure 8.2) cleverly picks up on a product feature (the hard shell prevents melting). But it also positions the ad in relation to a more restrained mood than Snickers (Figure 8.1). Gratification is relatively deferred – positioning the

**Figure 8.1** Snickers ad.

**Figure 8.2** Minstrels ad.

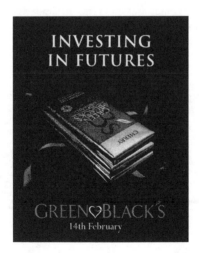

**Figure 8.3** Green and Black's ad.

products differentially in our emotional 'index'. Like many ads there is a play on an obsessive or otherwise eccentric relationship to product-consumption.

In the ad for Green and Black's chocolate (Figure 8.3) there is a reversal of the usual ad strategy where economic concerns are translated into emotional ones. Here emotional relations are reconceived in the language of finance. The ad pretends to appeal to a pragmatic motivation while, at the same time, providing a Valentine's joke. The choice of 'cherry' flavour may or may not be a hint at a sexual meaning.

The ad for Crunchy Nut Clusters (Figure 8.4) celebrates instant gratification. Crunchy 'nut' cornflakes have punningly played up the 'madness' of appetite-driven consumers in their 'id' oriented campaign. Many ads use the lexicon of mental disorder to distinguish normal consumer relations from the special relationship their product might provoke; this is in the manner of the office gag 'you'd have to be mad to work here'.

The Divine ad (Figure 8.5) offers a blend of appeals. The attractive woman is positioned, as in so many ads, as an object of desire. But the ad plays with the classic relational matrix of advertising. She is not a model, as such, but comes from the cocoa farmers' co-operative that co-owns the 'fair trade' brand 'Divine'. The joke slogan 'equality treat' puns on a well-known product name (the British confectionery assortment, Quality Street), and thereby emphasises difference in similarity as well as asserting an appeal to the moral sensibility of consumers seeking to relate to the market ethically.

**Figure 8.4** Ad for Kellogg's Crunchy Nut Clusters.

**Figure 8.5** Divine chocolate advert.

Source: © Divine Chocolate Ltd/St Lukes.

It is useful to consider these three 'principles' in their connection to the semiotic character of advertising. The chains of signifying association described by semiotics and the dynamic engagements in meaning described as 'unlimited semiosis' are not unconnected to the notion of free association, and specifically 'free association', which is also central to psychoanalysis. One useful way of thinking about what shapes and informs the subject's flow of semiosis is to propose that readers' engagements with advertisement texts are (in part) semiotic elaborations, judgements and interpretations mobilising signs in the service of the (developmentally) configured psycho-dynamics of the pleasure or reality principles; and perhaps concurrently, bringing to bear the evaluative precepts of the superego: a dynamic enacting and elaborating a complex and evolving 'self', in part through relationships and including but by no means restricted to those enacted in consumption and symbolised by advertising.

Advertising texts and attendant semiotic engagements may service the articulation of a variety of responses, responses which may be in conflict. A way of looking at the advertising genre is as a form designed specifically to provoke attention and conflict in subjects, but precisely with the aim of providing (in the sign of the product or brand) the symbolic means to a plausible, stabilising and momentary resolution or settlement in such conflict – this as a complementary perspective (Richards 1994; Richards *et al.* 2000) to set against critical analyses that automatically propose advertising as a source of evasion, defensive denial or pathological displacement of anxious conflict (Haineault and Roy 1993).

Figure 8.6 is an advertisement for Patek Philippe watches demonstrating the 'triple' appeal of advertising. The scene depicts a moment, a gesture of release, of freedom, with the child and his father bursting out of the house, through the constraining doors and out 'to play'. They are leaving something behind, momentarily suspending the adult world of the imposing middle-class home, and (symbolically) suggested implicature of (domestic/maternal) adult authority and responsibilities, in favour of the boundless outside; crossing a threshold and escaping. But in the same movement there is a reaffirmation of relations of authority: the child is bound to his father, eagerly following him, submitting to his lead. The tag line 'begin your own tradition' is supported by and supports both of these movements (escape *and* familial bonding). The slogan reaffirms this dynamic, situating the watch in a dramatic tension binding past, present and future, which is what ads (and a watch) aim to do: trace the product with the consumers' life events – connected to embodied or fantasised narratives.

The idea that 'You never actually own a Patek Philippe, you merely look after it for the next generation' is a classic evocation of the benign superego, protective, nurturing and authoritative. It also euphemises the economic fact of purchase, and perhaps offers a 'response' to the anticipated 'reality-based' objection provoked by what is probably an expensive and (in pragmatic terms) unnecessary purchase. The close detail, showing the product face on, open for scrutiny, is similarly satisfying: to the pragmatic sense that wants to see the product, and also to the 'id', which may add a tone of pleasure and longing to the contemplation of an impressive if indulgently crafted object.

**Figure 8.6** Patek Philippe ad.

The Patek Philippe ad offers a fantasy vision of oedipal harmony. The commercial element of ownership, as so often in advertising, is euphemised so as to represent the commodity as a *gift* (Offer 1996).

Critical examination of advertising, especially when speaking in general terms, often works on the assumption that advertising is socially damaging because of the over predominance in its aggregated appeals, to just one of the 'principles' of subjectivity: desire, rationality or ethical constraint.

For instance criticism of advertising that proposes rational action as the optimal mode of consumer choice (and social organisation), characterises advertising as preventing proper deliberation and calculation (ego) by representing products in the glamorous shadow of irrelevant seductions (id) or by appeals to obsolete, guilt-inducing and 'primitive' traditions or value systems (superego). On the other hand, social visions privileging tradition or encouraging the extension and elaboration of hedonism or enchantment might question the rationalistic character of some advertising appeals – and their problem solving or cost-benefit approach to life – as well as the limited or repetitive nature of the pleasures and values indexed in most advertising.

The flexibility of psychoanalytic concepts in thinking about advertising and consumption should not distract from the differences between psychoanalysis as a clinical encounter, and psychoanalysis as a useful theoretical resource. One realistically sceptical commentary recently observed in relation to a brand analysis pointed out: ' . . . advertising such as Tango or Peperami and brands like Persil . . . seem to speak to consumers of their deepest values and beliefs', but, he warned, echoing the scepticism with which psychoanalysis is treated in poplar culture, 'whatever kind of depth it is that we are concerned with in market research it is not the same as the depth of the Oedipus Conflict, Thanatos or Penis Envy' (Fletcher and Morgan 2000).

Nevertheless, the capacity of psychoanalytic conceptions to capture the dynamics of the psyche-soma – the hybrid body/mind posited by some psychoanalytic thinking that constitutes the subjective site for the movement of meaning and semiosis – ensures psychoanalysis has a relevance, alongside other means aiming to capture something of the complexity of audiences' experiences of advertising. Ads seemingly carry some of the mythic functions of traditional colloquial and folkloric genres – conveying truisms and affirming everyday 'wisdom' – that serve cultural communication.

A recent campaign for mortgage products uses a hot air balloon in the shape of a house as a metaphor. It makes a straightforward rational set of proposals about the product – but the accompanying film offers a glimpse into an emotional world of anxiety and desire. This is routine in the richly crafted and carefully made ads that cross audiences' TV screens daily.

The journey begins with the house shaped and painted hot air balloon alone, high in the stormy sky (symbolic sign of difficulties). The viewers will idly follow it into clear open skies, and down over streets of secure looking terraced homes. Perhaps some of the audience will read the balloon as both an iconic sign of a house – a containing accommodation for a young

This (40 second) TV ad has the following script:

Wish you could find a great mortgage deal that lasted more than
2 years? Here's an idea, moving to a different kind of mortgage one that
won't tie you in, one that will always track just above the base rate.
With the Abbey Flexible Plus mortgage you'll never need to change your
mortgage again. Visit your local branch call 0800 80 80 80 or go to
Abbey.com. Abbey more ideas for your money.

**Figure 8.7** Abbey: a simple proposal opens up audience's anxieties
and desires.

couple and an adventure – and others (simultaneously) as a symbolic one,
referring to the mortgage that supports home ownership. We might also
imagine, from a psychoanalytic perspective, the way the ad figures and
indexes the movements – ups and downs – of life in ways that might
resonate in subtle ways, with embodied feelings of holding and being held.
A balloon-house image is precisely suited to representing, the elusive
quality of substance and non-substance constituting a mortgaged house,
a condensation of solid bricks and mortar merged with the abstraction of
a finance product/service. Like a balloon, an embodiment of a kind of
emptiness, as well as of fullness, present and absent, so a mortgaged house
has a dual nature between ownership and debt, and by association to
feelings of security and insecurity – both financial and emotional. The ad
makes such feelings palpable to its audience, not spelling it out but also

not via any act of decoding as such, but rather in the materiality of the figured scene, associating to deep-seated (if only half registered) thoughts and feelings.

The couple inside are dependent on the balloon. Their journey appears risky. As the voice-over describes Abbey's products things become calmer – fulfilling the analogy Abbey might expect the audience to register and in the service of the brand. It would be possible to watch this ad footage and begin to imagine a variety of less reassuring journeys, perhaps (associatively) indexing fears about or experiences with mortgage finance; the iconography sparking off associative thinking and feelings about debt, dependence, responsibility and risk. The ad metaphorically alludes to such thoughts – dark skies and 'a bumpy ride' – while also, finally, allaying them in the presence of the name of the logo.

The ad charts a movement from sky to earth and from isolation to connection. The final scene shows the balloon hovering in the dusky light alongside other balloons just a few feet above the ground. The lone imperilled couple are safe alongside other (Abbey) owners; secure and calm. The ad articulates feelings about fear of abandonment, and the reassurance of being brought into the group – the 'brand family'. The ad affords the audience opportunities to 'feel' a sequence of moments linked to an argument charting homeowners' movement from danger (other insecure lenders/the market) to safety (Abbey) and from isolation to membership (with other consumers in a big branded bank).[7]

There is no reliable way of knowing that this will actually happen. Like balloons, interest rates (and 'market bubbles') go up as well as down. They can even burst. The market can crash or freeze. Yet the ad, semiotically, can incorporate, in the complexity of the associations it might provoke, both an acknowledgement of the risky nature of mortgages *and* a sense of their security *here with Abbey*. The ad binds the risk to 'the competition' and the security to its own brand – this without making specific comparisons.

The financial theme aside, we could map this ad's narrative onto a nursery rhyme and note, as Rustin and Rustin (2001) have, that narratives often begin with the provocation of anxiety (through signification), which produces (another sign, internally) excitement and fear, but which in the end is reframed, as in the ad, through more signification, asserting resolution, assurance and 'containment' of anxiety. 'Rock-a-Bye Baby' is the pattern for this; risk is followed by care and support (we might think of other children's games such as Peek-a-Boo and Hide and Seek where anxieties about separation and loss enervate the game to a point, and then reassurance is provided before the prospect of being lost or abandoned gets too scary).

This is the text of the nursery rhyme:

*Rock-a-Bye, Baby*

Rock-a-bye, baby
In the treetop
When the wind blows
The cradle will rock
When the bough breaks
The cradle will fall
And down will come baby
Cradle and all.

Baby is drowsing
Cosy and fair
Mother sits near
In her rocking chair
Forward and back
The cradle she swings
And though baby sleeps
He hears what she sings.

From the high rooftops
Down to the sea
No one's as dear
As baby to me
Wee little fingers
Eyes wide and bright
Now sound asleep
Until morning light.

Advertising depends on engaging attention by tapping consumers' desires, anxieties and apprehensions about novelties, indulgence, ongoing insecurities and guilt. They excite us (when they do) because they touch on and dramatise dilemmas we might relate to: are we depriving ourselves of sensual indulgence? Have we spent too much money? Are we damaging the planet? Are we excessively consumerist? We hardly turn to ads for 'advice', but, invited or not, ads can open up some of the interior monologuing connected to everyday life and thought – and propose forms of engagement and dialogue with the world and its object, through consumption: consumption that is, of course, of *this* product, and, preferably *now*! The ad also helps to provoke and resolve tensions to secure a sign (a brand symbol) as a locus for credibility, security and trust; not just for a single purchase but towards assuring a long-term relationship – i.e. affirming a complex of cultural meaning upon which brand loyalty is built (Holt 2004) and across which further exchange will habitually accrue (Lury 2004).

Necessarily truncated, advertisements' narratives echo some of the basic story-patterns found in nursery rhymes, fairytales, films and other cultural forms. The work of placing products within engaging stories has become a prominent element of marketing, including advertising, with brands, routinely now thinking about the relation between the brand story (Jensen 1999) and consumers' life stories. Arguments (see Chapter 5 in this book) continue to be raised against advertising as cultural-representational form that has typically evaded or occluded anxiety-provoking material – producing and facilitating complacency and evasion. However, the presumption that the genre comprehensively excludes meaningful engagements with audiences' underlying preoccupations (death, loss and other anxiety-provoking ideas) is questionable. An example cited in Chapter 7 (Figure 7.3) explicitly seeks the shock value of Death Row and criminality to arrest attention. Many ads allude gently, but assuredly, to serious emotional and ethical issues and dilemmas. Advertising is commonly understood (often deservedly) as a brake on thinking, an empty diversion and a cluttering out of ideas. However, it is possible to consider that ads are not just and are not always an empty interruption. Everyday ads – as they seek our attention and credibility – can and do produce pauses for thought. Richards (1994) suggests:

> One of the characteristics of advertisements that renders them so significant in the study of culture is their unavoidable presence in public space. Whatever particular goods they may be promoting, they set an agenda for our everyday experience in their use (usually through skilfully constructed rich and powerful imagery) of psychosocial themes. They do not create these themes: insecurity of various kinds, envy and guilt are not foisted upon an innocent public by manipulative copywriters. But they do articulate these themes in specific ways that help to shape the predominant experience of self and society, and of course to link the resolution of problems to the consumption of goods.
>
> (Richards 1994: 103)

The rationale behind production of intense and striking ad-images is, as ever, a commercial one – culturally 'good' ads grab attention and are crucial in certain product sectors. But to grab attention is not necessarily to control and guide the processes of reception – the semiosis that unfolds in the face of an arresting sign can, in certain circumstances, enable productive connections – inter- and intra-personal – and enliven thinking and the 'cultural conversation' (Richards 1994: Richards *et al.* 2000; Haineault and Roy 1993; Falk 1994: Holt 2004).

## CONCLUSION: MAKING YOUR MIND UP

Advertisements are momentary and ephemeral cultural events; 'incidents' (Barthes 1992); narratives and snapshots, montages which are at points spectacular and negligible, intrusive yet undemanding. Making such 'glimpses' intelligible is a part of the (not uncreative) work of individuals' and audiences' ongoing experience. Genre conventions for understanding advertising communication are instilled in us in the course of everyday living, allowing us to read advertisements without discernible effort. We grow up turning this interpretive capacity into a basic competence.

As part of that learning, in learning from experience, and, perhaps, also from science, religion, journalism and the humanities, we can acquire additional capacities to judge the kinds of proposition advertisements are making – ads are always critically under review. Consumers know advertising as a certain genre, and might permit it to express only certain kinds of 'truth', for example information to assist in marketplace choices (which they might supplement, or ignore, in favour of other, better sources). Even if readers are 'done with' the informational content (as if that could be conveniently split off in an engagement with an ad), in any advertisement there remains a coextensive element, one which is integral to the advertisement, which engages readers (and which is engaged) in ways distinct from the more binding logics of verification and falsification.

This remainder, extending across the surface and through any advertising communication, might serve as an (idle) source of pleasure: of play and entertainment, or of 'edutainment', quiet satisfaction, 'critical' insight, or aesthetic contemplation. Peirce (1908) called similar everyday encounters with materials objects 'musement', an activity he suggested we indulge in 'moderately'.[8] Advertising is one of the many modern sources of purposeless entertainment/leisure, one to which we may give a little too much time. Advertisers hope that, in engaging with the ad, aesthetically or in acts of daydreaming, interpretation or calculation, some further associative links might form in consumers' minds, or become reaffirmed. Such a process will (perhaps) establish the product-idea or the brand-idea, nudge it into a 'position' (Stern 1991; Bonney and Wilson 1990; Ries and Trout 1982) in readers' sensibility and lives, relative to other competitor brands and other valued signs, leading to further engagements and brand owners' profits.

To return to the analogy with 'Rock-a-Bye Baby' above, the pattern of cultural engagement with advertising (induced excitement and anxiety followed by reassuring resolution, common to many ads), invites the conclusion that such texts, as it were, sing us to sleep. The somnambulist mass consumer-subjects depicted by generations of criticism come to mind. We are reminded too of the reservations critics have had more generally about aesthetically ambitious postmodern advertising (Goldman 1992). The weight of cultural analysis of advertising remains with that view. Ads produce at best 'defensive' representations – opening up imagination long enough to provoke anxiety or desire but foreclosing on deeper dilemmas and emotions. Advertising stands as a predominant everyday form of cultural representation cutting us off and diverting from important sources of thinking and cultural apprehension (Haineault and Roy 1993; Jhally 1990; Williamson 1978). The semiosis inducing (potentially) rich, funny, dreamy engagement with a cultural text is foreclosed in the face of strapline or logo: associative chains collapse, the space of cultural relating constrained to the 'buy one get one free' dimensions of a market transaction.

That said, and as Richards (1994) has suggested, while advertising is functionally committed to a market-based understanding of human rela-tions – fostering a limited and limiting conception of audiences' subjective life – as a genre it faces a dilemma of its own. For ads to produce the authentic and culturally-credible attentiveness that they are required to produce (Davenport and Beck 2001; Lewis and Bridger 2000; Gilmore and Pine 2007), they must engage attention in registers and through ideas that are culturally more profound than the 'I shop therefore I am', 'consumer-centric' ideas fashionable in much neo-liberal political argument and which imbricates everyday commercial logics and logistics.

Through ad-based, and lately brand cultures, what Richards (1994) has called 'a projective system' of consumer goods emerges – one that is at once internal (our own significant reference points) and external (with cultural and material correlates). This 'system', which is not systematic, is sustained, interactive and continually revised; but only in part by advertisements. It should be noted too that product sectors actually constitute 'mini' projective systems within themselves; individuals and age groups and genders have profoundly varying knowledge about and interest in different product sectors. The power of some brands is to be able to use signification, for example logos, in the work of moving attention from one sector to another; advertising performs a proportion of this work.

Many ads are produced in the hope that audiences might draw certain conclusions (logically); but they mostly also seek to embed the product or brand within networks of personal and cultural association – memory and anticipation. For the consumer, the product more readily becomes an exemplar of some familiar feeling or perhaps unspoken conception such as 'good', 'home' or 'teenage kicks'. Ads engage and are engaged (interpretively) in thinking and daydreaming of this kind: processing, as semioticians have it, that is open, potentially endless, 'unlimited semiosis' – the semiotic correlate of 'going on being' or 'becoming'.

To pathologise such mental processes too readily is to mistake engage- ment *with* for subjection *to*: to celebrate them too readily, however, is to understate the ultimately perfunctory nature of the cultural material advertisements routinely present (however artful). 'Becoming', maybe; but becoming who or what? It is this polarisation between interpretive semiotic processes – 'unlimited semiosis' – and semiotically enforced sub- jection that enables Barthes (1988) to identify advertising contradictorily as both deluding and as among 'those great aliments of psychic nutrition . . . which for us include literature performances, movies, sports, the press, Fashion' (Barthes 1988: 178). He continues, describing advertising as a genre that:

> reintroduces the dream into the humanity of the purchasers: the dream: i.e., no doubt, a certain, alienation (that of competitive society), but also a certain truth (that of poetry).
>
> (Barthes 1988: 178)

However, Lury's essay on commercial imagery and consumers' semiosis offers a helpful observation to bring us back down to earth: 'rather than reaching towards infinity . . . we confront unlimited finitude' (Lury 2000: 179).

Advertising rests on a contradiction. It strives – ad by ad – in amongst and competing with numerous other cultural-semiotic and marketing resources – especially other advertisers/brands – to bind an array of incommensurable flows:

- economic productivity and innovation – producers' profit motive;
- rhythms and arrhythmias of the economic cycle – shifting credit/debt, affluence and relative poverty, consumer confidence, etc.;
- individuals' and audiences' shifting conceptions of consumer ethos, needs and desires;
- regulation issues – national and regional;
- the permeable boundaries between local and global sub and meta- cultures – notably fragmenting/transforming media technologies and habits of media use.

For ads to effectively navigate and connect these different spaces requires a creative act. Advertisers hope that the materiality of economic production (cars, shoes, banking services) can be transformed to enable 'goods' to move through audiences and resonate credibly within 'live' consumer cultures. Increasingly, and as networks of connection and disconnection become more complex (with technology and globalisation leading such processes), the work of binding products to living and working consumer cultures will require a continuing opening-out – even a turning-inside-out – of marketing interfaces such as advertising. The genre's capacity to deliver up cultural authenticity will be tested, possibly to destruction. Indeed 'branding' and not 'advertising' has become the most suitable term in thinking about the multi-dimensional engagements between audiences and systems of production and provision – extending analysis and scrutiny beyond texts, audiences and ad agencies and reconnecting with contexts of global production and trade, eco-consciousness, corporate managerialism and the utilisation of human resources by brand owners.

Advertising in future faces an intensification of long-exerted pressures. On the one hand the intensification of hyper-rational price-based marketing driven through information rich, hyper-searchable mobile/finger tip databases and direct consumer-provider interfaces will bypass some of the explicitly cultural and marketing information functions underpinned for decades in advertising. At the same time and conversely, as Donaton (2004) has suggested, brands will use advertising, and advertising derived aesthetics, in wider arrays of branded-cultural communications. In these communications (as opposed to the price-based data-ads) the marketing intention of advertising will become yet more elliptical and tangential, with brand cultures and cultural brands striving to produce a semiosphere combining social, market and cultural signification seamlessly – via sponsorship, event creation, product placements and celebrity-brand building. Without us noticing, some advertising modes will disappear – going the way of print-based classified ads – to re-emerge in new modes of mediation and new technology platforms.

Branding watchwords will reference product and service functionality, price competitiveness, trust, credibility and authenticity. But, in particular relationship and interactive responsiveness (allowing personalisation and stimulating/simulating decommodification) will become ever more prominent corporate-brand aspirations. Advertising, as has been suggested for some time, and as the genre is currently configured, is not fully equipped to provide the communicative interfaces demanded by either brand owners or consumers. We will continue to see web-based interfaces taking over and enhancing consumer and brand communications management. However, a degree of consumer scepticism about being at the wrong end of rationalising customer relationship marketing systems

– remote call-centre systems and depersonalising Internet-based interfaces are increasingly seen less as a convenience and more as (face-to-face) service limitation.

What might resemble a kind of de-commercialisation of media culture is in prospect, in the limited sense that there might be more channels and publications based on subscription income – displaying little or no advertising. Paradoxically such de-commercialisation of the media sphere will provoke a redistribution of the marketing function across many more numerous and fragmented (cultural) interfaces – and perhaps further into unlikely and hitherto largely sacrosanct places and spaces (notably with advertisers sponsoring educational institutions and yet further cultural activities). Indeed, if and as the boundaries between public and private provision of goods and services, e.g. in health, education and city infrastructure, become ever more porous, it is likely that commercially-based communications habits and expertise will continue to characterise reconfigured relationships to hospitals, school, and local and national government services.

Audiences, driven by daily irritation and boredom, might hope to strike advertising down. However, and even as and where it seems to recede and even disappear, there is the concomitant prospect that (refigured and further integrated in institutional and entertainment cultures) our engagements across commercial interfaces will continue to prompt, prod and provoke us to consume.

# NOTES

## INTRODUCTION

1   *Keep the Aspidistra Flying* is based on a novel by George Orwell. Orwell is an important critic of advertising, which he associated with other forms of propaganda. These topics are also explored in his most famous novels *Animal Farm* (Orwell 1945) and *1984* (Orwell 1949).

2   For instance in 2006 in the UK there is strong government support for banning media-based advertising for junk-foods during programmes likely to be watched by under 16s. However, McDonalds, regularly associated with the label 'junk-food', has successful sponsorship initiatives linked to sports (e.g. football) which ensures promotional exposure for the brand. Likewise McDonalds is amongst a number of major official sponsors for the Olympic Games – this coverage, less direct than advertising, escapes the regulatory scrutiny applied to broadcast and published items of promotional advertising.

3   The Advertising Association, an industry body in the UK working to oversee best practice in advertising, has a useful website providing, amongst other things, informative records of advertising complaints.

4   This has been an important advertising strategy in the twentieth century. Dotz and Husain (2003) provide many hundreds of familiar faces from the history of advertising. Michelin is amongst the oldest and one of the most widely known.

5   American media theorist Marshall McLuhan coined this phrase (with a different emphasis) for the title of his (1964) book *Understanding Media: the Extensions of Man*.

6   It should be noted here that it is increasingly inaccurate to talk about a 'typical' agency, or to identify 'the advertising process'. Included amongst the many changes facing advertising industry is a move away for traditional models of institutional organisation.

## 2   ADVERTISING AGENCIES

1    Of course tea bags are not 'natural', either; decades of advertising have striven to normalise the tea bag (as against loose leaves and a pot) in the normal domestic process of tea-making.

2    Suggestive is not to say subliminal, however. There is a temptation to see advertising's elliptical rhetoric as grounds for identifying its messages as having 'secret' or 'hidden' meanings. This is to misunderstand the processes of interpretation and association that underpin audience responses (or non-responses). Indeed the ancient 'if . . . then' propositional structure (Barnard 1995) is one which is sometimes reductively imposed on ads for the purposes of criticism of the genre's failure to persuade *logically* (Thompson 1990: 211) or products' failures to deliver 'promised' outcomes.

3    A useful shorthand way of differentiating product sectors and consumers' thinking/feeling about products is used in the industry. Known as the Foote Cone Belding Planning Grid, it was used by that agency in working up its advertising approaches and linking products to typical consumer orientations.

|  | THINK | FEEL |
|---|---|---|
| High involvement | High-involvement thinking. Decisions characterised by a high level of involvement and a primarily rational decision process. Examples of high-involvement thinking products include cars, homes, major appliances and consumer electronics. | High-involvement feeling. Important, high-involvement decisions in which the decision criteria are primarily affective or emotional. Examples include jewellery, cosmetics and fashion apparel. |
| Low involvement | Low-involvement, often routine product decisions, in which emotional motives are of little importance. Examples include household products such as food, tea, breakfast drinks, as well as many personal care products (razor blades) and detergents. | Everyday pleasures, low level of involvement but often emotional decision-making. Examples include snack foods, sweets and soft drinks. |

4    Of course both clothes and food can be heavily involving for consumers. The degree of involvement is not a function of the object in itself, but

of the relationship that emerges through mediation processes, consumption, use and ownership.

5 However, non-consumers arguably do have a function in the production of product image in so far as the social reputation of a brand or product becomes a component of the product's or brand's wider value and attraction.

6 ABC1 refers to acknowledged categories of probable readership – here professional, managerial and lower managerial middle- and lower-middle-class women.

7 The imprecision in measuring the impact (positive or negative) of ad campaigns on the commercial life of a brand gives judgements such as these a flavour of uncertainty.

## 3 MARKETING, MEDIA AND COMMUNICATION

1 In practice this requires identification of the best timeslot in the media schedule and the best media outlet, e.g. a national or local newspaper. 'Cultural' and social locations require a more subtle estimation based on a sense of the types of people who might be likely to engage with an advertising proposition – again media selection covers this process, but also creative work – tuning in to the cultural styles most relevant at the 'destination'.

2 More recently as the FCUK branding has become a tired cliché the brand has struggled. Some commentators attribute this directly to the absence of a new advertising-based direction for the brand.

3 The car company Audi now has a TV channel, as do a number of travel firms.

4 The Internet (e-shots and websites) provides a powerful tool in this effort.

5 A connected development has seen the diversification in the ways an advertising agency earns income. While in the past a commission was earned (c.15 per cent), derived from the advertisers' expenditure on advertising media within a campaign, today a number of remuneration models operate, respecting the variety of agency–client relationships entered into in the development and management of a 'brand'.

6 This issue, viewers' technological management of their interactive media environment, is supplementary to longer standing debates in media and advertising studies about active and/or passive media consumers.

## 4 ANALYSING AND HISTORICISING ADVERTISING

1 The ubiquity of advertising is sometimes overstated – but it is difficult not to be surprised at the continual ingenuity of the advertising industry as it penetrates new spaces, new media and new territories.

2    Other approaches for instance foreground the sign and signification (see Chapters 5, 6 and 7 of this volume) or particular themes: gender, ethnicity or social values. Analysis will often typically consider and integrate concepts and analytic techniques.

3    The successful documentary *Super Size Me* (2004) dramatises the potential ill effects emergent when 'appetite', a human system, is over-run by 'super size' commodity marketing – a corporate system.

4    Shoppers confronted with numberless racks of objects will report disillusionment. On another day and in another mood they will return, convinced of the value of their mission. Advertising audiences are the same: astonished one day at the banality of advertisements, but on another occasion they will find themselves enraptured by an image or a narrative.

5    Nixon (2003: 20) warns against inserting analyses of 'advertising' too readily within grander historical narratives and 'reductive' models of 'epochal' social and cultural change.

6    It is worth pointing out that such 'roles' are neither binding nor all-encompassing; they merely describe instituted instances (of varying duration) of identification, relationship and action.

7    And, as Nevett (1980) and Williams (1980) point out, advertising in the broadest and therefore the least helpful sense is as old as the most ancient societies. De Vreis is prepared to go further and writes: 'Advertising is as old as humanity: indeed, much older; for what are the flaunting colours of the flowers but so many invitations to the bees to "come buy our product"' (1968: 6).

8    *Caveat emptor*: buyer beware.

9    Presbrey (1929) is an often cited resource for UK and US early period advertising history; see also Turner 1952 and Nevett 1980 for the UK. For more recent treatments and revisions see McFall 2004, and McFall 2004.

10   Historians of modern (Nixon 2003) and early advertising (McFall 2004) have taken Williamson's point of view as an explanation for the (mistaken) and past neglect by academic critics of makers of advertisements (as opposed to the ads themselves).

11   A 'joynted baby' was a doll.

12   For instance McFall (2004: 80) cites Addison's 1710 essay in praise of advertising copywriters.

13   No formal research took place of course.

14   H. G. Wells was a socialist and intellectual and novelist most famous for his science fiction classic *The Time Machine*,1898.

15   However the word 'brand' appears in the novel only once.

16   Williams's occlusion of the early forms of 'advertising' and other sophisticated promotional forms (such as those identified by Wernick 1991 and McFall 2004) from his definition of 'modern advertising',

an exclusion extending forwards beyond Johnson's time (1759), is consistent with a definition of advertising precisely as a persuasive communicative form circulating because placed in paid-for media. Important too is the formalised and institutional nature of modern advertising, as an autonomous business in itself, not an offshoot of publication or trade. Williams perhaps excluded other promotional forms of marketing communication, ancestors of what has come to be known as 'below the line' advertising because, primarily, he wanted to give emphasis to the impact that paid for media-based advertising (and resultant dependencies) have had on public media. For Williams the aim of advertising history is to trace the development to an institutionalised system of commercial information and persuasion, to relate this to changes in society and in the economy, and to trace changes in method in the context of changing organisations and intentions. Williams (1980), McFall and others (Barnard 1995) have argued that to locate the emergence of persuasive advertising too precisely in the twentieth century ignores key evidence of a longstanding tradition of pre-modern creative advertising.

17  The critique of advertisements in this era typically trumped the 'magical' discourse of advertising with the authoritative discourse of science: facts over fiction. This is indicative from the *Daily Mail's* critique: 'An exposure by Sir William J. Pope, K.B.E., F.R.S., M.A., D.Sc., LL.D., Professor of Chemistry in the University of Cambridge. Sir William said he would set out to show that "Yadil" was not "trimethenal allylic carbide" as it professed to be, but a dilute solution of a well-known substance; that it was sold at a price some sixty times the actual cost of the materials used; and that no valid evidence had been produced to show that it had any efficacy in curing the maladies listed in its advertisements – namely consumption, cancer, bronchitis, pleurisy, pneumonia, malaria, scarlet fever, measles, diphtheria, pernicious anaemia, and others' (*Daily Mail* 1924, cited in Turner 1952: 185).

18  Early newspaper advertising remained predominantly a medium of the word: images came later. A curious interim stage saw advertising placed in newspapers in such a way that type was able to form larger words or other iconic patterns. Photography came in the ads of the 1920s (Marchand 1985: 149).

19  McFall (2002) usefully reminds us of the existence of the 'old cultural intermediaries'.

20  S.C.A.P.A society was founded in 1893 (Nevett 1981; Turner 1952: 112) and attacked advertising on grounds of taste and decency and in terms of environmental – landscape, protection.

## 5   ADVERTISING AND CULTURE

1   *Scrutiny* was a Cambridge periodical which ran for 19 volumes from 1932 to 1953, edited by L. C. Knights, Donald Culver, Denys Thompson, D. W. Harding and others, but dominated largely by F. R. Leavis; a 20th issue, with a 'Retrospect' by Leavis, appeared in 1963 (see *The Oxford Companion to English Literature* 1995).

2   See also Henry 1966; Hoggart 1957; Thompson 1943; Inglis 1971; Scruton 2000 for detailed examples of related critical approaches.

3   In the particular context of these errors, the spelling offence would be especially serious. The mistakes occur in an excerpt from a poem by Andrew Marvell who remains a particular hero to many scholars of classic English literature. The advertisers' casual treatment of one of the great voices of English poetry would mark the advertisement as especially unpalatable to their literary sensibility.

4   It would be left to a later generation (of feminist critics) to highlight another likely critical objection to this particular advertisement: the objectification and commoditisation of the female body – the metaphoric equation of a series of product parts with the feminine body (see for instance, Winship 1981; Moog 1990) justly provokes critical commentary

5   The still montage reproduced from the Müller website does not reflect the full range of ethnicities in the TV ad proper.

6   'Intertextual' meaning, when one text is made up of elements of one or more previous texts, bound together to make a new 'text' which draws on, but also elaborates on the past meanings of source texts, as well as generating its new textual meanings within new communicative contexts of reading and interpretive reception.

7   Including of course the various other types of real and virtual marketplaces: cultural events, online retailers and 'invisible' services – such as advice and care.

8   Frosch (2003) provides a detailed insight into the workings of the large industry which provides 'stock' images to advertising and other media. For a price advertisers can buy off-the-shelf images based on conventional and conventionalising poses in order to depict ideas visually – personal and social relationships to tag onto ads. The mass produced nature of these images – and the archive systems through which they are stored and searched – ensures a continuance in pre-specified typification as a 'ready-to-wear' outfit for quick turnaround low budget campaigns.

9   Largely Goffman's examples are from North American society and reflect the conventions of advertising in highly developed consumer societies of the West in the 1970s.

10  'Genderquake' is a term coined by Wolf (1993) to capture the various social and cultural shifts in the politics and experiences of genre in the twentieth century – and in particular in the period post-1960.

11 Note however Mcfall (2004) who makes useful points regarding the assumption of a too radical shift in advertising especially from a use focus to image focus.

12 C.S. Peirce, an highly influential thinker in this field proposed that: 'the universe . . . is perfused with signs, if it is not composed exclusively of signs' (Peirce 1931–58, 5.449n).

## 6   SIGNS AND TEXTUALITIES

1 It should be said however that advertising income can suppress novelty in media production as much as stimulating new ideas or formats.

2 Transport technologies such as cars and space travel are also profoundly implicated in changing the ways we experience and represent the world and its spaces – and these too are media for advertisements. Mobile and miniature technologies further disturb the 'natural' dimensions of everyday space and time – and will continue to provide new media opportunities for advertising and other brand-based communications.

3 The 'semiotic space of the culture in question' (Lotman 1990), or a 'semiotic ecology where different languages and media interact' (see Chandler 2002: 249).

4 Lury and Warde (1997) describe the work of advertising and branding consultancy Semiotic Solutions, who have been successful in turning the insights of semiotics to help planning advertising campaigns. Clark *et al.* (1994) argue semiotics has been a part of advertising practice since the 1950s, citing 'one of their better known studies of the 1950s' which revealed 'how intangible, and often accidental, symbolism in retail stores' advertising communicates 'my kind of store' to shoppers of different social classes (Clark *et al.* 1994: 27). They go on to point out that advertising professionals are especially adept at co-ordinating symbolic communication for advertising – without necessarily needing any specific or explicit grasp of 'semiotics'. However Valentine (2007) suggests that semiotics has made some serious contributions to marketing practice.

5 Sebeok (2002) outlines the ways that semiotics has a role in understanding natural animal and biological sign-making as much as human culture. Indeed semiotic approaches work to destabilise some of the distinctions between human and animal sign-making.

6 For instance a 2006 campaign from mobile network '3' showed ads including a singing cherry in a box and an enormous dancing jellyfish. The strong affinity between surrealist juxtaposition and advertising is explored, for instance, by Williamson (1986).

7 The favoured mode in the eighteenth and nineteenth centuries whereby painters displayed and cherished the objects of consumption: classically, fruit in bowls.

8    Williamson's influential *Decoding Advertisements* (1978) notion of en-
     coding and decoding, based heavily in linguistic models of signification,
     have supported a view of ad texts as carrying hidden codes – one taken
     to extreme in Key's work on subliminal messages (Key 1974; 1989;
     1992)

9    'Getting' used here in the sense of 'getting a joke' i.e. making sense
     of the dynamic elements of the message

10   We are prone to operate pragmatically in relation to signification, we
     understand much of what is going on around us. Communication
     depends upon a working acceptance of the system of meaning in
     operation at any point. We do not normally question the means
     of representation and signification – even while debating meanings
     within a system. Nor is it necessary to have an explicit or specialist
     grasp of semiotic concepts to communicate effectively and creatively.
     However quite profound intuitions about what semioticians would
     call the dynamics of 'sign processes' are evident as part of all kinds of
     communications and statements – from dinner party conversations,
     to makeover shows, to ad texts, to works of literature – and, as exem-
     plified e.g. by 'Banksy' in graffiti, pop art and, basically, to varying
     degrees, in most communication.

11   C.S. Peirce (1839–1914) was an American philosopher – and semioti-
     cian – working in the nineteenth century. Peirce developed 'semiotics'
     into a highly elaborated set of conceptions based on the sign – consisting
     of representamen, object and interpretant (see Figure 6.3).

12   Ferdinand de Saussure (1857–1913) was a highly influential scholar in
     the field of linguistics. Saussure proposed the development of
     semiology, a study of signs based, primarily, on his model of linguistic
     signs (i.e. signifier/signified) operating in an arbitrary system of
     differences.

13   Or, in the case of TV, radio and some Internet-based ads, *partially* verbal
     and multi-media communication.

14   Chandler suggests that academic applications (in Media and Cultural
     studies) 'most commonly employ the Peircean distinctions within a
     broadly Saussurean framework' (Chandler 2002: 36). Danesi (2002:
     31) points out a 'tendency within semiotics to amalgamate Saussurean
     and Peircean notions especially when it comes to the analysis of cultural
     phenomena', he also points out however that 'the paradigms of Saussure
     and Peirce are not isomorphic' (Danesi 2002: 31) (i.e. not readily
     interchangeable). For the purposes of this text, where the focus is on
     advertising and not semiotics as such, it is simply worth noting that
     terminologies have different genealogies. The key point is to recognise
     that advertising signification is a matter depending upon a dynamic
     operation of signifying elements – and that recognising such processes
     depends upon awareness of models of the sign.

15  Saussure studied, taught and wrote about linguistics in Switzerland in the early twentieth century.

## 7  NEW FORMS AND INTIMACIES

1  Unique selling proposition (or USP) was coined by Rosser Reeves in 1961 to describe a way of advertising products by focusing the ad on one special product feature, which could be used as a memorable and functionally distinguishing rationale by consumers selecting in a crowded marketplace. For example manufacturers adding adding additional blades and lubricating strips to razors so they stand out as the shaving implement with the best and most unique system.

2  To reiterate, the attempt to posit 'essential' or even normative characterisations of advertising today (in terms of aesthetics and culture) is to misunderstand the generative 'magpie' nature of advertising. There is always a further 'new' (or 'neo') example, and there is always a counter-example; bucking trends *is* the trend – including, of course, bucking the trend-bucking trend.

3  The use of cue cards to convey a message in this form can be traced to D.A. Pennebaker's film, *Don't Look Back* (a documentary about Bob Dylan's first tour of the UK in 1975) which has been used in many subsequent pop videos, ads (e.g. VW) and other 'edgy' programming, to the point that it becomes a cliché itself.

4  *The Office* is a UK sitcom based on a parody of the styles and gestures of workplace reality TV. It develops a trend evident in a number of precursors and has influenced many other film, ad and TV makers attracted to the ways that parody engages intimacy.

5  In the eighteenth and nineteenth centuries the use of royalty or religious figures in commercial endorsement was very commonplace. Likewise in the modern era sporting heroes and cinema icons stood as straightforward exemplars of cultural ideals in advertising. This tactic was based on an assumption that identification with exemplars and conformity were likely to be persuasive. Since the 1960s the emergence of counter-cultural trends has tended to support the cultural currency of anti-heroes; non-conformity and dis-indentification form 'mainstream' social values as a paradoxically normative stance. This to the point where the marginal, the alternative and the excluded, in suitably aestheticised ways, have become powerful mainstream discourses, with advertising chief amongst the genres trading on the aesthetic gestures of transgression, refusal and apathy. Since the 1990s the advertising industry has worked ever harder to attach the glamour of counter-cultural trends to aesthetic and the values-based appeal to the consumer.

6  The pop video and evolving cinematic styles feed and feed from such advertising developments.

7 MacLachlan and Logan (1993) reported average shot lengths: 1.6 seconds on MTV videos and 2.3 seconds in 30-second commercials (MacLachlan and Logan, 1993). A general tendency towards faster cutting has been interpreted as part of a move towards less 'rational' modes of advertising discourse. For MacLachlan and Logan the too short cuts had negative effects on the persuasiveness.

## 8    AUDIENCES AND PSYCHOLOGY

1 The nineteenth-century SCAPA Society simply removed offending ads. There is a spectrum at the end of which 'active reading' becomes activism. Protests against advertising texts have ranged from angry letters to newspaper editors, defacement, subversive doctoring and outright removal. Parody also has a long history and examples of advertising self-parody have become ever more numerous in recent years.

2 Ad 'clutter' and correlative ennui can be seen as conditions of the advertising genre rather than symptoms within 'a new phase' (see e.g. Johnson 1779, cited in Chapter 4).

3 Work of this kind on advertising readers (Alperstein 2003; O'Donohoe 1997; Nava and Nava 1992) emerged out of an emerging paradigm in cultural studies shaping work through the 1980s on a number of cultural studies projects examining various media genres, culture sectors and subjectivities, and producing some now classic studies: of readers of romance novels (Radway 1987), TV news (Morley 1980), soap opera (Ang 1985; Brunsdon 1981) and punk music.

4 Fordism describes the system of mass production dependent upon mass media – especially advertising – to induce mass consumption to maintain the levels of production and profit upon which capitalist accumulation rests.

5 *Bank of Mum and Dad* (BBC2) and *Spendaholics* are recent TV shows in the UK which situate consumption in a psychotherapeutic (if not psychoanalytic) frame. *Spendaholics* is described on its BBC programme website thus: 'Out-of-control shopaholics are put under the microscope to unravel the buried meanings behind their spiralling debt. Contributors receive a psychological make-over as their spending habits are recorded and tracked' (www.bbc.co.uk/programmes/b006t793). It is notable that these shows are both on non-commercial TV.

6 There is some doubt about the attribution of this quote but it is traced by *The Wordsworth Dictionary of Quotations* (Robertson 1998: 122) and is also linked to a paraphrase from psychoanalyst Erik Erickson's (1963) publication *Childhood and Society*.

7   The bank is now not a building society where membership was a different and firmer contractual relationship than is found in the consumer banking market.
8   He suggests some five to six percent of one's waking time, perhaps 'during a stroll'.

# BIBLIOGRAPHY

Aaker, D. 1996. *Building Strong Brands.* New York: The Free Press.

Abaitua, M. 2006. 'Letter from London', available at www.bonfireofthe brands.com/2006/04/essay-from-matthew-de-abaitua-only.html (accessed 19 December 2007).

Adorno, T. 1978. 'Culture and Administration', *TELOS* 11: 93–111.

Adorno, T. 1991. *The Culture Industry: Selected Essays on Mass Culture.* London: Routledge.

Adorno, T. 1994. *The Stars Down to Earth and other Essays on the Irrational in Culture.* London: Routledge.

Adorno, T. and Horkheimer, M. 1979. *Dialectic of Enlightenment.* London: Verso.

Ahuvia, A. 1998. 'Social Criticism of Advertising: On the Role of Literary Theory and the Use of Data', *Journal of Advertising* 27: 143–62.

Alfino, M., Caputo, J. and Wynyard, R. 1998. *McDonaldization Revisited: Critical Essays on Consumer Culture.* Westport: Praeger.

Allen, P. 2000. 'The Age of Noise: Establishing Successful Customer Relationships Amid All the Volume' *The Advertiser* (November).

Alperstein, N. 2003. *Advertising in Everyday Life.* Cresskill: Hampton Press.

Alvarado, M. and Thompson, J. 1990. *The Media Reader.* London: BFI Publishing.

Anderson, C. 2002. *The Big Lie: The Truth About Advertising.* London: Random Thoughts.

Anderson, C. 2006. *The Long Tail: How Endless Choice Is Creating Unlimited Demand.* London: Random House.

Ang, I. 1985. *Watching 'Dallas': Soap Opera and the Melodramatic Imagination.* London: Methuen.

Ang, I. 1992. 'Living-Room Wars: New Technologies, Audience Measurement and the Tactics of Television Consumption'. In R. Silverstone and

E. Hirsch (eds) *Consuming Technologies: Media and Information in Domestic Spaces*. London: Routledge, pp. 131–45.

Ang, I. 1996. *Living Room Wars: Rethinking Media Audiences for a Postmodern World*. London: Routledge.

Appadurai, A. 1986. *The Social Life of Things: Commodities in Cultural Perspective*. Cambridge: Cambridge University Press.

Appiah, O. 2001. 'Ethnic Identification on Adolescents' Evaluation of Advertisements'. *Journal of Advertising Research* 41(5): 7–22.

Arlen, M. 1980. *Thirty Seconds*. London: Penguin.

Arning, C. and Gordon, A. 2006. 'Sonic Semiotics – The Role of Music in Marketing Communications', ESOMAR Annual Conference, London.

Arvidsson, A. 2004. 'On the "Pre-History of the Panoptic Sort": Mobility in Market Research', *Surveillance and Society* 1(4): 456–74.

Arvidsson, A. 2005. 'Brands: A Critical Perspective', *Journal of Consumer Culture* 5: 235–58.

Auge, M. 1995. *Non-places: Introduction to an Anthropology of Supermodernity*. London: Verso.

Badiner, A.H. 2002. *Mindfulness in the Marketplace: Compassionate Responses to Consumerism*. Berkeley: Parallax.

Bagehot, W. 1873. *Lombard Street: A Description of the Money Markets*. London: Henry S. King & Co.

Baker, C.E. 1995. 'Advertising: Financial Support and Structural Subversion of a Democratic Press'. In *Advertising and a Democratic Press*. Princeton: Princeton University Press, pp. 7–43.

Bakhtin, M. 1981. *The Dialogic Imagination*. Austin: University of Texas Press.

Barnard, M. 1995. 'Advertising: The Rhetorical Imperative' in C. Jenks (ed.) *Visual Culture*. London: Routledge.

Barnes, M. 1975. *The Three Faces of Advertising: Economics Ethics Effects*. London: The Advertising Association.

Barnes, M. 1982. 'Public Attitudes to Advertising', *International Journal of Advertising* 1: 119–28.

Barnet, K. 2001. 'Sonic Branding Finds its Voice', Brandchannel.com/features_effect.asp?pf_id=63.

Barrett, N. 1996. *The State of the Cybernation: Cultural, Political and Economic Implications of the Internet*. London: Kogan Page.

Barthes, R. [1964] 1977. 'The Rhetoric of the Image'. In S. Heath (ed.) *Image Music Text*. New York: Hill & Wang.

Barthes, R. 1972. *Mythologies*. New York: Hill & Wang.

Barthes, R. 1977a. *Elements of Semiology*. New York: Hill & Wang.

Barthes, R. 1977b. *Image – Music – Text*. London: Fontana.

Barthes, R. 1977c. *The Pleasure of the Text*. London: Cape.

Barthes, R. 1986a. 'The Face of Garbo'. In *Mythologies*. London: Paladin.

Barthes, R. 1986b. 'One Always Fails in Speaking of What One Loves'. In *The Rustle of Language*. New York: Hill & Wang.

Barthes, R. 1988. 'The Advertising Message'. In *The Semiotic Challenge*. Oxford: Blackwell.

Barthes, R. 1992. *Incidents*. Oxford: University of California Press.

Bartolo, D.D. and Clarke, B. 1972. *Madvertising: Or Up Madison Avenue*. New York: Signet.

Baudrillard, J. 1988a. *The Ecstasy of Communication*. New York: Semiotext(e).

Baudrillard, J. 1988b. 'Simulacra and Simulations – extract'. In M. Poster (ed.) *Selected Writings*. Stanford: Stanford University Press, pp. 166–84.

Baudrillard, J. [1968] 1996. *The System of Objects*. London: Verso.

Bayley, S. 1986. *Sex, Drink and Fast Cars: The Creation and Consumption of Images*. London: Faber.

Beale, C. 2002. 'Why the Academic Take on TV Doesn't Affect Advertisers', *Campaign* (21 November).

Beale, C. 2004. 'The Creativity Conductor', *Campaign* (18 June).

Beasley, R. and Danesi, M. 2002. *Persuasive Signs: The Semiotics of Advertising*. New York: Mouton de Gruyer.

Beasley, R., Danesi, M. and Perron, P. 2000. *Signs for Sale: An Outline of Semiotic Analysis for Advertisers and Marketers*. New York: Legas.

Bech-Larsen, T. 2001. 'Model-Based Development and Testing of Advertising Messages: A Comparative Study of Two Campaign Proposals Based on the MECCAS Model and a Conventional Approach', *International Journal of Advertising: The Quarterly Review of Marketing Communications* 20(4): 499–519.

Beck, A. 2003. *Cultural Work: Understanding the Culture Industries*. London: Routledge.

Beckman, S. and Elliot, R. 2001. *Interpretive Consumer Research: Paradigms, Methodologies and Applications*. Copenhagen: Copenhagen Business School Press.

Bell, D. 1976. *The Cultural Contradictions of Capitalism*. New York: Basic Books.

Benjamin, W. 1999. *The Arcades Project*. Cambridge, MA: Harvard University Press.

Berger, A.A. 1992. *Popular Culture Genres: Theories and Texts*. London: Sage.

Berger, A.A. 2000. *Ads, Fads and Consumer Culture: Advertising's Impact on American Character and Society*. Lanham: Rowman & Littlefield.

Berger, J. 1973. *Ways of Seeing*. London: Pelican.

Berger, W. 2001. *Advertising Today*. London: Phaidon.

Bergson, H. 1911. *Laughter: An Essay on the Meaning of the Comic*. London: Macmillan.

Berman, R. 1981. 'Advertising and Social Change'. In *Advertising and Social Change*. London: Sage.

Betz, H.-G. 1992. 'Postmodernism and the New Middle Class', *Theory, Culture and Society* 9: 93–114.

Bevan, J. 2001. *The Rise and Fall of Marks and Spencer*. London: Profile Books.

Bignell, J. 2002. *Media Semiotics: An Introduction*. Manchester: Manchester University Press.

Billings, C. 2004. 'BBH to Develop New Branded TV Channel for Audi UK', *PR Week* (30 July). Available at www.prweek.co.uk/uk/news/article/217997/BBH-develop-new-branded-TV-channel-Audi-UK/.

Bivins, T. 2004. *Mixed Media: Moral Distinctions in Advertising, Public Relations, and Journalism*. London: Lawrence Erlbaum.

Blake, A. 1997. 'Listen to Britain: Music, Advertising and Postmodern Culture'. In M. Nava, A. Blake, I. MacRury and B. Richards (eds) *Buy This Book: Studies in Advertising and Consumption*. London: Routledge, pp. 224–38.

Bloom, H. 1973. *The Anxiety of Influence: A Theory of Poetry*. New York: Oxford University Press.

Bogart, L. 2000. *Commercial Culture: The Media System and the Public Interest*. Oxford: Oxford University Press.

Bond, G. and Griggs, S. 1996. 'Group Discussion Attendance and Attitudes to Advertising', *Journal of The Market Research Society* 38: 207–18.

Bonello, D. 2000. 'Advertising Receives 76 Percent Public Approval Rating', *Campaign* (4 August).

Bonnal, F. 1990. 'Attitudes to Advertising in Six European Countries', *Admap* (December): 19–23.

Booker, C. 1969. *The Neophilliacs: A Study of the Revolution in English Life in the Fifties and Sixties*. London: Collins.

Boorstin, D. [1961] 1992. *The Image: A Guide to Pseudo Events in America*. New York: Vintage Books.

Bordo, S. 1990. 'Reading the Slender Body'. In M. Jacobus, E.F. Keller, and S. Shuttleworth (eds) *Body Politics: Women and the Discourses of Science*. London: Routledge.

Bourdieu, P. 1972. 'Public Opinion Does Not Exist'. In A. Mattelart and S. Siegelaub (eds) *Communication and Class Struggle*, vol. 1. New York: International General, pp. 124–30.

Boutlis, P. 2000. 'A Theory of Postmodern Advertising', *International Journal of Advertising* 19(1): 3–23.

Bowlby, R. 1993. *Shopping with Freud*. London: Routledge.

Boyle, D. 2003. *Authenticity: Brands, Fakes, Spin and the Lust for Real Life*. London: Flamingo.

Brace, I. and Bond, G. 1997. 'Segmenting by Attitudes to TV Advertising – Eye Opener or Blind Alley', *International Journal of Market Research* 39(3): 481–508.

Bradshaw, D. 1994. *The Hidden Huxley*. London: Faber & Faber.

Braudel, F. 1982. *The Wheels of Commerce*. New York: Harper & Row.

Brierley, S. 1995. *The Advertising Handbook*, 1st edn. London: Routledge.

Brierley, S. 2002. *The Advertising Handbook*, 2nd edn. London: Routledge.

Briggs, A. and Cobley, P. 2002. *The Media: An Introduction*. London: Longman.

Brignull, T. 1996. 'Big Bang, Little Impact', *The Guardian* (12 February): 10–11.

Britton, R. 1998. *Belief and Imagination*. London: Routledge.

Broadbent, S., Ambler, T., Blight, I., Feldwick, P., Lind, H. and Waterson, M. 2000. 'Learning More About Ad Effects' *Green Paper*. London: Advertising Association.

Broadbent, T. 2000. *Advertising Works*, 11. London: IPA.

Brown, A. 2005. 'King Google', *Prospect* 117 ( December).

Brown, J. and Richards, B. 1998. 'The Humanist Freud'. In A. Elliot (ed.) *Freud 2000*. Cambridge: Polity Press.

Brown, J. and Richards, B. 2000. 'Introduction to the Psychoanalytic Sociology of Emotions', *Psychoanalytic Studies* 2: 31–3.

Brown, J. and Richards, B. 2000. 'The Humanist Freud'. In A. Elliot, *Freud 2000*. Cambridge: Polity.

Brunsdon, C. 1981. 'Crossroads, Notes on a Soap Opera', *Screen* 22 (4): 32–7.

Brvicevic, M. and Kay, G. 1998. 'Giving French Connection the F Factor', speech presented at the IPA Effectiveness Awards, London, Institute of Practitioners in Advertising.

Buijzen, M. and Valkenburg, P. 2000. 'The Impact of TV Advertising on Children's Christmas Wishes', *Journal of Broadcasting & Electronic Media* 44(3): 456–70.

Burk, K. 2003. 'Matter of Taste', *Prospect* 87 (June). Available at www.prospect-magazine.co.uk/article_details.php?id=5624 (accessed December 2007).

Burne, J. 2003. 'A Probe Inside the Mind of the Shopper', *Financial Times* (27 November).

Busch, T. and Landeck, T. 1980. *The Making of a Television Commercial: What Television Advertising Is All About*. New York: Macmillan.

Butterfield, L. 1999. *Excellence in Advertising*. London: IPA.

Buttle, F. 1991. 'What do People do with Advertising?', *International Journal of Advertising* 10 (2).

Cadley, J. 1992. 'About Men: Shoe Garnish'. In W. Leeds-Hurwitz *Semiotics and Communication: Signs, Codes, Cultures*. Hillsdale: Lawrence Erlbaum Associates, pp. 149. Originally published in *New York Times Magazine*, 13 September 1992, p. 24.

Campbell, C. 1987. *The Romantic Ethic and the Spirit of Modern Consumerism*. Oxford: Blackwell.

Caplin, R. 1959. *Advertising: A General Introduction*. London: IPA.

Cappo, J. 2003. *The Future of Advertising: New Media, New Clients, New Consumers in the Post Television Age*. London: McGraw-Hill.

Castells, M. 1996. *The Rise of Network Society*. Oxford: Blackwell.

Catterall, M., MacLaran, P. and Stevens, L. 2000. *Marketing and Feminism: Current Issues and Research*. London: Routledge.

Chandler, D. 2002. *Semiotics: The Basics*. London: Routledge.

Chandler, D. and Griffiths, M. 2000. 'Gender Differentiated Production Features in Toy Commercials', *Journal of Broadcast and Electronic Media* 44(3): 503–20.

Chapman, S. and Egger, G. 1983. 'Myth in Cigarette Advertising and Health Promotion'. In H. Davis and P. Walton (eds) *Language, Image Media*. Oxford: Blackwell.

Cheng, H. 1994. 'Reflections of Cultural Values: A Content Analysis of Chinese Magazine Adverts from 1982 and 1992', *International Journal of Advertising* 13: 167–83.

Churchill, R. 1944. 'Advertising and Civilization', *Scrutiny* XII: 64–6.

Clark, E. 1989. *The Want Makers: The World of Advertising and How They Make You Buy*. New York: Viking.

Clark, E., Brock, T. and Stewart, D. (eds) 1994. *Attention, Attitude, and Affect in Response to Advertising*. Hillsdale: Erlbaum.

Clifton, R. 1995. 'Do We Need Another Article About Women?', *Admap* (3 September).

Cobley, P. 2001. *The Routledge Companion to Semiotics and Linguistics*. London: Routledge.

Cobley, P. and Jansz, L. 1999. *Introducing Semiotics*. London: Icon.

Collins, R., Curran, J., Garnham, N., Scannell, P. and Schlesinger, P. 1986. *Media Culture and Society: A Critical Reader*. London: Sage.

Coltrane, S. and Messineo, M. 2000. 'The Perpetuation of Subtle Prejudice: Race and Gender Imagery in 1990s Television Advertising', *Sex Roles* 42: 363–89.

Cook, G. 1992. 'Ads as a Discourse Type'. In *The Discourse of Advertising*. London: Routledge.

Corcoran, N. 2007. *Communicating Health: Strategies for Health Promotion*. London: Sage.

Corner, J. 1999. *Critical Ideas in Television Studies*. Oxford: Oxford University Press.

Corry, D. 2003. 'Communications Bill: Inside Story', *Prospect*. April.

Cortese, A. 1999. *Provocateur; Images of Women and Minorities in Advertising*. Lanham: Rowman & Littlefield.

Costera Meijer, I. 1998. 'Advertising Citizenship: An Essay on the Performative Power of Consumer Culture'. *Media, Culture and Society* 20: 235–49.

Costera Meijer, I. and Van Zoonen, L. 2002. 'From Britney Spears to Erasmus: Women, Men and Representation'. In A. Briggs and P. Cobley *The Media: An Introduction*. London: Longman, pp. 327–39.

Courtney, A. and Whipple, T. 1983. *Sex Stereotyping in Advertising*. Lexington: Lexington Books.

Cozens, C. 2004. 'Advertisers Fail to Tap Ethnic Minority Markets', *The Guardian* (3 December).

Creer, V. 1994. 'Marks & Spencer's Sales Success – An Undercover Story', speech presented at IPA Effectiveness Awards, London, Institute of Practitioners in Advertising.

Cronin, A. 2000. *Advertising and Consumer Citizenship: Gender, Images and Rights*. London and New York: Routledge.

Cronin, A. 2004a. *Advertising Myths: The Strange Half Lives of Images and Commodities*. London: Routledge.

Cronin, A. 2004b. 'Currencies of Commercial Exchange', *Journal of Consumer Research* 4: 339–60.

Cronin, A. 2006. 'Advertising and the Metabolism of the City: Urban Space, Commodity Rhythms', *Environment & Planning D: Society and Space*, 24(4): 615–32.

Cross, G. 2000. *An All-Consuming Century: Why Commercialism Won in Modern America*. New York: Columbia University Press.

Cross, M. 1996. *Advertising and Culture: Theoretical Perpectives*. Westport: Praeger.

Curran, J. 1981. 'The Impact of Advertising on the British Mass Media', *Media, Culture and Society* 3: 43–69.

Curran, J. 2002. *Media and Power*. London: Routledge.

Curran, J. and Gurevitch, M. 2005. *Mass Media and Society*. London: Hodder Arnold.

Curti, M. 1967. 'The Changing Concept of "Human Nature" in the Literature of American Advertising', *Business History Review* XLI: 335–57.

Czikzentmihalyi, M. and Rochberg-Halton, E. 1981. *The Meaning of Things*. Cambridge: Cambridge University Press.

Danesi, M. 1999. *Of Cigarettes, High Heels, and Other Interesting Things*. New York: St Martin's Press.

Danesi, M. 2002. *Understanding Media Semiotics*. London: Arnold.

Danesi, M. 2003. *Forever Young: The 'Teen-Aging' of Modern Culture*. London: University of Toronto Press.

Danesi, M. 2006. *Brands*. London: Routledge.

Davenport, T. and Beck, J. 2001. *The Attention Economy: Understanding the New Currency of Business*. Boston: Harvard Business School Press.

Davidson, M. 1992. *The Consumerist Manifesto: Advertising in Postmodern Times*. London: Routledge.

Davies, J. 1998. *The Book of Guinness Advertising*. London: Guinness Publishing.

Davies, W. 2006. 'Digital Exuberance', *Prospect* (February). Available at www.prospect-magazine.co.uk/article_details.php?id=7294 (accessed December 2007).

Davis, H. and Scase, R. 2000. *Managing Creativity: The Dynamics of Work and Organisation*. Buckingham: Open University Press.

Dawson, N. and Hall, M. 2005. 'That's Brand Entertainment!', *Admap* 458 (February): 27–30.

De Botton, A. 2004. *Status Anxiety*. London: Penguin.

Delaney, S. 2007. *Get Smashed!: The Story of the Men Who Made the Adverts That Changed Our Lives*. London: Sceptre.

DeVries, L. 1968. *Victorian Advertisements*. London: John Murray.

De-Young, S. and Crane, F. 1992. 'Females' Attitudes Toward the Portrayal of Women in Advertising: A Canadian Study', *International Journal of Advertising* 11(3): 249–55.

Decker, C. 1998. *P&G99: 99 Principles and Practices of Procter and Gamble's Success*. London: Harper Collins Business.

Diamond, N. 1985. 'Thin is a Feminist Issue'. *Feminist Review* 19: 1–13.

Dichter, E. 1960. *The Strategy of Desire.* New York: Doubleday.

Dickason, R. 2000. *British Television Advertising: Cultural Identity and Communication.* Luton: University of Luton Press.

Dietmar, C. 2003. 'Mobile Communication in Couple Relationships', unpublished draft.

Dill Scott, W. 1910. *The Psychology of Advertising: A Simple Exposition of the Principles of Psychology in Their Relation to Successful Advertising.* New York: Small, Maynard & Co.

Dobrow, L. 1984. *When Advertising Tried Harder.* New York: Friendly Press.

Donaton, S. 2004. *Madison and Vine: Why the Entertainment and Advertising Industries Must Converge to Survive.* London: McGraw-Hill.

Dotz, W. and Husain, M. 2003. *Meet Mr. Product: The Art of Advertising Character.* San Francisco: Chronicle Books.

Douglas, M. 1966. *Purity and Danger.* London: Routledge.

Douglas, M. and Isherwood, B. 1978. *The World of Goods: Towards an Anthropology of Consumption.* London: Routledge.

Du-Plessis, E. 2005. *The Advertised Mind: Ground Breaking Insights into How Our Brains Respond to Advertising.* London: Kogan Page.

Dunn, R. 1991. 'Postmodernism: Populism, Mass Culture and Avant-Garde', *Theory, Culture and Society* 8: 111–35.

Dzamic, L. 2001. *No-Copy Advertising.* Brighton: Rotovision.

East, R. 1997. *Consumer Behaviour: Advances and Applications in Marketing.* Hemel Hempstead: Prentice Hall.

Eco, U. 1976. *A Theory of Semiotics.* Bloomington: Indiana University Press.

Eco, U. 1986. *Travels in Hyper-Reality.* London: Pan Books.

Eco, U. 1990. '*Intentio lectoris*: The State of the Art'. In *The Limits of Interpretation.* Bloomington: Indiana University Press.

Eco, U. 1994. 'Does the Audience have Bad Effects on Television'. In R. Lumley (ed.) *Apocalypse Postponed.* London: BFI; and Bloomington: Indiana University Press.

Ehrenberg, A. and Scriven, J. 1997. 'Added Values or Propensity to Buy?' *Admap* (January): 11–13.

Ehrenberg, A., Barnard, N. and Scriven J. 1998. 'Justifying Our Advertising Budgets: An Overview', *Admap* (March): 9.

Eliot, T.S. 1920. 'Tradition and the Individual Talent'. In *The Sacred Wood: Essays on Poetry and Criticism.* London: Faber & Faber.

Elliot, R. and Wattanasuwan, K. 1998. 'Brands as Symbolic Resources for the Construction of Identity', *International Journal of Advertising* 17(2): 131–44.

Enright, D.J. 1988. *Fields of Vision: Essays on Literature, Language and Television.* Oxford: Oxford University Press.

Eshun, E. 2001. *Surrealism and Advertising.* Available at www.bbc.co.uk/surrealism/ekow1.shtml (accessed May 2002).

Ewen, S. 2001. *Captains of Consciousness: Advertising and the Social Roots of Consumer Culture*. New York: Basic Books.

Ewen, S. 1976. *All Consuming Images: The Politics of Style in Contemporary Culture*. New York: Basic Books.

Ewen, S. 1988. *All Consuming Images: The Politics of Style in Contemporary Culture*. New York: Basic Books.

Ewen, S. 2000. 'Memoirs of a Commodity Fetishist', *Mass Communication and Society* 3: 439–52.

Ewing, M. and Jones, J.P. 2000. 'Agency Beliefs in the Power of Advertising', *International Journal of Advertising* 19.

Falk, P. 1994. *The Consuming Body*. London: Sage.

Falk, P. 1997. 'The Bennetton–Toscani Effect: Testing the Limits of Conventional Advertising', in M. Nava, A. Blake, I. MacRury, and B. Richards (eds) *Buy This Book: Studies in Advertising and Consumption*. London: Routledge, pp. 64–85.

Falk, P. and Campbell, C. 1997. *The Shopping Experience*. London: Sage.

Fallon, I. 1988. *The Brothers: The Rise and Rise of Saatchi and Saatchi*. London: Hutchinson.

Featherstone, M. 1991. *Consumer Culture and Postmodernism*. London: Sage.

Feldwick, P. 1996. 'The Four Ages of Ad Evaluation', *Admap* (April): 25–7.

Fine, B. 1995. 'From Political Economy to Consumption'. In D. Miller (ed.) *Acknowledging Consumption*. London: Routledge.

Fine, B. and Leopold, E. 1993. *The World of Consumption*. London: Routledge.

Fisher, J.C. 1993. *Advertising, Alcohol Consumption, and Abuse: A Worldwide Survey*. Westport: Greenwood Press.

Fiske, J. 1991. *Understanding Popular Culture*. London: Routledge.

Florida, R. 2002. *The Rise of the Creative Class: And How It's Transforming Work, Leisure, Community and Everyday Life*. New York: Basic Books.

Forceville, C. 1994. *Pictorial Metaphor in Advertising*. London: Routledge.

Fornas, J. 1995. *Cultural Theory and Late Modernity*. London: Sage.

Fornas, J., Becker, K., Bjurstrom, E. and Ganetz, H. 2007. *Consuming Media: Communication, Shopping and Everyday Life*. Oxford: Berg.

Fowles, J. 1996. *Advertising and Popular Culture*. London: Sage.

Fox, S. 1984. *The Mirror Makers*. New York: Random House.

Frank, T. 1997. *The Conquest of Cool: Business Culture, Counterculture and the Rise of Hip Consumerism*. Chicago: University of Chicago Press.

Friedan, B. 1963. *The Feminine Mystique*. London: W. W. Norton & Co.

Frith, K. (ed.) 1997. *Undressing the Ad: Reading Culture in Advertising*. New York: Peter Lang.

Frith, K. and Mueller, B. 2003. *Advertising and Societies: Global Issues*. New York: Peter Lang.

Fromm, E. 1976. *To Have or To Be?* London: Jonathan Cape.

Frosch, S. 1997. *For and Against Psychoanalysis*. London: Routledge.

Frosch, P. 2003. *The Image Factory: Consumer Culture, Photography and the Visual Content Industry*. Oxford: Berg.

Fuat Firat, A. and Dholakia, N. 1998. *Consuming People: From Political Economy to Theatres of Consumption*. London: Routledge.

Fukuyama, F. 2002. *Our Posthuman Future: Consequences of the Biotechnology Revolution*. London: Profile Books.

Fuller, L.K. 1997. 'We Can't Duck the Issue: Imbedded Advertising in the Motion Pictures'. In K.T. Frith (ed.) *Undressing the Ad: Reading Culture in Advertising*. New York: Peter Lang.

Fullerton, R. and Nevett, T. 1986. 'Advertising and Society: A Comparative Analysis of the Roots of Distrust in Germany and Great Britain', *International Journal of Advertising* 5.

Galbraith, J.K. 1958. *The Affluent Society*. London: Penguin.

Galbraith, J.K. 1977. *The Affluent Society*. London: Pelican Books.

Garfield, B. 2003. *And Now a Few Words From Me: Advertising's Leading Critic Lays Down the Law, Once and For All*. London: McGraw-Hill.

Giaccardi, C. 1995. 'Television Advertising and the Representation of Social Reality', *Theory, Culture and Society* 12: 109–31.

Gibson, O. 2006. 'Alcohol Advertising Regulation', *The Guardian* (11 January).

Gifford, C.H.P. 1934. 'Advertising and Economic Waste', *Scrutiny* 2 (September).

Gilmore, J. and Pine, J. 2007. *Authenticity*. Cambridge, MA: Harvard Business School Press.

Goddard, A. 1998. *The Language of Advertising*. London: Routledge.

Goffman, E. 1979. *Gender Advertisements*. London: Macmillan.

Goldman, R. 1992. *Reading Ads Socially*. London: Routledge.

Goldman, R. and Papson, S. 1994. 'Advertising in the Age of Hyper-Signification', *Theory, Culture and Society* 11: 23–53.

Goldman, R. and Papson, S. 1998. *Nike Culture*. London: Sage.

Gordon, W. 2006. 'Out with the New, In with the Old', *International Journal of Market Research* 48(1): 7–26.

Gordon, W. and Ryan, C. 1984. 'How do Consumers Feel Advertising Works', *Journal of the Market Research Society* 39(1).

Gough-Yates, A. 2003. *Understanding Women's Magazines*. London: Routledge.

Gray, R. 2004. 'Lifestage Marketing: The Seven Stages of Marketing'. Available at www.brandrepublic.com/Campaign/News/209744/Lifestage-marketing-seven-stages-targeting/ (accessed November 2008).

Grayling, A.C. 2002. *The Meaning of Things: Applying Philosophy to Life*. London: Phoenix.

Green, A. 1992. 'Death of the Full-service Agency', *Admap* (January).

Green, L. 2005. *Advertising Works and How: Winning Communication Strategies for Business*. London: IPA.

Green, M. 1987. 'Introduction: Points of Departure: "New" Subjects and "Old" '. In *Essays and Studies*. London: John Murray.

Gundlach, E.T. 1931. *Facts and Fetishes in Advertising*. Chicago: Consolidated Book Publishers.

Hackley, C. 2002. 'The Panoptic Role of Advertising Agencies in the Production of Consumer Culture', *Consumption Markets and Culture* 5: 211–29.

Hackley, C. 2003. 'From Consumer Insight to Advertising Strategy: The Account Planner's Integrative Role in Creating Advertising Development', *Marketing Intelligence and Planning* 21: 446–52.

Hackley, C. 2005. *Advertising and Promotion: Communicating Brands*. London: Sage.

Haefer, M. 1991. 'Ethical Problems of Advertising to Children', *Journal of Mass Media Ethics* 6: 63.

Haig, M. 2002. *Mobile Marketing*. London: Kogan Page.

Haineault, D.-L. and Roy, J.-Y. 1993. *Unconscious for Sale: Advertising, Psychoanalysis and the Public*. Minneapolis: University of Minnesota Press.

Hall, M. 1991. 'How Advertisers Think Marketing Works', British Market Research Society Annual Conference.

Hall, S. 1990. 'Encoding/Decoding'. In *Culture, Media, Language: Working Papers in Cultural Studies, 1972–79*. London: Routledge.

Hall, S. and Whannel, P. 1964. *The Popular Arts*. London: Hutchinson.

Hamilton, C. 1994. *Absolut: Biography of a Bottle*. London: Texere.

Harker, M., Harker, D. and Svensen, S. 2005. 'Attitudes Towards Gender Portrayal in Advertising: An Australian Perspective', *Journal of Marketing Management* 21(14): 251–64.

Hartley, J. 2005. *Creative Industries*. Oxford: Blackwell.

Harvey, D. 1989. *The Condition of Postmodernity: An Enquiry into the Origins of Cultural Change*. Oxford: Blackwell.

Haug, W.F. 1986. *Critique of Commodity Aesthetics: Appearance, Sexuality and Advertising in Capitalist Society*. Minneapolis: University of Minnesota Press.

Hennion, A. and Meadel, C. 1989. 'The Artisans of Desire: The Mediation of Advertising between Product and Consumer', *Sociological Theory* 7: 191–209.

Henry, J. 1966. 'Advertising as a Philosophical System'. In *Culture Against Man*. London: Tavistock.

Hesmondalgh, D. 2002. *The Culture Industries*. London: Sage.

Himpe, T. 2006. *Advertising Is Dead: Long Live Advertising*. London: Thames & Hudson.

Hindley, D. and Hindley, G. 1972. *Advertising in Victorian England 1837–1901*. London: Wayland Publishers.

Hodge, R. and Kress, G. 1988. *Social Semiotics*. Oxford: Polity.

Hodson, V. 1985. 'The "Lost" Women of Advertising', *Campaign* (22 March): 77–9.

Hoggart, R. 1957. *The Uses of Literacy*. London: Pelican.

Hoggart, R. 1968. 'Where Is It All Leading Us?'. In A. Wilson (ed.) *Advertising and the Community*. Manchester: Manchester University Press.

Holt, D. 2004. *How Brands Became Icons: The Principles of Cultural Branding*. Boston: Harvard Business School Press.

Hopkins, C. 1966. *My Life in Advertising and Scientific Advertising*. London: McGraw-Hill.

Horowitz, D. 1994. *Vance Packard and American Social Criticism*. Chapel Hill: University of North Carolina Press.

Horsley-Smith, G. 1954. *Motivation Research in Advertising and Marketing*. London: McGraw-Hill.

Huhmann, B. and Brotherton, T. 1997. 'A Content Analysis of Guilt Appeals in Popular Magazine Advertisements', *Journal of Advertising* XXVI: 35–45.

Huxley, A. 1932a. 'Advertisement'. In *Essays New and Old*. New York: H.W. Wilson.

Huxley A. 1932b. *Brave New World*. London: Penguin.

Huxley, A. 1959. 'Subconscious Persuasion'. In *Brave New world Revisited*. London: Chatto & Windus.

Inglis, F. 1971. *The Imagery of Power: A Critique of Advertising*. London: Heinemann.

IPA 1995. *Advertising Effectiveness: A Guide to Best Practice – Alcoholic Drinks*. London: IPA.

Irving, H. 1991. 'Little Elves and Mind Control: Advertising and Its Critics', *The Australian Journal of Media and Culture* 4(2): 98–111.

Jackson, P., Lowe, M., Miller, D. and Mort, F. 2000. *Commercial Cultures: Economies, Practices, Spaces*. Oxford: Berg.

Jackson, P., Stevenson, N. and Brooks, K. 2001. *Making Sense of Men's Magazines*. Cambridge: Polity.

Jaffe, L. and Berger, P. 1994. 'The Effect of Modern Female Sex Role Portrayal on Advertising Effectiveness', *Journal of Advertising Research* 34(4): 32.

Jakobson, R. 1960. 'Closing Statement: Linguistics and Poetics'. In T. Sebeok (ed.) *Style in Language*. Cambridge, MA: Harvard University Press.

James, O. 1997. *Britain on the Couch: Why We're Unhappier Compared with 1950, Despite Being Richer – A Treatment for the Low-serotonin Society*. London: Century.

James, O. 2007. *Affluenza*. London: Vermillion.

Jameson, F. 1991. *Postmodernism, Or, The Cultural Logic of Late Capitalism*. Durham: Duke University Press.

Jameson, F. 1998. 'Postmodernism and Consumer Society'. In *The Cultural Turn: Selected Writings on Postmodernism*. London: Verso.

Jenkins, S. 2005. 'End of the Standard', *Prospect* (March).

Jensen, R. 1999. *The Dream Society*. London: McGraw-Hill.

Jernigan, D., Ostroff, J. and Ross, C. 2004. 'Sex Differences in Adolescent Exposure to Alcohol Advertising in Magazines', *Archives of Pediatrics and Adolescent Medicine* 158: 629–34.

Jhally, S. 1990. *The Codes of Advertising: Fetishism and the Political Economy of Meaning in the Consumer Society*. London: Routledge.

Jhally, S. and Lewis, J. 1998. 'Unpopular Messages in an Age of Popularity'. In Roger Dickinson (ed.) *Approaches to Audiences: A Reader*. Arnold: London.

Johnson, G. 1999. 'From Pokemon to Palm Pilots, It Was the Year of the Consumer', *LA Times* (26 December). Available at http://articles. latimes.com/1999/dec/26/business/fi-47642.

Johnson, S. 1759. The Art of Advertising Exemplified, *The Idler* 40 (29 January).

Jones, J.P. 1999. *The Advertising Business: Operations, Creativity, Media Planning, Integrated Communications*. London: Sage.

Jones, J.P. 2004. *Fables, Fashions, and Facts About Advertising: A Study of 28 Enduring Myths*. London: Sage.

Josling, J. 1995. 'The Advertising Agency'. In N.A. Hart (ed.) *The Practice of Advertising*, 4th edn. Oxford: Butterworth-Heinemann.

Kaldor, N. 1950. 'The Economic Aspects of Advertising'. In M. Barnes (ed.) *The Three Faces of Advertising: Economics, Ethics, Effects*. London: The Advertising Association.

Kang, M.-E. 1997. 'The Portrayal of Women's Images in Magazine Advertisements: Goffman's Gender Analysis Revisited', *Sex Roles* 37(11–12): 979–97.

Keller, K. 1993. 'Memory Retreival Factors and Advertising Effectiveness'. In A. Mitchell (ed.) *Advertising Exposure, Memory and Choice*. Hillsdale: Lawrence Erlbaum Associates.

Kemper, S. 2003. 'How Advertising Makes its Object'. In T. de Waal Malefyt and B. Moeran (eds) *Advertising Cultures*. Oxford: Berg.

Kent, R. 1994. *Measuring Media Audiences*. London: Routledge.

Kern-Foxworth, M. 1994. *Aunt Jemima, Uncle Ben, and Rastus: Blacks in Advertising, Yesterday, Today, and Tomorrow*. Westport: Praeger.

Key, W.B. 1974. *Subliminal Seduction*. New York: Signet.

Key, W.B. 1989. *The Age of Manipulation*. Lanham: Madison Books.

Key, W.B. 1992. *Subliminal Ad-Ventures in Erotic Art*. Boston: Branden.

Kilbourne 1999. *Can't Buy My Love: How Advertising Changes the Way We Think and Feel*. London: Touchstone.

Kilbourne, J., Lysonski, S., Miller, M., Ford, J. and McDonald, C. 2005. 'Comments – Sexy vs. Sexism in Advertising', *International Journal of Advertising* 24 (1): 113–24.

Klitzner, M., Gruenewald, P. and Bamberger, E. 1991. 'Cigarette Advertising and Adolescent Experimentation with Smoking', *British Journal of Addiction*, 86: 287–98.

Klein, N. 2000. *No Logo*. London: Flamingo.

Kline, S. 1993. *Out of the Garden*. New York: Verso.

Kline, S. 1997. 'Image Politics: Negative Advertising Strategies and the Election Audience'. In M. Nava, A. Blake, I. MacRury and B. Richards, *Buy This Book: Studies in Advertising and Consumption*. London: Routledge.

Knobil, M. 2003. *Cool Brand Leaders: An Insight into Britain's Coolest Brands 2003*. London: The Brand Council.

Kolbe, R. and Albanese, P. 1996. 'Man to Man: A Content Analysis of Sole Male Images in Male-Audience magazines', *Journal of Advertising* XXV: 1–20.

Kotchemidova, C. 2005. 'Why We Say "Cheese": Producing the Smile in Snapshot Photography', *Critical Studies in Media Communication* 22: 2–25.

Kress, G. and Van Leeuwen, T. 1996. *Reading Images: The Grammar of Visual Design*. London: Routledge.

Laird, P. 1993. 'The Business of Progress: The Transformation of American Advertising', *Business and Economic History* 22: 13–18.

Laird, P. 1998. *Advertising Progress: American Business and the Rise of Consumer Marketing*. Baltimore, and London: Johns Hopkins University Press.

Lance, S. and Woll, J. 2006. *The Little Blue Book of Advertising*. London: Portfolio Penguin.

Landry, C. 2000. *The Creative City: A Toolkit for Urban Innovators*. London: Comedia.

Langer, R. 2003. 'New Subtle Advertising Formats: Characteristics, Causes and Consequences'. In F. Hansen and L. Christensen *Branding and Advertising*. Copenhagen: Copenhagen Business School Press.

Langholz-Leymore, V. 1975. *Hidden Myth: Structure and Symbolism in Advertising*. New York: Basic Books.

Langrehr, F. and Caywood, C. 1989. 'An Assessment of "Sins" and "Virtues" Portrayed in Advertising', *International Journal of Advertising* 8: 391–403.

Lasch, C. 1979. *The Culture of Narcissism*. London: Norton.

Lasswell, H. 1932. 'The Triple Appeal Principle', *The American Journal of Sociology* 57: 523–38.

Law, A. 1999. *Creative Company: How St. Lukes Became 'The Ad Agency to End All Ad Agencies'*. London: John Wiley.

Lawes, R. 2002. 'Demystifying Semiotics: Some Key Questions Answered', *International Journal of Market Research* 44.

Lawson, G. and Brahma, S. 2006. 'Women's Views on Their Portrayal in Advertising – "We Have Changed, Do Advertisers Know?"', *ESOMAR*, Paper presented at the *Asia Pacific Conference*, Mumbai, March.

Lazarsfeld, P. 1941. 'Remarks on Administrative and Critical Communications Research 9.1', *Studies in Philosophy and Social Science* 9: 2–16.

Lears, J. 1994. *Fables of Abundance: A Cultural History of Advertising in America*. New York: Basic Books.

Leavis, F.R. and Thompson, D. 1964. *Culture and Environment: The Training of Critical Awareness*. London: Chatto & Windus.

Lee, M. 1993. *Consumer Culture Reborn: The Cultural Politics of Consumption*. London: Routledge.

Leech, G. 1966. *English in Advertising: A Linguistic Study of Advertising in Great Britain*. London: Longmans.

Leiss, W., Kline, S. and Jhally, S. 1990a. 'Fantasia for the Citizen: The Nature and Uses of Political Marketing'. In *Social Communication in Advertising: Persons, Products, and Images of Well-Being*. London: Routledge.

Leiss, W., Kline, S. and Jhally, S. 1990b. *Social Communication in Advertising: Persons, Products, and Images of Well-Being*. London: Routledge.

Leiss, W., Kline, S., Jhally, S. and Botterill, J. 2005. *Social Communication in Advertising: Consumption in the Mediated Marketplace*. London: Routledge.

Leppert, R. 2002. 'Introduction'. In R. Leppert (ed.) *Essays on Music*. Berkeley: University of California Press.

Levy, S. 1999. 'Semiotician Ordinaire'. In D. Rook *Brands, Consumers, Symbols and Research: Sidney J. Levy on Marketing*. London: Sage.

Lewis, T. 2003. 'Consuming Children: Education–Entertainment–Advertising'. *Journal of Educational* 47(1): 107–11.

Lewis, D. and Bridger, D. 2001. *The Soul of the New Consumer*. London: Nicholas Brealey.

Lewis, R. and Rolley, K. 1997. '(Ad)dressing the Dyke: Lesbian Looks and Lesbians Looking'. In M. Nava, A. Blake, I. MacRury and B. Richards (eds) *Buy this Book: Studies in Advertising and Consumption*. London: Routledge, pp. 259–309.

Lewis, T. 2003. 'Consuming Children: Education–Entertainment–Advertising'. *Journal of Educational* 47(1): 107–11.

Leymore, V. 1975. *Hidden Myth: Structure and Symbolism in Advertising*. New York: Basic Books.

Lodziak, C. 2002. *The Myth of Consumerism*. London: Pluto Press.

Lopiano-Misdom, J. and Luca, J.D. 1997. *Street Trends: How Today's Alternative Youth Cultures are Creating Tomorrow's Mainstream Markets*. London: Harper Business.

Lotman, Y. 1990. *Universe of the Mind: A Semiotic Theory of Culture*. Bloomington: Indiana University Press.

Lukacs, J. 2001. *Five Days in London*. New Haven: Yale University Press.

Lury, A. 1994. 'Advertising: Moving Beyond the Stereotypes'. In R. Keat, N. Whiteley and N. Abercrombie (eds) *The Authority of the Consumer*. London: Routledge.

Lury, C. 2000. 'Thinking with Things'. In J. Pavitt (ed.), *Brand New*. London: V&A.

Lury, C. 2004. *Brands: The Logos of the Global Economy*. London: Routledge.

Lury, C. and Warde, A. 1997, 'Investments in the Imaginary Consumer: Conjectures Regarding Power, Knowledge and Advertising'. In M. Nava, A. Blake, I. MacRury and B. Richards (eds) *Buy This Book: Studies in Advertising and Consumption*. London: Routledge, pp. 87–102.

Lury, G. 2001. *Adwatching: Lifting the Lid on Advertising*. London: Blackhall.

McAllister, M.P. 1997. 'Sponsorship, Globalization, and the Summer Olympics'. In K.T. Frith (ed.) *Undressing the Ad: Reading Culture in Advertising*. New York: Peter Lang.

McChesney, R.W. 2004. *The Problem of the Media: US Communication Politics in the 21st Century*. New York: Monthly Review Press.

McCracken, G. 1990. *Culture and Consumption: New Approaches to the Symbolic Character of Consumer Goods and Activities*. Bloomington: Indiana University Press.

McDonald, C. 1997. 'Pre-testing Advertisements' *Admap*.

McDonald, C. 2003. 'The Human Factor' *Admap* 445 (December): 27–9.

McDonald, C. and King, S. 1996. *Sampling the Universe: The Growth, Development and Influence of Market Research in Britain Since 1945*. Henley-on-Thames: NTC Books.

MacDonald, M. 1995. *Representing Women: Myths of Femininity in the Popular Media*. London: Edward Arnold.

McEvoy, D. 2002. 'Outdoor: The Creative Medium', *Admap* 428 (May): 26–8.

McFall, L. 2002. 'Who Were the Old Cultural Intermediaries? An Historical Review of Advertising Producers', *Cultural Studies* 16: 532–52.

McFall, L. 2004. *Advertising: A Cultural Economy*. London: Sage.

McGuigan, J. 1992. *Cultural Populism*. London: Routledge.

MacKay, H. 1997. *Consumption and Everyday Life*. London: Sage.

McKendrick, N., Brewer, J. and Plumb, J.H. 1982. *The Birth of a Consumer Society: The Commercialisation of Eighteenth Century England*. Bloomington: Indiana University Press.

MacLachlan, J. and Logan, M. 1993. 'Camera Shot Length in TV Commercial and their Memorability and Persuasiveness', *Journal of Advertising Research* 33.

McLuhan, H.M. 1951. *The Mechanical Bride: Folklore of Industrial Man*. New York: Vanguard Press.

McLuhan, H.M. 1964. *Understanding Media: The Extension of Man*. London: Routledge & Kegan Paul.

McLuhan, E. and Zingrone, F. 1995. *Essential McLuhan*. London: Routledge.

McQuail, D. 1987. *Mass Communication Theory: An Introduction*. London: Sage.

McQuarrie, E. and Mick, D. 1992. 'On Resonance: A Critical Pluralistic Inquiry into Advertising Rhetoric', *Journal of Consumer Research* 19: 180–97.

McQuarrie, E. and Mick, D.G. 1996. 'Figures of Rhetoric in Advertising Language', *Journal of Consumer Research* 22: 424–38.

MacRury, I. 1997. 'Advertising and the Modulation of Narcissism: The Case of Adultery', in M. Nava, A. Blake, I. MacRury and B. Richards (eds) *Buy This Book: Studies in Advertising and Consumption*. London: Routledge.

Malefyt, T. and Moeran, B. (eds) 2003. *Advertising Cultures*. Oxford: Berg.

Mandese, J. 2004. 'This is the End, My Friend, the End-user', *Admap* 453 (September): 10.

Marchand, R. 1985. *Advertising the American Dream: Making Way for Modernity 1920–1940*. Berkeley: University of California Press.

Marcuse, H. 1972. *Eros and Civilisation*. London: Abacus.

Marsland, D. 1988. 'Against Advertising – Inadequacies in the Treatment of Advertising by Sociology', *International Journal of Advertising* 7: 223–36.

Mass Observation Archive. 1944. 'How Much Are You Influenced by Advertising', Mass Observation Archive, University of Sussex.

Mattelart, A. 1991. 'The Weapons of Criticism and the Criticism of Weapons'. In *Advertising International: The Privatization of Public Space*. London: Routledge.

Mayer, M. 1958. *Madison Avenue USA: The Inside Story of American Advertising*. London: Penguin.

Mayhew, L. 1997. *The New Public: Professional Communication and the Means of Social Influence*. Cambridge: Cambridge University Press.

Mayle, P. 1990. *Up the Agency*. London: Pan.

Mayne, I. 2000. 'The Inescapable Images: Gender and Advertising', *Equal Opportunities International* 19: 56–61.

Mazzarella, W. 2003a. 'Critical Publicity/Public Criticism'. In T.M.a.B. Moeran (ed.) *Advertising Cultures*. Oxford: Berg.

Mazzarella, W. 2003b. *Shovelling Smoke: Advertising and Globalization in Contemporary India*. Durham: Duke University Press.

Menzies Lyth, I. and Trist, E. 1988. 'The Development of Ice Cream as a Food'. In I. Menzies Lyth (ed.) *The Dynamics of the Social: Selected Essays*. London: Free Association Books, Chapter 5.

Merrell, F. 2001. 'Charles Sanders Peirce's Concept of the Sign'. In P. Cobley *The Routledge Companion to Semiotics and Linguistics*. London: Routledge, pp. 28–39.

Messaris, P. 1997. *Visual Persuasion: The Role of Images in Advertising*. London: Sage.

Micheletti, M. and Stolle, D. 2007. 'Mobilizing Consumers to Take Responsibility for Global Social Justice', *The Annals of the American Academy of Political and Social Science* 611: 157–75.

Mick, D.G. 1986. 'Consumer Research and Semiotics: Exploring the Morphology of Signs, Symbols and Significance', *Journal of Consumer Research* 13: 196–213.

Mick, D.G. 1992. 'Levels of Subjective Comprehension in Advertising Processing and Their Relations to Ad Perceptions, Attitudes and Memory', *Journal of Consumer Research* 18: 411–25.

Mick, D.G. and Buhl, C. 1992. 'A Meaning-Based Model of Advertising Experiences', *Journal of Consumer Research* 19: 317–38.

Miller, D. 1987. *Material Culture and Mass Consumption*. Oxford: Blackwell.

Miller, D. 1995. *Acknowledging Consumption: A Review of New Studies*. London: Routledge.

Miller, D. 2003. 'Advertising, Production and Consumption as Cultural Economy in Advertising Cultures'. In Timothy Dewaal Malefyt and Brian Moeran (eds) *Advertising Cultures*. Oxford, and New York: Berg, pp. 75–89.

Miller, M. and Kilbourne, J. 2005. 'Comments: Sexism in Advertising and Marketing to Women and What Else Does Sex Sell?', *International Journal of Advertising* 24(1): 113–24.

Millum, T. 1975. 'Images of Woman'. In *Images of Woman: Advertising in Women's Magazines*. Lanham: Rowman & Littlefield.

Milner, M. 1957. *On Not Being Able to Paint*. New York: International University Press.

Minsky, R. 1998. *Psychoanalysis and Culture: Contemporary States of Mind*. Cambridge: Polity.

Mitchell, A. 2007. 'Advertisers Turn to Science to Get Inside Consumers' Heads', *Financial Times* (5 January).

Moeran, B. 1996. *A Japanese Advertising Agency: An Anthropology of Media and Markets*. Richmond: Curzon.

Moody, N. 2000. 'Nation and Nostalgia: The Place of Advertising in Popular Fictions'. In Jackie Cannon, P.D. Baubeta and R. Warner (eds) *Advertising and Identity in Europe: The I of the Beholder*. Bristol: Intellect.

Moog, C. 1990. *Are They Selling her Lips: Advertising and Identity*. New York: William Morrow.

Moor, E. 2003. 'Branded Spaces: The Scope of "new marketing"', *Journal of Consumer Culture* 3: 39–60.

Moor, L. 2004. 'Brands, Property and Politics', *Soundings* 28: 49–61.

Moores, S. 1993. *Interpreting Audiences: The Ethnography of Media Consumption*. London: Sage.

Morgan, B. and Fletcher, J. 2000. 'New Directions in Qualitative Brand Research', Market Research Society Annual Conference.

Morley, D. 1980. *The eNationwide Audience: Structure and Decoding*. London: BFI.

Mort, F. 1996. *Cultures of Consumption: Masculinities and Social Space in Twentieth-Century Britain*. London: Routledge.

Mort, F. 1997. 'Paths to Mass Consumption: Britain and the USA Since 1945'. In M. Nava, A. Blake, I. MacRury and B. Richards, *Buy This Book: Studies in Advertising and Consumption*. London: Routledge, pp. 15–33.

Murdock, G. 2003. 'Back to Work'. In A. Beck (ed.) *Understanding the Cultural Industries*, London: Routledge, pp. 15–35.

Murphy, C. 2004. 'Chanel No. 5 turns to Hollywood', *Marketing* (17 November). Available at www.brandrepublic.com/Marketing/Analysis/228292/News-Analysis-Chanel-No-5-turns-Hollywood/ (accessed November 2008).

Myers, G. 1994. *Words in Ads*. Oxford: Arnold.

Myers, G. 1999. *Ad Worlds: Brands, Media, Audiences*. London: Arnold.

Myers, J. 2004. 'Tweens and Cool', *Admap* 448 (March): 37–9.

Myers, K. 1986. *Understains: The Sense and Seduction of Advertising*. London: Comedia.

Nava, M. 1997. 'Framing Advertising: Cultural Analysis and the Incrimination of Visual Texts'. In M. Nava, A. Blake, I. MacRury and B. Richards (eds) *Buy This Book: Studies in Advertising and Consumption*. London: Routledge.

Nava, M. and Nava, O. 1992. 'Discriminating or Duped? Young People as Consumers of Advertising/Art'. In *Changing Cultures: Feminism, Youth and Consumerism*. London: Sage.

Nava, M., Blake, A., MacRury, I. and Richards, B. 1997. *Buy This Book: Studies in Advertising and Consumption*. London: Routledge.

Negus, K. and Pickering, M. 2004. *Creativity, Communication and Cultural Value*. Sage: London.

Nevett, T. 1981. 'The Scapa Society: The First Organized Reaction Against Advertising', *Media, Culture and Society* 3: 179–87.

Nevett, T. 1982. *Advertising in Britain: A History*. London: Heinemann.

Nicholson, D.R. 1997. 'The Diesel Jeans and Workwear Advertising Campaign and the Commodification of Resistance'. In K.T. Frith (ed.) *Undressing the Ad: Reading Culture in Advertisements*. New York: Peter Lang.

Nixon, S. 1996. *Hard Looks: Masculinities, Spectatorship and Contemporary Consumption*. London: St Martin's Press.

Nixon, S. 2000. 'In Pursuit of the Professional Ideal: Advertising and the Construction of Commercial Expertise in Britain 1953–64'. In P. Jackson, M. Lowe, D. Miller and F. Mort (eds) *Commercial Cultures: Economies, Practices, Spaces*. Oxford: Berg, pp. 55–74.

Nixon, S. 2003. *Advertising Cultures*. London: Sage.

Norris, V. 1981. 'Advertising History – According to the Textbooks', *Journal of Advertising History* 16: 241–60.

O'Barr, W. 1994. *Culture and the Ad: Exploring Otherness in the World of Advertising*. New York: Harper Collins.

Obermiller, C. and Spangenberg, E.R. 1998. 'Development of a Scale to Measure Consumer Skepticism toward Advertising', *Journal of Consumer Psychology* 7: 159–86.

Odih, P. 2007. *Advertising in Modern and Postmodern Times*. London: Sage.

O'Donohoe, S. 1994. 'Advertising Uses and Gratifications', *European Journal of Marketing* 28: 52–75.

O'Donohoe, S. 1995. 'Attitudes to Advertising: A Review of British and American Research', *International Journal of Advertising* 14: 245–61.

O'Donohoe, S. 1997. 'Leaky Boundaries: Intertextuality and Young Adult Experiences of Advertising'. In M. Nava, A. Blake, I. MacRury and B. Richards (eds) *Buy this Book: Studies in Advertising and Consumption*. London: Routledge, pp. 257–75.

O'Donohoe, S. 2000. 'Women and Advertising: Reading the Relationship'. In M. Catterall, P. MacLaran and L. Stevens (eds) *Marketing and Feminism: Current Issues and Research*. London: Routledge.

O'Donohoe, S. 2006. 'Yummy Mummies: The Clamor of Glamour in Advertising to Mothers', *Advertising & Society Review* 7(3).

O'Donohoe, S. and Tynan, C. 1998. 'Beyond Sophistication: Dimensions of Advertising Literacy', *International Journal of Advertising* 17.

Ofcom 2004. 'Child Obesity – Food Advertising in Context', available at: www.ofcom.org.uk/research/tv/reports/food_ads/ (accessed 13 January 2005).

Offer, A. 1996. *In Pursuit of the Quality of Life*. Oxford: Oxford University Press.

Ogilvy, D. 1964. *Confessions of an Advertising Man*. London: Longmans, Green.

Ogilvy, D. 1983. *Ogilvy on Advertising*. London: Prion.

Ohmann, R. 1996. *Selling Culture: Magazines, Markets, and Class at the turn of the Century*. London: Verso.

Olins, W. 1999. *Trading Identities: Why Countries and Companies Are Taking on Each Others' Roles*. London: The Foreign Policy Centre.

Olins, W. 2003. *On Brand*. London: Thames & Hudson.

Orbach, S. 1993. *Hunger Strike*. London: Penguin.

O'Reilly, D. 1983. 'The New Faces of Eve', *Marketing* (26 May): 29–38.

Orwell, G. 1945. *Animal Farm*. London: Penguin.

Orwell, G. 1949. *Nineteen Eighty Four*. London: Secker & Warburg.

Orwell, G. 1954. *Keep the Aspidistra Flying*. London: Secker & Warburg.

Orwell, G. 1968a. 'As I Please – Letters'. In S. Orwell and I. Angus (eds) *As I Please: The Collected Essays Journalism and Letters of George Orwell*. New York: Harcourt Brace & World.

Orwell, G. 1968b. *My Country Right or Left*. London: Penguin.

O'Shaughnessy, J. and O'Shaughnessy, N. 2003. *Persuasion in Advertising*. London: Routledge.

Ostergaard, P. and Jantzen, C. 2000. 'Shifting Perspectives in Consumer Research: From Buyer Behaviour to Consumption Studies'. In S. Beckmann and R. H. Elliott (eds) *Interpretive Consumer Research: Paradigms, Methodologies and Applications*. Copenhagen: CBS Press, pp. 9–23.

Packard, V. 1957. *The Hidden Persuaders*. London: Pelican.

Packard, V. 1959. *The Status Seekers*. London: Pelican.

Packard, V. 1960. *The Waste Makers*. London: Pelican.

Packard, V. 1964. *The Naked Society*. London: Pelican.

Parker, B.J. 2003. 'Food for Health: The Use of Nutrient Content, Health, and Structure/Function Claims in Food Advertisements', *Journal of Advertising* 32(3): 47–55.

Pearlman, J. 2005. 'Marks & Spencer's Sales Increase Fuelled by Twiggy Ad Campaign', 11 October, available at www.brandrepublic.com/news/521449/marks-spencers-sales-increase-fuelled-twiggy-ad-campaign-/ (accessed 19 December 2005).

Pfanner, E. 2007. 'Saatchi Gets the Boot Over Use of Dead Rock Star', *International Herald Tribune* (3 June).

Pierce, P. 1999. 'Humour in Television Advertising: A Researcher's View'. In J.P. Jones *The Advertising Business*. London: Sage, pp.181–92.

Pine, J. and Gilmore, J. 1999. *The Experience Economy: Work is Theatre and Every Business is a Stage*. Boston: Harvard Business School Press.

Plessis, E.D. 2005. *The Advertised Mind: Ground-Breaking Insights into How Our Brains Respond to Advertising.* London: Kogan Page.

Pollay, R. 1986. 'The Distorted Mirror: Reflections on the Unintended Consequences of Advertising', *Journal of Marketing,* 50: 18–36.

Pollay, R. 1987. 'On the Value of Reflections on the Values in "The Distorted Mirror"', *Journal of Marketing,* 51: 104–9.

Pollay, R.W. 1993. 'Pertinent Research and Impertinent Opinions: Our Contributions to the Cigarette Advertising Policy Debate', *Journal of Advertising* 22: 110–17.

Pope, D. 1983. *The Making of Modern Advertising.* New York: Basic Books.

Poster, M. 1990b. *The Mode of Information: Poststructualism and Social Context.* Oxford: Polity.

Postman, N. 1986. *Amusing Ourselves to Death: Public Discourse in the Age of Show Business.* London: Penguin.

Presbrey, F. 1929. *The History and Development of Advertising.* New York: Doubleday.

Pringle, H. and Thompson, M. 1999. *Brand Spirit: How Cause Related Marketing Builds Brands.* London: John Wiley.

Quart, A. 2003. *Branded: The Buying and Selling of Teenagers.* London: Arrow.

Radway, J. 1987. *Reading the Romance: Women Patriarchy and Popular Literature.* London: Verso.

Ramamurthy, A. 2003. *Imperial Persuaders: Images of Africa and Asia in British Advertising.* Manchester: Manchester University Press.

Rawsthorn, A. 1984. 'What Katy Did Wrong', *Marketing* (9 February): 28–31.

Rettie, R. and Mojsa, M. 2002. 'Attitudes to Internet Advertising: A Cross Cultural Comparison'. Presented at the British Academy of Management Annual Conference, 9–11 September, London.

Rheingold, H. 2003. *Smart Mobs: The Next Social Revolution.* Cambridge, MA: Perseus Books.

Richards, B. 1994. *Disciplines of Delight.* London: Free Association Books.

Richards, B., MacRury, I. and Botterill, J. 2000. *The Dynamics of Advertising.* Amsterdam: Harwood.

Richards, J. 2000. 'Interactive Advertising Concentration: A First Attempt', *The Journal of Interactive Advertising* 1.

Ries, A. and Ries, L. 1999. *The 22 Immutable Laws of Branding.* London: Harper Collins Business.

Ries, A. and Ries, L. 2002. *The Fall of Advertising and the Rise of PR.* London: Harper Collins Business

Ries, A. and Trout, J. 1981. *Positioning: The Battle for Your Mind.* New York: McGraw-Hill.

Roberts, K. 2004. *Lovemarks: The Future Beyond Brands.* New York: Powerhouse Books.

Robinson, J. 1998. *The Manipulators: Unmasking the Hidden Persuaders.* London: Pocket Books.

Rose, G. 2001. *Visual Methodologies*. London: Sage.

Rosen, E. 2000. *The Anatomy of Buzz: Creating Word-of-Mouth Marketing*. London: Harper Collins Business.

Rothenberg, R. 1994. *Where the Suckers Moon: The Life and Death of an Advertising Campaign*. New York: Vintage.

Saatchi, M. 2006. 'The Strange Death of Modern Advertising', *Financial Times* (21 June).

Samuels, J. and Silman, R. 1996. 'Segmenting by Attitudes to TV Advertising; Towards the Development of a Major New Analysis Variable', *Proceedings of The Market Research Society Conference*, pp. 223–47.

Sandage, C. 1961. *The Promise of Advertising*. Homewood: Irwin.

Sardar, Z. 2002. *The A–Z of Postmodern Life*. London: Vision.

Savan, L. 1994. *The Sponsored Life: Ads, TV, and American Culture*. Philadelphia: Temple.

Sayers, D.L. 1933. *Murder Must Advertise*. London: New English Library.

Scammell, M. 2007. 'Political Brands and Consumer Citizens: The Rebranding of Tony Blair', *Annals of the American Academy of Political and Social Science* 611 (1): 176–92.

Schlosser, E. 2002. *Fast Food Nation: What the All-American Meal is Doing to the World*. London: Penguin.

Schoenbach, K. 2003. 'Advertising Effects: An inventory of Inventories' *Admap* 445 (December): 29–2.

Schor, J. 2004. *Born to Buy A New Book, Born to Buy: The Commercialized Child and the New Consumer Culture*. London: Scribner.

Schor, J. 2007. 'In Defense of Consumer Critique: Revisiting the Consumption Debates of the Twentieth Century', *The Annals of the American Academy of Political and Social Science* 611: 16–30.

Schor, J.B. 2004. *Born to Buy: The Commercialized Child and the New Consumer Culture*. New York: Scribner.

Schroeder, J. and Zwick, D. 2004a. 'Mirrors of Masculinity: Representations and Identity in Advertising Images', *Consumption, Markets and Cultures* 7: 21–52.

Schroeder, K.C. 1994. 'Audience Semiotics, Interpretive Communities and the 'Ethnographic Turn' in Media Research', *Media, Culture and Society* 16: 337–47.

Schudson, M. 1981. 'Criticizing the Critics of Advertising: Towards a Sociological View of Marketing', *Media, Culture and Society* 3: 3–12.

Schudson, M. 1993. *Advertising, the Uneasy Persuasion: Its Dubious Impact on American Society*. London: Routledge.

Scott, L.M. 1994. 'The Bridge from Text to Mind: Adapting Reader Response Theory to Consumer Research', *Journal of Consumer Research* 21: 461–80.

Scriven, J. and Ehrenberg, A. 1997. 'Added Values or Propensities to Buy?', *Admap* (September).

Scruton, R. 2000. *An Intelligent Person's Guide to Modern Culture*. Indiana: St Augustine Press.

Seabrook, J. 2004. *Consuming Cultures: Globalization and Local Lives*. Oxford: New Internationalist.

Sebeok, T. 1991. *A Sign is Just a Sign*. Bloomington: Indiana University Press.

Sebeok, T. 2002. *Signs: An Introduction to Semiotics*. Toronto: University of Toronto Press.

Seely, P. 1994. 'The Mirror and the Window on the Man of the Nineties: Portrayals of Males in Television Advertising'. In L. Manca *Gender & Utopia in Advertising*. Chicago: Procopian Press.

Shah, D., McLeod, D., Freidland, L. and Nelson, M. 2007. 'The Politics of Consumption/The Consumption of Politics', *The Annals of the American Academy of Political and Social Science* 611: 16–30.

Simmel, G. [1903] 1950. 'The Metropolis and Mental Life'. In K. H. Wolff (trans. and ed.) *The Sociology of Georg Simmel*. London: Collier-Macmillan, pp. 409–24.

Simmel, G. 1950. 'The Metropolis and Mental Life'. In *The Sociology of Georg Simmel*. New York: Free Press.

Siu, W.-s. 1997. 'Women in Advertising: Comparison of TV Advertisements in China and Singapore', *Marketing Intelligence and Planning* 15: 235–43.

Slater, D. 1997. *Consumer Culture and Modernity*. Cambridge: Polity.

Slater, D. and Tonkiss, F. 2001. *Market Society*. Oxford: Polity.

Smit, E., Van-Meurs, L. and Neijens, P. 2006. 'Effects of Likeability: A 10-Year Perspective', *Journal of Advertising Research* 46: 73–83.

Smith, T. 2005. 'Pumping Irony: The Construction of Masculinity in a Post-Feminist Advertising Campaign', *Advertising and Society Review* 6. Available at www.aef.com/on_campus/asr/contents (accessed November 2008).

Soar, M. 2000. 'Encoding Advertisements: Ideology and Meaning in Advertising Production', *Mass Communication and Society* 3: 415–37.

Spence, E. and Heekernen, B.V. 2005. *Advertising Ethics*. London: Pearson.

Springer, P. 2007. *Ads to Icons: How Advertising Succeeds in a Multimedia Age*. London: Kogan Page.

Sreberny, A. 1999. *Include Me In*. London: ITC & Broadcasting Standards Commission.

Stallabrass, J. 1996. *Gargantua*. London: Verso.

Stern, B. 1989. 'Literary Criticism and Consumer Research: Overview and Illustrative Analysis', *Journal of Consumer Research* 16: 322–34.

Stern, B. 1991. 'Detailed Image Analysis: Poetic Methodology for Advertising Research', *International Journal of Advertising* 10: 161–80.

Stern, B. 1996. 'Textual Analysis in Advertising Research: Construction and Deconstruction of Meanings', *Journal of Advertising* 25(3): 61–73.

Stern, B. 2000. 'Advertisements as Women's Texts'. In M. Catterall, P. Maclaran and L. Stevens (eds) *Marketing and Feminism: Current Issues and Research*. London: Routledge.

Sugar, A. 2005. *The Apprentice: How to Get Hired not Fired*. London: BBC Books.

Sweney, M. 2008. 'Mobile Firms to Develop Common Advertising System', *Guardian* (12 February).

Tadajewski, M. 2006. 'Remembering Motivation Research: Towards an Alternative Genealogy of Interpretive Consumer Research', *Marketing Theory* 6: 429–66.

Tanaka, K. 1999. *Advertising Language: A Pragmatic Approach to Advertisements in Britain and Japan*. London: Routledge.

Taylor, J. 1993. 'The Public Foetus and the Family Car: From Abortion Politics to a Volvo Advertisement', *Science as Culture* 3: 601–18.

Temporal, P. and Trott, M. 2001. *Romancing the Customer: Maximizing Brand Value through Powerful Relationship Management*. Chichester: John Wiley.

Thoman, E. 2002. 'Re-imagining the American Dream'. In A. Badiner *Mindfulness in the Marketplace: Compassionate Responses to Consumerism*. Berkeley: Parallax.

Thompson, D. 1932. 'Advertising God', *Scrutiny* 3 (December): 241–6.

Thompson, D. 1943. *The Voice of Civilization: An Enquiry into Advertising*. London: Frederick Muller.

Thompson, D. 1964. *Discrimination and Popular Culture*. London: Penguin.

Thompson, J.B. 1995. *The Media and Modernity: A Social Theory of the Media*. Oxford: Polity.

Thompson, J.O. 1990. 'Advertising's Rationality'. In M. Alvarado and J.O. Thompson (ed.) *The Media Reader*. London: British Film Institute.

Timmers, M. 1998. *The Power of the Poster*. London: V&A Publications.

Tjernlund, A. and Wiles, C. 1991. 'A Comparison of Role Portrayal of Men and Women in Magazine Advertising in the USA and Sweden'. *International Journal of Advertising* 10: 259–67.

Tomlinson, A. 2004. 'The Disneyfication of the Olympics: Theme Parks and Freak-Shows of the Body'. In J. Bale and M.K. Christensen (eds) *Post-Olympism?: Questioning Sport in the Twenty-first Century*. Oxford: Berg, pp. 147–63.

Toncar, M. 2001. 'The Use of Humour in Television Advertising: Revisiting the US–UK Comparison', *International Journal of Advertising* 20(4): 521–39.

Toole, J.O. 1981. *The Trouble with Advertising*. New York: Chelsea House.

Treneman, A. 1989. 'Cashing in on the Curse: Advertising and the Menstrual Taboo'. In L. Gamman and M. Marshment (eds) *In The Female Gaze: Women as Viewers of Popular Culture*. Seattle: The Real Comet Press.

Tui-Wright, L. and Kelemen, M. 2000. 'The Cultural Contexts of Advertising to Women Consumers: The Examples of Malaysia and Romania'. In M. Catterall, P. Maclaran and L. Stevens (eds) *Marketing and Feminism: Current Issues and Research*. London: Routledge.

Tungate, M. 2007. *Adland: A Global History of Advertising*. London: Kogan Page.

Tunstall, J. 1964. *The Advertising Man in London Advertising Agencies*. London: Chapman & Hall.

Tunstall. J. 1993. *Television Producers*. London: Routledge.

Turner, E.S. 1952. *The Shocking History of Advertising*. London: Penguin.

Twitchell, J. 1999. *Lead Us into Temptation: The Triumph of American Materialism*. New York: Colombia University Press.

Valdiva, A. 1997. 'The Secret of My Desire: Gender, Class and Sexuality in Lingerie Catalogues'. In K.T. Frith (ed.) *Undressing the Ad: Reading Culture in Advertising*. New York: Peter Lang.

Valentine, V. 2002. 'Using Semiotics to Build Powerful Brands for Young Consumers', *Young Consumers* 4.

Valentine, V. 2007. 'Semiotics, What Now My Love?', Market Research Society Annual Conference, 21–3 March, Brighton.

Van Leeuwen, T. 1999. *Speech, Music, Sound*. London: Macmillan.

Van Leeuwen, T. 2005. *Introducing Social Semiotics*. London: Routledge.

Vestergaard, T. and Schroeder, K. 1985. *The Language of Advertising*. Oxford: Blackwell.

Walker-Laird, P. 1998. *Advertising Progress: American Business and the Rise of Consumer Marketing*. London: Johns Hopkins Press.

Waller, D.S. 1999. 'Attitudes Towards Offensive Advertising: An Australian Study', *Journal of Consumer Marketing* 16: 288–94.

Webb, S. 1914. 'Introduction'. In G.W. Goodall *Advertising: A Study of a Modern Business Power*. London: Constable & Co.

Wells, H.G. [1909] 2005. *Tono-Bungay*. London: Penguin.

Wernick, A. 1991. *Promotional Culture: Advertising, Ideology and Symbolic Expression*. London: Sage.

Wernick, A. 1994. 'Vehicles for Myth: The Shifting Image of the Modern Car'. In M.A. Solomon (ed.) *Signs of Life in the USA: Readings in Popular Culture for Writers*. Boston: Bedford Books.

White, R. 2000. *Advertising*, 4th edn. London: McGraw-Hill.

White, R. 2003. 'Briefing Creative Agencies', *Admap* 440 (June): 12–13.

White, R. 2005. 'Semiotics Deciphered', WARC Best Practice, *Admap*, September (464): 16–17.

Whitehead, F. 1964. 'Advertising'. In D. Thompson (ed.) *Discrimination and Popular Culture*. London: Penguin, pp. 23–49.

Whitehead, J. 2004. 'UK Online Adspend Grew by 80% in 2003 to Top £350m', *Brand Republic* (21 July). Available at www.brandrepublic. com/News/216980/Uk-online-adspend-grew-80-2003-top-350m/ (accessed November 2008).

Whitehead, J. 2005. 'Heineken Questions Effectiveness of TV Advertising as it Shifts UK Budget', *Brand Republic* (21 October).

Wight, R. 1972. *The Day the Pigs Refused to be Driven to Market: Advertising and the Consumer Revolution*. New York: Random House.

Williams, F. 1951. *The Richardson Story*. London: Heinemann.

Williams, R. [1962] 1980. 'Advertising: The Magic System'. In *Culture and Materialism*. London: Verso, pp. 170–95.

Williams, R. 1969. *Communications*. London: Pelican.

Williams, R. 1983. *Writing in Society*. London: Verso.

Williams, R. 1987. *Culture and Society: Coleridge to Orwell*. London: Hogarth.

Williamson, J. 1978. *Decoding Advertisements: Ideology and Meaning in Advertising*. London: Marion Boyars.

Williamson, J. 1986. *Consuming Passions: The Dynamics of Popular Culture*. London: Marion Boyars.

Willmott, M. 2001. *Citizen Brands: Putting Society at the Heart of your Business*. Chichester: Wiley.

Wilson, E. 1999. 'The Bohemianization of Mass Culture', *International Journal of Cultural Studies* 2: 11–32.

Wilson, R. 2004. 'Whose Ad Is It Anyway?', *Creative Review* (1 November).

Winship, J. 1981. 'Handling Sex', *Media, Culture and Society* 3: 25–41.

Winship, J. 2000. 'Women Outdoors: Advertising, Controversy and Disputing Feminism in the 1990s', *International Journal of Cultural studies* 3: 27–55.

Wolf, N. 1993. *Fire with Fire*. London: Vintage.

Yeshin, T. 2006. *Advertising*. London: Thomson.

Zanlot, E. 1984. 'Public Attitudes to Advertising', *International Journal of Advertising* 3.

Zhou, D., Zhang, W. and Vertinsky, I. 2002. 'Advertising Trends in Urban China', *Journal of Advertising Research* 42(3): 73–81.

Zukin, S. 2004. *Point of Purchase: How Shopping Changed American Culture*. London: Routledge.

Zyman, S. 2002. *The End of Advertising As We Know It*. London: John Wiley.

Zyman, S. 2004. 'Advertising Doesn't Work', *Creative Review* (July): 44–5.

# INDEX